Cusco

Ancient Cities of the New World

UNIVERSITY PRESS OF FLORIDA

Florida A&M University, Tallahassee
Florida Atlantic University, Boca Raton
Florida Gulf Coast University, Ft. Myers
Florida International University, Miami
Florida State University, Tallahassee
New College of Florida, Sarasota
University of Central Florida, Orlando
University of Florida, Gainesville
University of North Florida, Jacksonville
University of South Florida, Tampa
University of West Florida, Pensacola

CUSCO

Urbanism and Archaeology in the Inka World

IAN FARRINGTON

Foreword by Michael E. Smith, Marilyn A. Masson, and John W. Janusek

University Press of Florida

Gainesville · Tallahassee · Tampa · Boca Raton

Pensacola · Orlando · Miami · Jacksonville · Ft. Myers · Sarasota

This book may be available in an electronic edition.

18 17 16 15 14 13   6 5 4 3 2 1

A copy of cataloging-in-publication data is available from Library of Congress.
ISBN 978-0-8130-4433-0

The University Press of Florida is the scholarly publishing agency for the State University
System of Florida, comprising Florida A&M University, Florida Atlantic University,
Florida Gulf Coast University, Florida International University, Florida State University,
New College of Florida, University of Central Florida, University of Florida, University of
North Florida, University of South Florida, and University of West Florida.

University Press of Florida
15 Northwest 15th Street
Gainesville, FL 32611-2079
http://www.upf.com

Contents

Figures

Tables

Foreword

Cuzco, Peru, was the center of the Inka world, and along with Tenochtitlan, the Aztec imperial capital in contemporary Mexico, it was one of the two most important cities in the Americas just prior to the arrival of Europeans in the sixteenth century. Today, when one thinks of the Inka or the South American Andes, the spectacular site of Machu Picchu inevitably comes to mind. Machu Picchu was a local estate established by a pivotal Inca ruler known as Pachakuti. He and his retinue of engineers and architects established at least two other estates in the same "sacred valley" near Cuzco. Yet Cuzco—not Machu Picchu—was the center of the Inka Empire and culture.

Cuzco has received relatively little systematic archaeological coverage over the past century. Most studies dedicated to the center have focused on historical documentation of the city by early Spanish conquerors and administrators or native and mestizo writers. Very few studies have developed an intensive focus on Cuzco's material archaeological record. The present volume seeks to rectify this situation. Ian Farrington, senior lecturer in archaeology at the Australian National University, has conducted research in the Andes for more than three decades. His approach to Cuzco meshes two analytical techniques: town plan analysis and urban archaeology. He develops a rich understanding of Inka urban planning, the interwoven functions of different sections of the city, and the social and symbolic dimensions of the city that were simultaneously transferred to a series of "new *cuscos*" that served as local imperial centers throughout the Andes. Farrington is the first to apply town plan analysis, a technique of the British "urban morphology" approach, to an ancient city in the New World. As such this book breaks new ground methodologically.

This book is the third in the series Ancient Cities of the New World. Books in this series provide accessible views of urban patterns in places where publication has not kept up with fieldwork and archival research. While the study of any past urban center can claim to be about ancient cities or urbanism, this book series features studies that employ specific theories, models, and approaches drawn from the scholarly literature on cities and urbanism. Volumes in this series will complement introductory textbooks as in-depth, theoretically driven case studies of urbanism in pre-Columbian Mesoamerica and South America.

Michael E. Smith, Marilyn A. Masson, and John W. Janusek
Series Editors

Preface

The work for this book began in the early 1980s during other archaeological field projects that I was directing in the Sacred Valley. Ancient urbanism had been a long-term interest of mine. I had been a student of Paul Wheatley at University College London and had had field experience in Britain of both geographical and archaeological approaches to the understanding of the medieval town. Therefore, when I first came to Cusco in 1977, I became concerned that so little was known about its archaeology and planning, despite the fact that it was being considered for nomination as a World Heritage city (a status which it achieved in 1983). Much of what was known about the old city had been derived solely from the analysis of the chronicles, and although there had been some excavations, little had been published. My thoughts were that I could use my urban observational skills and experience to good effect and spend a few days collecting data, walking round the streets, taking photographs, making measurements, and naturally visiting churches, bars, restaurants, discotheques, shops, and even banks. This produced an independent set of information and measurements that could, at some stage, be used to find a better understanding of the old city. Other commitments meant that this observational research phase eventually lasted almost twenty years, as more places became available to enter. During this time, I continued to do some recording, while working and excavating elsewhere in the inka heartland.

When I returned to Cusco in 1993 to continue my own researches, the old city was devoid of tourists, who had been kept away like myself by the activities of Sendero Luminoso. Nevertheless, it remained a living urban center, like a medieval European town, with its flourishing businesses and large residential population in close juxtaposition. It was a perfect opportunity to check basic results. However, in the years since then, the tourists have returned in greater and greater numbers, and gradually the urban economy has boomed. As a result, the face of the city has changed. Many of its inhabitants have been moved out to the suburbs as multinational companies have bought inner-city property to develop international quality hotels and other tourism infrastructure. This has meant that archaeological investigation has become a priority in advance of construction.

Generally, individual excavation projects have been small in scale and have encountered the universal urban phenomenon of a very disturbed, almost incomprehensible stratigraphy, a feature which has deterred most archaeologists from fully evaluating the meaning of their finds. But as the large-scale Kusikancha program has shown, these difficulties can be overcome. Increasingly, larger archaeological projects have been undertaken, and while these too remain largely unpublished, more data is now available at the Instituto Nacional de Cultura (INC), now the Dirección Regional de Cultura (DRC) library in Cusco.

Over the years I have been able to read and even acquire copies of several unpublished excavation reports that describe specific projects in various parts of the city and its environs. In some cases, I have been able to visit during excavation and discuss results with their directors. Nevertheless, there are still many reports I have not seen and excavations that I know nothing about. What can be said is that these excavations have yielded hundreds of thousands of potsherds, animal bones, and human bones, as well as metal, shell, wood, and stone artifact fragments. These have all been examined to some extent, but they have not been studied thoroughly or systematically, and invariably they have been barely reported. In recent times, the websites of the local and national newspapers, *El Sol* and *El Comercio*, and the Peruvian press agency, Andina, have become useful sources that describe important discoveries, while the DRC Museo Garcilaso in the city displays some of the more recent archaeological finds. The varied quality of the data presents a problem for analysis, yet these can be used effectively to proffer a new perspective on this ancient city.

In this book, I have combined the data at hand with my understanding of the archaeological city, and while not ignoring the historical descriptions, I find it is now possible to evaluate Cusco as the ancient inka capital not only in terms of its archaeological findings but also from a planning perspective. This can be enhanced by a comparative approach, utilizing data from other inka urban centers near Cusco and the distant provinces of Tawantinsuyu that enable this more rigorous interpretation to emerge. Nevertheless, this is only a first step. Intentionally, I raise interpretations and hypotheses that need to be tested by more excavation, publication of previous excavations, and a rigorous reevaluation of that knowledge.

A Note on Quechua Usage

Quechua has no standard orthography and was indeed an unwritten language until after the Spanish conquest. I have refrained from using anglicized or hispanized versions of their words to describe inka buildings, artifacts, and institutions and have adopted, wherever possible, the quechua term with its modern Cusco spelling. Therefore, inka is spelt with a *k*, *qhapaq* (*capac*) with *qh* and *q*, and *waka* (*huaca* or *guaca*) with a *w*. I have not simply made plurals by adding an *s*. While this may be challenging to readers who are familiar with those spellings, I have provided an extensive glossary with short definitions of these words. However, to simplify some of the words, I have tried not to use the apostrophe for glottal stops and aspirations in the spelling of, for example, *waka* or *mita*. I have used Inka with a capital "I" when referring only to the personage of the king, Sapa Inka or simply the Inka, while a lower case "i" is used in all other circumstances.

Acknowledgments

This work has benefited greatly from the efforts of three excellent field assistants and companions in Cusco: Eliana Gamarra, Julie Dalco, and Lisa Solling. I must also thank many Cusco archaeologists and students who have kindly given up their time to discuss their own work with me and who have provided me with unpublished reports and plans. These include Percy Ardiles, Fernando Astete, Ives Béjar, Luis Fernando Béjar Luksic, Raymundo Béjar, Javier Condori, Miguel Cornejo Gutierrez, Daniel Cabrera, Carmen Farfán, Octavio Fernández, Helen García, Raúl del Mar, Julio Maza, Antonia Miranda, Alfredo Mormontoy, Italo Oberti, Eliza Orellana, Rubén Orellana, Mónica Paredes, René Pilco, Juan Samaniego, Marcelino Soto, Walter Zanabria, and in particular, Julinho Zapata. The staff at the library of the Instituto Nacional de Cultura in Cusco enabled me to consult various other reports, while I am grateful to Antonia Miranda for allowing me access to the catalogue and storerooms of the Museo Inka. Field work in Argentina benefited from the support of Rodolfo Raffino, Dario Iturriza, and María Martha Toddere.

I have also had many discussions about inka planning and archaeology with my colleagues, who have sharpened my understandings and insight into this subject. These include Santiago Agurto, César Astuhuaman, Roberto Bárcena, John Hyslop, Albert Meyers, Alfredo Mormontoy, Italo Oberti, Mónica Paredes, Rodolfo Raffino, Rubén Stehberg, Julinho Zapata, Mariusz Ziolkowski, and Tom Zuidema as well as my former PhD students, Miguel Cornejo Guerrero, Ken Heffernan, and Idilio Santillana.

I am grateful to Lisa Solling, Tom Farrington, and Lindsay Smith, who worked tirelessly producing the maps and diagrams, and to Raymundo Béjar, Luis Fernando Béjar Luksic, and Lisa Solling, who have kindly provided some of the photographs used as illustrations. Other photographs have been reproduced with permission from Andina. All other photos were taken by me.

Overall, this book has benefited from the insights of Lisa Solling, who has critically read and contributed to the text. I am grateful to Julie Dalco and Ken Heffernan, who have read the developing manuscript and offered advice concerning its logic and flow. However, the arguments, interpretations, and explanations I have offered about inka Cusco remain strictly my own.

1

Urbanism in Prehispanic Andes

Cusco, the former capital of Tawantinsuyu, the inka empire, is a rapidly growing city in the southern highlands of Peru with a population of about 349,000 inhabitants. Despite its present tourist boom and downtown hotel growth, it remains a place readily overlooked by the visitor, who invariably flies in, stays a night or two in the city, and sees a few local sights, but whose main destination is the nearby spectacular World Heritage monument of Machu Picchu, only three hours away by train. Yet the Cusco historic center is also on the World Heritage list for its unique combination of baroque churches and inka remains. Its inka architecture can be seen at Qorikancha, Kusikancha, and along streets as well as in various cafés, restaurants, hotels, bars, and discotheques. These provide glimpses into the splendor of inka Cusco, but much remains invisible as a result of the development of the colonial city and the modern city on top. This book is an attempt to reveal what we know about this once great capital.

The nature of the inka city has been studied by archaeologists, mainly at abandoned settlements, such as Pumpu (Matos 1994) and Huánuco Pampa (Morris 2008; Morris and Thompson 1985), in central Peru (figure 1.1), and at Machu Picchu (Valencia and Gibaja 1992) and Patallaqta (Kendall 1991) in the Cusco area (figure 1.2). In these locations, the ancient urban infrastructure is readily discernible in the landscape through standing buildings, all roofless and some collapsed, terraces, platforms, plazas, and streets. These projects have enabled significant advances to be made in the interpretation of inka structures and their associated cultural deposits to yield a better understanding of inka urbanism.

Results suggest that these were functioning urban centers, but how do we interpret them, in a western or andean sense? Were they fully fledged western-style traditional cities? Were they elite-only centers that performed the ceremonies and rituals to control the rhythms of state political power?

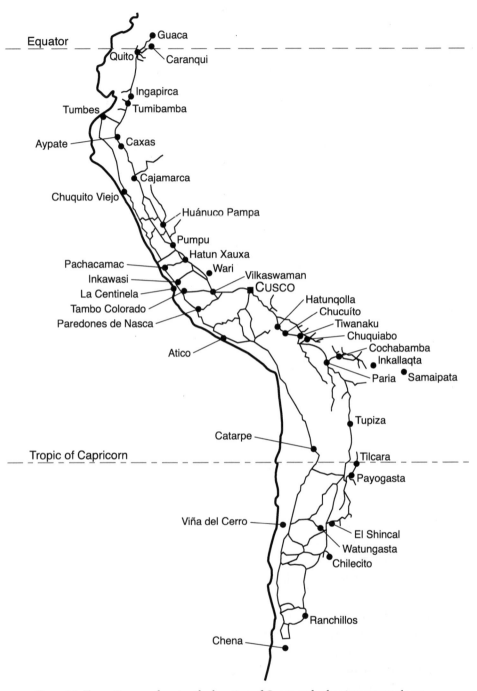

Figure 1.1. Tawantinsuyu, showing the location of Cusco and other important places (after Hyslop 1984).

Figure 1.2. The inka heartland.

Could they be regarded as periodically occupied places that attracted populations only at certain times for certain purposes but which were largely empty of permanent residential populations and which lacked the industrial and social organization of a city to be considered urban in a western sense?

It would be thought that these questions could be resolved by examining the evidence from the capital city, Cusco. However, in contrast to the abandoned centers, the study of Cusco has remained very much in the realm of an historical enquiry, based mainly on a series of sixteenth-century eyewitness chronicles and later accounts of the ancient city, of the inkas and their history, with some supporting evidence, gleaned from other colonial documents that refer to the city and its inka past. One significant problem

Table 1.1. A chronological sequence of the Cusco valley

Date	Andean period	Cusco valley period	Cusco ceramic styles
1500–BC 500	Middle Formative	Markavalle	Markavalle
BC 500–AD 200	Late Formative	Chanapata	Chanapata; Chanapata derived
AD 200–600	Early Intermediate	Qotakalli	Qotakalli, Muyu Orco
600–1000	Middle Horizon	Wari	Horizontal incised; Ccoipa; Araway
1000–1400	Late Intermediate	Killke	Killke, Lucre, Colcha, and other regional wares
1400–1533	Late Horizon	Inka	Classic (Polychrome A, B, C, Cusco White-on-Red); Killke; Sillustani, Urqosuyu, Pacajes, Chincha, Chimú

Sources: Barreda 1973; Bauer 2004.

has been that the chroniclers did not agree on the location, ownership, or function of many inka buildings. Nevertheless, from these studies a standard but rather static account has emerged of the location and probable function of particular inka buildings and spaces in the city, its social divisions as well as the ceremonial and ritual activities that occurred within the urban area and its environs.

The only archaeological evidence, which has been incorporated into such studies, is the distribution of standing architectural remnants, including ancient walls, doorways and niches, found throughout the city; but these have only been used to confirm the historically derived picture (e.g., Agurto 1980; Wurster 1999). In his 2004 book, *Ancient Cuzco*, the archaeologist Brian Bauer presented a well-researched chronological history of human settlement in the Cusco valley, based on his own fieldwork (table 1.1). He evaluated the historical issues concerning building location, but he failed to engage in any archaeological interpretation of the city. He briefly mentioned some of the more important archaeological finds but did not analyze their significance (Bauer 2004: 114–15, 152). As a consequence, his chapters on the city and its buildings lie firmly within the historical mold. Similarly, a paper by Covey (2009) on society and craft industry in inka Cusco offers little beyond a historical account.

For the inka archaeologist, it is as if there is nothing additional to say from their own data about the capital, Cusco, that is not included in this historical narrative. Another example of this approach can be seen in recent analyses of Machu Picchu as an inka royal palace and estate, based simply on the interpretation of a sixteenth century land document that mentions a Lord of Picchu and indicates that several properties along the lower Vilcanota had belonged to Pachakuti Inka Yupanki (Niles 2004; Rowe 1990a). It does not refer to a palace. Such a conclusion should demand comparison between known palaces and cities, but this has been ignored because of the belief that the document must be correct and inviolable. It can be said that inka archaeology has been clearly guided in its development and interpretation by the reading and analysis of the historical record; therefore, such issues as site description and chronology seem to be dictated by the written word. Indeed, inka archaeology has failed to establish its own independent view and interpretation of the past in many respects, serving in common with several other archaeologies of a "historical" period, as the "handmaiden to history" and historical interpretation (Hume 1964). Why should this be so, particularly when the documentary sources present varied and often confusing details about place and time?

History versus Archaeology

History and archaeology must be regarded as complementary windows on the human past; they utilize different sets of data specific to their discipline, with different analytical methods, and as such they have different goals for its presentation. They have different perspectives about what can or cannot be said about the past; but to claim, as some historians do, that "history represents the truth" and that "archaeology can only confirm that constructed picture" is nonsense. Each historical document deals with its particular subject at the moment in time it was written; it is complete with the biases of its author, as well as its means of and reasons for its preparation. In historical analysis and narrative, the historian pieces together evidence from many documents to interpret not only the nature and sequence of events but also the context, reasons, and motives that lie behind it, whether they be social, political, economic, or religious in origin. On the other hand, the archaeologist deals with material evidence in the form of building remains, food, and other discards from the activities of everyday life, such as cooking, eating, working, and socializing, as well as the residues of public rituals and ceremonies, including the disposal of the dead. Archaeological data is rarely able to deal with a particular set of events that occurred on a particular day in the past, although when it can, its results can be contrary to the standard historical narrative of that event (e.g., Fox 1997; Scott et al. 2000). In the majority of projects, the archaeologist collects, catalogues, analyzes, and interprets material culture and sediments that have been laid down at different times by varied activities and processes in order to construct a general picture of the events and lives in which people of the past engaged. Sequences of superimposed strata present a 'longue durée' record in which changes in materials, behavior, and environment can be noted through time.

Given the lack of archaeological information in any modern account of ancient Cusco, it might be suspected that the city is archaeologically sterile and/or that there have been no finds of significance. Yet there have been more than sixty separate excavation programs within the urban area since the early 1970s, although most remain unpublished (table 1.2; figure 1.3). Some may argue that these have little or no value because they were dug into disturbed urban deposits that had been thoroughly churned during the last five hundred years, leaving few sealed contexts that could tell us what was going on at particular locations within the city during inka times. As we shall see, none of these accusations are true. The city has suffered the depredations of urban land use change from the moment the Spaniards arrived on 15 November 1533. Since then, there have been many phases of destruction, demolition, construction, and encroachment throughout the inka town, including the installation of modern urban utilities, such as reticulated water, sewerage, electricity, and telephone systems, which have added significantly to the disturbance of archaeological deposits.

What the practice of archaeology in Cusco has lacked is not the quality of its archaeologists nor the quality of its finds, but a means of interpreting the vast range of data, mainly coming from disturbed deposits, to resolve particular research questions. This book is an attempt to assemble archaeological data and other field observations about its urban topography as well as the finds and historical information in order to examine the nature of the inka capital and posit new hypotheses that can be tested using a variety of analytical techniques. In this book, I examine the archaeological evidence from the city by combining research techniques that have been successfully developed in the inquiry into the medieval European town, namely, "town plan analysis" (Conzen 1960) and the principles of urban archaeology, as developed by Martin Biddle (1976a) and Martin Carver (1987a).

As a consequence, archaeology can offer a perspective on various urban themes, such as social organization, craft production, domestic and ritual activities, the disposal of the dead, and chronology, by discovering

Table 1.2a. Urban excavations in Cusco

Place	Plan-unit / seam	Street block	Year	Chief excavator
Pumaqchupan		Mz175	1947	Luis Llanos
Qorikancha (including fountain) Qorikancha church	B	Mz74	1970–71, 1971–72, 1974–79, 2001	Raymundo Béjar, Luis Barreda & José González José Lorenzo, Alfredo Valencia & Arminda Gibaja, Italo Oberti
Qorikancha terraces and esplanade	B	Mz74	1993–94	Raymundo Béjar
2nd Cloister S. Domingo	B	Mz74	2000–2001	Raymundo Béjar
Canchón	B	Mz74	1943, 1970	John Rowe Raymundo Béjar
Intipampa	B	Plaza	1995	INC-Cusco
Calle Arrayan	B	Street	1997 (2)	Walter Zanabria; Oscar Fernández
Limaqpampa Grande	B	Plaza	2008–9	Patricia Benavente
Intiqawarina #620	I	Mz73	2004–5	Erika Rodríguez; Patricia Arroyo
Tullumayu #698	I	Mz73	2006	Antonia Miranda
Calle Zetas	I	Mz72	1990s	INC-Cusco
Pampa del Castillo #347	IIE	Mz37	1988	Percy Ardiles
Plazoleta Sto Domingo #263	IIE	Mz37	1994, 2004	Nancy Olazábal, Luis Tomayconsa & Rene Pilco; Carlos Rosell
Kusikancha	IIE	Mz37	2001–5	Various, INC-Cusco
Casa de los Cuatro Bustos	IID	Mz36	1962	Fidel Ramos
Hotel Libertador	IID	Mz36	1981	José González
Limaqpampa Chico #473	IIC	Mz35	2005	Patricia Arroyo
Banco Wiese, Maruri #319–341	IIA	Mz16	1996	Julio Masa
Triunfo #338	IIA	Mz2	1997–98	Wilfredo Yepes
Triunfo #392	IIA	Mz2	1998	Walter Zanabria
Casa Concha	IIA	Mz16	2002, 2005 2006	Percy Paz & Eulogio Allacontor; Javier Condori; Luis Cuba Peña
Santa Catalina Ancha #342	IIA	Mz16	2005	E. García Calderón
Calle Triunfo	A/IIA	Street	2009	Carlos Rosell
Maruri #256	IIA	Mz3	2005	Erika Rodríguez

continued

Table 1.2a—*Continued*

Place	Plan-unit / seam	Street block	Year	Chief excavator
Hatunrumiyoq passage	A/IIB	Mz14	1979	Wilbert San Román
Herrajes #171, Pas Inka Roca	IIB	Mz14	2004	Patricia Arroyo
San Agustín--H. Marriot	IIB	Mz15	2009	Irwin Ferrándiz
San Agustín #239, Novotel	IIB	Mz34	1996	Miguel Cornejo
Compañía de Jésus	A	Mz4	1991–92	Alfredo Valencia
Paraninfo	A	Mz4	1992	Raúl Del Mar
Avenida del Sol #200	A	Mz4	1997	Italo Oberti
Loreto/Justicia	A	Mz4	2000	Claudio Cumpa
Loreto #208	A	Mz4	2003	Wilber Bolívar
Avenida del Sol #103	A	Mz4	2004	Calos Rosell
Hawkaypata pileta	A	Plaza	1996	Miguel Cornejo
Plateros #316	A	Mz8	2002	Italo Oberti
Plateros #348	A	Mz8	1999	Tula Castillo
Procuradores #366	A	Mz56	2004	Italo Oberti
Suecia #348	A	Mz9A	2001–2	Julinho Zapata
Iglesia Triunfo	A	Mz1	1998	J. Cahua
Catedral	A	Mz1	2002	Amelia Pérez Trujillo
Plaza Regocijo	A	Plaza	1940	José Franco Inojoso
Hotel Cusco	A	Mz19	2001	Mario Del Pezo
Palacio Municipal	A	Mz7	2005	Carlos Atapaucar
Calle Santa Teresa	A	Street	1997	Walter Zanabria
Colegio de las Mercedes	A	Mz7	2006	Carlos Atapaucar
Concebidayoq #174	A	Mz44	2001	Mónica Paredes
San Juan de Dios	A	Mz22	2002	Julinho Zapata
Márquez #24	A	Mz20	2002	Amelia Pérez Trujillo
Calle Márquez	A	Street	2008	INC-Cusco
Parque Tricentenario	III	Mz9D	1996	INC-Cusco
Casa Almirante	III	Mz10	1993	Julinho Zapata
Casa Cabrera	III	Mz11	2001	INC-Cusco
Beaterio de las Nazarenas	III	Mz12	2001, 2005, 2009	Miguel Colque, Walter Zanabria;
Wanaypata	III	Street	1957	Luis Pardo

Table 1.2b. Suburban village excavations in Cusco

Place	Suburban village	Street block	Year	Chief excavator
Colegio Salesiano	Qolqampata	Mz54B	2000, 2002	Walter Zanabria, Carmen Aguilar
Qolqampata	Qolqampata	Mz55	1974	Alfredo Valencia
Terraces below San Cristóbal	Qolqampata	Mz9C	1998	Julinho Zapata
San Cristóbal	Qolqampata	Church	2007	María del Carmen Martín Rubio
Teqsecocha #526	Terraces	Mz25	2002	Italo Oberti
Teqsecocha #415	Terraces		2001	Patricia Arroyo
Resbalosa #494	Terraces		2005	T. Aguilar
Casa Tigre	Wakapunku	Mz24	1992	Julinho Zapata
Amargura # 107	Wakapunku	Mz54A	1998	Walter Zanabria & Alfredo Mormontoy
Saphi #817	Wakapunku	Mz	2005	I. A. Fernándiz
Saphi grifo	Wakapunku	Mz54B	1996	Claudio Cumpa
Santa Ana, Carmenqa	Carmenqa		1973, 1995, 2006	Alfredo Valencia, INC-Cusco, Reynaldo Bustinza
Tambo de Montero #117A	Carmenqa	Mz23	2003	Italo Oberti
Sapantiana	Carved rock	Mz57	1934	Luis Valcárcel
Siete Borreguitos / Sapantiana	Terraces	Mz57	2005	L. M. Apaza & R. Béjar
Suytuqhato, Toqokachi	Toqokachi	Mz62	1970	Raymundo Béjar
Qoripata	Cayaokachi		1941, 1976, 1987, 1997	John Rowe, Miguel Cornejo, Percy Paz, Wilfredo Yepes, Walter Zanabria

and analyzing material evidence in combination with the field evidence of buildings and footings, the nature and type of material remains, burials, and the historical setting, in general and in detail of particular locations.

The Concept of the City

In general, a city can be defined as a large, dense, and permanent agglomeration of public buildings for economic, administrative, and religious purposes and residences that house people from a diversity of social grades who service those functions (e.g., Hardoy 1973). It is a central place whose functions impose hegemony over its hinterland (Smith 2007: 4–5), while it

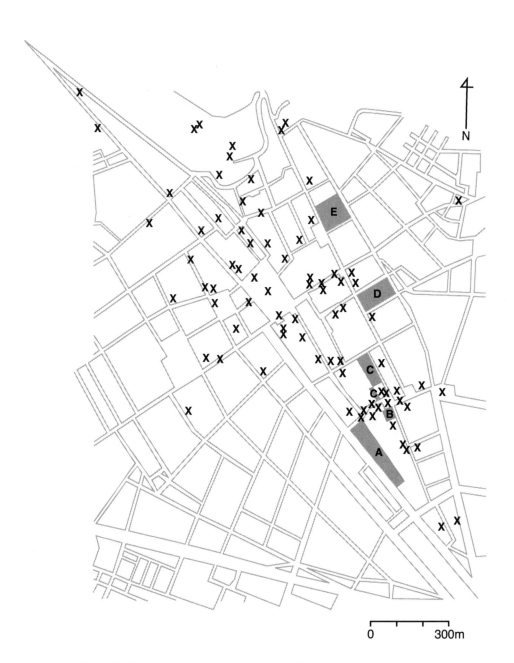

Figure 1.3. The location of excavations in Cusco. The shaded areas represent extensive archaeological programs. *A*, Qorikancha esplanade and terraces; *B*, Qorikancha; *C*, Kusikancha; *D*, San Agustín site; *E*, Beaterio de las Nazarenas. Smaller projects are marked with a cross.

draws resources, goods, and people from that area to sustain it. This neutral definition belies the fact that all cities do not look alike and that there are regional, temporal, and culturally specific forms that need to be understood. Nevertheless, the city has two critical components, its form and permanency on the one hand, and its function as a central place on the other. Having such a universal definition does not mean that the ancient city can be regarded in the same way as a modern western one. While the physical resemblance between them may suggest that they should both be viewed by the same criteria, it is the specific political, economic, social, cultural, and religious mechanisms of urbanism that make them different.

Comparison between modern western and traditional cities of the ancient world is possible only when we accept that a city is a "central place" within its hinterland from which it attracts people and resources and which it governs and influences from the center itself. This does not mean that it is a central place in the classic geographical sense, as articulated by the theories of Haggett (1965) and Berry (1967), that is, governed by the principles of western economics of unfettered supply and demand and the principle of least cost effort in its relations with the hierarchy of smaller settlements in its hinterland. In contrast, for the ancient city, particularly in those regions without a market economy or the use of money, the relationship between the city, its ruler, and the hinterland is structured differently. It is the political and cultural power of the ruler in the capital and his desire to display his authority and wealth by organizing tribute and corvée labor obligations from the hinterland to sustain his city and state. This is used to build monumental architecture in the form of temples to the gods and ancestors, palaces for himself as god's representative on earth, as well as royal tombs in which the ancestors can be glorified. In this version of central place theory, it is tribute obligation to a ruler and the gods that replaces the economic power wielded by the shops, industries, and markets of the center in the attraction of people and wealth from the hinterland. Paul Wheatley (1971: 257–61) described these as centripetal forces that brought people and goods into the city, while the redistribution of tribute, political, and spiritual protection was offered to the hinterland in recompense, that is, centrifugal forces. In order to assess such mechanisms, Wheatley (1971: 265–66) relied on tribute documents of the twelfth-century Khmer kings, while in the absence of such data among the Classic Maya, Adams and Jones (1981) chose the number, type, and mass of public monuments as a reflection of the extent of centripetal forces. Other studies have used relative settlement area as a hierarchical device within a given region to assess the importance of central place (e.g., Bauer and Covey 2004).

Therefore, ancient cities play political, administrative, and religious roles within their landscape to organize labor and resources to sustain the center and to redistribute largesse and protection in return. They are central places intimately connected with their hinterlands that sustain them economically, politically, and socially.

Another characteristic of the ancient city is its social diversity, composed of a series of elite and non-elite groups pursuing various roles within the urban framework. These could be considered kin-groups, but Adams (1966: chap. 3) in his comparative study of urbanism in Aztec Mexico and Early Dynastic Mesopotamia emphasized a gradual transformation from kin-based to communities related on the basis of living in specific urban neighborhoods. These were corporate entities of administrators, clerks, craftsmen, cooks, and domestic servants.

Each ancient culture had its particular architectural and planning canons that successfully expressed their beliefs about their own importance and power. Therefore, the morphology of the ancient city in any one culture can be varied with a central area full of state monumental buildings, such as temple, palace, and royal tomb, and a series of wards or neighborhoods containing the residences and workshops of elite-based lineages and non-elite groups, who maintained and managed them. Such places do not necessarily have any streets and often no hint of a readily understandable grid plan; yet they have been planned to enable the performance of the rituals and ceremonies necessary to maintain the state and the institutions of authority as well as rulers and their ancestors in power.

Many scholars, such as Paul Wheatley (1971) and Davíd Carrasco (1999), have argued that the principal driving force for the execution of a city plan and its architecture is that a culture's belief system, its cosmology, is reflected in the orientation and distribution of buildings as well as in their external and internal decoration, furniture, and the location and type of offerings. Indeed, such arguments have led to the understanding that certain cities could indeed be laid out as a "celestial archetype," a cosmogram, in which a culture's cosmological beliefs are displayed in its layout. While this may be the case, Smith (2007) has cautioned against the general acceptance of this concept for all ancient cities, and particularly for those with no written record. Therefore, the meaning of a plan, its buildings, architectural decoration, and landscape needs to be carefully tested against other archaeological data of that culture before being suggested as an hypothesis for further testing and refinement. Nevertheless, such symbolism reinforces both the religious and political powers wielded by the ruler, usually as "god king." As the ruler is divine, a god within the pantheon, his position is legitimated through his relationships with the gods and his equally divine ancestors; it is these who bestow and legitimize his right to political power and greatness.

Urban planning can be defined as the formal organization of space through the deliberate allocation of blocks of land for specific uses and constructions (Biddle 1976b), while Smith (2007: 7), following arguments by Carter (1983) and Ellis (1995), has suggested that urban planning in the ancient world has two components. The first is termed "coordination among the buildings and spaces of the city" and is composed of the arrangement of buildings, the formality and monumentality of layout, orthogonality, other forms of geometric order as well as access and visibility. The second is "standardization among cities in terms of architectural inventories, orientation, and metrology." In other words, within a culture, there are similarities of urban form and arrangement with all new foundations.

Ancient planning can assume various forms that may be influenced not only by standardized measurement, axiality, orientation, and/or cardinality but also by culturally standardized form and building placement that can position appropriately the essential elements of urban function: palace, plaza, temple, tomb, and residence. As a result, the planning process may result in a spatial separation of planned elements, to present a more diffuse spread of population and urban infrastructure. Orthogonal planning is only one of these types; it gives an impression of order and enables the evaluation and measurement of its components in the search for regularity.

An ancient city plan can be the result of a single phase of design and construction, or it can grow organically through time over several centuries as successive rulers reinterpret their sacred political missions (Smith 2007). Within such places, change needs to be evaluated and understood over time. It is fortunate that Cusco and other inka cities, discussed in this book, were built on relatively pristine sites, but older locations were also transformed to bear witness to an inka occupation that recognized the importance of its ancestral past.

The character of the ancient city therefore is composed of its political and religious power and authority, which it wields over its surrounding landscape and even beyond. Generally, it has a permanent residential population living in neighborhoods and a monumental arrangement of culturally standard types of buildings and spaces that accommodate the roles of temple, palace, royal tomb, and plaza. It is a place where authority is legitimated through ritual. Its resident population comprises the ruler's lineage and its associates as well as the officials and retainers that maintain the political and economic well-being of the city and the polity. While it does not have to have been built as a single unified plan, it often shares with other locations within the same culture a standardized arrangement of building and spatial components that make up the structural elements of authority.

Prehistoric Andean Urbanism

Wheatley (1971: 225) argued that if "we trace back the characteristic urban form to its beginnings we arrive not at a settlement that is dominated by commercial relations, a primordial market, or at one that is focused on a citadel, an archetypal fortress, but rather at a ceremonial complex." He stated that the central Andes can be regarded as one of the primary realms of nuclear urbanism and that the ceremonial complex can be traced back to Áspero, a collection of pyramids, mounds, and kitchen middens in the Supe valley, dating to about 1000 BC (Wheatley 1971: 235–38). This has been extended recently by Ruth Shady (2006), who has excavated at the large ceremonial city of Caral, also in the Supe valley, yielding an occupation dating between 3000 and 2000 BC.

In his review of ancient urban settlements in the Andes, the archaeologist, John Rowe (1963: 3–4) used a rather crude measure: "an urban settlement is an area of human habitation in which many dwellings are grouped closely together . . . [with only] space for gardens," and from this he estimated population size. He used twenty dwellings as the minimum criterion for urban, and two thousand inhabitants as a dividing line between small and large. He examined various places and determined that between 1500 and 1000 BC several ceremonial centers had urban populations and could be called cities. He reviewed the extant literature, noting, "The story of urban pattern in Peru in later times is not one of simple expansion through the growth of existing settlements and the establishment of new ones. . . . Many sites of large urban centers were occupied for relatively short periods and then abandoned. Whole districts with a flourishing urban tradition lost it and shifted to other patterns of settlement" (Rowe 1963: 1). He traced the rise and fall of cities throughout the prehistoric period, while noting that only two very important cult centers, Tiwanaku and Pachacamac, each displaying more than one thousand years of continuous urban occupation, defied this trend.

Recent work concurs with Rowe that prehistoric andean urban cultures waxed and waned for at least 5,000 years, and no single urban tradition was long lasting; each gradually declined and ceased to exist. In most parts, central places, whether they are defined as sacred or political centers, emerged, urbanized, and declined without leaving a lasting imprint of an urban tradition, even within their own region.

The reasons that underlie these processes and settlements have been debated; for some, it is the lack of a market economy which prevented the ability to sustain an urban settlement, while, for others, it is regarded as an andean phenomenon, a measure of the different principles by which central places were created and sustained. The role that regionalism has played, and continues to play, in this very mountainous environment and the need to gain and maintain access to people and resources to sustain a large settlement has meant that there would have been continuous pressure to maintain authority over anything larger than a small region for any great length of time. The urban breakdown after the fall of Tiwanaku and Wari between AD 1000 and 1150 is often attributed to the growth of regionalism and the rise of petty warfare between competing small polities, occupying defended hilltops (e.g., Hastorf 1993).

It is from this milieu that the inka state began to crystallize as a small polity in the Cusco valley in the twelfth and thirteen centuries. During the Late Intermediate period, Killke culture dominated the western end of the valley, where there were at least ten large villages, including a settlement of unknown size beneath the modern city (Bauer and Covey 2004: 74–78), while Lucre culture prevailed in the lower eastern basin (McEwan et al. 2002). Recent excavations in the largest Lucre site, Choqepukyo, about 28 km from Cusco, demonstrate a continuous occupation, culminating in the appearance of inka buildings and offerings (McEwan et al. 2002). Despite this evidence, whether inka urbanism can be traced directly to this site or to Killke antecedents remains unknown.

The inka urban tradition and political success in expanding its empire is in part a result of how they interacted with the importance of existing or abandoned cultural centers that existed in their oral tradition and which were located sufficiently distant from Cusco to remain important in the inka psyche, yet physically unknown. It is perhaps significant that, during the reign of Pachakuti Inka Yupanki, the first military campaigns beyond the Cusco heartland were westward toward Soras and Chincha and southeastward to Lake Titiqaqa (Julien 2000: 111–15), that is, into the spheres of influence of Pachacamac and Tiwanaku, respectively. With the conquest of the Qolla, a foothold was gained in the latter, which enabled the eventual conquest of Tiwanaku and further campaigns to the south. In contrast, the former proved much more difficult to overcome. Indeed, the inka armies moved northward through the highlands, eventually capturing much of Chinchaysuyu before Pachacamac and the Kingdom of Chimor were brought under their aegis during the reign of Thupaq Inka Yupanki.

The Inkas and the Tiwanaku Legacy

Like the Aztecs of Mexico, the emerging inka state, powerful in its local region, looked to a recent grand civilization as the ancestor of its noble classes and its polity. Many scholars have considered that the inkas, with no immediate tradition of government or urbanism in their region, must have gained their experience from the capture of ideas and peoples from other andean cultures. At various times, archaeologists have considered that the Chimú, Wari, and Tiwanaku cultures were vital in this development. However, such an approach denies the inkas their own tradition and abilities by simply promoting the idea that they were secondary users of institutions, ideas, and techniques that had already been successfully effected elsewhere. While this is certainly part of the process of cultural development, we must consider what the inkas may have known about certain places and why they were interested in gaining control of them. And indeed, what were the impacts of these on the inkas themselves?

It was toward Tiwanaku at the southern end of Lake Titiqaqa that the inkas looked for inspiration, legitimation, and guidance in their own governance, conquests, and the expansion of their political authority. On the other hand, Pachacamac and its oracle on the central coast was never, it seems, a major political player but a place with which any stronger polity needed contact, if it were to wield great religious influence over the south coast and the central highlands. For the northward expansion of the state, it became a place of influence that the inkas needed to control.

Tiwanaku and the Lake Titiqaqa featured in oral tradition throughout the southern Andes as the place where the world began and where humans were created, including the inkas themselves. From an inka perspective, one version of the myth suggests that, at the Sacred Rock on the Island of Titiqaqa, a deity, Wiraqocha Pachayachachiq, after several attempts, created the earth and the sun, moon, and stars and set them in motion to establish night and day. He populated it with wild plants and animals and then set about creating pairs of men and women out of wood and stone, painting them with the colors and designs of their clothing, and gave them language, domesticated plants, and animals (Cobo 1990: 13). He ordered them to travel underground from there to *paqarina*, origin places, where he would call them out in pairs to begin the process of village foundation and the establishment of a regional people. In another version, the ancient city itself was the place where Wiraqocha fabricated the men and women out of stone, and from there they were sent to populate the southern sierra. The inkas were one such group that believed that their own ancestors had been made in Tiwanaku and had been summoned by Wiraqocha to found their own city and polity.

For the inkas, Wiraqocha Pachayachachiq was their supreme creator god (Demarest 1981), whom they associated with the aymara god Thunupa at Tiwanaku. There, the latter was considered responsible for thunder and lightning and therefore with life-giving rains but also destructive hail. It was said that he cried tears of hail and that he could manifest as a feline. The inkas appear to have equated these attributes of Thunupa with their own ancestry because they, too, had a special relationship with felines, identifying themselves with the puma. They also had a tradition of a mythical feline, the *qoa*, which caused thunder, lightning, rain, and hail. The inkas must have understood themselves to be the descendants of Wiraqocha and Tiwanaku.

Tiwanaku had been an extensive urban complex for at least 1,000 years until AD 1150 (Janusek 2004). It had been regionally powerful across the southern Andes for several centuries and certainly was known about in the Cusco region, as pottery from there was found in contemporary local elite graves at Batan Urqo (Zapata 1997). Whether the inkas knew of the ancient city prior to their expansion or had simply heard stories about it, the presence of very large anthropomorphic statues throughout the site were probably thought to be vestiges of the humans created by Wiraqocha. Even the large statues of seated felines, called *chachapuma*, would have reinforced the importance of felines and feline deities to the inkas and given them a sense that, like themselves, the ancient Tiwanaqueños also revered the puma and identified with it. This would have been further enhanced by their observation of designs on Tiwanaku polychrome pottery and incense burners made in the shape of felines.

Tiwanaku pottery was quite different in style and decoration from that of the inka, but it must have been much admired by them. For example, a small offering was excavated at Saqsaywaman near Cusco, associated with the Muyuqmarka temple complex, that comprised a Tiwanaku style *qero* and a camelid bone *ruki* (Valcárcel 1935). However, this pot does not appear to be an antique fabricated in Tiwanaku but a copy, probably made by the inkas in Cusco for use as a symbolic offering. This is confirmed by the discovery of Tiwanaku-like wasters at an inka manufacturing site near Tambokancha and by sherds found in excavations in a large building at the main site itself (Farrington and Zapata 2003).

Archaeologists and architectural historians have believed for some time that the exquisite inka stone architectural techniques appeared so suddenly in the Cusco valley that they must have been deliberately copied from expert Tiwanaku masons (e.g., Gasparini and Margolies 1980), although this idea is not new. For example, Cieza de León (1959: 284) wrote that he had "heard Indians say that the Incas built their great edifices of Cuzco along the lines of the wall to be seen in this place (Tiwanaku)."[1] Various traits have been cited as proof of this, including fine stone cutting and the accurate fitting of rectangular flat blocks into walls to make them strong and aesthetically pleasing as well as the use of metal clamps set into adjacent blocks. For example, Gasparini and Margolies (1980) noted that ethnohistorical research indicated that the Lupaqa masons from the southern end of Lake Titiqaqa were deployed "to build houses and walls in Cusco." While these were highly valued by the inkas, did they influence the design and form of their buildings and settlements? Were not the inkas acquiring and learning skills from others to execute their own designs and plans in Cusco and elsewhere in the empire? Protzen and Nair (1997) have argued that, while the inkas may have been inspired by Tiwanaku, their architecture was technically and stylistically of a different order and included rounded sunken joints, so typical of inka stonework.

It has been argued that a number of other architectural and urban traits found at Tiwanaku influenced the canons of inka planning (e.g., Gasparini and Margolies 1980), such as the *kancha* arrangement of four buildings around a central patio to form a basic residential unit, a feature at both Tiwanaku and Wari. The latter certainly introduced this form into the Cusco valley at the urban site of Pikillaqata in the tenth century. Its main structural component is a long, narrow niched hall, considered to be the forerunner of the inka *kallanka* (McEwan 1998). Yaeger and López (2004) have argued that the Pumapunku pyramid at Tiwanaku was an *usnu* platform with a broad plaza to its east and that it could have been the stimulus for the inka adoption of this feature in urban design. Archaeologically, it had an intensive inka occupation, but it is probable that such structures were already part of the planning canon introduced into Tiwanaku to redevelop existing monumental structures. It could be argued that at Tiwanaku the inkas could have considered the stone stelae and statues found at many platform mounds and subterranean temples to be copies of their own *usnu* concept (see chapter 2).

Similarly, the concepts of cardinal orientation and directionality, such as facing a mountain, and to some extent orthogonal planning could be argued to be elements that the inkas at Tiwanaku had observed and took back to Cusco to become part of their architectural canon. Whether such individual traits could be considered part of the inka incorporation of Tiwanaku into its own worldview and architectural planning is moot; certainly some were known from elsewhere and could simply be seen as a part of a general late andean tradition of architectural arrangement at important places. Each culture developed its own characteristic traits for its own cities and monuments. The inka advantage was to acquire from their conquered provinces those craftsmen who could produce what the inka required in their landscape, urban centers, and material culture.

Cusco: An Ancient City

Several authors have explored the urban characteristics of inka Cusco, based on reviews of the chronicle and other historical literature (Chávez Ballón 1970; Rowe 1968; Hardoy 1973; Wurster 1999), while others have included the distribution of architectural remains (Agurto 1980; Hyslop 1990; Bauer 2004). In 1997, a team from the Centro de Educación y Comunicación Guaman Poma undertook extensive fieldwork expanding knowledge of extant wall remains and adding surface artifactual data to establish an independent picture of this ancient city (Paredes 1999, 2001). Overall, these have lacked broad analytical skills to evaluate inka planning canons beyond simply listing architectural and social attributes and their possible functions. This book provides the first comprehensive study of the urban topography of Cusco, using not only the documentary record and architectural studies but also the results of archaeological studies, such as mapping and excavation, to elaborate and test hypotheses. It will also propose a conceptual model for the understanding of the ideal city, the new *cusco* or other *cusco*.

Given the issues canvassed in this chapter, the introduction continues with four further chapters that outline the background details for the analysis that follows. Chapters 2 and 3 lay out our basic knowledge of inka construction techniques, architecture, and canons of urban planning, while chapter 4 presents two practical techniques, used in medieval European urban studies, that are used to interpret inka Cusco. In chapter 5, I consider the history and development of the urban plan and its fabric from its inka beginnings, outlining the various events and changes that have brought about the form of the city as it is today.

The next four chapters utilize the techniques described in chapter 4 to consider the Cusco town plan. Chapter 6 presents basic field data to describe streets, wall construction styles, building types, and measurements in order to divide it into plan-units. Chapter 7 examines the important plan-seams, containing public spaces, plazas, palaces, and temples. In chapter 8, the planning canons of the residential plan-units are considered, while a social archaeology of the city is presented in chapter 9. The range of settlements of the hinterland and their relationships with the city are examined in chapter 10, while in chapter 11, the ceremonies and rituals performed in the city and their extensions into the hinterland are considered. This leads naturally into chapter 12, a consideration of its urban symbolism and its setting through the geomantic myths, toponymic studies, and symbolism of the center in ritual and political practice. It is demonstrated that the concept of *cusco* was utilized in the expansion of empire through the establishment of new *cusco*, which imitated and performed as Cusco in the provinces.

2

Inka Architecture and Urban Buildings

The inkas were skilled architects and builders, who achieved a great deal with the resources at hand and without the use of iron tools or any mechanical devices, such as pulleys, wheels, and draft animals. Their basic technology and a large, efficient labor force enabled them to construct magnificent cities and individual buildings. The following two chapters present an understanding of the basic constructional, architectural, and planning processes, elements and concepts that were used in the erection of inka buildings and urban settlements. In this chapter, I review the main aspects of inka architecture, as outlined by a number of scholars (e.g., Agurto 1987; Gasparini and Margolies 1980; Kendall 1985; Protzen 1993, 1999), in order to describe construction methods and techniques, building forms, and constructional styles. It is divided into three sections. First, I deal with the construction process in order to ground any specific archaeological finding in an understanding of inka techniques. Second, I describe typical inka buildings and their location in relation to other architectural elements, including open spaces and terraces. The final section considers the concept of "style and time" and various schemes that use architectural differences as a relative chronology.

Construction

Much architectural study has focused on the visual, more aesthetic aspects of inka buildings, such as wall styles and niche distribution, and less on the practical aspects of construction, which are necessary for the field archaeologist to understand. It is vital to examine the building process from the digging and laying of footings through to the construction of walls, the assembly of the roof frame, and its thatching in order to be prepared to analyze building remains. In this section, I describe how each phase

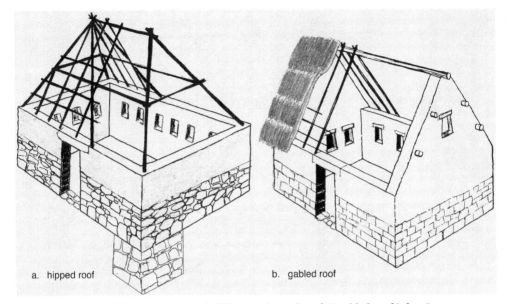

Figure 2.1. Small rectangular inka buildings. *A*, hipped roof; *B*, gabled roof (after Gasparini and Margolies 1980: fig. 149, fig. 164).

of inka building was accomplished, using basic tools, such as ropes and ramps, and the variations that can be found, using examples from around Tawantinsuyu.

The standard inka building is a one-room, one-story structure that is well made on a stable site. It is usually quite small, perhaps no larger than 10m by 7m. Its walls are wide, 80–85cm thick, and with an inward batter of between 2° and 7°.[1] Usually it has a single entrance, centrally placed in a long side, that is trapezoidal in form, with internal wall niches, also trapezoidal in form, on all four sides.[2] Its roof may be hipped or gabled (figure 2.1).

This technology is quite basic and in some respects can be regarded as modular in that the length and width can be extended and extra doors, niches, and windows placed according to the inka rules of symmetry. Some buildings, called *wayrana* or *masma*, have only three solid walls and the fourth side open, using a column to support the lintel and roof, if necessary. Additional structural height was gained either by simply using wider footings and walls to support the greater wall and roof weight or by changing upper wall assembly to adobe brick to reduce the overall weight. Therefore, a second story could be added, using adobe. However, as with the ancient

Maya, the limiting structural factor was building width because the short length of suitable and available timber for basic roof framing permitted a standard maximum of only around 10m. Therefore, wider buildings could only have been built with more technical roof frame constructions and/or the use of columns; with columns, the maximum width extended to about 26m (Agurto 1987).

Inka construction techniques were cautious, and their understanding of basic building physics was practical. While the thickness and batter of inka walls is distinctive, it is also mechanically very functional, since a wide wall enables a relatively heavy thatched roof to be supported without causing any wall to buckle or to settle and sink under the load. By the same token, the use of stone footings and walling with an adobe superstructure assists in the reduction of wall weight. The inkas were therefore very capable builders, spreading the structural load relatively evenly, using the four walls and any ancillary support columns effectively. Invariably, the footings were critical, and in certain sediments they needed to be set deep in the ground with a substantial width relative to the wall in order to avoid sinking.

Construction Materials

Inka construction involved the use of many types of materials, including fieldstone, quarried stone, rubble, gravel, sand, earth, clay, timber, and dried grass. In the Cusco region, most buildings were made out of stone or with a combination of a stone base and an adobe brick superstructure; all roofs had a timber frame that was thatched with dried grass. Elsewhere in the empire, adobe brick and tapia mud blocks were also used extensively for walling.[3]

In Cusco, the basic stone materials used in construction were either local fieldstone or locally quarried stone, chosen for its color, appearance, and how easily it could be worked and shaped. Naturally, such decisions must have been a function of where it was envisaged to use such blocks and in what kind of building. In the city, the favored building stones were andesite from quarries 15–35km distant and diorite and limestone from various outcrops to the north of the city. Local quartzite and granite were also used to some extent, but not sandstone. The exploitation of the andesite quarries at Rumiqolqa has been studied by Protzen (1980) and Béjar (2003) and at Waqoto by Miranda and Zanabria (1994). Stone building blocks were worked into four basic sizes at the quarry, then transported to the city via

Table 2.1. Standard sizes of stone blocks and adobe bricks in the Cusco region (in cm)

	Small	Medium	Large	Very large
Stone blocks	20 × 20 × 20	21–40 a side	41–80 a side	81–160 a side
Adobe bricks	39 × 19 × 16	50 × 30 × 15	90 × 20 × 10	—

a system of ramps and roads, using pack animals, people, poles, and ropes (Agurto 1987: 122).

Various local earths and clays were used to make adobe bricks by hand to a variety of dimensions (Moorehead 1978). Standard bricks varied in size between sites, but three general classes can be identified (table 2.1). Each brick had a flat base, vertical sides, and a plano-convex, slightly domed upper surface. They were generally made in the vicinity of each building site, by mixing sediments with water, dried grass, and even gravel and small sherds. Local earth and clays were also used to make mortar for laying up stone blocks and adobe bricks, whereas finer clays with dried grass were used to make wall plaster.

Certain local timbers were selected for building purposes, mainly to fabricate roof frames with beams, joists, rafters, and purlins, and they were used as lintels over doorways, niches, and windows. Among these species are *lambrán* (*Alnus jorullensis*), *kiswar* (*Buddleia incana*), *chachacomo* (*Escallonia* sp), *q'euña* (*Polylepis racemosa*), and *warango* (*Acacia macracantha*). These grow very slowly in valley and riverine locations with a maximum usable length of about 8–10m and a reasonable diameter of 12–20cm (Agurto 1987: 196). Timbers of high to very high density, such as *q'euña*, *warango*, *kiswar*, and *chachacomo*, have the strength to withstand heavy roof loads (table 2.2). It is also possible that, for special projects, timbers were imported from the upper valleys of the tropical forest.

The ubiquitous mountainside pasture grass, *ichu* (*Stipa ichu*), was dried to make thatch as well as string and rope of various ply and thicknesses. The latter were used to wrap lintel timbers and to tie the roof frame together and tie thatching to it and the structure itself.

Tools and Working

The basic inka builders' tool inventory would have consisted of several stone implements for both stone and woodworking. The *jiwaya* was a roughly oval hammerstone, made from various hard rock types and weighing between 1

Table 2.2. Available timbers for construction in the Cusco region

Botanical name	Vernacular name	Height (m)	Diameter (m)	Nature of trunk	Density
Acacia macracantha	*warango*	3–4	0.2	Cylindrical, twisted	Very high
Alnus jorullensis	*lambrán, aliso*	15–25	0.6	Straight, tapered	Low
Buddleia incana	*kiswar*	7–15	0.4–1.0	Straight, twisted	High
Escallonia resinosa	*chachacomo*	8–15	0.6	Cylindrical	High
Polylepis racemosa	*q'euña*	3–9	—	Twisted	Very high
Schinus molle	*molle*	6–8	0.5	Straight	High
Juglans neotropica	*nogal*	20	0.5	Straight, cylindrical	medium

Sources: Agurto 1987; Gade 1975.

and 10kg. Favored *jiwaya* materials were a black meteoritic stone, hematite, limonite, and a heavy, metamorphosed quartzite. These were used for initial flaking to form the rough shape, for pounding block faces to shape, and for fitting on-site. Flaked blades were used for scoring stone surfaces prior to finishing and for timber working, carpentry, and rope and thatch making. Other heavy, flat stones, and even potsherds, were utilized as building block face polishers.

Bronze chisels were used for timber working, particularly carpentry, while other bronze tools, such as T-shaped axes, chisels, and long bars, were used for splitting rocks and for finer percussion work in the trimming and shaping of stone blocks. For example, Gordon (1985) analyzed thirteen tools in the Bingham collection from Machu Picchu, concluding that only one had been used exclusively for woodworking, while ten were stone working chisels and two had remained unused.

Primitive drills, such as a fire-hardened wooden stake or a bow, were utilized with sand and water to perforate stone blocks that could be fitted into a gable end to tie a roof down. The digging of foundation trenches and postholes would have been achieved using a *chakitaqlla*, fitted with a bronze blade,[4] or a simple fire-hardened digging stick, with a doughnut-shaped stone weight, while earth and fill were probably moved using wooden hoes (*kuti*), baskets, and blankets.

Tall wall construction must have necessitated some form of working platform for bricklayers, stonemasons, and materials. It is known that ramps were built to access the top of a construction because there is a 20m long stone example adjacent to an unfinished *chullpa* at Sillustani. This method suits a small working area, but the long walls of a regular inka building must have required movable wooden scaffolding when it exceeded

2m in height. However, there is no physical evidence for such temporary constructions around any inka structure.

Platform Construction

In the Andes there is very little suitable flat land for construction, and it is necessary to build an artificial stable surface upon which to erect a structure. The inkas were accomplished terrace builders and simply used those skills to make large construction platforms. It required the erection of a battered stone retaining wall on the downhill side with a deliberately graded fill, layered behind to act as a stable matrix upon which to build. Alternatively, the platform was built by constructing a rough network of rubble walls to form cells, filling the spaces with stones, rubble, and gravel, and compacting them slightly before laying a series of progressively finer sediments on the surface. Both methods would serve to remove both surface and subsurface water. Once the platform sediments had settled, it could be built upon.

Footings

Once a site had been selected for a building, its outline would have been accurately marked out, and a footings trench dug, slightly wider than the proposed wall width to the depth of a firm natural clay or to an equivalent stable level and lined with clay. A basic foundation wall was then laid in the trench with large, relatively unworked blocks set firmly in a mud mortar. Its depth was generally in the order of two or three courses, between 40cm and 60cm, although in some cases footings have been recorded at over 1m deep. It was laid either vertically or with a slight batter; a very wide base was used to spread the load, particularly in more plastic soils. At this stage, surface drainage trenches would have been cut around a structure and filled with rubble or gravel in order to remove excess water from the site during construction and to dispose of rainwater afterwards.

Walls

A freestanding inka wall has two faces, both of which were carefully laid in accordance with the style required on either side. Therefore, the method of laying stone blocks always placed the worked faces outwards and the lesser worked ones to the interior, where the unseen core was filled with rubble, gravel, and earth. The sedimentary styles of stone ashlars were laid up in combinations of headers and stretchers without any internal fill. Each stone block was lowered into place along each course. If accurate fitting was required, as in polygonal or rectangular styles, this was done *in situ* by trial and error, using stone hammers and polishers to finish the joints and faces. Most wall assembly techniques also used a strong clay mortar to set the blocks in place. Adobe bricks were laid flat side up, in a clay mortar in "english bond," alternate courses of headers and stretchers, on top of a prepared double-faced, relatively level stone wall that stood between 1.2 and 1.5m above the floor (Moorehead 1978: 66, 90).

Wall width was a function of its projected height and the weight of the superstructure and roof. Irrespective of the materials used, there were two standard widths, 80–82cm and 1.05–1.10m, although others were also utilized. However, at Tambokancha, the lower courses of two free-standing walls are each more than 3m in width. They comprise three separate stone structures with cross-walls and buttresses at equal intervals to add strength, while the spaces in between were carefully filled with earth and rubble layers to lessen weight. Their height must have been over 10m, given the size of the elongated clay mounds from "melted" adobes that cover its lower stone walls (Farrington and Zapata 2003). Post-construction increase in wall width can be seen at Tambokancha, where external walls of certain structures were widened to about 2m using an 80cm veneer of fitted limestone blocks. Another technique designed to give walls additional strength to support a heavy roof is its distinctive batter, which may be at slightly different angles on the two faces with no structural consequences.

Great attention was paid to the construction of quoins in both structural corners and doors by carefully laying alternate courses of headers and stretchers (stone or adobe brick) to make all corners structurally sound. In the corners of some stone and adobe buildings, wooden braces were used at regular height intervals to reinforce the bonding and stability of the walls, quoins, and therefore the structure, such as at the Sayri Thupaq palace in Yucay (Moorehead 1978).

Wall Styles

The inkas were excellent stone masons, and many scholars have commented on the well-fitting nature, finish, and aesthetic appearance of inka stone working and wall construction, generally with the assumption that it must mean something. As a consequence, there have been several attempts

A

B

Figure 2.2. Inka wall construction styles. A, sedimentary style with rectangular andesite blocks in the Qorikancha enclosure wall in Awaqpinta; B, polygonal style limestone wall of the Colegio de Ciencias, lining the road to Kuntisuyu, just south of Kusipata (photo by Lisa Solling).

to classify wall styles in detail (e.g., Agurto 1987; Harth-Terré 1964). Indeed, Valencia and Gibaja (1992) identified eleven styles of wall at Machu Picchu, while Qorikancha displays at least four (Puelles 2005).

Essentially in the Cusco region, there are four basic wall styles: cellular or polygonal, sedimentary, *pirka*, and stone and adobe, of which the first two are the most aesthetically pleasing and frequently subdivided, according to the nature of the joint between the blocks or the profile and quality of the finish (figure 2.2). The polygonal style is essentially the fitting together of similar sized but irregularly shaped blocks, while sedimentary uses rectangular ashlars, laid in fairly level courses. Both are characterized by their fine finish, sunken joints, and good workmanship. It has often been stated that in these styles no mortar was used, and while that may be the case in certain walls, it is not universal. The third stone style is *pirka*, the wall assembly of roughly shaped stone rubble, laid randomly, although sometimes semi-coursed, in a thick clay mortar. Such walls would have been plastered inside and out.

Buildings made with stone and adobe walls are very common throughout the Cusco region, generally comprising a lower polygonal, sedimentary, or *pirka* wall, erected to a height of 1.2–1.5m and finished as a relatively level surface. On top of this were laid adobe bricks in english bond in a clay mortar up to 1.5cm thick (Moorehead 1978). The advantage of such a mixed wall was to reduce the overall weight of the structure, while not compromising its strength or stability. These walls were then plastered and painted, including even their lower polygonal or sedimentary stonework.

Wall Features

The standard inka wall features, such as doorways, niches, and windows invariably have a trapezoidal form that corresponds to a few standard sizes (figure 2.3a). All required the use of a lintel to support the wall above, and these were firmly embedded into the wall on either side. In many buildings, the lintel was a single stone that spanned the top of the feature, including doorways in excess of 4m. In the case of wide walls, two or more stones may have been set side by side. Alternative lintel materials were timber poles or thick bamboo canes that were individually bound in rope and clay before being set into the wall.

The placement of such features generally conforms to a concept of symmetry with emphasis placed on equal size, shape, and equidistance in separation. Single doors were invariably centrally placed in a front wall but were

A

Figure 2.3. Inka wall features. *A*, double-jamb doorway, Choqechaka #469; *B*, niche and barhold in structure E6 at Quispeguanca. This building has a random rubble base to the height of the niche base with an adobe superstructure and is covered in a red clay plaster. The barhold measures about 15cm square and is about 48cm to the left of the door jamb.

B

Table 2.3. Basic dimensions of trapezoidal niches (in cm)

	Basal width	Lintel width	Height	Depth	Height above floor
Small	≥30	~20	25–40	30	—
Standard A	28–42	25–38	55–65	25–30	125–50
Standard B	31–50	33–44	63–72	30–36	125–50, 220–40
Standard C	45–56	35–46	70–97	35–44	125–50
Large	60–63	43–55	96–102	35–48	125–50
Full length	115–200	67–148	184–250	32–79	~30

Sources: Agurto 1980; Kendall 1985: 31–35.

symmetrically spaced if there were more. The common façade doorway ranged between 0.8m and 1.65m in width, although wider ones are also found up to 4.6m (Kendall 1985: 25–27). Additional side doors are found only in certain types of building, such as *kallanka*.

Kendall (1985: 31–35) recognized five sizes of niche from small to full size and irregular (table 2.3); standard sized ones are found usually on internal walls at a height of 1.2 to 1.5m above floor level and are evenly spaced along a wall. These would have functioned as storage spaces and for the placement and display of special objects. Niches can also be found externally on a façade or retaining wall in order to add to the aesthetic and politico-religious meaning of a building or building complex; these can be either small, standard size or full length. For example, there are the full-length niches on the façade of the large hall of Casa de la Ñusta, the Palace of Sayri Thupaq, the Urqo round tower, and on retaining walls that define special areas at Vilkaswamán and Qolqampata, while at Quispeguanca there are standard niches on the lower wall of the palace complex. The distribution of doors and niches is invariably symmetrically planned and executed.

One common aesthetic device, which was used to enhance doors or niches, was setting them into the wall with a second jamb, architrave or frame on either side and at the lintel. This is thought to have increased the importance of a structure. There are large full-length external triple framed niches at Mawqa Llaqta as well as remnants of a triple-jamb gateway at Quispeguanca. The stepped niche is a decorative device added to a façade or internal wall, such as at Sayri Thupaq in Yucay, Iñak Uyu on Koati and Pilko Kayma on the Island of the Sun.[5]

Another wall feature is the trapezoidal window that can be full sized or small, but it is not very common. Such windows are found usually in gable ends or as an added feature within a larger niche. Cylindrical stone pegs are found in a building interior at the height of the lintel of a standard niche, as at Qosqo Ayllu and Machu Picchu. Their function is not known, but it is possible they were used for hanging personal items, such as clothing.

A rather common, but not universal, feature is the "barhold," a small hole in the stonework, 10–15cm square and about the same depth with an upright cylindrical stone placed in its internal center (figure 2.3b). Bouchard (1983: 42–43) has identified four types. They are usually found at 1.1–1.2m above the floor level on either side of a doorway either in the jamb or on the internal wall face, and they indicate how the "door was closed." The inkas did not have the hinged, swinging doors of the Old World, but as Mancio Serra Lejesma described in his 1589 will, the inkas used only a "little pole" tied across the entrance to prevent anyone entering (Prescott 1862).

Roof

A roof is a wooden framework upon which the builder lays some form of impermeable cover that will keep the weather out of the structure. Its erection over a building requires some basic technology and carpentry skills.

There are two standard roof forms for inka buildings: gabled and hipped, although single sloping roofs were also common for small structures. For round or sub-rectangular buildings, tall conical roofs were constructed (Bauer 2004: 120). Agurto (1987) has studied the angle of roof extant at several locations in the Cusco region, concluding that, irrespective of type, the preferred roof slope was between 50° and 65°. Several authors have discussed the probable designs for the inka roof frame (e.g., Agurto 1987; Bouchard 1976b; Protzen 1993).

Clearly, the length of suitable and available timber was a limiting factor in determining the distance to be spanned; however, the ability to tie lengths of wood together in order to construct frames with joists, trusses, and a ridge beam enabled the inkas to span up to 10m without difficulty. Greater widths were spanned using evenly spaced columns along the center line to support the ridge beam or by using two or three lines of columns to support a roof frame. Timber posts, 20–30cm in diameter, were used for ridge-line columns in a *kallanka* at Huánuco Pampa (Murra and Hadden 1966: 136) and the large hall at Quispeguanca (Farrington 1995), for a double line in the *kallanka* at Samaipata (Muñóz 2007), and a triple line in the large *kallanka* at Inkallaqta (Coben 2006). At the Wiraqocha temple in Raqchi, the builders adopted a different approach with the construction of a freestanding, 16m tall central wall, 2.7m in width, to support the ridge beam and roof frame. A line of evenly spaced stone and adobe columns were situated on either side, only 2.7m from the side walls to add support to the frame.

On top of the roof frame, closely spaced purlins were tied to provide a surface upon which bundles of *ichu* thatch, up to 1m thick, were laid and tied to the frame. In gabled buildings, a line of stone cylindrical and donut-shaped pegs were placed into the upper part of the gable and eaves for use as tying points for the thatch bundles. In the absence of any formal roof drainage, the thatching protruded the wall line by about 1m to allow rainwater to drip clear, thus reducing splashback and unwanted erosion of adobe brick or plaster.

Floor

As a building began to take shape, the inka builders laid an internal floor and constructed a patio surface. The internal floor level was set slightly below that of the threshold stones. There are three basic inka floor types: stone, wood, and compacted or tamped earth with grave. The latter is the most common and is found in almost every excavated inka settlement in the Cusco region. It is formed by compacting a wet clay and gravel matrix with a heavy *makana*. This surface can withstand heavy usage; it can be easily swept and easily relaid, using the same materials. Such floors can be colored with yellow, red, or white clays (Gyarmati and Varga 1999), while Alcina (1976: 27) noted that such floors were also hardened by fire.

The second type, paving, was formed by either flagstones laid horizontally in a clay mortar or cobbling with rounded river stones on top of a compacted clay base. The difficulty with these is that differential settling and treadage affects their levelness. The third kind was a wooden floor, which was invariably used for a second story; naturally none of these have survived. However, lines of large rectangular holes set in side walls, such as in Qosqo Ayllu or Huchuy Cusco, imply that timber beams had been fixed into them, and upon these a light timber frame would have been laid with planks and boards.

Internal Bench or Platform

An internal bench or platform is found in some inka rooms in the Cusco area. It comprises a small rubble and earth mound with a compacted upper surface, retained by a low stone or adobe wall. These may have been used as sleeping platforms. In storerooms, benches have rectangular clay bins on top and a system of ventilation ducts in the body. In some sites, a bench supported a platform only 10–15cm above the general floor level that was used to separate a kitchen area from other activities.

Decoration

Apart from the arrangements of niches and windows and the placement of stepped-fret niches, inka wall decoration usually took the form of a thick layer of plaster applied to both the external and internal faces. This was a 3–4cm thick layer of fine clay, mixed with gravel or sand and short pieces of dried grass. It was applied, then burned *in situ,* and therefore is black in color. Its surface was then painted with thin layers of fine clay, that is sometimes naturally red, pink, yellow, or cream, to a total thickness of about 5cm. Such render was applied to external surfaces of *pirka,* adobe, and even stone and adobe. It is suspected that polygonal and rectangular style external walls were not plastered; however, all internal walls were rendered irrespective of style, such as observed at Chinchero and Raqchi.

Pigments were added to the final layers to make individual buildings brighter and more distinctive. Such colors include red, yellow, white, blue, brown, and black. At Tambo Colorado, Protzen and Morris (2004) have recorded fourteen decorative combinations, using three colors, yellow, white, and red, including all white and all red walls, the use of horizontal stripes and triangles, as well as the painting of niche interiors in a color different from the adjacent walls. Certain patterns tend to be concentrated in particular compounds or structures. Various houses in *kancha* at Tarmatambo were also painted in red, yellow, and white (Arellano and Matos 2007). At Incarracay in Bolivia, Gyarmati and Varga (1999: 69–75) reported that an east facing *wayrana* was painted internally red on both its southern side and half its western wall, while yellow was on the northern wall and the remainder of the western wall. In the Lauca region of Bolivia, there was an inka period, local tradition of painting adobe *chullpas* with geometric designs, similar to patterns on inka *unku* in four colors, red, yellow, white, and green (Gisbert et al. 1996).

In the Cusco region, evidence for wall painting is quite rare, probably because of adverse climatic conditions; however, some sites have indications of painting. For example, at Qorikancha in Cusco, a 7.5cm wide horizontal grey-black band was painted at about 2.15m above the floor to pass through the internal niches of two buildings, R-3 and R-4 (Béjar 1990). A similar line was noted by Protzen (1993: 236–37) at Choqana near Ollantaytambo and inside the cave of Choqueilla. My own excavations at Tambokancha uncovered painted internal wall panels in white, yellow, and orange-red in a large building, a double stepped-fret form (Farrington and Zapata 2003), while at the Palace of Sayri Thupaq, painting was discovered in several niches. Sillar (2002: 229) has reported traces of a double stepped-fret design painted in red directly on the lower courses of the fine sedimentary style stone wall that forms the central column of the large hall at Raqchi.

As far as can be determined, the external and/or internal walls of inka buildings were decorated in single or multiple colors in designs of simple horizontal stripes and triangles, while some Bolivian *chullpas* had more elaborate geometric designs. It is uncertain whether these were found elsewhere. The inkas do not appear to have painted figurative friezes, although Xerez (1985: 134) reported that the main entrance to Paramonga on the central north coast was flanked by two painted jaguars.

One rare characteristic of inka dressed stone masonry in prestigious locations is zoomorphic bas-relief carving, such as snakes, felines, and other animals, on individual building blocks (van de Guchte 1990). For example, at Huánuco Pampa there are pumas carved in high relief in two contexts: on the *usnu* platform, at lintel level on the jambs of both entrances there are pairs of felines, arranged one behind the other; and in bas-relief on a block in the western wall and at each of four gateways between pairs of *kallanka* that lead into the innermost *kancha* of Sector IIB, the probable royal palace, where each double-jamb entrance is flanked at lintel height by carved pumas in profile that face inwards (Morris and Thompson 1985: 59–60, plates 25, IV). As such, they serve to protect and elaborate the route into the royal quarters. A similar carved block was found adjacent to the entrance into the main complex of Pumapongo, the "gate of the puma," at Tumibamba (Idrovo 2000: 116) and another at Vilkaswamán that had probably been removed from the *usnu* platform (Santillana 2001: 143). Some inka *chullpa* in Lupaqa cemeteries, such as at Cutimbo (Tantalean and Pérez 2000), have felines, snakes, and vizcacha carved on building blocks around their entrances. Clearly, such decoration must have had social, political, or religious meanings that should be explored.

Concepts of Symmetry and Aesthetics

In terms of aesthetic design, the inkas used the straight wall and the concept of symmetry to great effect in the design of individual buildings, both

Figure 2.4. The *kallanka* at Huchuy Cusco with a symmetrical distribution of double-jamb doorways and windows, facing the plaza.

internally and externally. For example, doorways and niches were symmetrically placed and at equidistant intervals along a wall (figure 2.4), although Lee (1997) argued that such distribution was by proportion for each wall and not by accurate measurement. In many locations, the building distribution about a plaza or in a *kancha* is also symmetrical. This principle enables the archaeologist to deal with ruins and excavation data that are incomplete, to reconstruct the possible building arrangement.

It is clear that the inkas had no difficulty in building a straight wall and a rectangular structure, and although the constructed right angle was rarely accurate, it was a reasonable approximation. The builders were skilled enough to compensate in the layout and erection of the four walls to the extent that most buildings were not perfectly square or rectangular but gave the impression of being so.

At special locations, they used other arrangements to build important structures. For example, the distinctive zigzag terrace walls of Saqsaywaman used short straight lengths and rounded acute corners to define the Muyuqmarka temple complex. There are at least six other sites in the Cusco region where this technique was used to mark a major cultural place such as a temple or *waka*.

At the site of Tambokancha, the inka architects required a monumental built form and chose to gain height and mass for each building with the use of thick, slightly convex walls made of stone and adobe. Such monumentality enabled several large tall towers to be constructed as well as other complex, double stepped-fret forms to create an exceptionally special place (Farrington and Zapata 2003).

Another design was to build round or oval buildings or to use significant curves in the erection or display of others. Throughout Tawantinsuyu, there are very few round buildings to the extent that each known example is thought to have had some special importance, such as at Muyuqmarka, Urqo (Squier 1877), and the oval platform at Ingapirka (Fresco 1983). Distinctively curved walls were used in combination with straight ones at Qorikancha in Cusco and at the probable Sun temples of Machu Picchu, Pisaq, and Tumibamba to add a degree of importance to their appearance.

Urban Components

The inka urban center was characterized by a number of distinctive architectural elements, arranged carefully with the planned use of open spaces that may or may not be enclosed. In this section, I shall briefly review the field characteristics of these.

Plaza

Plazas are found in most inka urban centers as well as in rural palaces, such as Quispeguanca and Chinchero. They vary in size from as quite small to 520m by 360m at Huánuco Pampa (table 2.4). They are rectilinear in form, ranging from square to trapezoidal. They can be "open," that is, with flanking buildings only on one, two, or three sides, as at Pumpu, or "closed," with buildings on all four sides, as at Huánuco Pampa, or surrounded by a free-standing wall, such as at Watungasta and El Shincal (Raffino et al. 1983–85). The plaza was used for public gatherings and the major ceremonies of the inka world, such as *inti raymi*, *qhapaq raymi*, *sitwa*, *warachiquy*, and *qhapaq hucha* as well as daily rituals, processions, dances, and ritual battles between urban social groups (e.g., Morris and Covey 2003).

Usnu Complex

One characteristic of the inka plaza is the *usnu* complex that may be located within it, as at Huánuco Pampa, or to one side of it, but always approached directly from it, such as at Tambo Colorado (Hyslop 1990; Raffino and

Table 2.4. Selected plaza dimensions and features in Tawantinsuyu (in meters)

	Length × width	Open or enclosed	Features
Aypate	E—85.0; S—130.0; W—165.0; N—230.0	Open on N side	*Usnu* platform on E side of plaza
Huánuco Pampa	520.0 × 360.0	Enclosed by structures	*Usnu* platform in plaza; streets exit in NW, NE, SW, SE corners
Pumpu	E—285.0; S—480.0; W—395.0; N—425.0	Open on N and W sides	*Usnu* platform in plaza
Ollantaytambo Qosqo Ayllu	97.0 × 72.5	Enclosed by structures and wall	Wall on E side; 2 *kallanka* on N side, 2 on S; street to W
Calca	321.8 × 149.5	Open on S side	*Kancha* on W, N, and E sides. Church in middle
Samaipata	100.0 × 100.0	Open on N side, partially walled E and W sides	*Kallanka* on S side; main rock complex to N
El Shincal	175.2 × 175.2	Enclosed by wall	*Usnu* platform in plaza, 1 *kallanka* in SW plaza corner
Watungasta west	115.0 × 98.0	Enclosed by wall	*Usnu* platform in plaza
Watungasta east	154.0 × 113.0	Enclosed by wall	No *usnu* platform

Sources: Astuhuaman 1998; Matos 1994; Meyers and Ulbert 1997; Morris 1987; Raffino 1983–85; Raffino 1993–98; Soto and Cabrera 1999.

Farrington 2004). It consists of two critical components that have physical and cosmological characteristics (Zuidema 1980). The first is that it must have some height, such as a platform with a staircase, a large modified or natural rock or even a rock erected on top of a platform. The second is a feature that enters the ground, such as a prepared round hole, as at La Centinela, a tomb, a rock fissure, or something that gives the impression of entering the ground, such as a water surface, a canal, as at Manyaraki,[6] or a river, as at Watungasta. The second is often ignored in most archaeological studies, but it is vital because it received offerings. Most urban locations have some aspect of these features in close proximity within a plaza.

The *usnu* platform is certainly a most readily identifiable feature and the focal point of any inka urban center, with more than 85 throughout Tawantinsuyu from Quitoloma in Ecuador (Connell et al. 2003) to Chena in central Chile (Stehberg 1995; Raffino and Farrington 2004). They are generally low and rectangular, but they could be terraced with up to five levels, as at Vilkaswamán. A centrally placed stone staircase usually leads to the top from one side (figure 2.5). They vary in size from 7.0m by 3.5m

Figure 2.5. *Usnu* platform with central staircase and high walled summit at El Shincal, northwest Argentina.

at Hualfín to 48.0m by 32.0m at Huánuco Pampa, and stand from as little as 1.0m high at Oma Porco to 8.0m at Vilkaswamán and Caxas (table 2.5).

In several excavated examples, such as Huánuco Pampa, Pumpu, and El Shincal, the platform summit consists of a patio, surrounded by a low bench and an outer wall, where ceremonies and feasting could be practiced (see chapter 12). Orientation is usually measured by the azimuth of the staircase, which may be oriented toward a critical sunrise or sunset, such as at Pumpu, or toward a particular geographical feature, such as a mountain at Mitupampa (Astuhuamán 1998). It varies from place to place, with no apparent consistency.

Kallanka

A *kallanka* is a long, relatively narrow, multi-doored, single-room building that is always aligned with its long façade and doorways fronting a plaza (Gasparini and Margolies 1980; Meinken 2000–2001; Barraza 2010).[7] It has a symmetrical arrangement of external façade doors and internal niches, and it usually has a gabled roof with an additional door at each end (figure 2.4). Its doorways are wide and sometimes double-jamb. In most urban locations, *kallanka* range in length from 15m to 104m at Aypate and 105m

Table 2.5. Selected *usnu* platforms in Tawantinsuyu

	Basal dimensions (m)	Height (m)	No. of terraces	Access orientation	Construction material	Location in site	Elements on top of platform
Tumibamba	26.0 × 28.0	1.2	1?	SW?	Not known	On E side of plaza	Not known
Aypate	31.5 × 33.6 irregular	4.2	3	SW	*Pirka*	On side of plaza	Stone hole (*utqu*); fox cranium offering
Caxas	19.0 × 16.0 trapezoidal	8.0	2	W cardinal	*Pirka*	In plaza	Stone hole (*utqu*)
Mitupampa (Sondor)	16.7 × 14.8	2.0	2	ESE	*Pirka*	In plaza	Two carved felines in horizontal circles
Huánuco Pampa	48.0 × 32.0	3.5	3	S cardinal; steps to two entrances	Sedimentary laid dressed stone	In plaza	Walled; bench; structures on terraces, offerings?
Pumpu	25.5 × 20.5	2.9	3	E	*Pirka*	In plaza	Bench; hole; structures
Hatun Xauxa	28.0 × 32.0	2.7	2	SW	*Pirka*	In plaza	Chapel
Vilkaswamán	26.0 × 24.0	8.0	5	E cardinal	Sedimentary laid dressed stone	On W side of plaza	Paved; carved stone seat
Cochacajas	24.0 × 24.0	4.0	2	S	*Pirka*	In plaza	Not known

Usno Moqò	20.60 × 19.95	7.5	3	NW	*Pirka*	Not known	Paved; offerings
Oma Porco	5.0 × 5.0	1.0	1	?	*Pirka*	In plaza	Not known
Chipihuayco	5.0 × 4.0	1.0	1	—	*Pirka*	In plaza	Not known
Potrero de Payogasta	9.0 × 7.0	1.5	2	?	*Pirka*	In plaza	Not known
El Shincal	16.0 × 16.0	1.3	1	W	*Pirka*	In plaza	Walled; benches; offerings
Hualfin	3.5 × 7.0	1.0	1	W	*Pirka*	In plaza	Not known
Watungasta	3.0 × 4.0	1.0	1	W	*Pirka*	In plaza	Not known
Chilecito	12.73 × 10.3	1.4	1	SE	*Pirka*	In plaza	Not known
Paso del Lamar	6.1 × 11.6	1.2	1	E?	*Pirka*	20m S from plaza	Not known
Cerro Verde (Caspana)	20.7 × 19.6	1.5?	2	NE	Plastered *pirka*	On promontory	Not known
Viña del Cerro	N 6.1 × E 5.9 × S 6.2 × W 6.1	1.1	1	SW	*Pirka*	In plaza	Stair in SW corner

Source: Raffino and Farrington 2004.

at Pumpu (table 2.6), while they tend to be quite narrow, only 8 to 15m in width. Morris (Morris and Thompson 1985: 89) has excavated several at Huánuco Pampa and in one, measuring 74.0m by 13.4m, he revealed a central line of seven evenly spaced stone rings that originally held wooden posts to support the roof ridge. At Samaipata, Muñóz (2007: 259) has reported that its *kallanka* measures 68m by 16m and has two parallel lines of nine postholes, 6m apart, to support its roof. Each was 1m in diameter and dug into the sandstone bedrock to a depth of 1.8m, and in two of these, there were still the remains of timber posts, each 30cm in diameter.

Kallanka can occur singly, such as at Aypate and Samaipata, or in lines around a plaza, as at Huánuco Pampa. Gasparini and Margolies (1980: 196–97) noted that the pattern of *kallanka* placement varied from place to place, which could represent "a hierarchical distinction between administrative centers of regional importance."

Kancha

A *kancha* is an enclosed compound containing three or more inward facing, symmetrically placed buildings that open on to a central courtyard (figure 2.6; Gasparini and Margolies 1980; Hyslop 1990). It is a standard housing unit in inka urban centers and can be found from Callo in Ecuador to Tambillos in Argentina. In its basic form, the structures are generally built into the enclosure wall, leaving an open space in the corners, where burials occurred, animals were kept, and rubbish was dumped. *Kancha* can be arranged as separate street blocks, such as at Calca, Palkay, and Avijay, or can be arranged side by side in pairs, also surrounded by streets as at Ollantaytambo (Bouchard 1976a, 1983). In a *kancha*, all buildings may be either identical or individually different, including some arranged back to back, sharing a common wall, and a combination of closed buildings with doors, with two stories or even *wayrana*. The *kancha* usually have one or two entrances that, in the more important compounds, are double-jamb. Variations on this design include a similar arrangement of four or more buildings with internal patio but no enclosure wall, and a pair of identical buildings arranged on opposite sides of a small patio.

At several urban sites, there are other types of large walled enclosures that either contain parallel and perpendicular rows of relatively uniform buildings, such as V-B-5 at Huánuco Pampa (Morris and Thompson 1985: 70–71), or have a much less formal internal plan, such as *kancha* Ad-14 at Pumpu (Matos 1994: 165) and III-C-4 at Huánuco Pampa (Morris

Table 2.6. Selected *kallanka* dimensions in Tawantinsuyu (in meters)

	External / internal length	External / internal width	No of façade doors, windows	Rear wall details	Wall thickness	Internal gable details. End A; end B	No. of columns / no. of rows	Location
Aypate	104.0/ 102.0	11.8/ 9.8	9; not known	—	1.0	—	—	Plaza edge
Huancacarpa	99.0/ 97.6	14.5/ 12.9	8; not known	—	0.8	—	—	
Pukarumi	25.5/ 23.6	6.9/ 4.8	3; not known	—	1.05	—	—	Plaza edge
Huánuco Pampa II-B-1a	74.0/ 72.0	13.4/ 11.85	9; not known	10 windows	0.8?	2 windows; 1 door, 2 windows	7/1	Plaza edge
Pumpu K1, K2	105.0/ 103.6	9.5/ 8.1	4; not known	—	0.7	—	0	Plaza edge
Chinchero CH1	42.7/ 40.53	8.64/ 6.48	6 double jamb; 0	13 niches	1.07	Door and niche at each end	0	Plaza edge
Huchuy Cusco	41.5/ 39.6	11.25/ 9.89	5 double jamb; 6	6? niches, 5 doors	1.16	Door at each end	—	Plaza edge
Samaipata	68.0/ 65.2	16.0/ 13.2	8; not known	Door or window	1.4	—	18/2	Plaza edge
Inkallaqta	78.0/ 75.80	26.0/ 24.3	12; 13	44 niches	0.85	10 niches; 4 windows at each end	24/3	Plaza edge
El Shincal k2	47.9/ 45.8	10.4/ 8.8	3; 0	—	0.8	Door at each end	—	SW corner of plaza

Sources: Alcina 1976; Astuhuaman 1998; Gasparini and Margolies 1980; Matos 1994; Meyers and Ulbert 1997; Muñoz 2007; Raffino 2004; Schjellerup 1997.

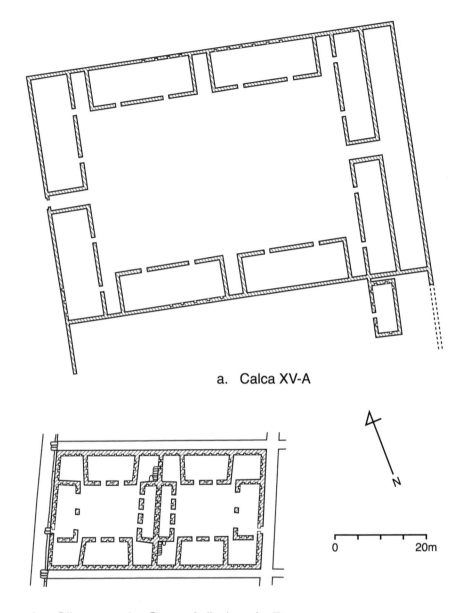

a. Calca XV-A

b. Ollantaytambo Qosqo Ayllu *kancha* 7

0   20m

Figure 2.6. Urban *kancha*. *A*, Calca mz XVA (after Castillo and Jurado 1996); *B*, Qosqo Ayllu, Ollantaytambo *kancha* 7 (after Protzen 1993: fig. 2.13; Soto and Cabrera 1999).

and Thompson 1985: 69). Both have structures and spaces, while access throughout is controlled by the placement of walls between buildings. The compound V-B-5 in Huánuco Pampa measures about 120m by 140m with only a single entrance on its southern side from the main plaza into a patio. This leads through an internal building into a small plaza, surrounded by several elongated buildings over 40m in length. From there, access to several lines of two-doored structures of two sizes (18.2m by 6.4m, 13.7m by 6.4m) is restricted.

While various archaeologists (e.g., Bouchard 1976a) have suggested that the kancha must reflect a social grouping that is somehow linked in terms of kin, craft, or other relationships, it is not known if identical buildings represent similar functions. However, in the absence of detailed archaeological analyses, such specific social and economic functions must remain hypotheses.

Palace with Large Hall

An inka palace is one of many urban elements that has been chiefly understood from the documentary sources, such as Murúa's description (1987: 345–49), which Craig Morris (2004) has interpreted to refine his work on the provincial inka palaces at Huánuco Pampa, La Centinela, and Tambo Colorado. From the survey and excavation of known rural palaces in the Sacred Valley and adjacent areas, such as Quispeguanca and Chinchero, a clear pattern of building layout can be described that comprises a plaza with a residential kancha on one side, adjacent to which there is a large hall (Farrington 1995)(figure 2.7a). A series of other rectangular buildings, arranged along streets within the general area, probably functioned as kitchens, workshops, storerooms, and retainer dwellings.

The large hall is generally monumental in its length, width, and height, and in contrast to a kallanka, its façade is a narrow gabled end that faces onto the plaza that, in several examples, displays a tall central niche and a pair of doorways. Guaman Poma (1980: 329 [331]) illustrated the buildings of a royal palace, including large halls.[8] From the archaeological evidence, there can be two to four lateral entrances along each long wall, and all standing examples are niched internally (table 2.7). The majority seem to be from 10m to 14m in width, while excavations at Quispeguanca have revealed centrally placed stone rings and postholes for wooden columns (Farrington 1995) (figure 2.7b). This distinctive pattern is repeated at other sites, such as Pumawanka, Canchispukyo, and Tambokancha, whereas the

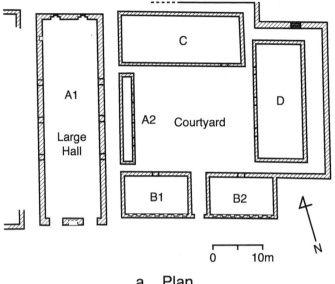

a. Plan

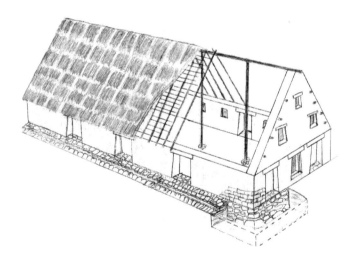

b. Large hall

Figure 2.7. The royal palace and large hall at Quispeguanca. *A*, plan of residential *kancha* and large hall; *B*, isometric drawing of the large hall (after Gasparini and Margolies 1980: fig. 249).

Table 2.7. Large halls in the Cusco heartland (in meters)

Site and structure	External/internal length	External/internal width	Wall width	No of doors per long side	Width of doors	Internal side wall niches by panels	Façade details	Overlooking
Quispeguanca A1	44.92/42.0	14.35/12.05	1.16	3	1.12	6 [2/1//1/1//2]	Stone corners; central niche and two doors	Plaza
Quispeguanca	—	8.85/	—	—	—	—	Stone corners only in field boundary wall	Plaza
Pumaguanca	33.35/31.18	12.78/10.40	1.1	1	1.3	10 [2,1,2//2,1,2]	Stone corners; central niche	Plaza
Casa de la Ñusta, Yucay	35.0e/32.60e	14.80/12.80	1.0	3	1.08	8 [0//3//2//3/0]	Stone corners; central niche and two doors	Plaza
Chinchero, CH-IV	43.20 43.7/ 40.8	12.93/10.53	1.2	3	0.96–1.10	—	Stone corners; possible footing in center; colonial door	Plaza
Chinchero, CH-VI	34.45/32.10	12.15/9.7	1.1	3	1.08–1.10	8 [2/2/2/2//2]	Stone corners; rebuilt with three irregular niches	Small Plaza
Canchispuqyo, Qochoq valley	27.1e/25.1	9.8/8.05	0.9	2	1.10	6 [2/2/2/2]	Destroyed by road	Qochoq valley
Tambokancha D5	34.3/32.1	12.86/10.54	1.12	4	0.90	—	Stone wall; probable central niche	Sector II-A + part of plaza

Note: e = estimated.

Casa de la Ñusta on the eastern side of the Yucay plaza is a large hall, but no adjacent buildings have yet been found.[9]

Streets (*Kiqllu*)

Inka streets (*kiqllu*) within urban areas were generally quite narrow (2.0–2.5m), giving access to the various *kancha* and other buildings. They were constructed with a paved surface on top of a compacted earth and gravel base and a stone-lined central or lateral drain. Wider streets (3.2–5.6m), built in the same manner, probably served as ceremonial routes, linking important locations while enabling the passage of litters carrying the Inka, mummies, and statues, as well as dancers, musicians, and other participants.

Town Walls

Prior to the rise of the inkas, the andean region is portrayed as one of regional polities with many walled hilltop settlements. In the Cusco region, few inka towns were surrounded by walls. For example, Machu Picchu has a wall separating its agricultural terraces from the urban sector, and a similar situation is found in the more dispersed settlements of Pisaq and Ollantaytambo. The towns of Patallaqta, Calca, and Cusco itself were not defensively walled, nor were any of the rural palaces. Walls, where they do occur in these settlements, may be free-standing or terraced, but they do not surround a place completely. They serve to define and separate spaces, possibly dividing the urban and sacred from the mundane and profane. Nevertheless, with or without a town wall, everyone must have known where the boundaries lay because, in Cusco, all foreigners had to leave the city during some festivals.

Gates (*punku*)

Like the town wall, the gate is a very clear indicator of passing from one cultural space and into another. Gate towers have been found, flanking the approaches to Huchuy Cusco, Ollantaytambo, and the palace of Quispeguanca. At the former site, there are the remains of partly destroyed gates that originally controlled access to the central plaza (Kendall et al. 1992). They display barholds in the jambs to indicate a pole was tied across to prevent entry. However, not all inka urban settlements had gate towers. The word *punku* is used as a suffix to mean a point of entry; therefore, the toponym Wakapunku referred to a place where the road from Chinchay-suyu entered Cusco, only 150m from Hawkaypata.[10]

Temple and *Waka*

Inka sacred places, *waka*, could be either natural features, such as mountains, rocks, caves, springs, lakes, waterfalls, and trees, or built structures, like fountains, platforms, buildings, or even parts of them, such as doorways. There was no definitive design for a temple as a place of worship; these could be simply basic rectangular buildings that were arranged in a *kancha*. However, the location itself could be made distinctive, using either zigzag or curved walls (see earlier). Some natural *waka* were also similarly walled, including the rock and caverns at Chingana Chico, Amarumarka-wasi, and Sapantiana and the scree stones at Salapunku (Km 82), below Ollantaytambo.

It has already been mentioned that Qorikancha and the Sun temples at Machu Picchu, Pisaq, and Tumibamba were characterized by a curved wall, either as part of the outer wall of the complex or as part of the particular building itself. In addition, there was also a tunnel or cave under the temples at Machu Picchu, Tumibamba, and possibly Cusco.

Qolqa

There are several types of storeroom, *qolqa*, found in association with inka urban centers and *tampu* throughout the empire (e.g., LeVine 1992). These tend to be individual buildings (rectangular or round), arranged in rows and invariably on hillsides, overlooking major production areas, such as in the Cochabamba valley, or at provincial towns, such as Hatun Xauxa and Huánuco Pampa. In the Cusco area, the *qolqa* were elongated and not only held agricultural produce but also cloth, clothing, metal goods, and weapons (Morris 1967).

Water Distribution Systems

Several inka towns had a water reticulation system that supplied fresh spring or river water for domestic and ritual use (Hyslop 1990, chap. 5). There were both open channels and subterranean stone culverts to deliver water to critical locations at fountains or baths throughout the urban area. There was also a more fundamental stone drainage system for the removal of surface rainwater from plazas, roofs, and patios in open channels down the middle of streets to a river. The disposal of food remains and human waste may also have been through the drainage network.

For the inkas, water surfaces were regarded as liminal phenomena that served as gateways into *ukhu pacha*, the underworld. For example, it was necessary that the *usnu* complex had a river or canal flowing past for it to receive and remove offerings and ashes. In addition, the fertilizing qualities of water were recognized. Hence the seeping of springs in urban and rural locations was regarded as a sacred occurrence, and therefore these became sacred places, *waka*.

Integration of Other Physical Features into the Townscape

Caves, rocks, hills, and even trees were also incorporated into the urban landscape and often served as *waka* for the local population (Hyslop 1990: chap. 4). In several locations, a large rock was incorporated within some form of inka structure, thus enhancing the sacred qualities of that particular feature, such as at Urqo, Huchuy Cusco, and Machu Picchu.

Function

I have tried to restrict this chapter to the constructional and architectural aspects of the principal elements of inka urban settlement without discussing building function. However, function has naturally interceded with such specific buildings as *usnu* complex, palace, temple and *qolqa*, for which there is some archaeological evidence to confirm such activities.

The chroniclers have named other buildings, mentioning their function but without meaningful descriptions; the only evidence for some are drawings by Guaman Poma (1980) (figure 2.8). These include such terms as *aqllawasi*, the house of the chosen women, *sinchiwasi*, military barracks, and *cuyusmango*, a palace or house of justice. Some archaeologists have attempted, either generally or specifically, to define these buildings. For example, Craig Morris (1971) concluded that a walled group of structures (V-B-5) at Huánuco Pampa was probably the *aqllawasi* on the basis of a large number of excavated spindle whorls and *chicha* making pottery found there. César Astuhuaman (2000, 2004) has attempted to define the spatial arrangement of certain *kancha* as *aqllawasi*, while Matos (1994) assumed a barracks function of *sinchiwasi* for a compound at Pumpu. While these studies have produced certain characteristics to sustain the definitions, it

Figure 2.8. The inka royal palace, drawn by Guaman Poma de Ayala (1980: 329 [331]).

is uncertain whether such functions can be attributed to similar building forms without excavation.

Architectural Style as Chronology and Function

A standard art historical maxim is that an art style, once developed, will evolve and change through time and that by monitoring subtle differences, various phases can be discerned that purport to show the rise, development, and eventual demise of a particular style. In Peruvian archaeology this method has been used to develop relative chronology of pan-andean horizons and regional intermediate periods. It was initially controlled by comparisons with grave ceramics from the Ica valley (Menzel 1976). It has also been used to establish particular cultural chronologies, using ceramics for the Middle Horizon (Menzel 1964), adobe bricks (Kolata 1982), and architectural form at Chan Chan (e.g., Conrad 1982).

For the inka period, Rowe (1946) used the king list of Cabello Valboa (2011) to establish a historical sequence, by attributing absolute dates from that chronicle to the reigns of particular Inkas and to certain events. He considered that the year 1438 marked the transition between the period of political consolidation (Late Intermediate) and the beginning of imperial expansion (Late Horizon). Using this as a fixed sequence, the method of "style and time" has then been applied by several scholars to account for the subtle changes they have noted in inka architecture and planning and to present an architectural chronology (e.g., Kendall 1985; Niles 1987, 1999; but see Protzen 1993: 263–69).

In this approach, both Kendall and Niles used documentary evidence to indicate that a particular place was associated with a particular Inka, either as builder or owner. Then, by examining the architectural characteristics of each place, they could establish the style of that ruler. They assumed that the named Inka was responsible for the construction to completion of each project and that each ruler built in new locations and endeavored to develop a particular style for himself. For example, they have argued that, since it is known that Pachakuti Inka Yupanki rebuilt the city of Cusco, then his style was manifest there, and that it was elaborated upon by each ruler in turn, including Waskar and even into the immediate post-conquest, Neo-Inka, period. Each ruler, they have argued, innovated a new style and made the simple inka forms more complex (table 2.8).

There are many difficulties inherent in such a scheme that need to be highlighted. For example, in his 1984 study of the church at Pacariqtambo,

Table 2.8. Architectural traits thought to be characteristic of the reigns of Inka kings

King and probable dates of reign	Associated places	Architectural traits
Viracocha Inka Pre-1438	Huchuy Cusco	Roughly coursed, random rubble masonry with large stones, use of small chips and mortar; perpendicular walls; double row of niches.
Pachacuti Inka Yupanki 1438–71	Cusco, Qorikancha, Pisaq, Ollantaytambo, Patallaqta, Machu Picchu	Simple single-room, rectangular, standardized floor plans and unadorned exterior walls, arranged in *kancha*; finely fitted rectangular masonry with subtly sunken joints; polygonal masonry; *pirka* construction; use of adobe superstructures; use of battered walls; symmetrical placements along interior and exterior walls.
Thupaq Inka Yupanki 1471–94	Chinchero, Wayllabamba	Increased complexity with introduction of interconnecting rooms; construction of single *usnu* platforms; use of round columns; elaboration of niches, i.e., several jambs, double rows, stepped detailing; use of carving and combinations of stone types; use of corbelling.
Wayna Qhapaq 1494–1525/8	Yucay (Quispeguanca), Tumibamba	Further elaboration and "increased secularism"; smaller scale projects; freer approach to building with stone and semi-fitted masonry; introduction of small, rectangular masonry style; more construction in less prestigious materials, such as *pirka* and adobe; highly decorated external walls; plaster stucco used as a sophisticated and effective decorative feature; more use of color; surface carving; use of corbelling in roofing and to enhance the decorative quality of niches with the use of stepped stones; the use of several jambs; oversize doorways, tall rooms, and relatively wide outer jambs.
Waskar 1525/8–1533	Calca, Muyna	Continued use of smaller, rectangular masonry style with more adobe and *pirka* construction and superstructures.
Neo-Inka Manco II, Paullu Post-1533	Ollantaytambo, Espiritu Pampa, Vitcos, Vilkabamba	Increased deviation from the canons of inka architecture; reduction in importance of symmetry, such as the irregular placement and distribution of doorways, windows, and niches as well as structures.

Sources: Kendall 1985; Niles 1999; Protzen 1993.

Gary Urton demonstrated that differences in architectural style and decoration can be related to many issues and not simply time, while Jean-Pierre
Protzen (1993) in his study of Ollantaytambo has cautioned against the
use of such a scheme. From her detailed studies of Chinchero, Stella Nair
(2003) has indicated that indigenous vernacular architecture continued
into the colonial period as a one-room dwelling, traditionally built with
stone bases for adobe walls except for the use of tiled roofs. She noted that
gradually this form utilized a Spanish design through the adoption of a
hall and the use of arches in niches. Further, she added that the characteristic inka wall batter was retained for some time in indigenously built
stone walls. Her studies suggested that stone tool marks distinguished inka
walling from metal marks on similar colonial walls and block faces (Nair
2007). However, metal reworking of an original inka wall *in situ* or simply
an individual block could throw such an observation into difficulty.

There are many logical problems with this approach that render it worth-
less, and it has not been adopted in this study.

First, it was assumed that the colonial documents were perfect memo-
ries of past events and associations, which may or may not be true. Such
evidence does not necessarily mean that the associated Inka was exclusively
responsible for its construction, if at all. To resolve this, it would be necessary to get corroborating evidence from several sources and disciplines.

Second, it was assumed that there were deliberate attempts by each Inka
to do things differently and that each had to establish a new settlement
and estate for himself. While there is some evidence to this effect, not all
sources agree, and it does not necessarily mean a new reign demands new
construction, new settlement, or new area. On the basis of the distribution
of settlement types in the Cusco heartland and the extension of the *seqe*
system, Farrington (1992) has proposed an alternative approach in which
the socio-spatial organization had remained relatively fixed throughout the
inka period. Therefore, the lands of Qhapaq Ayllu to the west were always
those of the incumbent ruler, and the recently deceased rulers were relocated to estates in Yucay and Chinchero after death.

Third, it was assumed that each particular settlement was built to a
single plan in a single phase and was never altered. While there may be
some sites that show no structural changes, most have had some alterations and even some reconstruction, such as at Huchuy Cusco (Kendall et
al. 1992). Protzen (1993) has argued that in order to establish such an architectural chronology, it is important to examine individual construction
histories for each place using traditional observational techniques, such

as superposition, because form and appearance can become similar, despite differing formation processes. He noted that conclusions should be checked against the archaeological record, adding that different architectural styles appear in the same settlements.

Fourth, it was assumed that every project had been completed at the time of conquest, except for those locations being developed by Waskar. Yet the field evidence demonstrates that most inka settlements were still in the process of construction, when the conquest happened.

Fifth, it was thought that these differences are somehow very apparent. However, the basic inka methods of building do not appear to have changed through time. Some buildings may have been remodeled and embellishments introduced, but this does not seem to have happened at the same time as a change in ruler.

Given these issues, it is very difficult to use style alone to determine period of construction and occupation. It would be archaeologically preferable if these relative dates for particular towns, suburbs, palaces, and temples were rejected, and the architecture could be reexamined without any historical influence. In addition, archaeologists should also refer more samples, from both architectural features and occupation deposits, for absolute dating, which could be used to date any changes in architectural or planning canons. Methods, such as thermoluminescence and radiocarbon dating, have had some impact on our understanding of inka chronology as a whole. For example, Adamska and Michczynski (1996) have reexamined calibrated dates against Rowe's standard dynastic chronology and have determined certain problems in the accepted historical sequence of conquest. They have suggested that the inka period must be longer than ninety-four years, perhaps by between forty and eighty years.

3

Canons of Inka Settlement Planning

The ordered nature of the inka landscape with its magnificent flights of terracing, river channelization schemes, and integrated road and settlement systems of cities, *tampu*, palace, temples, and storehouses demonstrate that the inkas were highly skilled urban and landscape planners and engineers, a fact remarked upon by numerous chroniclers (e.g., Betanzos 1996: chap. 16; Cobo 1990: 227; Garcilaso de la Vega 1966: 462–63; Sarmiento de Gamboa 2007: 115–21). The placement of individual buildings and rural and urban centers, controlled with the use of principles of symmetry and orientation, has led many scholars to consider the nature of inka planning. Apart from the work of John Hyslop (1984, 1990), there has been little formal analysis of the reasoning and methods that lay behind such schemes.

Like any state-level organization, the inkas needed to develop vast tracts of conquered country, administer conquered populations with some degree of humanity, whilst pursuing the glorification of their state and their gods. They needed to acquire and manage resources, including labor, in the right quantities, at the right time, and in the right places for certain annual events to happen, special projects to be built, or wars to be waged. As such, the inkas relied on political persuasion and native infrastructures to provide these, while minimally imposing their own administrators, governors, or will on the affected people or territory. Nevertheless, populations were moved around the landscape both as temporary workers (*mitayoq*) and as permanent migrants (*mitmaqkuna*) to ensure the stability of the state as well as the success of various projects.

Such imposing public works were carried out for economic benefit, but they also had political and social consequences and almost certainly were subject to various cultural constraints, geomantic precautions, and aesthetic considerations. In this chapter, I discuss the nature of inka urban and rural planning from the perspective of several sources, ethnohistorical documentation, archaeology and planning, their measurement system, and field evidence from two planned towns.

Ethnohistorical Documents

From the chronicles it is known that the last six Sapa Inka ordered the construction of certain buildings, towns, storehouses, and roads, but only five individuals are mentioned by name as "hands-on" planners and architects. These are the Inka ruler, Pachakuti Inka Yupanki, Thupaq Inka Yupanki, Waskar and Atawallpa, and the brother of Wayna Qhapaq, Sinchi Roca.

Betanzos (1996: chaps. 11–13, 16) has attributed the planning and construction of Cusco and its hinterland to the work of Pachakuti Inka Yupanki during a period of at least twenty years after the Chanka war. Indeed, the sequence in which he reported these projects suggests that great care had been taken to get the order right. The program began with the construction of Qorikancha, a major but small-scale job with a relatively small labor force that required good stone, timber, and clay resources and that was achieved "in a short time." It was followed by a much larger project, the depopulation and improvement of the countryside and the reallocation of lands to his loyal subjects. The third phase was an engineering masterpiece that involved the channelization of the two rivers that pass through the city from their headwaters to Pumaqchupan at the eastern edge of town. Subsequently, this was extended as far as Muyna, a distance of over 40km. This required straightening and bank stabilization with large stones set in mortar. According to Betanzos (1996: 57), this project took four years to complete and was designed to prevent bank erosion and flooding of the city and to reclaim valuable floodplain land for farming and reallocation downstream. The final task was the total replanning and rebuilding of the city, which took about twenty years.

The degree of organization required in these separate projects was significant, and Pachakuti Inka is described as being intimately involved in each one. The key to his success was the use of his own authority over the local lords to organize labor for specific tasks at each phase of construction as well as the supply of resources at appropriate times delivered to appropriate places.

Indeed, such large-scale projects needed many tasks to be fulfilled simultaneously and resources on hand to permit efficient progress. For example, a large labor force was required with a range of expertise that was organized into separate jobs, such as quarrymen, masons, builders, brickmakers, bricklayers, carpenters, plasterers, hauliers, porters, and laborers. Betanzos (1996: 71) noted that building work was never continuous, and a total of 50,000 men were used on the reconstruction of the city. It is presumed that the majority of these were *mitayoq* (corvée laborers) from the Cusco region; however, surviving documents show that the provinces were also obliged to provide skilled labor as tribute. For example, the provinces of Huánuco and Lupaqa sent stone masons and builders to Cusco (see Julien 1982: 136–41).[1] All had to be housed and fed, and both provinces sent farmers to provide for their specialists. In addition, each local community allocated a portion of its fields to the state, the produce of which was to sustain such projects, while storerooms were built around the city to house this surplus. This labor force was probably housed in several planned villages.

Construction materials had to be sourced, prepared, and transported to the appropriate building sites throughout the city. Pachakuti Inka ordered that all stone sources be examined before quarries were developed to provide the right kind of stone. According to Betanzos (1996: 69), Pachakuti Inka decided that the quarries at Salu, about 5 leagues from the city, were the most suitable. Almost certainly these are the andesite quarries at Waqoto on the flanks of Picol and Pachatusan on the northern side of the valley. There were other andesite quarries at Rumiqolqa about 35km downvalley, while limestone boulders and outcrops immediately above the city to the north were also exploited. At these locations, villages were built and administrative buildings, *kallanka*, erected among the pits, working floors, and ramps (e.g., Béjar 2003). At these quarries, rock was excavated, split, trimmed, and partially prepared. The pre-forms were transported to the city, using tree trunks and teams of hauliers with strong ropes to pull them over graded roads.[2] Smaller blocks would have been carried by pack animal or by porters.

Betanzos (1996: 70) noted that Pachakuti Inka also ordered that the correct species and timber lengths should be harvested for roof joists and beams. The riverside tree *lambrán* (*Alnus jorullensis*) produces straight strong limbs, ideal for building, although *kiswar* (*Buddleia incana*) would have served equally well (Gade 1975: 79). Both grew above 2,700m in the Cusco valley and in the Vilcanota valley.

In addition, appropriate clay sources had to be exploited to make adobe bricks and a strong mortar for use in wall construction and plaster (Betanzos 1996: 70). The areas chosen were probably the limestone rich clays on the Saqsaywaman plateau and valley floor. It is understood that the management and organization of this part of these projects extended as far as the provision of blankets for those who were carrying clay to and within building sites (Betanzos 1996: 56).

The inkas produced three-dimensional scaled models for various projects. For example, Betanzos (1996: chap. 16) mentioned that Pachakuti Inka used clay models in the conception and display of his plan for Cusco. Garcilaso (1966: 124) reported seeing one made of clay, pebbles, and sticks at Muyna that had been fashioned for the official visit of Damián de la Bandera in 1558 to demonstrate native population numbers and lands in Cusco and its region; it included houses, streets, squares, hills, streams, and valleys. Models were also made of each conquered province to illustrate the topographical location of its settlements to determine which to abandon and where to develop new ones. None of these have survived, but in the Museo Inka there is a ceramic model *kancha* as well as stone models of individual buildings, including towers.

Prior to the commencement of construction of Qorikancha, Pachakuti Inka measured and marked the outline of its buildings and patios, using a rope, a *ñañu waska*,[3] and he also helped lay out the *kancha* and streets of the city (Betanzos 1996: 45, 71). Local lords had also used cords in planning the channelization of the two rivers through the city. Its use in all three projects would suggest that the inkas had a standard linear unit that could be used accurately to organize the urban space for houses, palaces, temples, patios, and streets.

Another architect was Wayna Qhapaq's brother, Sinchi Roca, the governor of Cusco, who commenced a number of projects during one of the ruler's absences (Sarmiento 2007: 174). It is known that he built both the royal apartments in the Qasana palace and some other structures "in suitable places," such as the buildings on the royal estate of Yucay, including Quispeguanca (Farrington 1995). Inka Waskar founded, built, and settled the town of Calca in the Vilcanota valley, but information on his abilities as a planner is not extensive, while Atawallpa organized the construction of a palace at Caranqui in Ecuador (Betanzos 1996: 195, 200).

With regard to the management of these plans, the chroniclers are not very precise, except for Betanzos, who found that each project required considerable site works prior to construction. He added that Pachakuti Inka ordered that the existing inhabitants be removed, old houses pulled down, debris cleared, and the site leveled before the new lots, houses, and streets were marked out using the cord (Betanzos 1996: 70–71). He also ensured that every spring in the city was canalized to provide water in stone culverts to all urban houses and fountains. Such systems would also remove excessive water from each building site.

Considerable time was spent in making construction platforms for building foundations by digging as deep as the water table and using rubble and clay as fill to keep the footings dry. Betanzos (1996: 70) noted that stone walls were built to a reasonable height before adobe bricks, using clay, sticky earth, and straw, were placed on top to the required height. This was followed by sawing wooden poles to size to make a frame to support a thatched roof. Finally, the interior and exterior walls were plastered, using a mortar mixed with wool or finely ground straw as a binding agent, while the juice from an *haguacolla quisca* cactus (*Trichocereus cuzcoensis*) was painted on to prevent the plaster from cracking and to present a glossy surface.[4]

The distribution of urban allotments also took place using a clay model. The lots between the Qorikancha and Pumaqchupan were allocated to the lords of Hurin Cusco, while those above the temple as far as Qolqampata went to those of Hanan. The original inhabitants, the Alcaviza, were also settled in a suburban village called Cayaokachi (Betanzos 1996: 73).

The Archaeology of Inka Planning

While many scholars have commented on the inka ability to plan towns and their society and economy successfully, only John Hyslop (1990) has evaluated the nature of inka settlement planning through a consideration of several underlying cultural themes that may have been determinants in establishing the elements of an urban plan. These include an *usnu* complex, rocks and water features, and the principles of orientation and astronomical alignment that determine the layout of centers and their specialized functions. One important concern must have been how to transform preexisting settlements into inka centers. His analysis was enhanced by an examination of sites, plans, and archaeologies from numerous settlements throughout Tawantinsuyu, noting that no two places had the same plan and that "Inka concepts of settlement design were more varied and complex than . . . the Spanish . . . grid" (Hyslop 1990: 191). Nevertheless, he added that there was a degree of organization in each plan, agreeing with the archaeologist Craig Morris (1987: 32), who had commented that Huánuco Pampa had been built "in accordance to an elaborate pre-conceived plan."

Hyslop (1990: chap. 7) proposed that, by utilizing certain components of the urban "center," such as the *usnu* and plaza, as well as the focal importance of topographical features, and/or astronomical alignments, the inkas had developed two basic types of urban plan: orthogonal and radial. He noted that orthogonal plans, comprising a grid of roughly parallel streets, divided the urban area into rectangular or rhomboidal blocks, occupied by one or more *kancha,* and he described some examples, including Cusco, Ollantaytambo, and Chinchero in the heartland and Hatunqolla, Chucuito, Hatun Xauxa, and Nieve Nieve elsewhere, while Cornejo (1999: 93–102) has added several others from the coastal province of Ischma. Hyslop suggested that these centers may have housed a permanent population in contrast to the temporary accommodation provided for *mitayoq.* He remarked that, if Cusco were omitted, then the number of street blocks per settlement, despite variations in size, was generally in the order of twenty or forty, figures he thought might have something to do with the underlying social organization of Cusco itself.[5]

In contrast, Hyslop (1990: 202) noted that radial towns were more numerous and widespread. Each had a central focus, such as an *usnu* platform at Huánuco Pampa and Chilecito, or a carved outcrop as at Mawqa Llaqta, from which the urban pattern radiated. The resulting segments could be defined by streets that separated neighborhoods, as at Huánuco Pampa and Pumpu, dry stream courses at Mawqa Llaqta, or simply as scattered buildings at Chilecito.

His interpretations of radial urban plans led him into a discussion of the social organization of Cusco. First, he considered that the spatial distribution of twelve suburban villages around Cusco confirmed the bipartite social division of *hanan* and *hurin* and that this extended to the countryside as well. Second, he noted that the principal radiating feature in Cusco were the *waka* arranged on roads called *seqe,* emanating from Qorikancha. This system has been interpreted to underpin fundamental social, political, and land use divisions within the city (Sherbondy 1982; Zuidema 1964). Morris (1987) used this to divide Huánuco Pampa into twelve architectural sectors, three in each *suyu,* and to separate that city into *hanan* and *hurin,* and he demonstrated both tripartite and quadripartite divisions. Hyslop perceived that such social patterning determined urban plan and that it could be used to illustrate particular sub-sectors of the *seqe* scheme. For example, he argued that a southwestern sector of Inkawasi was a spatial representation of the fourteen *seqe* of Kuntisuyu, the southwestern *suyu* in Cusco. Its individual segments comprise three to five rooms that can only be accessed from a small plaza with an *usnu* platform. Although he acknowledged that local topography had played a role in developing the urban plan, such as at Mawqa Llaqta and Inkawasi, he suggested that the parallels with the *seqe* system and the concepts of social and spatial bipartition, tripartition, and quadripartition were too overwhelming to ignore. While this analysis suggested an underlying relationship between planned urban radiality and social organization, it has not been tested archaeologically.

To date, there has been little research on inka settlements to establish the regularity of the placement of buildings and spaces. For example, there are similarities in the layout of the central area of Huánuco Pampa and Pumpu that suggest a deliberate spatial organization of critical plan elements. In each, a large plaza is flanked by *kallanka*; an *usnu* platform sits inside it with a canal passing to one side en route to the architectural unit with the highest quality stonework, the so-called royal apartments, where it terminates in a bath or fountain. While the meaning of this arrangement can be considered, the orientation of the *usnu* platforms is different: to the east at Huánuco Pampa; to the south at Pumpu. This may prove significant in determining a higher level plan. Unfortunately, there are no other examples to test this observation.

Gasparini (1993: 84) thought that the similar orientations of the grids of Hatunqolla, Paucarqolla, and Chucuito were not coincidental but a design imposed by the inkas in their colonization of the Titiqaqa region. By examining the detailed plans of Huánuco Pampa, Pumpu, Inkawasi, and other inka sites, it can be seen that many sectors appear well-planned, rectangular or rectilinear, and even orthogonal in form. This implies that whatever the underlying motive for choice of building type or placement, the basic execution at this level was to utilize straight lines, regular spacing of features, and symmetry to lay out an urban block or even a whole settlement. In other words, the inkas used the principles of orthogonal planning within certain environmentally constrained areas.

Curved walls are usually found in inka settlements where the plan has been adapted to the topography with the curve forming a terrace alignment or where there are special structures, such as Qorikancha and the probable Sun temples at Pisaq and Machu Picchu. At Tambokancha, the urban plan is made up of many buildings with outwardly curving walls, either on all four sides or simply the front and back walls, while the plaza and its surrounding buildings are straight and rectangular. Its eastern sector was built as three parallel rows of eight large buildings, separated by streets that collectively form a semicircular shape (Farrington and Zapata 2003).

The inkas clearly had some interest in the orientation of buildings toward a prominent sunrise, sunset, or an important physical landscape feature. However, there has been little consideration of their understanding of the cardinal points, although El Shincal and Calca do exhibit such organization, while some important buildings, such as the *usnu* platform at Vilkaswamán, are also oriented to the cardinal directions. As will be argued in chapter 12, there are significant physical and cultural features around Cusco located cardinally with reference to the city.

The Determination of Ancient Planning

According to the archaeologist Martin Biddle (1976b: 20), a planned town is "an urban place which has been laid out in a regular plan at one moment in time with the purpose of dividing and apportioning the ground for permanent settlement. . . . The deliberate organization of space is the critical factor in the definition of a planned town."

There are a number of key factors that need to be determined to establish a notion of planning in any urban construction scheme. The first includes what might be seen as a degree of recognized order in the plan, its regularity at a large scale. For the inkas, this allocated space for appropriate buildings, plazas, and vistas. The second is the medium-scale arrangement of streets and street-blocks as a grid of straight, parallel, and perpendicular lines with even spacing between them and therefore conceived with a practical understanding of a right angle. This attribution may be enhanced if the streets or plaza are oriented toward the cardinal directions or if there is consistent orientation in a particular direction. A neighborhood can also comprise parallel curved arrangements of streets and street-blocks. Third, at the smallest scale is the construction of individual structures that make up the *kancha*, palaces, and temples.

A fourth factor of equal importance and one which archaeological enquiry should be capable of determining is whether a particular scheme was executed from its inception to completion within a short time frame and therefore constructed to a single design. It should be noted that a similar layout can be achieved by gradual accretion over a long period, perhaps several generations or even centuries, which would suggest that the end product, and its regularity, is an afterthought and not what had originally been conceived.

With regard to single planning phases, Philip Crummy (1979, 1982, 1985), an English archaeologist, has attempted to resolve questions similar to these in his analyses of Romano-British and Anglo-Saxon towns, which are characterized by roughly parallel and perpendicular street and block patterns and which show some degree of regularity in spacing between streets. Each town had experienced considerable encroachment along street frontages since its original conception, making accurate reconstruction and measurement difficult. His conclusions indicate that Romano-British towns were planned, using the Roman foot (0.925m) in multiples of 200, 250, 300, and 600, and that Anglo-Saxon towns were planned using a pole or perch of 16½ ft (5.03m) as a standard quantum. Both Terry Slater (1990) and James Bond (1990) have examined the mensuration of urban lots known as burgages in several planned towns of the twelfth and thirteenth centuries in central England. They have demonstrated consistency in the use of a linear measurement, the perch, and areal measurement, the acre (0.41ha), in the laying out of individual, contiguous plots in these plans.[6]

In a comparative study, Keith Lilley and his colleagues (2005, 2007) used sophisticated GPS and GIS mapping to analyze the plans of the twelve new towns of Edward I in North Wales between 1276 and 1296. They noted that these had been designed and built under the same political circumstances over a short space of time, yet they were "subtly and significantly different" in layout as well as overall dimensions, block size, street width, and plot size, even though many were in similar topographical locations. Their detailed field recordings enabled them to reconstruct the sequence of how these plans had been executed, while both field and documentary evidence informed them that it was not the king or the aristocracy who were responsible for the development of these plans but the on-site engineers, surveyors, masons, and ditch diggers (Lilley et al. 2007: 289–91). What this research suggests is that well-conceived plans have been subject to change and variation to suit local conditions and therefore are not always rigidly imposed.

Although Protzen (2008: 204) argued that "there is simply not enough empirical evidence available to induce a set of formal town planning rules by which, if they existed, the Incas laid out their settlements," it is within this framework that we can set up rules to identify the nature of planning in the construction of any particular scheme. These should include an

Table 3.1. Estimates of inka linear measurements (in meters)

Quechua name	Agurto	Baudin	Rostworowski	Rowe	Farrington
Waska (w)	6.40	—	—	—	6.46
Rikra (r)	1.60	1.60–1.62	1.68	1.62	1.615
Sikya (s)	0.80	—	—	0.81	0.8075

Sources: Agurto 1987; Baudin 2003; Farrington 1984b; Rostworowski 1978; Rowe 1946.

understanding of a codified system of linear mensuration, using whatever device, which enabled builders to space streets, structures, and other required features regularly, and in proportion to the area available. This would be indicated by the intervals along a straight wall that separate particular features, such as corners, streets, and doorways. It should also be possible to note the use of the right angle and that certain features are parallel or perpendicular. More sophisticated examples may imply greater knowledge of the practicalities of euclidian geometry in the use of curves, trapezoids, and other geometric shapes in the conception and execution of a plan. If such a measurement system can be established, then it is possible not only to test for accuracy in planning but also to discover errors in construction, such as placing a feature in the wrong place, and variations as a result of topographical difficulty.

The Inka Linear Mensuration System

There have been a few studies of the inka system of linear mensuration (e.g., Agurto 1978, 1987; Farrington 1984b; Rostworowski 1978; Rowe 1946). These have noted that, in common with most traditional cultures, inka measurements were based on the length of certain parts of the body, such as the foot, hand, palm, span, and pace, and this is confirmed by a study of contemporary indigenous units in Canas department (Valencia 1982). As far as is known, it appears that there were three related measurements of length, namely, the *sikya, rikra,* and *waska* (table 3.1). Each author has suggested that a wooden or metal rod was used for short measurements, such as the *sikya*, while a rope or cord, called a *ñañu waska*, was used for longer lengths. Its name would suggest that it was probably one *waska* in length; it was this, the chroniclers stated, that was used to lay out buildings and towns.

Farrington (1984b) mapped several terracing systems in the Sacred Valley, such as those at Yucay and Urubamba, using an electronic theodolite, before the results were field-checked with a 50m tape measure. A total of over 400 linear measurements were collected, ranging from about 4m to over 900m. Each system is located on a relatively gently sloping alluvial fan and therefore each has extremely long walls with good spacing between them to make large irrigable fields. In all systems, the walls themselves have in-built features, such as steps, staircases, and drainage channels, placed at regular intervals.

The task of estimating standard units of measurement from a set of field data and establishing within it the presence of a basic quantum, with its multiples and divisions, is not easy. For archaeologists, it is exceptionally difficult, because surviving features may be only a part of the original construction, unless there is some written evidence for potential quanta, such as those used by Crummy (1979, 1982, 1985) in the analysis of Romano-British and Anglo-Saxon town plans. This area of statistics has not been well developed, and the only serious attempts to find any ancient quantum have been the various studies to isolate the "megalithic yard," and it was one of these, D. G. Kendall's (1974) cosine quantogram method, that was chosen to analyze these data.[7]

This research concluded that the inka quantum, the *rikra* (r), was 1.615m±0.001m in length and that this result was highly significant at a level of probability in excess of 0.1% (Farrington 1984b). This was confirmed when the measurements for each individual terrace system with a data set of at least 50 measurements, such as those at Yucay, Urubamba, and Urquillos in the Sacred Valley and at Hacienda Andenes near Zurite, were tested. The raw field data suggest that this unit was used in multiples, such as four times equaling the *waska* (4r = 6.46m); and it was also subdivided into half, the *sikya* (0.5r = 0.8075m), quarters, and even tenths. Given this degree of accuracy over such long distances, it is probable that a cord of a length longer than one *waska*, perhaps 2, 4 or 5 *waska*, was used. It is extremely likely that this system may have been used in town planning and the construction of individual structures and public buildings.

An Analysis of Selected Inka Town Plans

Basic field research at inka towns in the Cusco area enables me to reconstruct the canons of town planning and explore the use of the *rikra* in this process. In this section, I analyze the plans of two small towns in the Vilcanota valley, Calca and the Qosqo Ayllu sector of Ollantaytambo, in order to understand how the inka planners went about their task of dividing up the land and erecting structures. Some brief archaeological notes offer some clues about structure and function.

Calca

The inka town of Calca was laid out on gently sloping ground on the eastern side of the Qochoq river about 600m north of its confluence with the Vilcanota.[8] Like other urban locations, since its construction it has suffered encroachment onto its plaza and subdivision of its *kancha*, but its original plan is readily discernible. Its planned area was extensive, about 487.75m (302r) square and parallel to and 8.05m (5r) from the walled bank of the river (figure 3.1). The planners laid out a large plaza with a grid of eight north-south streets and five transverse ones to its north, while its extent to the south is not known.

The plaza is located in the center of the southern end and measures 323m (200r) from east to west and by 150.15m (93r) from north to south. It has been encroached upon by four urban blocks and market stalls at its eastern end and also by the town church in the middle of the remainder. There is no evidence for an *usnu* complex, but the church may be on its location and an inka channel in Grau street could have provided water to it.

On the eastern and western sides of the plaza, there is a modern streetblock (XV, XIV), measuring 137.4m (85r) from north to south and 82.10m (50.875r) from east to west. Each is bounded to the north by a 6.46m (4r) wide street and by a narrower one, only 5.65m (3.5r), to the south. Each is subdivided into three by internal east-west walls, which reveal two similar sized *kancha* at the northern and southern ends, each with plaza frontage of 54.90m (34r), while the central space has a 26.6m (17r) frontage. Only in XV is there an inka construction, a rectangular stone structure, 12.9m (8r) by 6.45m (4r), with internal niches and an off-center doorway.

These four *kancha* have external walls of good quality masonry, comprising lower courses of finely finished, polygonal stonework made from small blocks of andesite, diorite, and grandiorite that stand to about 1.7m in height and are capped with plastered *pirka* set in a mud mortar. Each had one double-jamb entrance from the plaza, 2.45m (1.5r) in width, in the center of its façade. The internal arrangement has been studied by Castillo and Jurado (1996), who have identified by excavation and field observation a symmetrical arrangement of eight large buildings that surround a central patio (figure 2.6a). In *kancha* XVA, the six structures on the north,

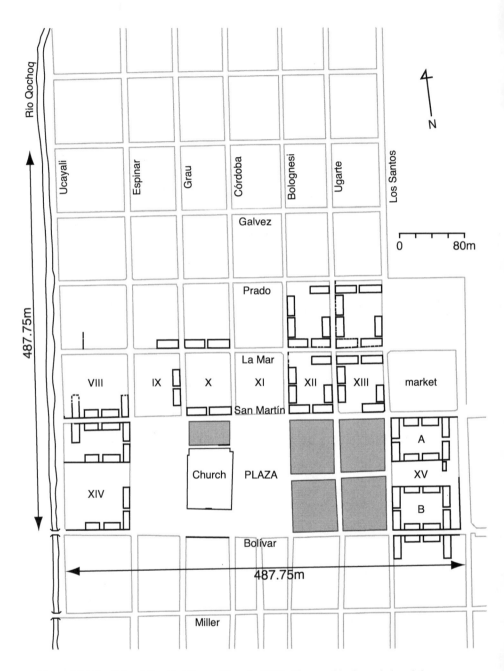

Figure 3.1. Inka Calca (after Castillo and Jurado 1996). The gray blocks and church have infilled the original plaza.

west, and south sides are incorporated into the enclosure wall; they range in length from 24.2m (15r) to 26.7m (16.5r) and are about 8.8m (5.5r) in width. Each has two doorways accessed from the patio and would have had at least eight equidistantly placed interior niches on its rear wall. They surround a broad patio with alcoves between each building. On the eastern side, there are two similar structures, 26.7m (16.5r) by 8.05m (5r) with a 2.5m (1.5r) alleyway between them that leads into an open space, 6.45m (4r) in width, which runs the whole length of the *kancha*. A similar arrangement was constructed in XVB and XVI.

On the northern side of the plaza, there are the remains of polygonal masonry and *pirka* enclosure walls in four blocks (IX, X, XII, XIII) but nothing in the central block (XI). Indeed, these four are similar in size, 56.45m (35r) in width and 80.75m (50r) in length, and are separated by streets, 6.45m (4r) in width. The modern arrangement of properties in these blocks would suggest that each had been divided into four equal-sized *kancha*. However, detailed analysis of the surviving external walls and some internal ones concludes that they also contained an arrangement of eight large buildings around a central patio with a vacant space, about 6.5m (4r) wide, across the northern end. The main entrance into each *kancha* lay in the middle of a long side, perhaps facing each other along the streets Ugarte and Grau (Castillo and Jurado 1996), although there is also evidence for a simple door at 9.7m from the southeast corner of each block, which would have entered a lateral patio. The modern central block (XI) is wider, 59.8m, than the others and is flanked by streets only 5.1m wide. It is not known if this contained any inka buildings.

To the north of La Mar, there are three rows of *kancha*, identical to those fronting the plaza, separated by transverse streets only 5.1m (3.5r) wide. Where walls have survived, they are constructed of *pirka* in a coarse mud mortar and presumably finished with plaster. They have the same external dimensions as those fronting the plaza and five demonstrate the same internal layout. All central blocks are devoid of inka structures.

On the western side adjacent to the river, the street pattern indicates that the block size was the same as XIV and XV. In two of these, some external walling and internal walls have been found, which indicate a similar *kancha* arrangement. A similar arrangement was also found in XVI to the south.

Both Betanzos (1996: 195) and Murúa (1987: 163) stated that Inka Waskar was engaged in the planning and construction of this town immediately prior to the Conquest. Niles (1988) thought that *kancha* XVA was his palace. However, it has none of the architectural attributes of a palace and is no different internally than any other *kancha* in Calca, suggesting that the town was merely a location of elite residences. Indeed, a mid-sixteenth-century document indicates that it was a town for the inka elite, as several nobles laid claims to various street-blocks as their rightful inheritance (Rostworowski 1962: 156). Small-scale excavations in *kancha* XVA by Castillo and Jurado (1996) have clearly determined the building layout and that, on the basis of ceramics, the town plan and its occupation are definitely inka. No offerings or burials were found.

Ollantaytambo Qosqo Ayllu

The inka settlement of Ollantaytambo has two major nuclei located on either side of the channelized Patakancha river, one a temple complex, known as the "fortress," and the other a residential sector, known as Qosqo Ayllu, which forms the nucleus of the modern town[9] (Protzen 1993, 2008; Soto and Cabrera 1999). The latter is located on a fairly flat terrace on the eastern side of the river about 1km north of its confluence with the Vilcanota. This site is confined by the steep slopes of Pincuylluna mountain to the east and north and by terraces to the west, and it extends southward as far as the structures of Pilkowasi.

Qosqo Ayllu has an orthogonal grid of seven parallel transverse streets (east-west), which average 1.68m (1.05r) in width, and four longitudinal streets, which are not parallel but which have a consistent width of about 2.45m (1.5r) (figure 3.2). Only the eastern interior longitudinal street, Horno, is perpendicular to the cross streets, while the others have different orientations: Pata, -4.5°, Chaupi, -3.5°, Horno, 0°, and Lari, +3.5°. Therefore, the overall plan is trapezoidal. However, not all streets continue to exist. For example, the cross street, Atoq, is now only a block in length, while the eastern street, Lari, runs for only 2½ blocks, while its alignment is continued with a drystone wall, as the boundary of the trapezoid.[10] The western street, Pata, widens slightly as it progresses northward from 4.08m (2.5r) wide at the southwestern corner of the grid to 4.45m (2.75r) further north.

Much inka architecture survives in Qosqo Ayllu today as houses, sheds, and yards, although there has been some reconstruction and alteration. There are two distinctive inka masonry styles which are spatially separated by the fifth cross street, Sipas, and its adjacent terrace wall. The southern five rows have magnificent, tall enclosure walls of well-fitting, cyclopean granite blocks that extend to a height of 1.5 to 1.7m with a superstructure

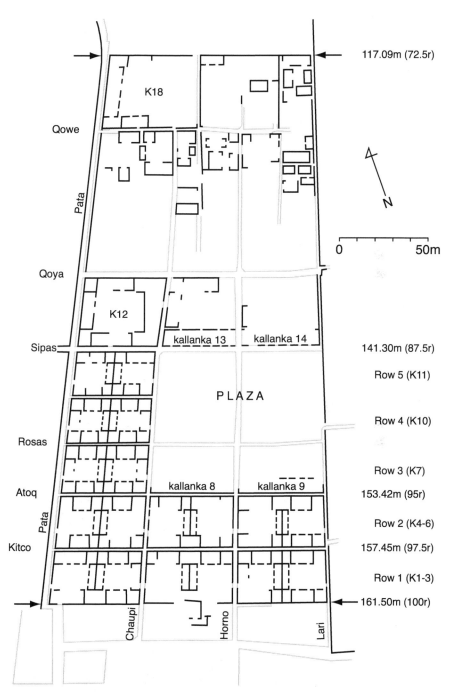

Figure 3.2. Inka Qosqo Ayllu, Ollantaytambo (after Protzen 1993: fig. 2.10, and Soto and Cabrera 1999).

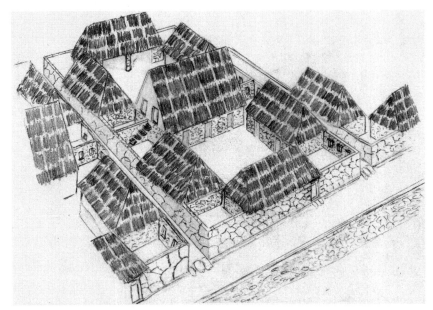

Figure 3.3. Isometric drawing of an Ollantaytambo Qosqo Ayllu *kancha* (after Gasparini and Margolies 1980: fig. 179).

in *pirka*. Internally, each is divided by a north-south wall into two *kancha*, with identical sets of four buildings around a central patio and four empty corner spaces. They comprise an entrance room with access from the street and two wide openings onto the patio, two identical, two-door structures on the northern and southern sides, and a three-door, two-story, back-to-back building on the rear wall, with only a half in each *kancha*, and with *saruna* to access the second floor on the left-hand side (figure 3.3). All buildings have *pirka*-style masonry with hipped roofs, except for the two-story gabled structure. Each has internal wall niches and cylindrical stones for hanging (Gasparini and Margolies 1980: 188, fig. 175; Protzen 1993). Each *kancha* is entered separately through a double-jamb doorway, 1.61m (1r) wide, from its respective north-south street at a set distance from the southern corner of the block. Within this sector, there is a small plaza, 97.0m (60r) by 78.75m (48.75r), that occupies the space of six street blocks in rows 3, 4, and 5. Two 43.5m (27r) long *kallanka*, each with seven doors, face onto it on its southern side, while two similar structures overlook from the north (Soto and Cabrera 1999).

The town plan to the north of Sipas street is not as formal with several irregularly shaped and sized *kancha*. All internal street blocks and structures are built in *pirka* masonry, although both the outer western wall along Pata street and the northern boundary wall are made of well finished cyclopean granite blocks, topped with *pirka*. The sixth row has three large *kancha*, of which K12 has four substantial buildings and is entered through a double-jamb doorway. According to Gibaja (1984: 228–30), the other two *kancha* are perhaps the most important in this sector, fronting the central plaza across Sipas street with seven-doored *kallanka* and other large buildings. Through this sector the two longitudinal streets, Chaupi and Horno, deviate slightly in direction and, with two cross streets, Qoya and Qowe, produce unevenly sized blocks. The archaeologists Marcelino Soto and Daniel Cabrera (1999) have surveyed around the private houses in this area and have recorded many inka walls and structures. They have also revealed through careful excavation many small irregular *kancha* and at least one other large one, K18, in the northwest corner. They demonstrated that the longitudinal streets are recent and that two other streets ran south from the northern boundary to the middle of the *kallanka* blocks.

The trapezoidal nature of the overall town plan and the fact that the parallel cross streets are not equidistantly separated means that block and *kancha* sizes are only similar within each row (table 8.1). Indeed, when individual street block dimensions are assessed, they do not conform to whole numbers of *rikra* or even halves or quarters, as at Calca. Similarly, the widths of cross streets do not appear to conform either, although it is possible that this merely reflects the difficulty in constructing a perfectly straight wall with large, irregular granite blocks. It is possible that the cross street Kitco was intended to be 1.615m (1r) wide. In contrast, all longitudinal street widths are more consistent.

Despite this apparent lack of conformity between individual blocks and *kancha*, it is clear that the inka measuring system was utilized in the planning of Qosqo Ayllu, if total lengths are considered. In the field, the first five blocks along the perpendicular street Horno measure 138.9m (86r) in length exactly, while the length of the first cross street, Kitco, from the extreme edge of the terrace overlooking the Patakancha to the boundary wall of Lari, measures 157.45m (97.5r). The next cross street, Atoq, has only one measurable block, but if that distance is tripled and the missing street widths are added, then it would have equaled 153.42m (95r). Examination of the next two cross streets and their extensions through the plaza shows that their total lengths are about 149.4m (92.5r) and 146.4 (90r), respectively. These results indicate that at each cross street the width of the trapezoid was diminished by 4.0375m (2.5r). This would mean that its base width, facing the southern plaza, would have been exactly 161.5m (100r). The width of Pata, the western street, probably served to control the field accuracy of these measurements.

The southern plaza has been encroached upon on all sides by houses, shops, and government buildings. Its original dimensions were probably about 100r for its northern side, 65r on its eastern, 107.5r on its southern, and 70r on the western side. Gibaja (1984) reported that encroachment had began in the neo-Inca period, immediately following Manqo II's occupation in 1536–37, when there was partial demolition of the southern wall of the middle block and the construction of several new buildings straddling its alignment. There is no evidence of an *usnu* complex, but there are stone-lined channels that run down the main longitudinal streets to enter this open space.

Overall, such a regular design implies careful planning; however, some difficulties in its execution can be detected, particularly in the northern sector.

i. At the northern end, the mountain cliff and many large boulders at its foot encroach into the plan, so that the enclosing wall of the trapezoid is not quite parallel to its base. Its perpendicular width at this point should have been 117.09m (72.5r). At the point where the boundary wall intersects with the prolongation of Horno, it is 302.8m (187.5r) from the plaza.

ii. The reconstructed details for the southern part should have allowed for five rows of equal-sized blocks, each 32m in length (16r), separated by a 1.05r (0.65r) cross street. However, this was not the case. The rows diminish in length from 28.38m in row 1 to 24.2m in rows 4 and 5, while the cross street widths remain constant. This means that the dimensions of each block and *kancha* are reduced on all four sides from row to row. The consequence is that the standard identical set of buildings for each *kancha* are themselves reduced in floor dimensions to fit into the available space. This could have been overcome differently by reducing the size of each corner alcove and central patio, not the size of each building.

iii. In accordance with the reconstructed plan, the width of the trapezoid at the fifth cross street, 141.3m (87.5r), should have been measured on the northern side of Sipas, but it is only accurate on the southern, because the street was accommodated along the top of the terrace wall overlooking the central plaza.

iv. To the north of Sipas, the original plan is completely disrupted, as both Horno and Chaupi are angled off-line. The resultant block widths are unequal and the two cross streets have non-standard lengths, 134.85m (83.5r) and 124.35m (77r).

These differences in plan and construction type have also stimulated certain cultural explanations, implying either that the northern sector was built later or that it was under construction at the conquest (Gasparini and Margolies 1980: 71), and/or that it may represent a social division, perhaps into upper (*hanan*) and lower (*hurin*) districts (Gibaja 1984: 228). While the distribution of wall construction types may define, at first glance, certain social areas, all internal structures in every *kancha* are built in *pirka*. The fine cyclopean walls enclose every street block of two *kancha* in the southern five rows, while they form only the outer boundary of the nine larger blocks in the north. Perhaps they are indicative of the activities that took place within them.

It might be expected that such a social division would be manifest archaeologically. However, the extensive excavation program by Cabrera and Soto (1999) has revealed no significant differences in the proportions, quality, and types of pottery or other artifacts, implying that similar domestic and ritual activities were performed in both sectors. Only three primary burials have been located, all against the rear wall of *kallanka* 9, while miscellaneous human bone was found in the central patio of *kancha* 6A, which might mean that standard inka dedicatory burials were practiced in certain structures or there was also some domestic disposal of the dead. No human bone has so far been found in the northern sector. Ceremonial activity may also be identified by fragments of a silver alloy llama figurine and by several stone *maran* found in the central plaza.

According to the documentary record, Tambo[11] was associated with Pachakuti Inka Yupanki (Rostworowski 1962; Rowe 1990a), but this does not mean that it contained a royal palace or was part of a royal estate. It was certainly part of the inka development along the Vilcanota river of small towns, *tampu,* and terraces as far as Machu Picchu. Its alternative name, Qosqo Ayllu, together with documentary evidence for a resident noble inka lineage of the same name in 1595, would suggest that, like Calca, this town was built for and inhabited by the elite (Glave and Remy 1983: 10–14).

Discussion

These two studies indicate some of the canons of inka town planning. The *rikra* (1.615m) was used in all three levels of planning: to lay out long lengths (at least up to 488m) and to establish a basic urban grid. It was also used for individual buildings, doorways, and streets. The methods by which this was executed seem to have been to measure initially not just a street block itself but also its adjoining street, so that each measurement was between points that were planned to have similar function, such as the eastern corner of a *kancha*. This is particularly revealed in the trapezoidal plan of Ollantaytambo, which can only be understood when the *kancha* dimensions and street widths are added together; but errors did occur.

The principles of town planning for residential purposes seems to have been to build on the basic household unit of four or more houses arranged around an interior patio in an enclosed *kancha*. These had only one entrance from the street, and often, as in the case of Qosqo Ayllu, doors were placed directly across the street from one another. *Kancha* may have been conjoined as at Ollantaytambo to form a single street block or comprise the whole of the street block itself. They were separated by streets whose widths were carefully measured and integral to the overall plan. Orthogonal street plans can be simple as at Calca, or trapezoidal as at Qosqo Ayllu, or even more complex to accommodate restricted amounts of leveled space, such as at Patallaqta and Machu Picchu.

4

Archaeology and the Town

Most studies of inka architecture and urban archaeology have been conducted in places that were abandoned shortly after the arrival of the Spaniards, such as at Pumpu (Matos 1994), Machu Picchu (Bingham 1930; Valencia and Gibaja 1992), Patallaqta (Kendall 1991), and El Shincal (Raffino 2004). In these locations, some buildings were standing in ruins at the time of archaeological inquiry. Many inka places had attracted an early Spanish urban foundation, such as Hatun Xauxa and Huánuco Pampa, but these were soon abandoned in favor of alternative sites. However, others, including Cusco, Ollantaytambo, Calca, Cajamarca, Vilkaswamán, and Tumibamba (Cuenca), have been continuously occupied and have therefore suffered various degrees of demolition, modification, and transformation to the inka plan and individual buildings.

The original inka center of these towns may be manifest today only by some lengths of walling along a street, perhaps with evidence for a niche, doorway, or plaster coating, because most buildings were demolished and replaced by brick, adobe, stone, timber, and wattle and daub structures during the colonial and subsequent eras. While their street plans are believed to be prehistoric in origin, they may have been substantially altered since the initial layout. Such places require analytical tools to tease out information about the underlying city, its buildings, frame, and planning and to establish its occupation sequence, noting changes to fabric and function that have occurred as it has grown and declined.[1]

In the 1960s, in order to resolve these questions for the study of medieval European urban topography, two field-based approaches were developed. These are "town plan analysis," a methodology developed under M.R.G. Conzen (1960; Lilley 2000), a historical geographer, and "urban archaeology," which became a vital adjunct to urban historical studies under the intellectual guidance of Martin Biddle (1968, 1976a, 1984) and Martin Carver

(1987a, 1987b). In this chapter, these two methodologies will be discussed for use in the analysis of inka Cusco.

The Study of Townscapes and Town Plan Analysis

Town plan analysis is a cartographic, documentary, and field approach that can be readily utilized in archaeological investigations, and from it, the remains of past settlements can be traced in "the present varied topography" of the town (Aston and Bond 1976: 219). Conzen (1960: 4) wrote that "by adopting an evolutionary approach, it seeks to establish some basic concepts applicable to recurrent phenomena in urban morphology and to lead to an explanation of the arrangement and diversity of an urban area in terms of its plan-types and resulting geographical decisions." Its techniques incorporate several principles, developed by Conzen in his analysis of the morphology of the small Northumbrian market town of Alnwick in England. He identified three interrelated components of the "townscape": the town plan, the pattern of land use, and the building form.[2] These are rarely treated together but are critical for analytical purposes.

The town plan refers to "the geographical arrangement of an urban built-up area," as is manifest on large-scale maps (Conzen 1960: 4–7). It has three essential elements: *streets, plots,* and *buildings.* Streets are open linear features for traffic of any kind that link places (e.g., houses, factories, churches, markets) and are organized into a *street-system.* The streets themselves serve to define and enclose spaces, known as *street-blocks,* which are made up of many individual contiguous land parcels, called *plots.* The distribution and orientation of property boundaries within a street-block is called a *plot pattern.* It is on this basic framework that the urban infrastructure is constructed. Buildings are erected on one or more plots, and their distribution describes a *block-plan.*

Conzen established that the plan and matrix of a town are largely immutable through time and that as new building forms are introduced, they are adapted to fit the pre-existing matrix. Of all the elements that make up a plan, he argued that the most important were plot or property boundaries because they were legally sanctioned and measured and therefore persistent in the landscape. The street-system, including other open spaces, and a town wall, if present, also show a degree of persistency through time as boundaries. Nevertheless, there are certain common types of change, such as plot and property subdivision and/or amalgamation, that alter the plot pattern and invariably produce a change in building distribution (Conzen 1960: 6); yet the outer boundary enclosing the new plot remains an unaltered vestige in the landscape (Aston and Bond 1976: 99). In addition, all public open areas, including streets, lanes, squares, and plazas, can be encroached upon initially by temporary construction, such as market stalls, which eventually may become legally permanent and incorporated into the plot. This process may also begin by the construction of an upper floor beyond the building line into the street. In Britain and Europe, these processes have led to the infilling of market squares, to irregular street alignments as individual properties have extended outwards into public spaces, and to the closing of some streets and to the opening of others. Nevertheless, despite such subtle changes in urban topography, the original street, street-block, and plot patterns tend to persist through the centuries and can still be recognized.

Through the examination of street, street-block, and plot patterns and standing architecture, it is possible to discern *plan-units*, in which there is some noticeable consistency in street and plot patterns, architectural design, and building cover. This probably indicates that it was established or constructed at a particular point in time and/or that it has evolved in a detectably similar manner through time. Plan-units vary in complexity and pattern, and the modern town can be made up of several of them (Conzen 1960). The history of any urban center reveals plan-units that have been established at separate times with different functions and that have changed at differing rates. A *plan-seam* is where plan-units abut each other, such as at major streets and/or topographic features, and where they sit uncomformably adjacent to each other, often creating urban spaces with forms and structures that do not have the definable characteristics of a plan-unit.[3]

One of the methodological requirements to perform such an analysis is a good sequence of urban maps and other illustrations. The late sixteenth century saw the beginnings of modern cartography and the publication of many urban atlases.[4] In later periods, plans and illustrations were drawn by property owners, travelers, etc., and in more recent times topographic maps at very large scales that illustrate block-pattern, plot boundaries, and building cover have become available around the world. There are also dated aerial photographs and satellite images that can be consulted. Such sequences of maps and illustrations should reveal the areas occupied at particular points in time and therefore present the scholar with an opportunity to describe a city's evolution.

An understanding of the city's history is also required, particularly with regard to urban services, censuses, property, taxation, court, rental, and market records as well as other urban activities, such as industrial production and employment. It is also necessary to understand the relationship between the city and its hinterland, as they are economically and culturally intertwined. Therefore, the dynamic forces of urban change can be understood and dated.

Detailed field observation is imperative for this type of study. It includes a recording of individual buildings, construction materials, methods of construction, wall features (i.e., windows, doors), and general architectural style. This should permit the scholar to gain insight into how each structure was built and how it has evolved (Bond 1987: 108; Schofield 1987), particularly with regard to evidence of sealed windows and doorways and even for narrower structures that may indicate encroachment. Furthermore, by defining the architectural characteristics of a particular period, it may also provide an insight into possible function and the "lifestyle" and "social structure" of its inhabitants (Perring 1987: 16). Buildings should always be studied in relationship with their surrounding features; for example, churches should always be analyzed with their precincts (R. Morris 1987: 184). In addition, any architectural data recovered from excavation can also provide evidence for constructional history (Bond 1987: 108).

Town plan analysis has been used as an interpretative tool for more than fifty years in many parts of the world, including a recent study of a traditional Chinese city (Whitehand and Gu 2007), but despite its potential, it has not been used to research the ancient city in the Americas (Smith 2011). In a review of the Conzenian approach, Lilley (2000: 11–13) has proposed that town plan analysis should follow a methodological procedure of four stages:

1. The production of an accurate, detailed cadastral plan of the city with its streets, blocks, and plots, which should be based on the earliest maps available.
2. The identification of the plan-units of the city, focusing on such characteristics as their size, shape, and orientation. The relationship between the plan-units should also be observed, particularly to define boundaries and anomalous zones, such as "plan-seams."
3. The incorporation of any historical information, relevant to the street, block, or plot, toponyms, and archaeological information

about buildings, footings, occupation, and dates to the extent that the morphological history of each is mapped.

4. This cartographic information should be interpreted to demonstrate the changing nature of the urban landscape.

Principles of Urban Archaeology

The practice of archaeology in "living" urban areas was developed in Europe after World War II, where urban renewal programs during the 1950s and 1960s led to the realization that valuable archaeological data was being lost that could offer clues to understanding urban histories. Indeed, Martin Biddle (1968) advocated that the purpose of urban archaeology was to provide urban history and enhance it through its discoveries. Prior to this, urban excavations had tended to be small and unfocused, or focused entirely on one period, usually the Roman occupation, at the expense of other contextual knowledge that overlay or was below the relevant strata.

During the 1960s, urban archaeology pioneered the technique of open area excavation because it allowed a spatially more comprehensive view of both vertical and horizontal stratigraphy of complex sites. It can deal with intrusive contexts, such as posts, pits, and trenches, in three dimensions, and note in detail how residual floors and layers were cut by such activities. Piecing together contemporary elements also required a sophisticated method of stratigraphical understanding and recording (Barker 1982; Harris 1979).

In general, urban sites possess deep stratigraphical layers, which may be sealed or have been disturbed and mixed. Indeed, urban archaeologists have been at the forefront of developing the notion of site formation processes to deal with the latter (Carver 1987b). Urban excavations can present evidence for occupation sequences through detailed stratigraphic analysis, revealing foundations, walls, pits, drains, postholes, and floors, while yielding a vast array of cultural materials that can define activities and occupation phases. From this, it is quite clear that urban archaeology can fill some of the lacunae in the historical record. Yet this is not so simple. There are a number of obstacles that need to be overcome in order for it to be successful.

The first is concerned with a detailed stratigraphical analysis and interpretation. Since urban deposits are deep, complex, and usually culturally mixed, they rarely form a single cumulative sequence (figure 4.1). Martin

Carver (1987b: 14–20) observed that continuous occupation of an urban location can result in numerous processes in addition to those of normal superimposition. These include

> "leveling up," when additional fill is brought into a location in order to build a terrace or platform;
>
> "leveling down," which is the deliberate removal of materials and earth from a plot; and
>
> "gradual rising," in which deeper, earlier cultural materials are mixed by the process of digging surface sediments, such as the digging of pits, graves, and even gardening.

As a result, the nature and function of excavated features are not immediately clear; only detailed stratigraphical observation enables some understanding to be gained (Carver 1987b: 20).

The second problem is that because of urban occupation intensity, archaeological deposits have been substantially disturbed and mixed, to the extent that sealed, untouched deposits are quite rare in an urban setting. Surface and lower strata have been punctured over centuries by the digging of pits for rubbish and latrines, the provision of water, gas, and electricity, and the disposal of sewage as well as the dead. These processes result not only in the building up of surface sediment (as above), but also that the holes eventually fill with later materials. This means that the depth of a deposit does not necessarily equal its age and that the material culture is generally mixed, with later and even earlier pieces found together (Grimes 1968: 6).

A third issue is that because urban archaeology today generally takes place ahead of redevelopment, then excavation sites are usually spread across a city and not conveniently located side by side and that they are only available for a very short time. This means that the archaeologist must have long-term research goals in order to make sense of the evidence from one particular excavation and to be able to link disparate excavations together in terms of stratigraphy, chronology, material culture, and function to form a comprehensive picture at one or several points in time. Generally, each site is relatively small, usually only one or two plots in size, and therefore it makes up a very small proportion of the total urban area.

In order to establish a more relevant, intellectual basis for such expensive archaeology, Martin Biddle (1968, 1976a, 1984) proposed a composite model as a form of spatial analysis in which archaeological research is conducted alongside detailed historical inquiry into the appropriate building

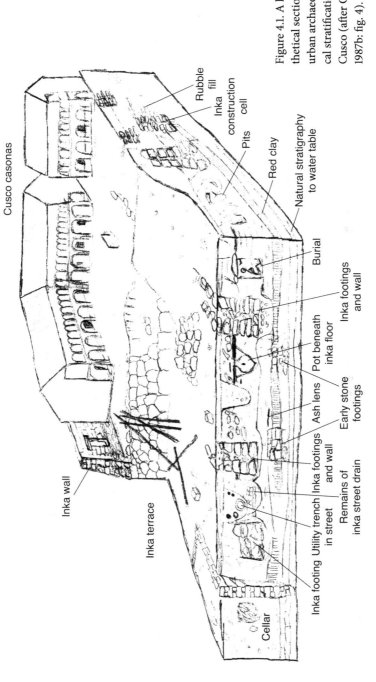

Cusco casonas

Inka wall

Inka terrace

Cellar

Inka footing | Utility trench | Inka footings and wall

Remains of
inka street drain

in street

Early stone
footings

Ash lens

Pot beneath
inka floor

Inka footings
and wall

Burial

Natural stratigraphy
to water table

Red clay

Pits

Inka
construction
cell

Rubble
fill

Figure 4.1. A hypo-
thetical section of
urban archaeologi-
cal stratification in
Cusco (after Carver
1987b: fig. 4).

plots, properties, and streets as well as the analysis of old maps and plans (Schofield 1987: 6). Its essential function is to enable researchers to weave together all threads of evidence in order to reconstruct the urban fabric at a particular point in time and to be concerned with tracing its evolution. At the site itself, the archaeologist has to understand the later history of the city, both in general and in detail, in order to interpret its stratigraphy and formation processes, which have actively produced what is observed. These include the nature of human activity (domestic, industrial, ritual) as well as superimposition, demolition, rebuilding, "leveling up," and "leveling down."

Therefore, in order for archaeology to be successful, a town must be well-researched historically and must also be subject to long-term archaeological exploration with constant reevaluation of results to refine and develop specific research questions for each location (Biddle 1984: 128–29). Nevertheless, Martin Biddle (1984: 95–105) has commented on the limitations of the urban archaeological approach. For example, he observed that excavations continue to be small-scale with limited resources. As a consequence, only a very small proportion of any town may be investigated; for example, by 1983, only 2% of the walled area of Winchester had been dug (Biddle 1984: 102) and therefore only general observations could be made about its nature and evolution. However, he argued that such difficulties could be diminished by a more precise definition of research aims, while taking into account the "practical considerations" (Biddle 1984: 94, 128). In addition, he considered it essential that various types of location be excavated, so that the results could be compared; for instance, at Winchester, he examined the cathedral, churches, bishop's palace, castle, and medieval house sites (Biddle 1984: 95–97).

For urban archaeologists, it is the understanding of stratigraphy that is paramount to achieving many of their goals. Its investigation and interpretation will enable a sequence of events to be suggested. For example, Vince (1987) noted that potsherds commonly found on urban sites are critical to relative dating; however, he suggested that three concepts need to be addressed for the construction of a ceramic chronology: association, intrusion, and residuality. It is accepted that there are few sealed deposits of single events, such as a burial or an offering, that provide associated items deposited at specific points in time, while what is usually encountered is an inevitable mixing of deposits through normal site formation processes of trampling, pit excavation and filling, and building demolition and construction. As such, a deposit may contain intrusive elements from later as well as residual elements from earlier occupations. In some cases, mixing of deposits during excavation is possible through the archaeologist's failure to recognize pits or other intrusive features, mainly because of the excavation strategy used. Nevertheless, irrespective of their condition, these strata must be dealt with and not be simply ignored as disturbed and therefore useless because there would be little for the urban archaeologist to report. To overcome this problem, the archaeologist needs to examine the complete artifact assemblage from a particular layer, evaluate the varied proportions of finds per context, and make assessments based on comparative knowledge with sealed contexts and clearly associated finds. In addition, there is a need to be rigorous in examining the relationships between the movable materials in a mixed stratum and the fixed items in the stratigraphy, such as footings, walls, floors, or even postholes and pits in order to suggest further possible associations.

Toward a Coherent Approach

These two approaches are complementary. Both are intent on augmenting and developing urban history by using a combination of field observation and documentary evidence to reveal the history of a town plan that would embrace the histories of its street system, street-blocks, individual plots, and individual buildings.

Town plan analysis seeks to provide this in two ways. At a macro-level it divides the urban area into plan-units to determine a sequence of urban development and change. At a micro-level it investigates the general history of plots through the analysis of large-scale maps, the architectural history of individual buildings, and the basic understanding of land-use changes through time.

The urban archaeological approach, advocated by Biddle, requires much of the work already completed by town plan analysis in order to develop hypotheses about a city, its land use, history, social organization, and functions. These can be tested at the micro-level through the use of open area excavation and the detailed analysis of building remains and stratigraphy as well as a thorough analysis of the recovered material culture. This enables at least a sequence of building phases characterized by specific material assemblages to be deduced and possibly more accurately dated. Interpretation, based on the archaeological record, should not be dictated by the known urban history, but it should be seen as local information that complements and enhances it. Therefore, it will enable new hypotheses to be developed for testing under further archaeological investigation.

The development of GIS mapping programs and accurate GPS survey techniques offers the potential to coordinate both the historical sequence of urban maps with the results of archaeological surveys and excavations as a powerful research tool. The work of Keith Lilley and his colleagues (2005, 2007, 2008) on the "new towns" of Edward I and Chester has highlighted this potential and raised many questions.

In the next section, I utilize both approaches to provide the first systematic and comprehensive study of the urban topography of inka Cusco. Both are suitable for application in Cusco and other inka towns because they were probably constructed over a short period to an urban plan that has been subsequently altered over five hundred years of European occupation. I will use not only the documentary record and architectural studies but also the results of other types of archaeological study, such as mapping and excavation, to elaborate and test hypotheses.

5

A Historical Topography of Cusco

Inca Cuzco lies at ground level and beneath the colonial city. It consists
of beautifully fashioned walls—massive, inert, and irreplaceable. Colonial
Cuzco overlies it with religious buildings and courtyard dwellings. . . .
[while] Modern Cuzco . . . requires all the varied structures of a large
regional capital.

Kubler 1952: 1

The modern city of Cusco lies at the western end of the broad, inter-mon-
tane Watanay valley, immediately below the plateaux of Saqsaywaman and
steep hills of Picchu. Today it stretches up these slopes and beyond, extending across several interfluvial ridges and along the floodplain to the southeast for a distance of over 10km, yet it remains almost entirely confined by
the valley itself (figure 5.1). In the last century, it developed rapidly from
only 18,617 inhabitants in 1906 (Azevedo 1982: 25) to 348,935 in 2007.[1] It
derives much of its wealth from the recent development of mass tourism
to visit it and, of course, Machu Picchu. However, large-scale tourism has
placed many constraints upon its original center and its surviving inka and
colonial buildings with an increase in vehicular traffic and hotel, restaurant,
and bar construction, some of which have threatened the townscape and
the archaeological deposits beneath the surface. Such developments, as well
as the awareness of the Instituto Nacional de Cultura (INC) in Cusco and
the Municipality to investigate and restore standing buildings and to excavate vacant lots prior to new construction, have provided opportunities for
archaeological inquiry.

In order to be successful, the methods of town plan analysis and urban
archaeology require a detailed understanding of the urban historical topography of Cusco, from its foundation through its transformations during
the colonial and republican periods to the World Heritage tourist center
that it is today. In this chapter, we need to examine its history throughout
the whole period in order to be able to understand the processes that have

Figure 5.1. Cusco from Qolqampata (San Cristóbal).

Qorikancha
(Santo Domingo)

Muyu Orqo

Kiswarkancha
(Cathedral/Triunfo)

Houses of Waskar
(Colegio San Borja)

Hatunkancha

Amarukancha
(La Compañia)

La Merced

Kusipata
(Hotel Cusco)

Qasana

Hawkaypata
(Plaza de Armas)

formed the modern city and those that have affected the quality and quantity of surviving archaeological evidence of the inka city.

The historical data is derived from the chronicles, including eyewitness accounts, the town council records, and accounts of travelers to the city. In contrast to many medieval English and European cities, Cusco does not have an extensive cartographic coverage of detailed street and plot plans. Nevertheless, there are several graphical sources that assist in charting the topographical history of the city and the processes of change after the Spanish conquest (table 5.1), and although few, it is possible to use them to

Table 5.1. Selected historical maps and other illustrations of Cusco, 1556–1907

Year	Compiler or source	Title (date of survey, if known)	Type
1556	Giovanni Battista Ramusio	Il Cuscho Citta Principale della Provincia del Peru	View
1564	Antoine de Pinet	Du Royaume de Cusco	View
1572	Georg Braun & Frans Hogenberg	Cuzco, in *Civitates Orbis Terrarum* vol. 1 (published in Cologne)	View
1596	Theodorum de Bry	Cusco urbs nobilissima . . .	View
1615	Felipe Guaman Poma de Ayala	La Gran Ciudad Inca 1051	View
1625	Francesco Vallego		Map
1643	Not known	Dos parroquias de la ciudad vistas en 1643	Map
1651	Don Alonso de Monroy y Cortes		Painting
1670	John Ogilby	Cusco	View
ca. 1673	Olfert Dapper	Cusco (published in Amsterdam)	View
1683	Alain Manesson Mallet	Cusco De L'Amerique Figure CLXV (published in Paris)	View
1709	John Stevens	Plan of Cuzco	Map
1713	Francesco Valegio	Cusco (Lasor a Varea, published in Padua)	View
18th C	Plano en Archivo Regional del Cusco	Plano . . . el curzo del Arroyo de la Avenida [Ejército]	Map
1791	Mapas de América, pertencientes a la Real Académica de la Historia	Ciudad del Cusco antigua Corte de los Reyes Ingas . . .	Map
1838	J. M. Pentland	Plano del Cuzco (1827, 1828, 1837, 1838)	Map
1865	Federico Hohagen	Plano topográfico de la Ciudad del Cuzco (1861)	Map
1877	Ephraim George Squier	Cuzco: Ancient and modern (1867)	Map
1880	Charles Wiener	Le Cuzco (Ccozcco) (1876–77)	Map
1900	Silgado & Valderrama	Plano del Cuzco	Map
1907	Max Uhle	Annotated sketch plan of Cusco (1907)	Map

advantage in this study. There are only a few good property histories; as a consequence, the focus is on streets and blocks, rather than plot and plot histories, with the use of detailed field data. The later urban history and transformations, using these methods, enable a better observation of inka design and its archaeological trace. It also serves to develop research questions beyond simple confirmatory ones of establishing the veracity of the historical record.

This chapter is organized under a series of subheadings that describe the city, its functions, and changes at various times in its development, from what the Spaniards first saw, the flourishing inka capital, to that of the modern era (figure 5.2).[2] The periods are chosen on the basis of quality of historical description and the completion of significant maps and other illustrations of the city.

Natural Setting

The built-up area of the inka city is located on an interfluvial ridge between two mountain streams, the Saphi and the Tullumayu, that cut through the plateau edge and into the valley. It stretches southeastward for about 1,400m from the lower slopes of Saqsaywaman toward the confluence of the two rivers at Pumaqchupan, the "tail of the puma," and has a maximum width of about 460m. Its main plaza, Hawkaypata, extended southwestward across the Saphi river onto a terraced area, Kusipata, while the other, Limaqpampa, stretched northeastward onto an alluvial terrace on the opposite bank of the Tullumayu. The steep colluvial slopes surrounding the city were occupied by small villages, terraces, and storerooms.

Early History of Cusco

Both the city and the valley were occupied prior to the entry of the inkas. The area of the city was called Aqhamama,[3] and the inkas would have had to negotiate with its inhabitants in order to live there. Little is known of these pre-inka peoples or their settlement, apart from inka legends that relate many versions of the city's foundation (see chapter 12) and the *seqe waka* indicating that many pre-inka ancestors and their *paqarina* remained enshrined in the landscape, although eventually their people were removed and resettled elsewhere (Cobo 1990). For example the Alcaviza were moved to the suburban village of Cayaokachi.

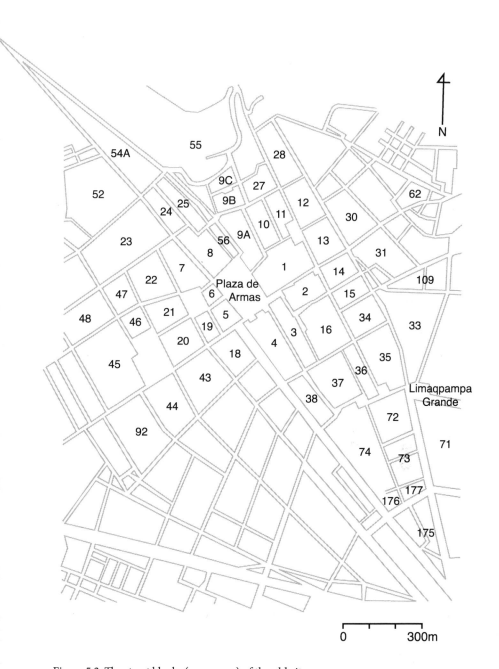

Figure 5.2. The street blocks (*manzanas*) of the old city.

As mentioned in chapter 3, several historical sources stated that, after the Chanka war, the city was rebuilt under the aegis of the great reforming king, Pachakuti Inka Yupanki, who ordered the existing town and temples dismantled and its reconstruction on a different plan. Subsequent Inka kings, including Thupaq Inka Yupanki and Wayna Qhapaq, are said to have added buildings themselves to the urban infrastructure.

The Inka City in 1533

The first Spaniards to arrive in Cusco were a party of three soldiers,[4] sent by Pizarro to oversee the collection of gold and silver objects for Atawallpa's ransom from certain designated temples and palaces in the city. They stayed for eight days in March and April 1533 before returning to Cajamarca with the looted treasures. While none of them wrote an account, they told their colleagues about what they had seen, and some of these experiences were recorded. For example, Francisco de Xerez (1985: 149), who returned to Spain and never saw the capital, retold what he had learned from Zárate: that the city was large and located on hillsides near a plain, and that the streets were well planned and paved. He noted that they had seen a house, certainly Qorikancha, clad in gold that measured 350 paces from corner to corner from which seven hundred gold panels had been prized. Cristóbal de Mena (1967: 93), another who never went to Cusco, added that there were other houses containing mummies and one so rich that the Spaniards sealed it to await their return.

Francisco Pizarro and his conquering army eventually took the city on 15 November 1533, about a week after they had won a victory at the Battle of Vilcaconga pass, a natural gateway, 45km west of the capital. With him there were five other chroniclers.[5] Most wrote their accounts, including information on Cusco in 1534 or 1535, although Pedro Pizarro (1986) did not publish his until 1571.

Juan Ruiz de Arce (2002:96) estimated that there were four thousand houses between the two rivers, while others noted that there were also satellite villages. Pizarro's secretary, Pedro Sancho de la Hoz (1917: 192–93), wrote that the city was populated exclusively by nobles and that no poor people lived there. He added that urban buildings were built either entirely of stone, of half stone and adobe, or simply of adobe brick and were well ordered in a planned grid of straight, narrow, and paved streets with a central stone channel. Various chroniclers listed its principal features, including the plaza, palaces, and temples (figure 5.3). For example, Miguel

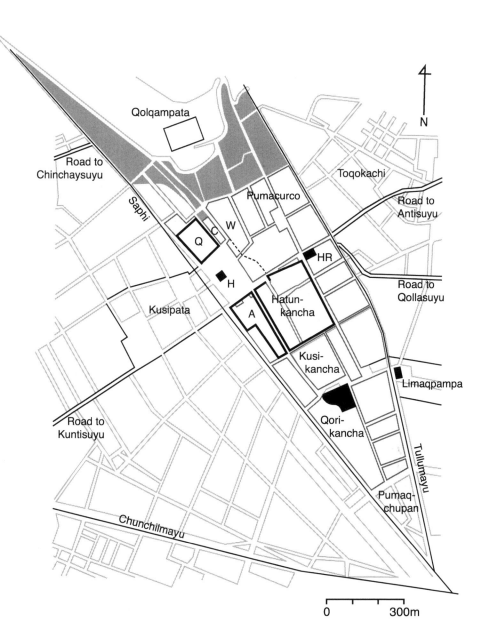

Figure 5.3. Inka Cusco in 1533. *A*, Amarukancha; *C*, Qora Qora; *H*, Hawkaypata and *usnu* platform; *HR*, Hatunrumiyoq; *Q*, Qasana; *W*, Houses and fortress of Waskar.

de Estete (1924: 45) wrote that it was almost square, while Sancho (1917: 154) added that it was mainly flat, cobbled, and surrounded by four palaces built of stone and with decorated entrances. Estete (1924: 45) noted that the palace of Atawallpa also had two towers, although Pedro Pizarro (1986: 161) indicated that these were round and made of well worked masonry with thickly thatched roofs and stood in front of Wayna Qhapaq's palace, called Qasana. The latter also discussed the daily rituals in honor of the Sun and attended by the ancestral mummies at the *usnu* complex in the center of the plaza, which he described as a small bench upon which sat a round stone as the idol of the Sun (Pizarro 1986: 89–90). There was also a small hole in the ground that received the ashes of burnt food and *chicha* that had been consumed by the mummies and the Sun.

Miguel de Estete (1924: 45) stated that adjacent to the plaza there was a compound known as Hatunkancha that was enclosed by a fine stone wall with only one entrance. It contained over 100 structures, while Pedro Pizarro (1986: 88) added that the *mamakuna* were residents of part of it. Several large buildings were noted around the plaza, including one in which the troops were first billeted, and another in which Hernando Pizarro lived that had a large doorway and no internal partitions. The Amarukancha palace was also mentioned. Qorikancha remained a focus of attention with several commenting upon its buildings, golden panels and fine, tall masonry enclosure wall. The Spaniards also admired the quantity and richness of the goods contained in the storerooms surrounding the city.

The victorious army immediately looted the city. Qorikancha suffered further deprivations as the remainder of its gold panels was removed, rooms stripped of their ritual paraphernalia, and several walls demolished. Elsewhere, the buildings belonging to Wayna Qhapaq, which had been left untouched during the initial visit, were systematically ransacked and many graves were robbed of gold and silver artifacts. The extent of looting was so dramatic that in December, these objects were melted down for the distribution of gold and silver among the men in appropriate proportions, while saving the royal fifth (Hemming 1970: 132).[6] Sancho (1917: 180–81) reported that they had acquired many life-sized statues, made of 18 carat gold, including at least ten women, each weighing about 29.1kg, and four llamas, each about 26.4kg.

The later sixteenth-century chroniclers, such as Betanzos, Cieza de León, Garcilaso de la Vega, Sarmiento de Gamboa, and Martín de Murúa, added more detail to these early descriptions of the city, its plan, and major buildings. It is unfortunate that overall the chroniclers present confusing details of the location and function of specific buildings, their inhabitants, and owners. As a city, Cusco was much admired by the first Spaniards. For example, Sancho (1917) had compared it favorably with the cities of Spain, while others viewed it as another ancient Rome (MacCormack 2001a).[7]

The Founding of the Spanish City

On 23 March 1534 Francisco Pizarro formally took possession of the inka Cusco with a ritual act of foundation by the erection in the main plaza of a wooden *picota*, a post, and by ceremonially cutting a notch out of it with his dagger. This very formal way of new town foundation in Spanish America seems to have its roots in classical and medieval Europe (Fraser 1990: 53–64) and was chosen to establish symbolically Spanish rule in the former capital. The *picota* was approached by climbing stone steps, which would probably place it on the *usnu* platform. Pizarro had summoned all of the men who intended to settle in the city to witness this act and to register themselves for the formal allocation of an urban property. He also designated a large hall on the terraces of the northside plaza for the church, which was to be dedicated to Nuestra Señora de la Asunción.[8]

This was confirmed on 29 October 1534 in the plaza, when Pedro del Barco, a town councilor, read to the assembled Spaniards a letter from Francisco Pizarro officially distributing the urban lots. Its purpose was to ratify the Spanish occupation of inka buildings in the city. The published document contains a list of names, allocations, and some locational information (Rivera Serna 1965). Each man received at least one *solar*, or in some cases several.[9] For each allocation, at least one of its boundaries, neighbors, or the name or function of an adjacent property is mentioned or the name of a particular building, plaza, street, hill or river. The document names several prominent inka compounds, including Qasana, Amarukancha, Hatunkancha, Apocomarka, the "houses" of the Sun, the "house of Waskar," and the large house of Atabilca;[10] the location of these can be discovered by cross-referencing with other sources or through the analysis of the lot allocation. There are also several street names, of which one, the street of the Sun, is probably an inka name. All the others are named after individuals, Spaniard or inka, who lived on that street or after a place from which the roads had come, such as Collao and Xauxa.

The allocation placed the Spanish leadership around the plaza (Rivera Serna 1965). For example, Francisco Pizarro took the largest and most prestigious compound, Qasana, an enclosure of four *solares*, while his brother

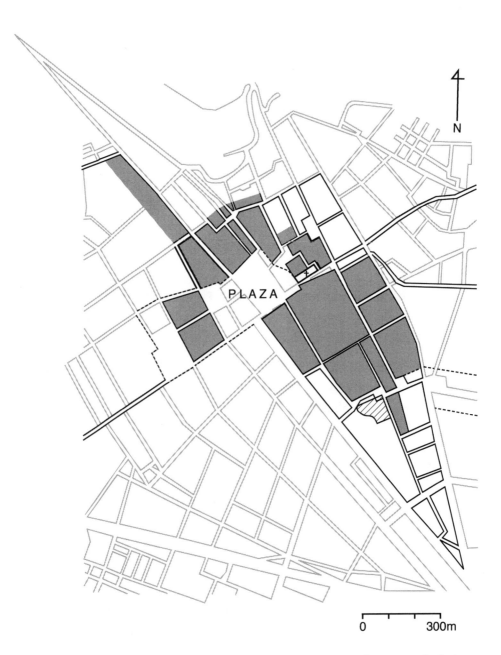

Figure 5.4. The distribution of Spanish *solares* in October 1534. The cross marks the location of the church Nuestra Señora de la Asunción (Triunfo).

Gonzalo was allocated two *solares* next door, a large hall called Qora Qora. Diego de Almagro took the houses of Waskar on the terrace above as his two *solares*, while Hernando de Soto was accommodated in two *solares* in Amarukancha. A large hall on the corner of Triunfo and the plaza were set aside for the church, while the *alcalde*, Beltran de Castro, occupied the adjacent property called Ochullo. The remaining eighty-five conquistadores were each allocated one *solar*, distributed mainly in *kancha* to the southeast of the plaza (figure 5.4). It is difficult to be entirely precise about the location of each lot, because the document is damaged; ninety-one men were allocated plots, but including neighbors, a total of ninety-nine are listed.[11]

The distribution map therefore reveals which *kancha* were vacant in the city and available for the Spaniards to occupy at this time; presumably this implies that some inka nobles also remained in residence. It is clear that the Spaniards had difficulty with the openness of the plaza itself, perceiving that it detracted from their European sense of a city, and they were determined to enclose it. To do this, seventeen *solares* were allocated on the second and third terraces of Kusipata.[12] The fact that some chose to settle on such vacant ground meant that during 1534 the Cabildo had to debate the size of a *solar*, agreeing to a frontage of 200 feet (55.8m).[13] The allocation of these plots effectively closed the southwestern side of Kusipata with four new street-blocks, mz20, mz21, mz22, and mz7.

Throughout 1534, the Cabildo met to discuss such pressing urban matters as the dumping of horse dung in the river, the fouling of drinking water, the gathering of wood, the illegal search for "treasure," the molestation of inka nobles, and the unlawful taking of servants (Rivera Serna 1965). Medieval Spain had become established in the Andes.

Remodeling the City in the Sixteenth Century

The Spanish occupation had commenced by retaining most of the *kancha*, buildings, streets, and open spaces of the city with encroachment only on Kusipata and the area close to the Saphi river. However, several events, decisions, and processes occurred during the following fifty to seventy years that substantially changed the character of the inka city.

The next major changes came with the inka uprising of 1536. As a result of a lack of respect and abuse by the Spaniards, relations had broken down to the extent that the puppet Inka, Manqo II, assembled a large army and surrounded the city. On 6 May he captured Qora Qora on the plaza and used this as a base from which to sling red-hot stones onto the thatched roofs of the city.[14] Most burned with much smoke for several days before eventually being destroyed; only that of the church failed to burn (Hemming 1970: 192–94). Hand-to-hand fighting ensued, and the inkas gradually recaptured their city. Although the siege was maintained for a year, poor decision making by Manqo eventually gave the victory to the Spaniards. He retreated, leading his men first to Ollantaytambo and finally into exile in Vilkabamba.

As a consequence, the exposure of each roofless building led to further structural decay as adobe walls 'melted' and clay floors were destroyed by rain and frost. This event had provided the new occupants with an opportunity to remodel the buildings on their property to more suitable Spanish-style houses. Progressively, the thick walls of many *kancha* buildings were dismantled, or partly so, to receive lighter wattle-and-daub framed walls, with bricks, second stories, wooden staircases, and balconies with windows and heavy wooden doors. Baked tiles replaced thatch as roofing material. Even the church received a tiled roof, while its façade was altered with the construction of a brick and stone portal in front of the main doors (Garcilaso 1966: 424). Indeed, the Cabildo issued licenses to tear down buildings. While fabric replacement did not happen overnight, it was progressive. This period probably saw the closure of many lanes between *kancha*, as they became incorporated into colonial structures. With the construction of the major monasteries and churches during the later sixteenth century, there was an increased demand for building stone, which led to the dismantling of even more buildings. The inka water distribution system had broken down by the 1550s (see Garcilaso 1966: 186). New sources had to be tapped and new pipes laid for domestic supply and to service the growing needs of the urban population, ecclesiastical institutions, and the plaza fountains (Viñuales 2004: 20–24).

In the mid-1530s, Cusco began to acquire many of the institutions that characterized the medieval towns so familiar to the Spaniards (Aston and Bond 1976). Between the eleventh and fifteenth centuries, religious houses in Europe were built on vacant land on urban fringes or in donated or purchased plots in the center itself; these processes continued in Cusco. In 1535 the three main religious orders were awarded urban locations for their churches and convents. The Dominicans received the prestigious Qorikancha from Francisco Pizarro and set about remodeling it as a monastery. The Mercedarians were allocated the open southeast side of Kusipata (mz18) for their establishment. The Franciscans initially took a plot on the northern terraces in Toqokachi overlooking the city, but after the uprising, they felt it was unsafe and were given part of Qasana by Francisco Pizarro. However, this location was considered too cramped for their purposes, and finally they settled on the terrace above Kusipata to build their church and convent. The Augustinians took street-block mz15 on the northern edge of the city, which contained *kancha* and terraces overlooking the Tullumayu River. The Jesuits arrived in Cusco in 1571 and purchased Amarukancha in the plaza for their church, convent, and school. At least two institutions were convents and hospitals for the poor and the local population: Santa Clara on the southern terraces beyond Kusipata was established between 1551 and 1560, and San Juan de Dios (1549) was initially located in a plot next to the church but moved in 1609 to mz22.

In 1559, Polo de Ondegardo, the corregidor of Cusco, established five parish churches for the native population in the suburban villages (Julien 1998). San Blas (Toqokachi), San Cristóbal (Qolqampata), Santa Ana (Carmenqa), and Belén (Cayaokachi) were located close to the city on the approaches from the north, west, and south, whereas San Sebastián (Cachipampa) was located about 5km downvalley (southeast) on the road from Qollasuyu. Three others were established in 1572: the Hospital de los Naturales, adjacent to Santa Clara on the edge of Kusipata, Santiago in Chakillchaca, and San Jerónimo about 10km downvalley.

The year 1559 witnessed another major development of religious building activity, the commencement of the new cathedral church on the plaza. The townsfolk had been concerned that the existing church was merely a converted inka large hall and that they wanted a European-style cathedral to underline the status of their city. In January 1553, the bishop purchased for 2,300 pesos the house lots adjacent to the existing church for the new structure. Like other ecclesiastical projects, except for the parish churches, the cathedral was to be a monumental structure in stone. Its construction required encroachment onto the plaza, as it was to extend 42.5m beyond the façade of Triunfo. This meant that a terrace extension had to be built that would be mechanically strong enough to support such a large building. It required a large amount of rubble to build up the level in order to dig the footings.

The old city had an abundance of stone buildings that their Spanish owners wished to dismantle to make room for the erection of commodious Spanish-style buildings. The cathedral also required so much stone that on 6 October 1559 the Cabildo gave permission for Saqsaywaman, the inka temple above the city, to be dismantled for this purpose (Dean 1998). Although the Cabildo rescinded this decision in May 1561, by all intents, the destruction continued, so that later Murúa (1987: 500) was able to comment that all Spanish buildings in the city were built from the stones of Saqsaywaman.

Deliberate alterations to the basic inka plan continued throughout this period (figure 5.5). The plaza served as a marketplace, and gradually shops appeared in the front of the surrounding buildings. During the 1540s the Cabildo decided to make it more European with the declaration that all shops had to have arcades in front, thus allowing encroachment onto the plaza with a supported upper story. In 1548, the Cabildo approved the division of the plaza into two smaller spaces with the construction of houses and shops over the Saphi river between the two bridges; these were completed in 1551. They too were provided with arcades to shade the businesses and shoppers. Then Kusipata became the principal marketplace for the city, although six shops were also erected on the terraces in the northwestern corner of the plaza. In another decision by the Cabildo in 1545, a street (probably Mesón de la Estrella) was opened to run from Kusipata to the fields. In 1551 it received a petition from one citizen to widen the street, approaching his property. The Cabildo itself moved from Amarukancha to its new building on the western side of the Plaza Regocijo in the early seventeenth century (Azevedo 1982: 50).

The chronicler Garcilaso de la Vega (1966), who was born in the city, left Cusco in 1560.[15] His most interesting chapters are in Book 7, in which he described the city prior to his departure. It is clearly the best eyewitness report of the city during this era, as he systematically walked through, noting its principal buildings in inka and contemporary times as well as the locations of the houses of particular individuals. He confirmed much of the urban geography as well as the architectural changes and alterations that had taken place up to this time.

One of the characteristics of urban historical studies of sixteenth-century Europe is the development of cartography and urban atlases, and for most places, these drawings were based on intimate knowledge of the particular cities. However, some atlases included illustrations that are certainly fanciful depictions, such as eight views of Cusco published between 1556 and 1713 (table 5.1). The probable inspiration for these was Pedro de Cieza de León [1986, cap xcii–xciii], who in 1553 had included in his *Crónica del Perú* a line drawing of a medieval walled city under the title "Cuzco" but whose popular description conveys much of the evidence translated in these woodcuts. For example, an illustration by Antoine de Pinet was included in Braun and Hogenburg's famous atlas of 1572 (2011), *Civitates*

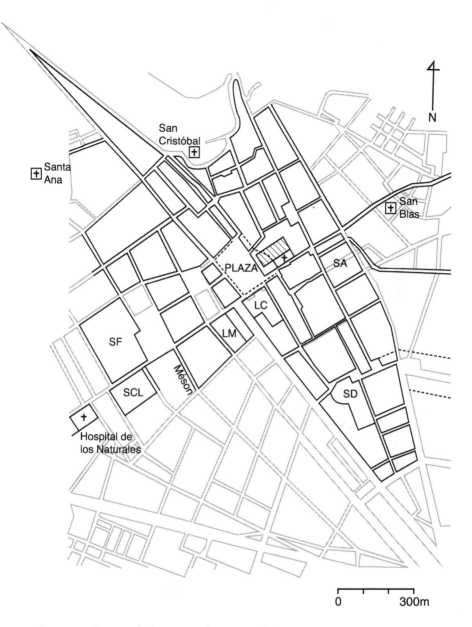

Figure 5.5. Cusco in the late sixteenth century. Black outlined streets demarcate the inhabited area. The hatched area is the building site of the cathedral. Monasteries: *LM*, La Merced; *LC*, La Compañía de Jésus; *SA*, San Agustín; *SD*, Santo Domingo; *SCL*, Santa Clara; *SF*, San Francisco. Parish churches (cross in rectangle).

Orbis Terrarum. It shows a walled city, set in a mountainous country between two rivers, with a small plaza and a grid of streets, each with a central channel, and dominated on the left-hand side by a fortress surrounded by three defensive walls. While this bears no resemblance to Cusco itself, it does suggest that the illustrator knew of the grid of streets with central drains, the "fortress" on a hill and the town square immediately below.

The first useful illustration is a drawing by the indigenous chronicler Felipe Guaman Poma de Ayala (1980: 1051[1059]) (figure 5.6). He illustrated numerous Spanish foundations in South America in a very standard manner, but he produced a most complex drawing of Cusco. While this is stylized, it can be deciphered to show that he was familiar with much detail of the city, its buildings, and spatial organization in the late sixteenth and early seventeenth centuries. It has a perspective from the southwest and looks across Kusipata toward Hawkaypata and San Blas beyond with a church façade (El Triunfo) to the right. The Saphi river divides it into two halves across the middle. The left-hand side presents places and buildings on the western side, ranging from Saqsaywaman to the churches of San Cristóbal and Carmenqa, and the Wakapunku entrance to the plaza, while the right-hand side depicts places on the eastern side, such as Qorikancha with its rounded wall and Belén and the open church of San Sebastián further downstream. It shows that the channelized river had been built over with arcades and shops, thus dividing the main inka plaza into two. The smaller Hawkaypata, the present Plaza de Armas, by this time had a fountain in the middle (erected in 1583), while Kusipata, also colonnaded for shops, was used as a market with booths and men arriving with loads or pack animals; there is a church tower, presumably La Merced, on its right-hand side.

The only serious problem is the inclusion at the bottom of the drawing of two places that should have been arranged to the east of the plaza: Kusikancha and Pumaqchupan. However, in his zeal to show the two plazas, he has had to take some artistic license, as much of the town would have been to the east of Hawkaypata, and he has compensated for this by drawing more buildings in an area that would have been open fields at the turn of the sixteenth century.

By the end of the first hundred years of Spanish Cusco, the inka city had significantly changed, mainly in its extent and building stock. The most important changes were related to a desire to make the city more "Hispanic" and to follow the royal instructions of urban plantation generally being practiced in Mexico and Panama at the time, including the need to locate the church and Cabildo on the plaza, with the former in a raised,

Figure 5.6. A drawing of Cusco by Guaman Poma de Ayala (1980: 1051[1059]).

prominent position, and to enclose the plaza as a European marketplace, surrounded by colonnaded arcades (Fraser 1990; Smith 1955). This process began in 1534, with a second phase in 1551, making three relatively small plazas. Another change, encouraged by the burning of the city in 1536, enabled individual owners to alter the layout of their plot, dismantle certain buildings, and build desirable two-story buildings in lighter materials with courtyards. The major ecclesiastical developments added to the European feel of this changing city whose major buildings, and in particular the cathedral, required vast quantities of building stone and provided a ready market for the dismantled structural materials. The Spaniards preferred to extend the city over the terraces surrounding Kusipata between the Saphi and Chunchulmayu streams.

The City in the Mid-Seventeenth Century

On 31 March 1650, an earthquake devastated Cusco, which promoted further urban change. This event marks the end of the first major phase of European urbanism, as it promoted massive reconstruction and redevelopment efforts. The documentary evidence includes a 1643 map of two urban parishes, a 1649 description of the city, a painting of the city center, and the assessments of damage to property conducted by the town council in May 1650 (figure 5.7).

A map of two parishes, Santa Ana and Hospital de los Naturales, was drawn as part of a legal dispute over parish boundaries and is the earliest cartographic representation of any part of Cusco (Rowe 1990b). It shows urban development adjacent to San Francisco, the *nueva calle* district. It can be seen that the large inka terrace on the western side of the Kuntisuyu road had been punctured to allow new streets access to it.

Contreras y Valverde (1982) provided a very brief description of the city in 1649, preferring to focus on the history of the bishops of Cusco and the churches. However, he did note that inka buildings were so well made of stone that they could have been made by "giants" and that the modern buildings were as sumptuous as those of Spain, while the streets were grand but narrow, yet a coach could still pass through them.

Immediately after the earthquake, the artist Don Alonso de Monroy y Cortes was commissioned to paint a vista of the damaged city. This painting, now hanging in Triunfo church, provides a valuable tool for the urban archaeologist, a view from the northeast overlooking the roof of Triunfo, the cathedral, and plazas as far as San Francisco and beyond (see Bauer

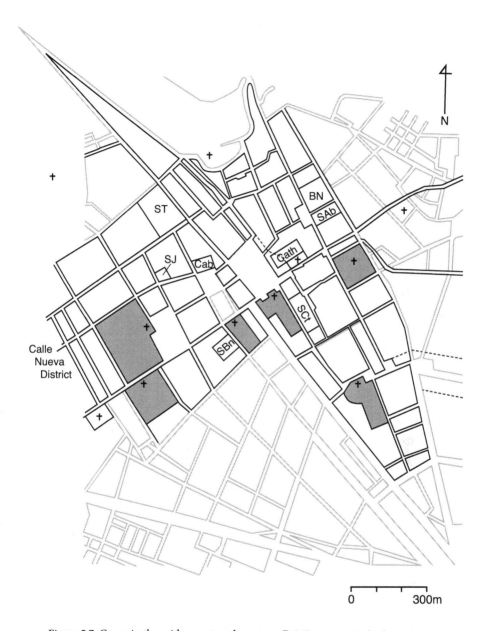

Figure 5.7. Cusco in the mid-seventeenth century. Existing monasteries in gray; crosses mark existing parish churches. New monastery, convent, school, and hospital foundations: *BN*, Beaterio de las Nazarenas; *SAb*, San Antonio Abad; *SCt*, Santa Catalina; *SBn*, San Bernardo; *SJ*, San Juan de Dios; *ST*, Santa Teresa; *Cath*, cathedral; *Cab*, cabildo.

2004: 108). Hawkaypata is shown divided into three sections not only by housing between the Plaza San Francisco from Kusipata but also by shops and arcades erected over the river. Each of the two main plazas has a central fountain, and Monroy has illustrated market stalls, a religious service, and other activities in them.

Each building is depicted so carefully that the urban plan can be readily discerned, showing dramatically how much the inka city had changed in the previous 116 years to the extent that no inka building is illustrated. The standard architecture is the two-story house, facing the street or plaza with single-story structures surrounding its patio. The former Qasana had been rebuilt in an interesting fashion that may indicate its underlying inka structure. A row of houses, shops, and arcades front the plaza, while behind there is a series of parallel buildings with few buildings at right angles to form courtyards. It can be interpreted that the shops and arcades with a second story have filled the space between the palace enclosure wall and the first internal *kancha*.

The Monroy painting clearly illustrates the earthquake damage; there are cracked walls, collapsed and damaged roofs, problems with gable ends, as well as clouds of smoke and/or dust billowing from house fires. It seems that the façades of La Merced, La Compañía, and the cathedral have collapsed; there appear to be no towers. There are many people gathering in the main plaza, and two men are inspecting the roof of Triunfo.

The urban community acted swiftly to assess the damage, and the Cabildo organized inspection teams in the first week of May, only four weeks after the earthquake. Good records were kept of these inspections and of the cost of the damage, incurred by each building and house (Julien 1995). Sixteen ecclesiastical complexes, including churches, convents, colleges, and hospitals, were visited as well as 603 urban properties and a great many more suburban ones.

The main religious structures were all under construction and suffered greatly as did existing churches and monasteries. The total damages were estimated as 1.7 million pesos, 82% of which was for repairs to Santo Domingo, San Francisco, La Merced, Santa Catalina, Santa Clara, and La Compañía. The three churches under construction, La Compañía, La Merced, and San Francisco, had collapsed significantly, while others had damaged arches, pilasters, domes, and leaning and/or collapsed walls. Convent accommodation and cloisters were also badly affected and even collapsed. However, the new cathedral suffered minor damage to its domes, windows, arches, and pilasters with the cost of repair estimated at only 27,800 pesos. In contrast, the modified inka large hall, the "old" church of Triunfo, had very little damage, mainly to its internal wooden walls and fittings, such as the choir, sacristy, baptistery, and a side chapel, while Monroy showed that some roof tiles had been lost. The total cost of these repairs was estimated to be only 4,000 pesos. It is significant that the inka large hall had suffered only damage to its Spanish additions. Its walls were not cracked or leaning but remained upright and continued to support its roof.

For the 603 residential and business properties throughout the city, the repair bill was estimated to be 1.265 million pesos, that is, 2,776 pesos per property. In the old town, about 275 properties were inspected and analysis of this data provides excellent commentary on the extent of architectural change. They ranged from elaborate multi-building, two-story houses in much of the central and upper parts of the city to individual huts, arranged in *kancha*, to the southeast of Santo Domingo in Awaqpinta, the barrio of Pumaqchupan. The total repair bill for the old city houses was estimated at 663,200 pesos, or 2,412 pesos each, but this is not the full story.

The new two-story houses with balconies and courtyards, erected in redeveloped *kancha*, suffered major structural problems. These included roof and even total building collapse, leaning and cracked walls, particularly quoins, and gables, allowing many to be left exposed, cold, damp, dangerous, and uninhabitable. There were 53 (19.25%) properties that suffered over 5,000 pesos worth of damage, of which three had repair estimates of 20,000 pesos. In contrast, 33 (12%) required no repairs whatsoever, and 173 (63%) had damage bills of 1,000 pesos or less, including all those in the *kancha* of Awaqpinta. The reasons for these differences are suggested by one entry in the inspection: a property (#76) along San Agustín, owned by the nuns of Santa Catalina, that was in good repair because it was largely an inka building[16] (Julien 1995: 323). Certainly, the inka structures with their thicker walls and strong footings were better constructed to withstand earthquakes than their flimsy replacements with two stories and balconies, supported on thinner walls, shallower footings, and with heavy tiled roofs that must have sat unconformably on dismantled inka foundations. As far as is known, inka enclosure walls remained along most streets, even if many of the internal buildings had been changed. The reason that most buildings in the old city had at least some structural damage is probably because tiles had replaced thatch as the preferred roofing material, and these would have broken readily.

Urban Rebuilding in the Late Seventeenth and Eighteenth Centuries

A major reconstruction began in the aftermath of the 1650 earthquake. All the main churches, ecclesiastical buildings, and new private houses were completed. During this period, the economy of the Cusco region was based on agriculture, woolen textiles, and mining, and coupled with its location on the royal road from Lima to the silver mining town of Potosí, the city flourished into the early nineteenth century (Mörner 1978).

Work on the cathedral had not been significantly delayed by the earthquake, and it was completed in 1654. This large structure, with its two towers framing a broad elaborate, baroque retablo-façade, carved in 1649, and central arched door, was designed progressively by several architects over the ninety-four years of its construction (Donahue-Wallace 2006; Viñuales 2004: 66–74). The churches and convents of Santo Domingo, La Compañía, Santa Catalina, La Merced, and San Francisco, the most badly damaged, were cleared of rubble, and rebuilding in the new baroque style commenced during the 1650s, but these were not finished until twenty or thirty years later; the Santo Domingo tower was not completed until 1780. The style of these and many of the suburban churches became clearly baroque, and this architecture distinguishes the city as one of the most impressive in Spanish America.

With the completion of the cathedral, the old church of Triunfo continued as a large side-chapel until 1729, when some of its walls and its main door were dismantled. It reopened in 1733, retaining some inka walling, particularly along Triunfo street, but it was now a new baroque church with a magnificent retablo-façade.

Convent foundation continued in peripheral locations with the establishment of the church and monastery of Santa Teresa by the order of the Carmelitas Descalzas in Wakapunku.[17] The church was commenced in 1673 and opened in 1676, followed by the construction of its cloister and convent, using many inka building stones acquired from several sites, including Saqsaywaman.

During this period, house repairs and new construction developed many of the fine *casonas* that characterize the city today. These generally have elaborate stone portals in baroque style with a coat-of-arms above the main door and wooden balconies and windows overlooking the street. Inka stonework was often blended into these Spanish-style mansions. These are two-story constructions built parallel to the street with gable roofs, internal patios, fountains, and gardens. However, not all repairs to existing dwellings were carried out immediately, and some structures remained in ruins for many years.

In town planning terms, this period witnessed a number of changes (figure 5.8). The cathedral and its terrace had encroached upon the plaza, while in the late seventeenth century the Plaza de Regocijo was further

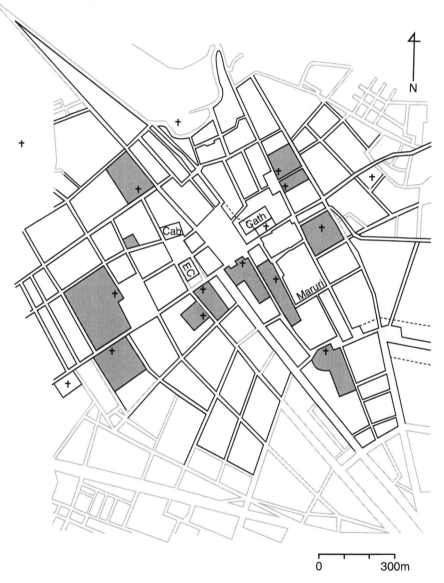

Figure 5.8. Cusco in the late eighteenth century. *EC*, the Mint in El Cuadro. Crosses mark parish and monastery churches.

reduced in size by the construction of the Mint (Casa de la Moneda), built in 1697–99 to take advantage of the burgeoning trade with Alto Perú, particularly Potosí. Several shops were located in this building, also known as El Cuadro, the rent from which went to provide alms for the urban poor. Plaza Regocijo then consisted of two small plazas, a larger one in front of the Cabildo and a smaller one beside the tower and façade of La Merced. The provision of water continued to be a problem, and pipes were always in need of repair (Viñuales 2004).

Another significant change to the old city was the widening of the street, now called Maruri. During inka times, this had been a narrow lane, an extension of Cabrakancha. Probably in the early colonial period, the wall of Pukamarka was breached to open Arequipa street as a route to the plaza. However, by 1763, it was known as Pampa or Plazoleta of Maruri or Loaysa, suggesting that it had been widened by this date (Vargas 2007: 284). The Loaysa family had owned a two-story *casona* and an adjacent property at what is now Maruri #340, better known as Kusikancha. Its doorway is an ordinary example of a late eighteenth-century stone portal, and as we shall see later, its façade was erected on top of the front of an inka building that had faced the other way. In other words, about 8.5m of these buildings had been removed to widen the street before 1763; the probable reason was to give access to a coach and horses. The name of the house owner, who had opened the street, became acknowledged in the street name. In the documents about this property, the narrow lanes, separating the inka *kancha*, remained open throughout this period (Vargas 2007). A late eighteenth-century map illustrates a street-block distribution of the old city and the urban spread as far as the parish churches of Belén, Santiago, Santa Ana, San Cristóbal, and San Blas but few other details (López and Manso 2006: 437).

The City in the Nineteenth Century, 1820–1880

During the nineteenth century the city led a checkered history. Its prosperity continued briefly, and during the Wars of Independence, it became the capital of the Viceroyalty between 1821 and 1824. It gained a munitions industry, bureaucracy and the Mint flourished, but this wealth was dissipated after the Battle of Ayacucho in 1824. Lima became the capital again; political strife and uncertainty left Cusco with only local interests as its access to Alto Perú, now Bolivia, had been cut off. It became strengthened again during the short-lived confederation of Peru and Bolivia in the 1830s, but was finally severed by the Civil War in 1839. As a result, Cusco's role in the new republic was drastically reduced. The growing world economy in the nineteenth century saw the city gradually excised from its textile-making role, while the problems of mountain topography prevented the establishment of modern transport connections to the capital, the coast, and therefore to the rest of the world. As a consequence, the urban economy declined severely after 1840. The population of the city fell by half during this period; in terms of population density, it had 198 persons per hectare in 1834, but by 1876 it had fallen to only 90.9 per hectare (Azevedo 1982: 26).

The city fell into decay, streets were not repaired, suburbs, such as Santiago, became abandoned ruins, and there was no investment in the new late nineteenth-century urban facilities of lighting, reticulated water, or sewerage systems. Cusco was visited by a number of foreign travelers who described its run-down nature, the piles of rubbish, and its smell *inter alia*. The Mint was closed, various hospitals and schools also ceased activities, while monasteries lost personnel. Several properties in the old city became *tambo*, a quechua word meaning "traveler's inn or lodging." These provided accommodation, stabling, shops, and warehousing and were located at the entrances to the city from the southeast, south, and west.

This period brought a number of changes to the old city (figure 5.9). These are documented on several maps published between 1827 and 1880, including those of Pentland, Hohagen, Marcoy, Squier (1877: 428), and Wiener (1880).[18] The first occurred in 1840 during a political dispute with the Augustinian congregation, when government troops under President Mariscal Agustín Gamarra fired cannon along the street called Ancha de Santa Catalina at the monastery of San Agustín, destroying both its church and parts of its cloister (Azevedo 1982: 61). This large urban site, overlooking the Tullumayu river, lay in ruins for about thirty years until the prefect, General Andres Segura, removed the rubble and built a new street, now called Ruinas, through where the church nave had once stood. It first appears as "calle del General Segura" on the Wiener map, surveyed in 1876–77.

A second alteration can be seen when comparing the Pentland, Hohagen, and Squier maps with that of Wiener; this is the extension of Pampa de Maruri to join Afligidos street and Avenida del Sol. The earlier ones show that this street-block (mz4) was bounded by the Plaza, Loreto, and Angosto de Santa Catalina-Arequipa and extended southeastward into what is now mz37. Its southeastern end was defined by a narrow lane with a circuitous

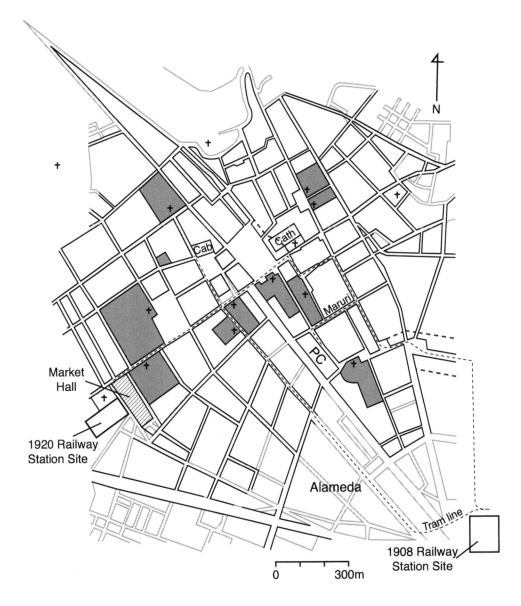

Figure 5.9. Cusco in the late nineteenth century and early twentieth century. Dashed line represents the horse-drawn tramway system. *PC*, Pampa del Castillo.

path that linked Maruri with Pampa del Castillo. By the 1860s, it was decided that Maruri should be continued in order to improve the traffic flow in the city center. After lengthy negotiations in 1865, the prefect allowed the compulsory purchase of part of the Santa Catalina property, and the new street extension was opened by pulling down inka walls on both sides and dismantling the structures within (Vargas 2007: 147). Other lanes in mz37 were probably closed during this period. The maps also indicated the extent of surviving inka channelization of the two major rivers.

Changes in the Twentieth-Century Townscape

The early twentieth century brought a change of fortune to Cusco. New roads opened up the upper jungle to sugar and tea production, thus diversifying its dependency upon wool. The railway from Mollendo, Arequipa, and Puno reached Sicuani by 1896 but arrived in Cusco only in 1908, instantly providing the city with a swift, reliable means of export and import. The opening of a second line to Santa Ana in the jungle in the 1920s further increased the development of that area. As a consequence, Cusco grew steadily, but slowly, and by 1940 it had a population of 46,000. A devastating earthquake in 1950 brought it to the attention of the newly formed UNESCO as a historic city in danger. Subsequently, the growth of world tourism and the establishment of both Cusco and Machu Picchu on the World Heritage list have promoted significant urban growth. Throughout the century, the fabric and plan of the old city have been adapted to deal with changes (Azevedo 1982: 142–45).

Urban Transport

The coming of the railway meant that, as in most cities, its stations were placed on the edge of the existing urban area. The first was built in 1908 on vacant land at Wanchaq to the northeast of Pumaqchupan, while the second was erected on the ruins of the Hospital de los Naturales near San Pedro church in 1920 (figure 5.9). Much of the Santa Clara convent was pulled down for the erection of an iron-framed market hall adjacent to Santa Ana station.[19]

In 1910, an urban transit company was formed to run horse-drawn trams between the two stations and the Plaza de Armas with one branch line to the Municipality in Plaza Regocijo and another into the center of the old town at Pampa del Castillo. As far as can be seen, no significant street alterations were necessary to accommodate this mode of transport. Trams continued until 1946, when bus lines took over. Many travelers had noted that there were very few cars in the city during the 1930s and that this did not change until the late 1940s. While there have been several attempts to regulate motor vehicles and buses through the old city since the 1980s, only two involved street widening, although some streets have been closed to vehicles.

In the 1930s, a military barracks (Cuartel 22 de Noviembre) was established in the old *tambo* San Jose in mz37 (Vargas 2007: 314). Once this urban lot of over 6,000sqm had been purchased, the military set about remodeling it into a barracks. Therefore, many colonial buildings and inka walls were dismantled to their foundations. In addition, the inka lane known as Romeritos, which runs between Maruri and the Plazuela de Santo Domingo, was widened to allow larger vehicles to use the military yard. This required the destruction of inka enclosure walls to increase the road width by about 1.2m for a distance of about 90m.

During the same period, many minor streets in the old city were paved: Pumacurco, Waynapata, Ataúd, Cuesta de San Cristóbal, Quiscapata, Arco Iris, Teqsecocha, and Tullumayu. In 1920, the Tullumayu channelization was covered between Ladrillo and Ruinas and that of Saphi from Santa Teresa to Rosario and extended in 1931 to Tambo de Montero. A new street, Avenida Garcilaso, was cut through the southeastern end of the old city.

Public Utilities

Public utilities in Cusco remained very primitive for much of the twentieth century. For example, in the 1920s drinking water was provided by only 150 public taps scattered throughout the city; but in 1927, a reticulated distribution system was opened to service 1,200 houses (Azevedo 1982: 63). This system was further expanded over the next few years, and by 1940 85.4% of households were supplied. In 1940, 77.3% of houses had some form of sewerage, mainly internal cesspools, while an integrated system was gradually introduced. Electricity was supplied to only 33.9% of households in 1940 (Azevedo 1982: 83). These services as well as telephone lines have been improved and extended, and as a consequence, streets and properties have been dug up to lay various pipes and cables.

Consequences of the 1950 and 1986 Earthquakes

Two earthquakes have affected the old city. The first, on 21 May 1950, brought considerable damage, destroying more than 3,000 houses, leaving only 1,200 habitable. It was estimated that private buildings suffered 300 million soles of damage, while that for churches and other public structures was about 100 million soles (Kubler 1952: 3).[20] The churches and monastery buildings all suffered considerably, and the damage pattern seems to mirror that of the 1650 earthquake with the most serious at Santo Domingo and La Merced, and those colonial buildings, built of adobe, stone, timber, and wattle and daub. The UNESCO mission to the city brought world experts to advise on heritage conservation, urban reconstruction, and town planning (Kubler 1952). Detailed surveys were conducted throughout the city not only to evaluate the damage but also to elaborate on the conservation plans. For example, a map of the extent of inka walling was produced.

This earthquake brought to light aspects of the old city that had been forgotten over the years. For example, the convent of Santa Catalina had been rebuilt after the 1650 earthquake on top of a rubble-filled platform that had not only raised the floor level and blocked entrances from Loreto but also buried details of twenty-nine evenly spaced niches that were found in the second cloister on the interior of that same wall (Kubler 1952).

While this was a great opportunity for major reform of the traffic congestion, it was advised that all inka and colonial façades that lined streets in the old city were not to be touched. The narrow streets were retained, and particularly difficult tight corners, such as Plazuela de Santo Domingo and Zetas, where the thoroughfare is only 3m wide, were allowed to remain. In the fullness of time, reorganization of traffic flow and the closure of some streets to cars has reduced some of these difficulties. However, immediately after the earthquake, bulldozers removed about 5m in width of colonial and republican façades along Ancha Santa Catalina to make it a better route for traffic from the plaza. This exposed an inka wall perpendicular to the street, but at least part of it, including a doorway, was destroyed.

The earthquake of 5 April 1986 was less devastating in comparison. While there was still damage to the towers and domes of the cathedral, La Compañía, Santo Domingo, and other churches, only 154 private properties in the old city were damaged, eighty of which were classified in the serious damage category (Aparicio and Marmonilla 1989). The problems were the same as earlier: the poor construction of colonial, republican, and modern buildings in adobe, stone, and timber.

Urban Renewal and Hotel Construction

In the old city, nineteenth-century decadence had allowed many build-ings to quietly fall apart. Urban renewal of houses was slow, but population growth and the rise of tourism has seen many private dwellings converted into shops, restaurants, and hotels. Nevertheless, such redevelopment has retained the essentials of the plan. In 1938 the old Mint building in Plaza Regocijo was pulled down and replaced by the Hotel de Turistas in 1944. Nowadays, any development activity is preceded by heritage surveys under the auspices of the INC, and there has been substantial rescue archaeology in advance of hotel reconstruction in several locations, such as at Hotel Libertadores in 1981, Novotel in 1998, and the Hotel Marriott in 2009. But many other properties in the old city have been subjected to archaeological enquiry during heritage investigations, such as Casa del Almirante, Casa Concha, Beaterio de las Nazarenas, and Kusikancha.

The twentieth century presented significant challenges to the old city with regard to the survival of its inka and colonial past. Nevertheless, the national cultural heritage laws from 1929 onward and the eventual estab-lishment of a government authority, the Instituto Nacional de Cultura (now the Dirección Regional de Cultura), to oversee the protection, conserva-tion, and investigation of the inka and colonial sites and the support of the Municipality on these matters has considerably changed our knowledge of the city. The growing tourism to the inka capital and the baroque city guarantees that these investigations will continue.

Analysis of the Cusco Town Plan

The majority of houses are made of stone, while others have a half-stone façade and many adobe. They are very ordered. The very straight streets are paved, with a stone-lined channel in the middle and they form a cross.

Sancho 1917: 192

The historical processes of urban change form the backdrop for an intensive field study of the inka capital. The layers of time that have gradually transformed the city into a modern tourist mecca need to be peeled away. This does not mean to say that the later city does not merit scholarly attention by town plan analysis in its own right, but in this book this approach is only used to examine the original town plan and its functions.

In this chapter, I collate basic field information to conduct a town plan analysis of Cusco by considering five topics: the street plan; the distribution of architectural styles; types of inka building; the relationship between the later courtyarded groups and inka *kancha*; and use of the inka mensuration system. These will present the data for a more comprehensive analysis of the extant built environment of Cusco, using the "Conzen" principles of medieval town plan analysis, in two subsequent chapters.

Street Plan

The studies of Calca and Ollantaytambo demonstrate that the inkas were skilled planners of orthogonal towns, who could execute single phase plans with a simple grid but also were capable of skewing it geometrically to form a favored shape on the ground, a trapezoid. The street plan of inka Cusco is largely reconstructable from the field survey of architectural remains, although many narrow lanes have been infilled, some streets widened, and new ones opened through inka blocks, while encroachment has occurred around the plazas. The basic grid was observed by Sancho in 1533 and has

A

B

C

Figure 6.1. Inka streets and lanes. *A*, San Agustín looking down from Ruinas with the enclosure wall of Hatunkancha (mz16) on the right and the remains of San Agustín monastery on the left; *B*, Cabrakancha, with a side street entrance on far right and a door jamb with a carved snake on left; *C*, the entrance into Cabrakancha from Tullumayu is highlighted in cyclopean green diorite, while the walls of Tullumayu are in polygonal limestone (photo by Lisa Solling).

Table 6.1. Cusco street alignments (in degrees magnetic)

Plan-unit	Main street	Side streets	Orientation
I	Awaqpinta		341°
		Pantipata,	71°
		Intiqawarina	71°
II	San Agustín		331°
		Maruri,	241°
		Cabrakancha,	61°
		Santa Mónica	61°
		Romeritos	331°
III	Pumacurco		331°
		Siete Culebras,	61°
		Tucuman,	62°
		Ataúd	331.5°
A	Loreto		324°
A	Triunfo-Hatunrumiyoq		241.5°
A	Procuradores		139.5°
		Portal de Panes (Plaza)	48.5°

been interpreted by Hyslop (1990: chap. 2) as orthogonal, comprising four longitudinal streets, including those that run alongside the two channelized rivers, and at least five transverse ones. However, it does not have a simple single phase grid but uses a series of grids and open spaces to create the civic, imperial, royal, sacred, and residential spaces required for it to function. There are no main streets that are strictly parallel, although some side lanes are perpendicular (figure 6.1). While this variation from a single grid might indicate chronological development, it probably reflects the simple adaptation by the inka planners to the contours of the ridge line, slope, and valley terraces.

The main axis of the city is composed of a sequence of two streets, Awaqpinta in the southeast and San Agustín–Pumacurco,[1] which runs through the urban core toward the northwest (figure 6.1a). These were laid out successively along the ridge-line, but did not join. Yet they are the key to understanding the planning process with a series of cross-streets and plazas as well as some parallel lanes that form rough grids. There are four main street orientations, with that of San Agustín dominating much of the center of the old city (table 6.1).

Basic fieldwork in the old city requires the detailed observation of major and minor clues to determine the principles of town planning, including not only the obvious examination of the construction style of walls and

A

B

Figure 6.2. Closed inka lanes. *A*, entrance to first side lane off Awaqpinta (mz72), now the door to a residence (photo by Lisa Solling); *B*, side lane entrance off Palacio (mz1).

buildings but also the recording of footings that can be seen at ground level along certain streets and blocks. Since inka walls are always battered, examination of the exposed ones along street frontages can reveal the stone courses of corners and the battered angles of original doors and streets. If the batter is inwards on both sides, then a trapezoidal doorway is indicated; if it is the reverse, then a wider opening, such as a street or lane, is present (figure 6.2).

Today, there are very few extant trapezoidal doorways leading into structures or *kancha* in the city that remain in use; many are intact but have been blocked, such as along Loreto (mz3, mz4) and in Casa Concha (mz16), while others exist as simple vestiges of a few courses of one or both jambs, such as along San Agustín between Cabrakancha and Santa Mónica (mz34), along Romeritos (mz37), and in Ataúd (mz10).

A number of former lane entrances have been detected across the old city, such as the first side lane to the north off Awaqpinta (mz72) (figure 6.2a), one on the east side of Cabrakancha (mz35), several in Kusikancha (mz37) in Plazuela de Santo Domingo, Pampa de Castillo, and Romeritos and on the southern side of Palacio (mz1) (figure 6.2b), and one, now isolated as the support for stone steps, on the southern side of Ataúd (mz9A).

The location of former terrace walls was also studied across the broader area of Cusco, not only extant lengths but also by noting significant breaks of slope, where a street is steepened over a short distance to reach a different level. Side walls with a battered façade, facing downhill, may also be noted. Areas of terracing have been noted around Kusipata to the south and east as well as in the San Blas, San Cristóbal, and Santa Ana districts.

Spatial Distribution of Wall Construction Styles

The inkas used several construction styles and rock types, including the use of adobe, in the city walls, often using different styles for enclosure walls and the buildings within them. There have been two major studies of wall construction styles: one by Santiago Agurto (1980, 1987), which was part of the PER-39 study of the heritage resources of the city,[2] and a second by Mónica Paredes (1999, 2001) for her dissertation. Agurto (1987: 161–62) noted that there is some consistency in the relationship between construction style and location, but he did not attach sociocultural meaning to it. However, he did suggest that the various styles could reflect a chronological sequence of construction or were used to emphasize the power of the *panaqa*, who lived in the city.

Recent field observations essentially concur with the conclusions of both Agurto and Paredes, who have discerned two distinct distributions. Fine, sedimentary laid andesite walls are concentrated around Hawkaypata and between it and Qorikancha, in other words, in the main urban compounds, *kancha,* and temple. In contrast, polygonal limestone walls are found more on the periphery in the southeast, north, and northwest, at some distance from the plaza (figure 6.3). These patterns are derived from the lengths of

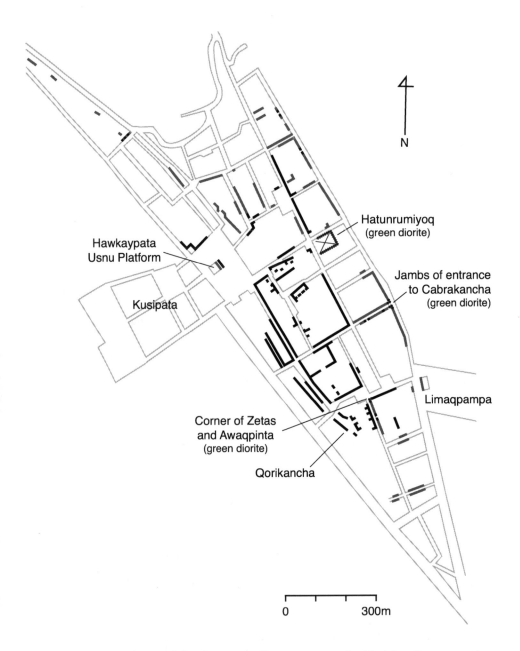

Figure 6.3. The spatial distribution of wall construction styles. Black is sedimentary style, in andesite; gray is polygonal style, in limestone; marked with a cross in a rectangle is encased style, in green diorite at Hatunrumiyoq; the simple crosses are the location of green diorite corners.

wall visible along and from the streets, but as far as is known, it also holds for the structures inside each street-block. The only exception is in mz12 at the Beaterio de las Nazarenas, which has both types in its enclosure walls with sedimentary along Pumacurco and polygonal on Choqechaka, but its external walls were probably reconstructed in the seventeenth century. A third, an elaborate polygonal style, uses large blocks of green diorite, which presents a well-fitting, polished, and pillowed wall that is incredibly strong but that was rarely used. There are no extant *pirka* walls in the old city.

The use of rose-black andesite appears to be related to the importance of the structure. It was generally shaped into either large or small rectangular blocks at the Waqoto and Rumiqolqa quarries and finished on all four sides at the building site. It was laid horizontally in english bond with the blocks of each higher course being slightly narrower and shorter. The main palace on Hawkaypata, Qasana, the large halls of Triunfo and Amarukancha, and the Hatunkancha compound had high walls of sedimentary andesite walling facing the plaza. The Sun temple, Qorikancha, and the main streets and blocks in between it and the plaza were built in the same way, including Kusikancha (mz37). Internal buildings within Hatunkancha and in Kusikancha are similarly built in andesite. It has been suggested that the use of large andesite blocks for some structures and smaller ones for others is a function of construction at different times, but within Hatunkancha, both types are found opposite each other along Arequipa. The distribution of andesite walling continues to the north of the plaza as far as the Beaterio de las Nazarenas (mz13). In some structures built in the polygonal style using limestone blocks, inka architects used andesite to highlight corners and doors.

The second important wall construction style in the city is polygonal, that is, invariably made with easily worked and readily available greyish-white limestone. Its distribution on the urban periphery, surrounding the andesite sedimentary core, is most distinctive. It is found both in enclosure and *kancha* walls along streets, such as Awaqpinta, Cabrakancha, Santa Mónica, Pumacurco, Ladrillos, and Tullumayu as well as in many parts as the typical inka terrace style. The latter are found in the area around the palace of Qolqampata to the west and the large terrace wall along Santa Clara, which has footings of small rectangular andesite, but also on the flanks of Carmenqa, San Blas, and to the south of the Avenida del Sol. Agurto (1987: 152–55) has suggested that its distribution may be simply a result of its availability, workability, and the fact that it makes very strong retaining walls. The river channelization walls of both Saphi and Tullumayu are made also of polygonal limestone.

Limestone polygonal walls were made of large and small blocks that were polished and pillowed, well-fitting but which could also be set in a clay mortar. Some also include other stones, such as diorite and sandstone. The most elaborate constructions in this style include the façade wall of Qolqampata, doorways within the Beaterio de las Nazarenas, and terraces in calle Suecia. However, there is also a cruder, more rustic version in some streets, such as in Pantipata. In certain locations, such enclosure walls have been interrupted to situate a sedimentary andesite doorway, such as along Choqechaka, or enclosure walls have been enhanced by andesite corners (mz56).

Despite the proximity of a diorite quarry just to the north of the city, it was rarely used by inka architects. Some have suggested that it was a preferred stone in the early inka period before Pachakuti's rebuilding and that it fell out of favor because it could not be acquired in quantity. However, it was used to build the magnificent Hatunrumiyoq platform in mz14 and to emphasize the entrance from the north into the side street of Cabrakancha (figure 6.1c). This style was also used in the Plazuela de Santo Domingo on the corner between Awaqpinta and Zetas to add color and majesty to a rounded corner close to the Sun temple. The lower terrace of Qorikancha also has rows of smaller rectangular blocks of diorite, laid in sedimentary fashion.

It is interesting to note that on the eastern side of the Hatunrumiyoq platform, its diorite wall has been clad with a limestone polygonal wall. This phenomenon has also been noted at Tambokancha, where original buildings have been clothed in a thick veneer of another construction style, presumably for both aesthetic and structural reasons.

Among the eyewitness chroniclers, Sancho (1917: 192) reported that adobe was widely used in Cusco as a building material but not for enclosure walls. Most modern architectural studies have tended to ignore its use by the inkas, preferring to study the aesthetics of stoneworking. Therefore, no examples of inka adobe walling had been noted in the city until recently, when with more thorough fieldwork, original stone walls are being found to have a capping of inka adobe bricks. For example, in mz13 Paredes (2001: 73) has recorded a lower polygonal limestone wall with a series of trapezoidal niches in its upper adobe section, each resting directly on the stone wall; each has wooden lintels, wrapped in rope. A similar wall was found in Kusikancha (mz37) in 2006, while the site was being prepared for display as a tourist venue. This process necessitated the conservation of all walls, and during the removal of plaster from an internal wall in *kancha* 5 building #8, five standard niches with wooden lintels were exposed. Each was resting on a course of adobe bricks on top of a sedimentary andesite wall. During the colonial period, these had been merely filled and plastered over. Further coats of plaster and paint left no surface indications of what lay underneath, and they were lost. It is not known how many other buildings in the old city continue to have original adobes sitting on top of fine inka walls.

Adobe was used mainly on top of stone walls because it reduced the overall weight of a roof and was particularly useful for the construction of gables. Paredes (2001) has recorded two buildings with adobe gable ends and inka cylindrical stone pegs set just below the roofline to tie down a thatched roof. One is the Casa de Cartagena in Pumacurco #336 (mz12) (figure 6.4), and the other is located in Márquez street (mz45). While the first is clearly a reused inka building, the second is probably a colonial construction using inka builders.

Figure 6.4. Adobe gable-end with roof pegs in a two-story building, Casa Cartagena, Pumacurco (photo by Lisa Solling).

The use of andesite for the most prestigious buildings in Cusco begs an important question: why was this stone chosen ahead of the more widely available limestone and diorite of the area immediately around the city that were also used distinctively within it? Certainly, andesite is a hard, heavy rock[3] with a fine color, when worked, but it requires considerable effort to shape it into a rough rectangular block and transport it from the distant quarries (Protzen 1980). Confirmation of its cultural importance to the inkas can be found 1,600km away in southern Ecuador, where Dennis Ogburn (2004a, 2004b) has located at least 450 well-dressed andesite blocks, some weighing as much as 700kg, at Puquishalpa near Saraguro. Using an X-ray fluorescence spectrometer, he was able to determine that these had come from the Rumiqolqa quarry and were probably en route to Tumibamba. He noted that, while there was good quality andesite locally available, the inkas had chosen, for cultural reasons, to use materials from their homeland in the construction of their new *cusco*.

This conclusion does not mean that the other building styles lacked any value or prestige. For example, at Quispeguanca, Tambokancha, and Raqchi, important royal centers, the main buildings were made of either random rubble, *pirka*, or cellular walls capped with adobe superstructures. Many buildings at Machu Picchu and Patallaqta were made of fairly roughly worked granite *pirka* in a mud mortar with a fine plaster coating. The distribution of rectangular ashlars laid in sedimentary style is quite rare beyond Cusco and is confined to some of the most prestigious places in Tawantinsuyu, including Vilkaswamán, Huánuco Pampa, Tumibamba, Chachapoyas, and Cerro Azul along the coast. Indeed, the importance of such ashlars for the inkas on the coast is highlighted by the use of rectangular adobe architecture and the discovery of a single cut stone in the northern jamb of the double-jamb entrance to the palace area of La Centinela[4] (Santillana pers. comm.). Despite its importance, this type of masonry is not used in any Qollasuyu center south of Lake Titiqaqa.

There is no field evidence for architectural painting in inka Cusco except for the horizontal band in the interior of buildings R-3 and R-4 in Qorikancha (Béjar 1990). However, there are more than sixty-five carved stone building blocks that are generally located in external walls. Whereas several can be considered *in situ*, many have been relocated since 1533 and occur in walls fabricated during the colonial period. They comprise mainly animals of which the majority (more than fifty) are serpents, but there are also carved felines or quadrupeds and humans standing beneath an arching rainbow (van de Guchte 1990: 37; Senchyshyn 2005) (table 6.2). They

Table 6.2. Zoomorphic and other bas-relief carvings on building blocks

Plan-unit / seam	Street block (mz)	Location	Type and location on wall	Rock type
B	72	Zetas #400	Three serpents near jambs; two serpents on vestibule wall	Andesite
B	72	Zetas #390	Serpent to north of door	Andesite
IIA	3	Loreto	Serpent north side wall (high)	Andesite
IIC	15	Cabrakancha	Serpent on west side door jamb	Andesite
IID	36	Amb 44, *kancha* 4, Hotel Libertador	Deer on reconstructed wall in *kancha*	Andesite
IIE	37	Plazoleta Sto Domingo #285	four serpents	Andesite
IIE	37	Maruri #340 (Kusikancha)	Seven serpents and two quadrupeds	Andesite
III	10	Casa del Almirante, Tucuman	Two serpents on one ashlar (low)	Andesite
III	10	Casa del Almirante, Ataud	two serpents	Andesite
III	10	Ataud #154	Two serpents on lintel; west jamb: one faint serpent	Andesite
III	12	Beaterio de las Nazarenas–Pumacurco	Three serpents (two on jamb stones) west of main door; two on east jamb stones; a four-legged animal (puma); six serpents near corner	Andesite
III	12	Beaterio de las Nazarenas–Siete Culebras	Eight serpents, human figure under rainbow	Andesite
III	12	Pumacurco #336	Two serpents to west of door, one to east	Andesite
A	4	Loreto door on south side	Two serpents on lintel, another to west of lintel	Andesite
A	1	Cuesta del Almirante #282	Two serpents on south door jamb, one adjacent; one to north	Andesite
A	22	Santa Teresa #385	Six ashlars, each with a carved puma, three either side of lintel	Andesite
A	45	San Francisco church N exterior wall	Serpent; two figures under rainbow	Andesite

Sources: González 1981; van de Guchte 1990; Pardo 1957; Senchyshyn 2005; Solling 2007.

Figure 6.5. Bas-relief serpents and a figure beneath a rainbow on a wall of Beaterio de las Nazarenas (mz12) in the lane Siete Culebras. This wall was recorded by Agurto as inka transitional, thought by others to be colonial, yet retains its inka footings and is clearly inka internally near the *kancha* corner (Colque 2001).

are mainly found in locations in the northwestern and northern parts of the old town. For example, snakes of various serpentine forms, some in pairs, on individual lintels and ashlars along Pumacurco, Ataúd, Cuesta de Tucuman, but others found in Loreto, Zetas, and Intipampa, while the human/rainbow figures are located on the Beaterio de las Nazarenas and in San Francisco church (figure 6.5). Six feline blocks are found above the lintel of a colonial house at Santa Teresa #385, while there is another quadruped in the façade of the Beaterio de las Nazarenas and others in Triunfo.

Pardo (1957: 120) has interpreted these zoomorphic reliefs as indicative of a heraldic custom, commemorating inka ancestors. In contrast, van de Guchte (1990) and Senchyshyn (2005) have argued that, since they appear in colonial buildings or in transitional walls, they should be considered colonial in origin, while the latter also noted scars from metal chiseling on some blocks to confirm this. While this may be true, it does not necessarily imply that the blocks themselves were not originally carved in this way and have been subsequently enhanced. As already mentioned, the built fabric has been radically altered from its days of inka glory and its past has been continually incorporated and remodeled into its colonial and later appearance. Examples from elsewhere in Tawantinsuyu, such as Huánuco Pampa and Tumibamba, highlight the importance of such carvings, particularly felines, on the jambs and lintels of entrances to inka buildings of high status, such as palaces and temple platforms, presumably as symbols for, and protectors of, sacred space. Clearly, with reference to the examples from the Lupaqa region, carved serpents also played a significant role in demarcating such space. The six carved feline blocks in Santa Teresa may therefore have come from the dismantling of entrances at Qasana nearby. There is no reason to deny that other blocks were also relocated from other places in the city.

Types of Inka Building

Very few inka standing buildings remain intact in the city today. These are rectangular in shape with one or more doorways, such as in Qorikancha. Prior to the excavations in Kusikancha (mz37), the *kancha* form could be discerned in the plan of its above-ground wall remains and in other street-blocks, such as the Beaterio de las Nazarenas (mz12). Other rectangular buildings can be inferred along Loreto (mz4) from surviving niches and wall stubs. There are no towers, and except for the curved wall at Qorikancha, no circular structures have survived. However, two other rectangular building types can be identified in the city: large halls and *kallanka*.

The street plan, property boundaries, and distribution of certain walls confirm Garcilaso's observation that there were three large halls facing Hawkaypata. Each appears to be located alongside a "palace" complex, similar to their placement within the rural palaces of the Sacred Valley (Farrington 1995; figure 2.8). However, these buildings were much larger than those associated with the country palaces (table 6.3).

The location of the first church, Triunfo, was chosen because it was a large hall in an elevated position above the plaza on its northern side, a key principle of the Royal Ordinances. Through its function, it was kept largely intact until the mid-eighteenth century, when it was remodeled into the building that is seen today with only one surviving length of sedimentary andesite wall along the street. Judging by the property boundaries to its rear, the size of the church, and the distribution of other inka walls, it may have been about 90m (56r) in length and perhaps 32m (20r) in width, which would have made it one of the largest buildings in Tawantinsuyu.

The building called Qora Qora stood on the plaza between Qasana and

Table 6.3. Large halls in Cusco and its hinterland (in meters)

	External length	External width	Wall width	Façade details	Columns	Overlooking
Qora Qora	90.0e (56r)	28.3 (17.5r)	—	Not known	Not known	Hawkaypata
Amarukancha	68.0e (42r)	9.7e (6r)	80–82	Not known	Not known	Hawkaypata
Triunfo	90.0e (56r)	32.0e (20r)	—	Not known	Not known	Hawkaypata
Qolqampata	25.8e (16r)	9.7 (6r)	80–82	Central double-jamb door; with a small window on each side	Not known	City
Muyuqmarka E (Sallaqmarka)	21.8	10.2	1.10	Not known	Three rectangular footings on center line	City
Muyuqmarka W	17.95	11.45	1.10	Not known	Two lines of rectangular footings	To west

Note: e = estimated length.

the houses of Waskar, identified as the long, narrow street-block (mz56) between the streets Suecia and Procuradores. Its width was about 28.3m (17.5r), and its length may have been up to 100m, but probably much less. It became the property of Gonzalo Pizarro, but was destroyed in 1548 and the site was sown with salt (Esquivel y Navia 1980: 148–49). There are no vestiges of any inka walls or footings in this location.

The third hall housed the *cabildo* in the 1530s and was located adjacent to Amarukancha and alongside Loreto street (mz4). It was probably removed during the construction of the Capilla de Loreto in the early seventeenth century, which is mainly built from reused andesite blocks; however, there is a length of inka walling on the street side that formed part of its northern wall. An excavation by Valencia (1991) confirmed that this hall extended 7m beyond the chapel façade into the plaza. Its overall dimensions were probably 9.7m (6r) in width and about 68m (42r) in length.

It is commonly believed that there are no surviving *kallanka* in the city, because they would have been located on a plaza and none have been recorded historically in either Hawkaypata or Limaqpampa (Hyslop 1990: 18; Paredes 1999: 132). However, detailed analysis of the standing architecture of extant structures suggests that there may have been at least two examples.

One lies on the north side of Angosta Santa Catalina at the Hotel Conquistador (mz2), where there is a battered wall of sedimentary, rectangular andesite, facing east that extends into the street. It contains at least six wall sections, each 3.4m (2.1r) in length, with two standard internal niches and five trapezoidal doorways, each 1.48m (0.9r) in width, separating them, some with lintels *in situ*. The section on the pavement is shaped for another doorway, which means that there would have been at least one other wall section in the street. A length of 32.68m can be readily measured, but there are indications in other properties that it extends further into the block, making it a *kallanka* with probably nine doors and about 48.5m (30r) in length. This wall has survived because it is a long established property boundary; unfortunately, its rear and side walls have been destroyed without trace.

The other is Casa Concha in Ancha Santa Catalina #320, an inka structure and colonial *casona*, facing west in mz16. It is oriented at an odd angle (58°), relative to San Agustín and other streets, yet it is roughly parallel to, and about 60m from, the first. It comprises a 45.5m (28r) long façade of thirteen to fifteen courses of rectangular andesite wall, standing 2.5 and 3.0m tall, in which there are eight doorways of different periods, including the filled-in locations of two inka trapezoidal doors, located about 3.56m (2.2r) apart, a spacing which confirms that other doorways were destroyed by the placement of colonial wooden doors. This building has survived because its façade was located on the new street, Ancha Santa Catalina, and it was converted into a colonial *casona*. It has retained both sides and was probably about 9.65m (6r) in width. It has standard inka niches on internal walls.

The Relationship between Colonial and Later Buildings and the Inka *Kancha*

Ever since the arrival of the Spaniards in 1534, Cusco has been rebuilt continually on the inka plan, retaining to a large extent its original street and *kancha* layout with only some slight modifications in the form of widening and closing of some streets and encroachment onto all plazas. At plot-level, individual properties have been subjected to much subdivision and amalgamation, while much of the original building fabric has been replaced with European courtyarded structures. In this section, I examine the relationship between such colonial and later buildings and the shape and form of the original inka *kancha*.

This enquiry is based largely on air photo interpretation and cartography, supported with some information on modern property boundaries and ownership changes. These different sources provide some clues to understanding the nature of this question and offer some answers. However, very little archival work has been done to date on property ownership changes over the last 480 years, except for a few colonial *casonas* that have been subject to recent restoration programs, Maruri #340, part of Kusikancha (Vargas 2007), and the Beaterio de las Nazarenas (Amado 2003). They indicate the times at which adjacent property was acquired, new structures were built, and narrow lanes were enclosed.

The process of conversion from a *kancha* to a courtyarded, Spanish-style house took place over the first two centuries after the conquest. It is the product of a simple desire to have two-story, enclosed, and courtyarded urban villas, with elaborate external portals, balconies, windows, and an inner patio, as in Spain. The *kancha* with its individual structures, corner spaces, and patio offered an ideal platform to do this, but it could not have been simple. The nature of private property meant that the newly occupied *solar* had fixed boundaries that could be measured and checked at any time. As in Europe, the only means of extending an urban property were either by purchase of a neighboring one and amalgamating the two or by encroachment onto public open space with a temporary structure that became permanent or by the incorporation of the narrow lanes between *kancha* into a plot. This simple action would have been especially effective if its enclosure was timed to coincide with the dismantling of the *kancha* and the erection of a new house. In these processes the majority of property boundaries would have survived, albeit with some of slightly larger area than others.

Subdivision also could have occurred at any time, but apart from the new internal boundaries, the outer boundaries of the original lot should still be traceable. For example, in Kusikancha (mz37), the *kancha* in the northeastern corner maintained its outer walls on two sides, enclosed the adjacent east-west lane, and became subdivided into three separate properties probably during the colonial period, progressively dismantling many inka buildings and walls, before becoming a single property again in recent years (Paredes 1999).

Property maps of the city and building cover with property boundaries have been used to assess the persistence of the *kancha* in the boundary arrangements across the old city. This information has been augmented by the 1956 vertical air photo and contemporary satellite images from Google

Earth to plot the patios and building edges. It is quite clear that there is some relationship between these features when the maps of the distribution of inka walls are also added. In the Awaqpinta area, along the northern side of San Agustín and in mz37, there is some relationship between these various factors which would suggest that original *kancha* can be traced. The area between Ataúd and Pumacurco has some indications of *kancha* subdivisions. In contrast, the property boundaries along San Agustín and Maruri (mz16, mz2) appear to be based not on dismantled *kancha* but on some other arrangement of buildings.

Measurements

The collection of raw data took place on various occasions from 1984 onward and involved the measurement of all street lengths and widths as well as other surviving inka architectural features throughout the old city.[5] They include lengths between street corners, as indicated by inka walling or the modern street pattern; street widths between known exposures of inka walling or footings; and the distances from and to like places, which would enable evaluation of longer measurements and greater planned areas.

On the basis of the results from Calca and Ollantaytambo, it was expected that there should be some consistency in the use of measurements, and this has proved to be correct. The *rikra*, its multiples, and divisions were utilized in the layout of various grids at a macro-level to such an extent that particular survey methods and origin points can be discerned. Among the smaller measurements, street and building widths show evidence of its use.

The measurement of street width is generally made between two lengths of good inka wall or footings; however, this is not always possible, and distance between one wall and the opposite building line have been substituted where appropriate. The overall accuracy is compromised by two factors: the irregular nature of the face of an inka wall, and the change in street level relative to the walls since original construction; this situation is made worse with the inka use of wall batter.

According to Sancho (1917: 192), Cusco streets were quite narrow and paved, with barely enough space for two horsemen to pass, and this is borne out by these results. The widest is the main artery of San Agustín between Limaqpampa Chico and Triunfo, with 5.25m (3.25r), while the short Zetas street between Plazuela Santo Domingo and Limaqpampa Chico is 4.84m (3r). Together these would have formed part of the main processional route

Table 6.4. Street widths in Cusco

Modern street name	Plan unit / plan-seam	Mean width (m)	Mean width in *rikra*
San Agustín	II	5.23	3.25
Palacio (Pumacurco)	III	4.705	2.875–3.0
Zetas	B	4.82*	3.00
Pumacurco	III	4.60	2.85
Ataúd	III	3.82	2.365
Procuradores	A	3.40	2.10
Loreto	A	3.23	2.0
Closed lane Ataúd south	A	3.22	2.0
Triunfo (original width)	A	2.80	1.73
Hatunrumiyoq	A	2.66–2.77	1.65–1.70
Tucuman	III	2.63–2.93	1.65–1.8
Awaqpinta	I	2.70	1.675
Romeritos	II	2.58	1.60
Kusikancha internal (E-W)	II	2.52–2.60	1.60
Siete Culebras	III	2.45	1.50
Ladrillos	III	2.42	1.50
Santa Mónica	II	2.43	1.50
Cabrakancha	II	2.42	1.50
Closed lane—Palacio south	III	2.33	1.45
Kusikancha internal (N-S)	II	2.13–2.36	1.35
Closed lane Ataúd north	III	2.07	1.275
Beaterio internal	III	2.00	1.25
Intiqawarina (Lane 3)	I	1.98	1.225
Closed lane—Awaqpinta (Lane 1)	I	1.96	1.20
Awaqpinta (Lane 4)	I	1.95–2.02	1.20–1.25
Pantipata (Lane 6)	I	1.90	1.175
Closed lane—Cabrakancha east	II	1.41	0.875

* Zetas has been widened by 1.5–1.6m; original width probably was 3.25m (2r).

from Qorikancha to Hawkaypata, which turned left into an open space now partly occupied by the Plazuela Lambarrí and along Triunfo to the plaza. Two other wide streets also enter the plaza: one from the east, Loreto, measures about 3.25m (2r), and from the west, Procuradores, is 3.4m (2.1r).

In the residential areas there are three common street widths: 2.65–2.75m (1.65–1.70r), such as Awaqpinta and Hatunrumiyoq; 2.38–2.50m (1.5r) for the south-north streets; and 1.95–2.0m (1.25r) for the Awaqpinta side streets (table 6.4). The excavated east-west streets in mz37 are about 2.25m (1.4r). All of the closed streets fit into these size categories. For example, along Arequipa (mz16) there are three spaces between buildings that measure (A) 2.4m, (B) 2.5m, and (C) 2.5m. The entrance off Ataúd to the south (mz9A) is 3.22m (2r) wide, and it probably enters a palace area overlooking the plaza; the one on Palacio (mz1) is 2.33m (1.45r), while the one on Cabrakancha's east side (mz34) is the narrowest, only 1.41m (0.875r).

At its greatest extent the inka city was 1.25km in length and between 180m and 460m in width. The urban area is not one continuous grid but is divided into several interlinked, but distinct, plan units with different orientations. Like Qosqo Ayllu, the block lengths were not laid out in whole *rikra*; for example, there are measurements that convert to 65.23r and 24.4r. These make more sense when block lengths and street widths are added together to the extent that, according to inka surveying logic, measurements would have been done in whole units between like points in the plan.

In this section, I shall only consider the use of longer measurements from probable survey origin points that form the basis of these grids because a more detailed discussion occurs in the following two chapters. The two main arteries have each been laid out with a high degree of accuracy. A residential sector lies on either side of Awaqpinta street with its survey origin point in the Plazuela de Santo Domingo, the corner of Zetas and Awaqpinta. Its end point was a remnant of an inka wall on the steps above Avenida Garcilaso, a distance of 323m (200r). The length of San Agustín from Limaqpampa Chico to the terrace wall at Ese street is 807.84m, or a little over 500 *rikra*;[6] the height difference is about 45m. A second survey origin point is the southwestern corner of San Agustín and Maruri, which enabled the establishment of a grid on either side of San Agustín. This point is exactly 161.5m (100r) along San Agustín from Limaqpampa Chico and the same distance to the street Ancha Santa Catalina, although there is no extant inka walling at the latter point. The transverse distance from the Tullumayu entrance along Cabrakancha and Maruri to the last terrace above Avenida del Sol is 323m (200r), passing through the origin point at 125.15m (77.5r).

There is an anomaly in this planning argument in that the distance between the second origin point and the equivalent corner of Triunfo and San Agustín does not equate with the whole number of *rikra*. This may suggest that the cross street was not part of the planned area from the corner of Maruri and San Agustín. To the northwest of Triunfo, there is a third survey origin point in Plaza Nazarenas that served to lay out five large *kancha* in mz10, 11, 12, 13, and 14.

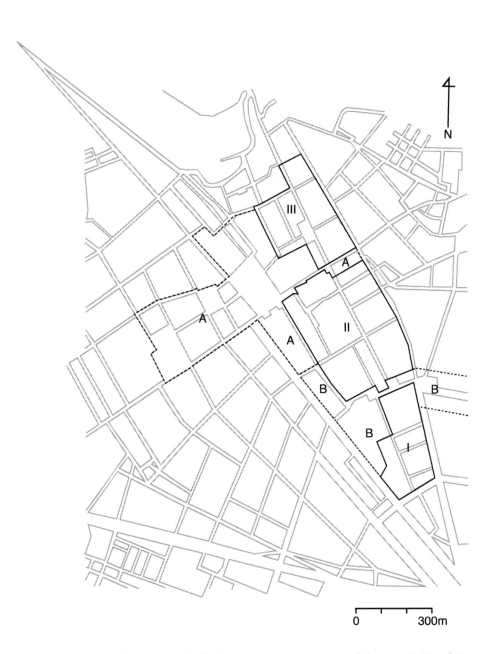

Figure 6.6. Plan analysis of inka Cusco, showing the location of plan-units I, II, and III and plan-seams A and B.

The Plan-Units of the Old City

The "Conzen principles" of town plan analysis in which plan-units can be distinguished on the basis of similarity of orientation and regularity of spacing of streets as well as similarity in construction style and rock type suggests that Cusco has a complex town plan. Essentially, it is composed of three separate but internally coherent plan-units that were planned at the same time (figure 6.6). They can be distinguished along the main axes: one is associated with Awaqpinta (plan-unit I) and two with the San Agustín–Pumacurco artery, one on either side of the street Hatunrumiyoq–Triunfo (plan-units II and III). These are separated by two irregular plan-seams (A and B), which contain the major public open spaces, as well as the principal temples and palaces, and which cross the city from one side to the other.

This analysis demonstrates that the inka concept of planning was modular and quite small-scale. Five separately planned areas were brought together as a single city that integrated the three regular residential grids of *kancha* with the two separate focal elements of inka society, the temple to the southeast and the politico-religious center of Hawkaypata and its surrounds. Indeed, plan-unit II is itself made up of five separate sub-units that further complicate this basic understanding. The plan-units and plan-seams will be analyzed in detail in the next two chapters.

Inka Public Spaces, Palaces, and Temples

The plaza was square, paved and mainly flat; around it were the four houses
of the important lords of the city, painted and well-made.

Sancho 1917: 192

Cusco played two very important roles in inka society. First, it was the political and administrative capital and hence contained the principal royal residence and, second, it was the supreme religious center where the Sun was worshipped and two other deities, the Creator god, Tiqsi Wiraqocha Pachayachachiq and the thunder god, Illapa, were venerated. It was also where the Inka ancestors, including the founding Ayar siblings as well as the mummies of former kings, were fed and honored as sons of the Sun. Cusco was the navel of the world about which everything was regulated and revolved. These roles were intertwined both in the person of the king and in the social fabric of the city and its environs. It was the place where ancestral stories, myths, and legends were told and retold, where origin stories were enacted and reenacted, and where political decisions were wrapped in oracular utterings, ceremonial dances, sacrifices, and provincial diplomacy.

In the design of the city, these two functions, administrative and religious, were kept spatially separate, about 400m apart, in plan-seams of public and private spaces, with one residential plan-unit between them. The other two plan-units lay to the west of seam A and east of seam B (figure 6.6). In this chapter, I consider the planning and archaeology of the plan-seams to establish function more clearly.

Plan-Seam A

The main plaza, Hawkaypata, was located on the southwestern edge of the city, where the alluvial fan was relatively wide and more level. It was surrounded on three sides by palaces, large halls, and a temple (Rowe 2003b).

To its southwest across the Saphi river was the extensive terraced plaza of Kusipata, and to its northwest along Triunfo street were assembly spaces and the Hatunrumiyoq platform (figure 7.1).

Plaza and *Usnu*

This large public area was described by John Hyslop (1990: 37) as a "dual plaza" on either side of the channelized Saphi with two adjacent trapezoidal spaces: Hawkaypata, now the Plaza de Armas on the city side, and Kusipata to its southwest. It measured in the order of 525m (325r) from end to end with a series of leveled terraces that descend from the Plaza San Francisco to the river and then up to the level of Triunfo Church. At its narrowest point, at the river, it was 170m (105r) wide. Hawkaypata was surrounded by palaces and compounds, while around Kusipata there is some evidence from excavations for structures along Teatro, San Juan de Dios, and Márquez, despite a lack of chronicle information.

Hawkaypata was clearly the more important, measuring about 143m (88.5r) along its northwest side, about 205m (127r) on the northeast, and 167m (103.5) on the southeast, with a total area of 2.91 hectares (Fernández 2004). Sancho (1917: 192) noted that it was almost square, level, and cobbled. In 1559, Polo de Ondegardo (1965: 109) stated that the inkas had covered its surface with ocean beach sand to a depth of 2½ *palmos*, about 54cm.[1] He had this removed for use in mortar for the construction of the cathedral because only poor quality sand was available locally. During this work, he reported that "many gold and silver vessels, small sheep [llamas], and small humans" were found in it, presumably from inka offerings. According to chronicle sources, there were several structures in Hawkaypata, including an *usnu* complex and some towers, and it was surrounded by at least three palaces and associated buildings (Protzen and Rowe 1994; Rowe 1991).

Archaeo-astronomical inquiries suggest certain functions. For example, Aveni (1981) and Zuidema (1981) were able to determine the location of the *usnu* platform, which they believed would have been the place from which sunset observations were made. They used a reverse reading from a place on Picchu mountain, where the antizenith sun set, when generally observed from the plaza to indicate that the most probable location for the platform lay between the fountain and Medio street. Bauer and Dearborn (1995: figs. 5, 7) noted that all critical sunsets could be observed from a location in the center of Hawkaypata.[2] While all sunrises can also be seen from the plaza,

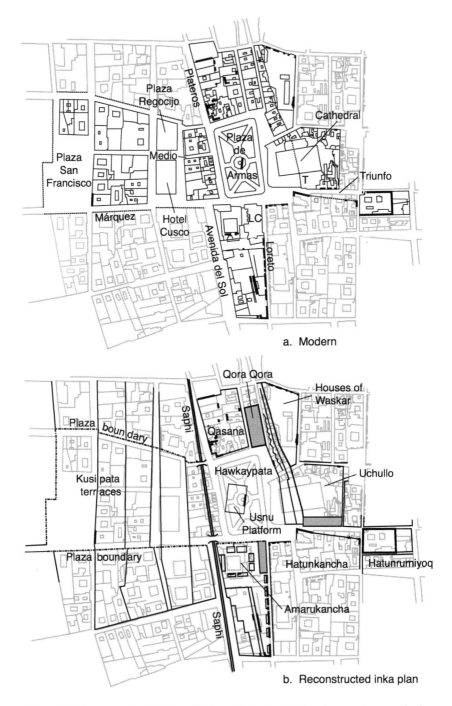

a. Modern

b. Reconstructed inka plan

Figure 7.1. Plan-seam A. *A*, Modern blocks and streets; *B*, Inka plazas, palaces, and other buildings.

the culturally important December solstice sunrise, *qhapaq raymi*, an event that culminated in the important *warachiquy* initiation rituals, would have been observed rising behind the snowy peaks of Awsangati, 80km away, as if emerging from it. From the center of the plaza, the northeastern horizon is relatively close, and while the June solstice sunrise can be seen, both urbanization on the hilltop and the height of the cathedral nowadays make knowing its precise observation alignment difficult to determine.

There have been several excavations in the plaza revealing ancient deposits. For example, in August 1994 Seda Qosqo[3] opened a trench in Medio street that enabled examination of the original inka channelization of the Saphi river, which at this point was about 4.5m wide and 6m deep, and of the colonial bridge built with reused andesite and basalt blocks in lime mortar in 1559–60. In 1997, long trenches were dug around the plaza to lay electricity and telephone cables, which were monitored for prehispanic evidence by Walter Zanabria (1997). He noted that there was a yellowish sand layer in two locations, in front of La Compañía and in front of the Portal de Panes. Along the eastern side, stone canals were observed running from the cathedral to the river, and in front of the Portal de Carnes, some structures were found built with "re-utilized" inka blocks.

The Usnu Complex

The *usnu* complex lay in the middle of Hawkaypata. It had a worked stone, shaped like a ninepin, with a golden sleeve, as an image of the Sun, and a round hole to receive libations (Anonymous Chronicler 1906: 151; Betanzos 1996: 48; Molina 1989: 74). According to Cieza de León (1959: 182–83), it stood on a small bench that he described as a theater or throne, whereas Segovia (1968: 22) indicated it was a square platform with a staircase. Beside it stood a stone brazier and initially a stone-lined hole into which *chicha*, charcoal, and ashes from the offerings were tipped and into which people also urinated during major ceremonies. At some stage, this had been replaced by a stone font, 83.5cm tall,[4] which stood over a stone channel to carry these offerings to Qorikancha and beyond. A small round reed hut covered this at night (Pizarro 1986: 90). Without doubt, the *usnu* complex was the *waka* that Cobo (1990: 57) called Aucaypata (CH-5:4).[5] It received "universal sacrifice" to the Sun, which was subsequently divided and sent to other parts of Tawantinsuyu, presumably as *qhapaq hucha*. It was also the focus of daily rituals and sacrifices as well as monthly and annual ones and was where major ceremonies were performed.

In 1996, the Municipality began a works project for the refurbishment of the nineteenth-century fountain in the middle of the Plaza de Armas. Long, deep trenches were dug in order to access its mechanism and pipework. During these interventions, the top of an inka wall was discovered at a depth of 1.9m. Archaeologists from the INC-Cusco, under the direction of Miguel Cornejo (1996, 1998), began a rescue program to record as much of this structure that could potentially be damaged by these works. In total, nineteen trenches were excavated around the fountain, some to a depth of over 3m as far as sterile alluvial deposits, and many contexts were recorded (figure 7.2). Despite much disturbance, five general stratigraphical layers were distinguished: modern, republican, colonial, and inka occupations on top of sterile clay. In addition, no clear evidence of either an extensive sandy layer or cobbling was discovered to indicate the original plaza surface.

The inka wall was exposed for a total length of 19.25m on an alignment of 310°, but there was no evidence for any corners, sidewalls, or stone steps that would have given some indication of the size and disposition of this structure.[6] Its footings are rustic, while it is made in polygonal style with well fashioned diorite and limestone blocks (Cornejo 1996). It reaches a maximum height of 1.8m, and it was found 2.17m from the surface in the northwest trench but only 1.04m below in the southeast. It is an inka retaining wall, facing north (i.e., battered to the south). It was associated with decorated inka pottery, charcoal, and camelid bone. About 1m to the north, remnants were found of a second wall, parallel to the first, and made of finely fitting, rectangular, polished andesite blocks. Many similar stones were scattered to the north of its trajectory. This structure must have been enlarged at some stage and clad with a rectangular veneer, a style in keeping with all the buildings surrounding the plaza.

To the west of the fountain, a series of superimposed floors were found. A typical inka floor, consisting of a compacted layer of clay and small stones, was discovered at a depth of about 80cm in several adjacent trenches, below both a colonial floor and a republican paving, confirming that the structure was a platform. Although colonial and republican canals were found, no inka canal could be identified because this level was the platform summit.

The excavation yielded large amounts of pottery of all periods, as well as animal bone and other items of material culture.[7] Preliminary analyses suggest that the prehispanic pottery is mainly inka decorated wares (types A and B) from *maka*, *aysana*, plates, and jars—an assemblage indicative of feasting and drinking, possibly associated with the ceremonies that were practiced in this vicinity. There was only a small quantity of killke sherds.

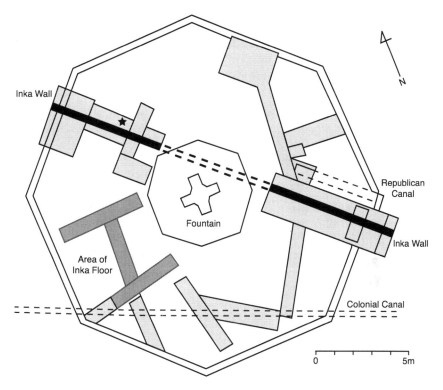

Figure 7.2. Excavations at the fountain in Hawkaypata and the location of trenches. Thick black line is the inka platform wall; dark gray areas are inka flooring; the black star marks the location of the llama figurines (after Cornejo Guerrero 1996).

Much camelid bone was also found, including carbonized and charred elements in ash lenses. These finds suggest some evidence for the rituals during which at least one llama was killed each day and burned in a perpetual brazier. Nevertheless, the collection contained other animal bones, including sheep and pig.

The most important find was a line of four upright llama figurines, discovered near the platform wall in a clay and gravel matrix. They were pointed toward the southeast and Wanakawri mountain in single file, in the following order: gold, silver, gold, and spondylus (figure 7.3). Each is miniature, standing only 5.0 to 6.5cm in height. Betanzos (1996: 48) mentioned that small gold statues of llamas had been placed in the ground adjacent to the *usnu* complex as offerings, while Polo de Ondegardo (1965: 118–19) reported that many gold and silver figurines of humans and llamas had been removed in 1559 along with the sand. This particular find may have been deposited as part of the inaugural dedication rituals for the *usnu*

Figure 7.3. Line of four llama figurines found in the Hawkaypata *usnu* excavations (after Vargas 2007: gráf. 5.1).

complex, as described by Betanzos, and it may have been disturbed by the sand removal by Polo.

Kusipata

Kusipata was separated from Hawkaypata by the channelized course of the river and only connected to it by two stone bridges across the Saphi. It extended a further 319m (197.5r) along its western side, about 236.5m (146.5r) on its southern side, and 352m (218r) on its eastern side, covering an area of 6.82 hectares. It was terraced with five or six broad, parallel levels to cover the 15m height difference between San Francisco and the river. Kusipata is often described as a place from which public ceremonies in Hawkaypata were viewed. There is no indication that it contained an *usnu* complex or any other inka structure within it, although the *waka* called Aucaypata paccha, (CH-8:3), a fountain, was located somewhere within it (Cobo 1990: 60). It was associated with the priests of Chuquilla and was where the thunder deity, Illapa, bathed. No inka buildings were reported historically fronting the plaza, although a trapezoidal doorway and rectangular sedimentary wall has been recorded in Márquez street on the southeastern side and another in the Municipality on the western side (Agurto 1980). Recent excavations have revealed evidence for structures along Teatro, San Juan de Dios, and Márquez streets.

The colonial encroachments on the Kusipata terraces produced a grid of seven street blocks across the former plaza extending onto the adjacent terraces. This has meant that in this area urban renewal of buildings and heritage conservation projects have produced an opportunity to excavate within the plaza and in properties on its periphery.

There have been at least seven rescue excavations in and around this plaza, but these have been poorly published to date. The first took place within the Plaza de Regocijo, where an inka occupation layer was found, 80cm thick, associated with inka sherds, lithic fragments, and organic materials. It lay on top of a sterile natural layer of fine sand and stones (Franco 1941: 108–9). During the early 1940s, some artifacts were recovered from the construction site of the new Hotel de Turistas, known as El Cuadro. These included at least one disturbed cache of pottery that contained two conjoining fragments of a black polished Chimú double-bodied pot modeled as a condor, a red bowl with a puma handle, and a neck of a decorated *maka* (Museo Inka Inventory: 33/1427–31).

On its western side (mz7), recent excavations in the patio of the Municipality prior to the construction of a convention hall have produced some inka walls and much pottery as well as a colonial canal, near where Agurto (1980) had reported a standing inka doorway and wall. In the same area, rescue excavations during trenching for electricity and telephone cabling located a terrace wall along the northern side of Santa Teresa between the Municipality and the San Antonio restaurant (Zanabria 1997). It was found below several former street pavings, modern fill, and old metal piping. It is 70m long and made from limestone and green diorite blocks in a clay mortar with its footings resting on a red clay bed at a depth of about 80cm. In front of it, there was an ashy lens containing plenty of charcoal and inka pottery. At the Hotel Málaga (#344), a second wall, 1.2m wide and of similar construction, was found to run perpendicular to the main alignment. It is associated with a disturbed deposit that could imply a later building, but its size and association with the main wall suggest it to be a terrace segment to shape the landscape beyond the plaza. At the far end of this trench near the Plazuela Silva, a deep offering pit was discovered that contained only a very large, fragmented *maka*, surrounded by a circular arrangement of ash-coated stones. Zanabria (1997) suggested that this was probably an offering to Pachamama.

On the fourth terrace above the river on the western side, an excavation program was conducted in 2002 at the Hospital of San Juan de Dios (mz22). It uncovered the footings of inka structures, abundant inka polychrome, and plain pottery, mainly *maka* and plates, as well as some inka burials with grave goods (Zapata pers. comm.).

On the eastern side, there are no major indications of inka walling except for a trapezoidal doorway in fine rectangular stonework, set within an elaborate colonial portal in Márquez (Agurto 1980), while in the same streetblock (mz43) there is also an adobe gable end with cylindrical roof pegs (Paredes 2001: 75–76). In recent excavations in the same street, INC-Cusco archaeologists have found, at a depth of 1m below surface, the footings of an inka wall and a 40cm wide, stone-lined canal (El Comercio 09/04/2008). This 1m wide wall has three courses of finely worked rectangular andesite. It is probably part of the plaza boundary wall, although it is thought that there were also inka structures in this area to the south of the plaza. In mz18 a recent excavation in the Colegio Mercedario has revealed some inka materials, but this has not been well reported. In the 1940s, a cache of pottery was donated to the museum from Casa Trelles, a property adjacent to La Merced convent. This included three fine *maka*, a *maka* neck, a casserole dish, and a pedestalled pot, a typical inka burial assemblage that had been found during renovations at the property.

Palaces and Large Halls

Historical sources (e.g., Garcilaso 1966: 320) noted that there were three inka palaces, each associated with a large entertainment hall fronting onto Hawkaypata and a fourth on a higher terrace in the northwest corner. Qasana, the main royal palace, lay on the western side with the Qora Qora large hall to its north (figure 7.4). Amarukancha was on the southeastern side with a hall to its north, and Uchullo, associated with Pachakuti Inka, was located on the terraces to the north with its hall to its east (figure 7.1b). This pattern is typical of inka rural palaces, such as Quispeguanca, Pumawanka, and Chinchero in the Sacred Valley, where large halls were found adjacent to residential and administrative *kancha* (Farrington 1995). Unfortunately, in Cusco very little standing architecture survives in these areas to confirm such an interpretation.

Plan analysis indicates that Qasana occupied the street block (mz8) between the modern streets of Plateros and Procuradores. It was described by Sancho (1917: 154) as the finest of the palaces, which were all "painted and well worked in stone." It had a magnificent red and white portal, fronting onto the plaza, that was also a *waka* (CH-6:4), called Wayra, through which the wind howled, and in its threshold there was a pit in which sacrifices were buried (Cobo 1990: 58).[8] Pedro Pizarro (1986: 161–62; Estete 1924: 45) reported that there were two round towers, one on either side of the

Figure 7.4. Qasana palace, beneath the arcades, facing the Plaza de Armas. The church of San Cristóbal (Qolqampata) is on the hillside and Saqsaywaman on the hilltop.

portal, which were burned in 1536 and demolished soon afterward. Martín de Murúa (1987: 345–49) described the royal palace, which he called Cuyusmango. Its main gate was guarded, and beyond it, the palace was divided into two sections, each with an internal plaza. The outer one was for reception and also held the armory, while a second guarded entrance led into the inner sector, characterized by spacious apartments, containing the royal residences, administrative offices, the treasury, gardens, and a zoo. In its grounds, there was another *waka*, a pond called Tiqsicocha (CH-6:5), to which "great sacrifices" were made (Cobo 1990: 58).

Qasana was awarded to Francisco Pizarro as four *solares* in 1534. It has undergone many architectural changes subsequently, including the loss of almost all its original structures, to the extent that very little standing architecture survives, including only ten lengths of wall and some footings. There are remnants of the façade wall and footings along Portal de Panes (Agurto 1980), while the distribution demonstrates a rectilinear plan of parallel and perpendicular walls. These include a lane between #369 and #348 Plateros; a 15m long wall at the rear of a property on Procuradores that now forms a property boundary; and a 30m long wall, parallel to the façade and about 125m from it, that also forms a property boundary, which was possibly the western enclosure wall.

The façade itself, under the arcades of the Portal de Panes, has been largely destroyed by the insertion of wide doorways, windows, and the construction of an adobe and timber second story (figure 7.5a). There are only intermittent lengths of its original limestone footings supporting a few courses of fine sedimentary andesite ashlars with an inward batter and no indication of the location of the original gateway. Its total length from Procuradores to a tall original corner at the Café Roma is 72.78m (45r). The corner and southern wall can be seen in the adjacent travel agency (figure 7.5b). Inside the café, the internal wall stands about 4m in height, with three evenly spaced standard niches (60cm wide, 80cm high) and about 2.5m above the floor. These are characteristic of a tall, freestanding enclosure wall with no attached buildings. About 15m along Plateros, it turns south and then west, and its footings can be seen under the modern building line.

There has only been one archaeological excavation within Qasana, although there have been several unreported finds. At Plateros #348, Castillo (1999) revealed limestone footings, over 1m in width, of a large inka building, lying just below the surface. Its function had been food and *aqha* preparation, because there were large quantities of charcoal, ash, and potsherds on the inka floor. From all excavation units, she found that about 60% of the pottery was from inka plainwares, mainly cooking pots, jars, and plates, while the finely decorated sherds were mainly from large *chicha* storage jars.

Elsewhere in Qasana, construction and infrastructural work in many properties have often yielded quantities of inka ceramics, but these have not been formally recorded. One find was a cache of gold and silver human and llama figurines, discovered in the early 1980s during the digging of footings for an extension to an existing shop in Portal de Panes, about 10–15m from the inka façade. This is clearly an offering deposited within what would have been the first patio of the palace.

The Qora Qora large hall stood to the north of Qasana between the modern streets of Procuradores and Suecia. It was a *waka* itself (CH-5:5), renowned as a place where Pachakuti Inka used to sleep, and it received llamas and clothing as offerings for burning (Cobo 1990: 57). Its size was such that its first Spanish owner, Gonzalo Pizarro, had received it as two *solares,* and he held jousting competitions within it. It was pulled down in 1548 (Rowe 1991: 88). This location has no visible inka architecture or footings, while the only excavation yielded a disturbed deposit, including inka pottery and some footings (Oberti 2004). In 2011, a second excavation

Figure 7.5. Qasana enclosure wall. *A*, inka façade and modern shops; *B*, the internal wall and niches in the Café Roma.

in the westernmost property of mz54, Procuradores #394 has yielded inka floors with inka and killke pottery, stone *qonopa*, and wall footings (Béjar Luksic et al. 2011).

The Amarukancha palace is less well known historically than Qasana. Various chroniclers considered it the palace of different Inkas, including both Wayna Qhapaq and Waskar.[9] It lay on the southeastern side of the plaza on terraces between Loreto street and the Saphi river (mz4) and consisted of a large hall on the street corner with a series of residential *kancha* alongside (figure 7.6a). The large hall and some residential buildings were handed as two *solares* to Hernando de Soto in 1534, while four others took property of one *solar* each in the area to the rear (Rivera Serna 1965). Garcilaso de la Vega (1966: 69) reported that the inkas had sealed one room because it had been struck by lightning.[10] He reported that most buildings were destroyed during the 1536 uprising and that only the large hall and the Sunturwasi tower remained (Garcilaso 1966: 426–27).[11] He also noted that Antonio Altamirano had found a large gold vessel in the patio of his plot (Garcilaso 1966: 749).[12]

This site is occupied by the Jesuit church, La Compañía de Jésus, its chapels and former cloisters with frontages on the plaza, measuring 116.2m (72r). The rear of the street-block mz4 between Loreto and Avenida del Sol features terraces, a craft cooperative, a commercial center, a bank, and the Palacio de Justicia. As we have seen, the large hall was probably in the location now occupied by the Capilla de Loreto, while the area of the church and cloister held residential and administrative buildings. According to Agurto (1980), very few standing walls and footings of inka construction remain. The most important is the enclosure wall, which has been recently conserved, that runs for about 160m along Loreto from the rear of the church to Afligidos. In addition, there are three inka walls parallel and perpendicular to the façade within the university cloister that indicate two rectangular inka buildings of one side of a *kancha*.

There have been five excavation projects in various parts of this compound since 1990, of which three are available. One was conducted within the church itself and involved ten excavation units, only four of which yielded any inka structural and occupational evidence (Valencia 1991). Its somewhat disappointing results are not surprising, because the construction of the church with its high walls, towers, columns, roof, and dome had required such deep footings to support the weight that most prehispanic structures and deposits would have been removed. Therefore, the excavations inside the church proved difficult to obtain inka contexts, particularly since the trenches were quite small.

One important trench was dug to a depth of 4.9m in the crypt beneath the high altar. In stratum IV at a depth of 1.95m, an inka wall was found, running east to west (Valencia 1991: 22–23). This consists of four courses of rectangular andesite, 1.4m high, set on a foundation of three limestone

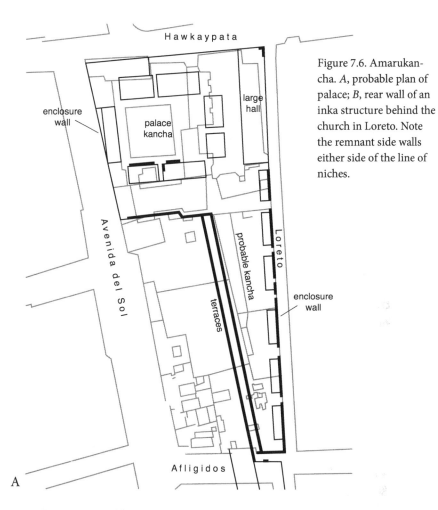

Figure 7.6. Amarukancha. *A*, probable plan of palace; *B*, rear wall of an inka structure behind the church in Loreto. Note the remnant side walls either side of the line of niches.

Hawkaypata

enclosure wall

palace kancha

large hall

Avenida del Sol

Loreto

probable kancha

enclosure wall

terraces

Afligidos

A

B

courses with clay mortar, which itself sits on a red clay base. It has a 2° batter toward the east and is the external façade of a building facing the plaza. It is associated with a paved floor, upon which there were inka sherds, calcined animal bone, and an ashy lens. More than 75% of all ceramic finds were inka pottery. Colonial wall foundations were found above this level and adjacent to it. The inka structures in this part of Amarukancha were on a lower terrace level than the church floor and the plaza.

A second trench was placed in the nave adjacent to the southeastern column of the main dome between the Sacred Family and San Juan de Dios altars. It revealed mixed deposits to a depth of 7m alongside the wide footings. Nevertheless, inka sherds dominated its assemblage with animal bone, while the fragmentary remains of two infant crania were also found (Valencia 1991).

Two other trenches investigated the exterior wall of the large hall. One was located at the entrance to the rear patio, finding twelve rectangular courses of thin andesite blocks set in a fine clay mortar with a 5% batter standing on top of an andesite footing sat on a red clay base at a depth of 3.06m. The other, located 68m from the first, explored the wall alignment into the plaza. It uncovered the top of an andesite wall only 61cm below street paving and electricity and telephone cables. Several courses were dug as far as andesite footings. This ended at a corner 7m in front of the Capilla de Loreto in line with the church façade (Valencia 1991: 28). This wall has a limestone veneer abutting it with its face to the interior of the building. This technique has been seen at Tambokancha, where it was used in a redevelopment of an original building to make it wider, perhaps to support a higher, heavier roof. These results indicate that this large hall underwent two phases of construction.

The Agurto survey (1980) and Compañía excavations revealed several unconnected, parallel and perpendicular walls to the south and east of the church that imply that the palace residential area consisted of *kancha*. The adjacent convent cloister, now a university property known as Paraninfo, was investigated during works to repair its patio fountain. Raúl del Mar (1992) excavated five pits, in which he reported disturbed layers containing inka, colonial, and republican sherds, although he did note an accumulation of limestone and green diorite flakes and dust in stratum II, indicating fine stoneworking *in situ*. He discovered a curious offering that consisted of fragments of a large rimless but decorated *urpu* that had six drilled holes in its lower body. It had been filled with ground mica, which would have gradually trickled out, while at its base a pair of decorated plates, a deer-handled plate, and a simple tripod cooking pot had been placed. He suggested that this must have been placed beneath the floor of this patio as an offering to Pachamama. In stratum II of a second pit, he found a rough limestone wall, about 1m high, that was associated with a gravel lens and inka pottery. There were sherds embedded in its mud mortar. This lay below inka floor level and was probably part of a cell that had been filled with rubble in order to build a construction platform.

There have been two archaeological investigations to the rear, associated with conservation work on the Loreto enclosure wall itself. These have confirmed that there were a series of inka buildings, keyed into the outer wall along its conserved length, each consisting of nine standard niches on its interior face with a wall stub at either end (figure 7.6b). Each has an external length of about 16.3m (10r), and from excavation, their width was about 5.92m (3.25r), although the number of doorways is not known (Bolívar 2004; Cumpa 2000). Various later walls and footings have been built up against it but were not keyed into it. It is possible that a plan of three *kancha* with six to eight buildings in each may have been built.

Along Loreto the enclosure wall is 80cm wide and made of small, coursed andesite blocks in a clay mortar, while the footings are slightly wider, comprising a mixture of limestone, sandstone, andesite, and diorite blocks, set into a clay base at a depth of 60cm. Eight doorways perforate the wall, but only three are relatively unaltered inka openings. The material culture provides a mixture of killke, inka, colonial, republican, and even modern objects, with a majority of inka period sherds. The assemblage includes decorated *maka* and plates as well as two large jars that had been placed in the floor and against the wall of one structure (Cumpa 2000).

Hawkaypata itself must have been relatively flat, although its northern side had two terrace walls, close together. In the northeast corner stood the large hall, used as the first church, Triunfo (figure 7.7), while in the center was the palace compound, Uchullo, which was attributed to Pachakuti Inka and granted to Beltrán del Castro in 1534 (Rowe 1968). This area has been substantially altered since the conquest, with the construction of the cathedral and its associated chapel (1559–54), which extend into the plaza. Apart from the wall on Triunfo street, no standing inka walls survive in the front half of this block (mz1), although behind the present ecclesiastical buildings, there is evidence of an east-west street that leads to a *kancha* with at least one double-jamb entrance on its northern side (see chapter 8).

In the cathedral, an excavation program was conducted in association with restoration works, following the 1986 earthquake (Perez 2001). It was

Figure 7.7. Triunfo church, the former large hall of Uchullo. Note the Portal de Belén rounded corner of the Hatunkancha enclosure wall at the far right.

designed to examine the cathedral foundations, record any prehispanic levels, and assess the nature of subterranean flow. As with La Compañía and other churches, its construction required deep footings to bear the load of its high stone walls, columns, towers, roof, and dome; at the rear these were dug into the original terrace, while at the front they were dug into the later construction terrace. As a consequence, the strata are very disturbed and no inka footings or floors of Uchullo were found, only some decorated and plain potsherds (Perez 2001: 37). Perhaps the most significant find was a number of natural springs, drained by a network of stone-lined canals that date from the inka period onwards (Perez 2001: 40). The archaeological strata in Triunfo church showed less disturbance, and despite the fact there were many inka sherds, there were no sealed contexts (Cahua 1998).

In the northwestern corner of the plaza lies a large terraced platform (mz9A), that stands about 12m above it. Today it is occupied by the Colegio San Borja and was probably the location of the "fortress" and houses of Waskar, but there are few visible remains, although the façade of the school displays a footing of pillowed limestone blocks (Farrington 2010a). In Ataúd, there is a remnant of inka wall that now serves as a footpath and steps to a school door. It stands only a few courses high, but its fitted polygonal limestone coursing clearly reveals a 3.22m (2r) wide street that has been infilled and that would have led into the area occupied by the school. There is no standing evidence in the school grounds. A steep slope defines the southern limits of this platform. An inka terrace wall of limestone blocks in polygonal style runs through properties #368, #348, #326, #320, and #310 Suecia and at least two other lower ones in the street façade of Suecia #310 and the other in the façade of Portal de Carnes (Agurto 1980; Vargas 2007: 59–64).

There have been no excavations at the school, but there has been one on the platform in the Parque Tricentenario on the corner of Cuesta del Almirante and Ataúd and another on the southern terraces. The first contained mixed deposits, including several finely worked andesite and limestone building blocks from a dismantled inka structure, a large quantity of camelid bone, and finely decorated inka potsherds. The latter included typical ceramic offering components, such as *maka* rims and zoomorphic plate handles.

The second was a series of fourteen trenches dug in the rooms, patio, and backyard of Suecia #348 (Zapata 2003). This project aimed to understand the function of an inka terrace wall at the rear of the patio. A 10m long wall of finely worked limestone blocks, carefully fitted in polygonal style, was found. This was not part of a building, because no transverse walls were encountered along its length, only a terrace facing south. Zapata (2003) discovered a monumental double-jamb doorway, measuring in width 2.14m (1.32r) and 1.22m (0.75r), that has a canal and stone staircase from the upper level. It is cyclopean in style and rests on substantial footings. It stands in a salient, implying that the wall followed a zigzag course (figure 7.8). A second terrace wall was found in the backyard, while the property boundary had a third up to the height of the school platform. This type of wall arrangement is found in several important locations in Cusco. For example, three similar monumental doorways occur in each zigzag wall leading from Choqepampa to the Muyuqmarka temple at Saqsaywaman, a complex that also acquired the name "fortress."

Vestiges of a tamped red clay and gravel inka floor were found about 1.95m in front of this doorway, which was associated with a large quantity of inka potsherds, ash, charcoal, and animal bone. A disturbed ritual deposit was also discovered near the second terrace wall, 2.70m below the surface in a sandy context, that contained inka ceramics, charcoal, ochre and clay lumps, burnt animal bones, a tooth, a slate fragment, and some small stones (Zapata 2003).

A large number of inka sherds were recovered from these excavations, including a variety of two-handled pots, bowls, jars, large plates, and *maka*,

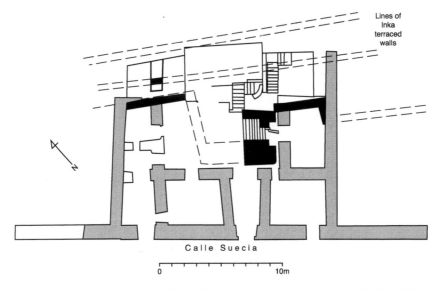

Figure 7.8. Terrace walls and double-jamb entrance and steps at Suecia #348. *Black fill,* excavated inka walls, with double-jamb entrance, zigzag salient and terraces; *dashed line,* probable trajectory of terraced walls; *gray fill,* existing fabric (after Zapata 2003).

but the most notable characteristic of the assemblage is the high quality of both vessel finish and decoration. There are numerous designs, ranging from the standard inka geometric patterns on *maka* and plates through crosses and dots to unusual figurative designs, including felines, humans, camelids, birds, *suri,* spotted frogs, scorpions, flies, butterflies, snails, and spondylus shells. Some human figures are dressed and carry a staff or *chakitaqlla,* as well as several plants, such as maize and chili peppers. This rare collection is matched to some extent by the material found at Parque Tricentenario and would probably confirm the existence of an important structure, perhaps a royal residence, on the platform above.

Stratigraphically, this site proved to be a typical urban deposit with few sealed prehispanic contexts. There were no inka buildings, but there was an accessway from the plaza through the zigzag wall to the palace. Burnt offerings were noted on the terrace levels, overlooking the plaza. This property was certainly colonized for housing in the early colonial period. It is possible that the large amount of inka material culture could have been rubbish thrown over the edge of the terrace from the platform when its buildings were dismantled, because footings of colonial terraces, arches, and walls were discovered to be grounded within this deposit.

Plan-seam A continues along the streets Triunfo and Hatunrumiyoq as far as the Tullumayu river. The main roads to Antisuyu and Qollasuyu left the plaza along this route. The corner walls of the Hatunkancha compound in mz2 and an excavation at Triunfo #392 show that the street opens gradually toward San Agustín, probably to serve as an assembly area for processions, musicians, and dancers prior to entry into Hawkaypata. However, recent excavations have demonstrated that this thoroughfare had been originally only 2.8m (1.75r) wide with a green diorite wall on its eastern side that had been dismantled during the inka period (figure 7.9). At that time, three adults were buried with inka pottery adjacent to its footings (El Sol 06/17/2009).

Figure 7.9. Excavations in Triunfo street, looking south (photo by Andina). Note the utility pipes and disturbed stratigraphy in the trench with the original street green diorite wall on the left.

Figure 7.10. The Hatunrumiyoq platform (north side) with its cyclopean green diorite retaining wall.

The Hatunrumiyoq platform, now occupied by the Museum of Religious Art, is a large, almost rectangular building in mz14.[13] It was originally built on a sloping site with retaining walls of cyclopean green diorite blocks in polygonal style (figure 7.10). Part of its eastern wall is clad with a polygonal limestone veneer, about 60cm thick, which must have served to strengthen it and allow it to withstand a greater load and support a taller building. It is probable that at one stage the whole platform was covered by a limestone veneer. Its walls stand from 3m to 5m high along its intact northern and eastern sides, while its western wall, which contains the famous stone of twelve angles, diminishes to about 2.2m in height as it stretches for about 45m from the northwest corner. In front of the main museum door, it has been dismantled, but its broken blocks protrude at pavement level. This aligns with the recently excavated section of similar construction on Triunfo. Its southern wall along San Agustín was dismantled and replaced by the external wall of the colonial *casona*. There are no inka doors or niches evident in the extant walls.

In the late seventeenth and early eighteenth centuries, a two-storied *casona* was constructed into the platform mass with access through a grand portal and steps from Hatunrumiyoq street. Largely, this building has preserved the original platform height and mass, but a basement was also excavated, which must have disrupted its original drainage system. In the

1970s, the eastern wall collapsed into the Pasaje Inka Roca as a result of drainage problems. In the subsequent conservation works, archaeological investigations were carried out, under the direction of Wilbert San Román (Vargas 2007: 8). These determined that the wall width of 80cm and batter of 20% was insufficient to retain its unstratified earth, clay, and stone mass without adequate drainage. In an internal patio on the summit, a short length of rectangular, sedimentary andesite walling was exposed, and numerous similar blocks were found scattered in it and the adjacent garden. This would suggest that there had been inka structures on top (Vargas 2007, photo i.6). Unfortunately, there have been no further excavations in either the patio or garden to verify the nature of these structures or activities on the summit.

Vargas (2007: 5–9) thought that this was an *usnu* platform, while others have labeled it, for no apparent reason, the palace of Inka Roca. What is clear is that it is a substantial platform that was probably built in the early inka period and subsequently clad in polygonal limestone masonry during the imperial period. Given that its original southern wall has been replaced, its exact location may have been inside the colonial one to accommodate a stone staircase to the summit. This building must have been important for the inkas to have left it intact during the remodeling of the city, although its limestone cladding and summit structures may indicate that it assumed a different role.

Discussion

This plan-seam with its palaces, large halls, plazas, and streets represents the politico-administrative focus of the city. Hawkaypata and its *usnu* was the main location for the rituals and ceremonies performed for the overall well-being of the Inka, the Sun, the state, the city, and the people. The wide streets, Triunfo, Procuradores, and Loreto, would have been *vomitoria* into the plaza for ceremonial processions of mummies, idols, dancers, musicians, and members of the *panaqa* and *ayllu* from all four urban *suyu* and tribute from the provinces. Kusipata was probably the location from which the provincial elite and other non-inkas could watch these activities, observing but not participating, although the two bridges over the river may suggest other processional access points. The palaces, particularly Qasana, had an inner patio with the royal apartments, a water feature, as well as an outer patio and a large hall for more public audiences with the Sapa Inka and his advisors. This would mean that the various structures and spaces of this plan-seam were exclusive to particular social groups and that there should be some archaeological signature of these differences. For example, in his analysis of the palace area of Huánuco Pampa, Morris and his colleagues (2011) noted that various pottery styles predominated in different sectors of the palace area and in the plaza. The most prestigious were found in the inner patio, while the forms for feasting and drinking remained the same. Unfortunately, for Cusco there has been insufficient excavation in these palaces to test this hypothesis.

Plan-Seam B

Plan-scam B plays a similar public role in the urban plan as plan-seam A, separating the well-planned residential units of Awaqpinta from those of San Agustín, but its function is both secular and religious. It is also irregularly shaped, consisting of a large plaza, Limaqpampa, a smaller one, Intipampa, and the Temple of the Sun, Qorikancha (figure 7.11). The terraced park area to the south alongside the Saphi river is also integral to this plan-seam.

Plaza and *Usnu*: Limaqpampa

The large public plaza, Limaqpampa, also known as Hurin Hawkaypata (Cobo 1990: 66), straddled the channelized Tullumayu river. Today it consists of the two open spaces of Limaqpampa Chico and Limaqpampa Grande, both of which have been encroached upon since 1533. On the city side, it was flanked by residential *kancha*. Across the river, it perhaps extended about 320m as far as the Estadio Universitario. Its maximum width between a terrace wall and a property boundary between Tullumayu and Qollacalle was about 100m.

Little is known historically about this plaza, although Cobo (1990: 66) reported that it contained an *usnu* complex, as the first *waka* on the fifth *seqe* of Antisuyu (AN-5:1) was a stone called Usno. The young men made offerings to it when they visited it during the *warachiquy* initiation ceremony. There was a second *waka* (QO-2:1), a flat place called Limapampa, where the maize harvest festival was celebrated in May (Betanzos 1996: 66; Cobo 1990: 71). A similar ceremony was held in July to pray for a productive year (Molina 1873: 20). It was also the scene of the inauguration ceremony of the Sapa Inka (Cobo 1990: 154), or certainly the place where the new king was presented to the people of Cusco (Sarmiento 2007: 173).

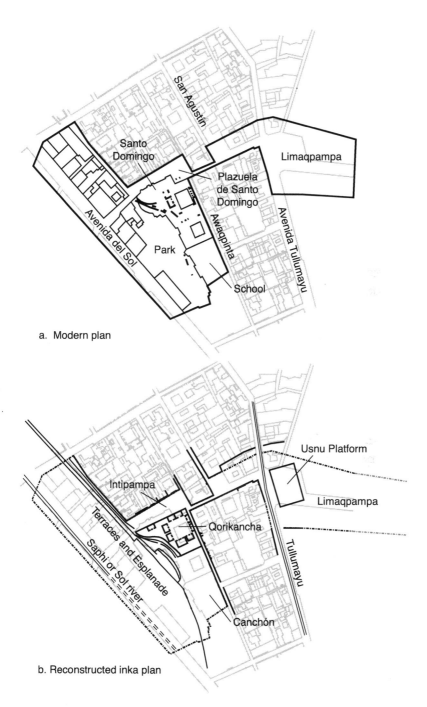

Figure 7.11. Plan-seam B. *A*, modern blocks and streets; *B*, Qorikancha, plazas, and other open spaces.

Bauer and Dearborn (1995: 68, 97, 98) postulated that Limaqpampa was probably a location for observations of sunsets on 23 May and 23 July behind a stone foundation on Picchu and that of the December solstice on the western shoulder of Killke hill. Important sunrise observations may also have been on the mornings of the passage of the sun through zenith and at the June and December solstices.

There is no standing architecture that categorically defines this large plaza. There are only a few short lengths of wall, including a *kancha* façade in Abracitos (mz72) and a terraced wall along Arcopunku. Its extent is determined by modern property boundaries and archaeology, such as the excavations at Limaqpampa Chico #343, where Arroyo (2005a) discovered that it had been terraced open space in inka times and only encroached upon during the colonial era.

On 26 March 2008, workers from Seda Qosqo were opening trenches in Limaqpampa Grande for the installation of sewer pipes. Within minutes they encountered the top of an inka wall and some potsherds, only 40cm below the surface (El Comercio 03/28/2008). A rescue excavation revealed a fine pillowed limestone wall, in polygonal style (Benavente 2009). It is 18m long and stands about 3m tall; its footings sit on a gravel base. Its orientation is ~345° and its 9% batter indicates that it faced southwards (figure 7.12). At its western end, there are five curved stone steps that lead to a higher level, indicating this was a platform, while 10m from the stair there are vestiges of an outward-facing niche.

A terrace, 2.8m in width, is defined by a second coursed polygonal limestone wall, parallel to the first, that stands five courses, about 1.2m tall, suggesting that this structure had at least two levels. A 1m wide canal terrace runs for about 6m along this terrace level adjacent to the main wall. The excavations produced many fine inka ceramics, including three decorated *maka*, a large plate, and a pedestalled pot, as well as some killke sherds (El Sol 08/08/2008, 12/30/2009; Benavente 2009). Other finds include metal objects, a stone knife, a camelid bone flute, bone *ruki*, spindle whorls, and a camelid mandible. A test pit about 15m behind the upper wall close to the modern monument found, at a depth of only 70cm below the surface, an occupation deposit on an inka floor that contained evidence of burning, camelid bones, spindle whorls, stone knives, and inka sherds. This indicates that this must be the *usnu* platform[14] Its material associations are similar to those found at other platforms, such as Hawkaypata and El Shincal

In 1926 some soldiers were employed leveling Limaqpampa, and in one trench they found a collection of inka pottery and other items (Comercial

Figure 7.12. The Limaqpampa *usnu* platform, looking toward the stone staircase (photo by Luis Béjar).

6/25/1926, 6/26/1926). It included *urpu*, jars, cooking pots, small pots, *qero*, and clay llama figurines. The most impressive find was a finely decorated, long-necked *tticachurana* (Pardo 1957: 581–82, lám 7a). In subsequent years, two burials have been recorded from the former plaza. One was found in a property in Abracitos and included a human cranium, a small *urpu*, two miniature bowls, and the base of a pedestalled pot. The other was uncovered during construction of the Estadio Universitario. It was quite rich, containing a human cranium, a decorated face neck jar, a neckless *maka*, a neckless bottle, five plates, decorated *maka* necks, three bronze and two silver *tupu*, some bronze needle shafts, a pair of bronze pectoral plates, and a spondylus shell trapezoidal bead. Some metal working objects were also found.

Temple: Qorikancha and Surrounds

The Sun temple, Qorikancha, was rebuilt on the site of the earlier Inti-kancha by Pachakuti Inka Yupanki as the first of his major construction projects. Xerez (1985: 152) commented on its high quality stonework and the squareness of the enclosure and its buildings. Other eyewitnesses were overwhelmed by the fact that it was paneled in gold and silver and that there was a garden with golden maize plants and many other gold objects, including "sheep, women, and jars" (e.g., Ruiz de Arce 2002: 103).[15] Some did note that a woman who kept flies away from a mummy insisted on the removal of boots prior to entry, but these early accounts did not consider other temple rituals. In contrast, the later chroniclers discussed how the Sun image was kept and fed, the perpetual brazier to burn offerings, its fountain and drain, and the rituals of the *mamakuna*, who served the deity. They also reported in more detail on its fine ashlar stonework architecture, noting that its main gate lay on the western side, and claimed that some buildings were set aside for the worship of separate deities, including the Moon, Venus, Pleiades and the Stars, Thunder, and the Rainbow. Cobo (1990: 49), in summarizing the work of others, indicated that Qorikancha was about 400–500' square (111.6m to 139.5m).[16]

The golden image of the Sun, Punchaw, was kept there, and important ceremonies, rituals, and sacrifices were held before it beyond the gaze of the public. Information collected by Polo de Ondegardo and published by Cobo (1990: 47–84) considered Qorikancha as the *axis mundi* of the inka world because it was the place where the Sun was worshipped and the focal point of the shrine system of 41 *seqe*. Several *waka* were even located in the temple itself and its immediate vicinity.

In 1535, the buildings were given to the Dominican order, who dismantled parts to build a church and monastery. The 1650 earthquake damaged these additions, which were subsequently rebuilt. These construction phases removed several original buildings and modified others to accommodate cells around the cloister itself by dismantling some walls and erecting others and encroaching into Intipampa. The 1950 earthquake enabled UNESCO and the INC-Cusco to commence a project of consolidation of its surviving standing architecture and sponsor various archaeological investigations within the complex.

Today, the inka temple is defined by some standing architecture, including much of the tall northern enclosure wall along Awaqpinta and the famous curved wall on the southern side (figures 7.13). The church was built over its western enclosure wall, while the eastern is probably represented by the boundary between the first and second cloisters. Internally, there are inka buildings with trapezoidal niches and doorways in the cloister that were liberated from convent buildings during the 1970s (Béjar 1990) (figure 7.14). On the northern side, there is an intact building R-2 (figure 7.15a) and the eastern part of the identical R-1, with an alcove, 4.19m

Figure 7.13. The curved wall at Qorikancha.

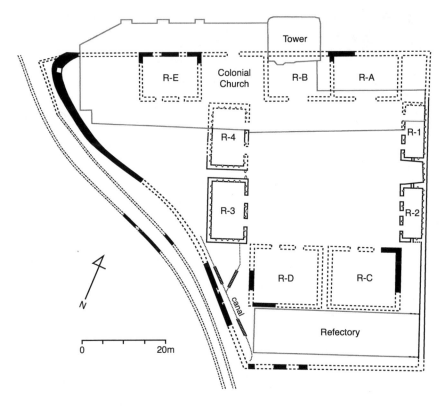

Figure 7.14. The temple enclosure of Qorikancha, showing walls found in excavation (after Béjar 1990: lámina 05).

in depth and 5.15m in width, between them (table 7.1). On the southern side, there were also two identical buildings, the now complete R-3 (figures 7.15b,c)[17] and the eastern end of R-4 with other remnants near the church wall (figure 7.15d); these are separated by a corridor, which has a double-jamb door onto the patio. The inka patio was located slightly further to the west than the colonial cloister, but it was rectangular in shape, measuring about 36.3m (22.5r) by 30.69m (19r). The post-1950 consolidation of the curved wall moved the external church wall back from the terrace edge and enabled architects to examine its internal face and discover an internal niche (Kubler 1952).

The enclosure wall and internal buildings are all built from reddish-gray andesite ashlars, laid in a sedimentary style; they were dry-fitted, using metal clamps, or set in a clay mortar. Puelles (2005: 93–113) has noted that, while this architectural style is consistent throughout the complex, the quality of finish is varied, particularly along the enclosure wall in Awaqpinta,

Table 7.1. Dimensions of standing buildings in Qorikancha (in meters and *rikra*)

Structure	External length	External width	Internal length	Internal width	Wall width	No. of doors	No. internal niches	No. external niches
R-2	13.10 (8.10)	5.03 (3.11)	11.50 (7.12)	4.20 (2.6r)	0.81, rear = 1.0m	3	17 (with a window in each end)	0
R-3	14.51 (9.0)	10.00 (6.2)	12.95 (8.0)	8.05 (5.0r)	0.81	2	25	1

while the internal and external faces of the patio buildings are quite uniform with very slight beveling to the joint. The footings throughout the complex are mainly of andesite, although in some places green diorite and limestone have been observed.

It is clear that certain solar observations must have been made from Qorikancha, particularly of the sunrises and sunsets thought to be critical to the inkas, such as solstice, zenith, and anti-zenith. Various scholars have speculated about what was observed. For example, Zuidema (1982: 214) argued that both the June solstice sunrise and heliacal rise of Pleiades could have been viewed above the alcove wall from the doorway between R-3 and R-4. The December solstice sunrise could have been observed from the southern terrace. In terms of sunsets, Bauer and Dearborn (1995: 77–78) provided evidence that the December solstice sunset behind Killke mountain could have been viewed from the corridor between R-3 and R-4 as well as from Intipampa.

From an archaeological perspective, the exploration of Qorikancha has yielded interesting results, both structurally and materially, that shed some light on the nature of the original buildings and their usage. Although sub-floor observations were made in the late nineteenth and early twentieth centuries, scientific excavations only began in 1970.

Enclosure Wall

The enclosure wall stands at its full height, 4.5m in 12 courses, only on the north side along Awaqpinta, where it is 81cm in width (figure 2.2a). It is 65.72m long to an excavated corner with the east wall. It is clear that, in contrast to both Qasana and Hatunkancha, it also formed the back wall of its internal buildings. There are three short sections of the east wall,

A

B

Figure 7.15. Qorikancha buildings. *A*, inside R-2, showing niches and end window, looking west (photo by Lisa Solling); *B*, façade of R-3 with the double-jamb passage door on the right and holes for attaching gold panels; *C*, central niche of R-3 that had originally been clad in gold panels; *D*, internal remnant of R-4, note the colonial roof arch built into the niched southern wall (photo by Lisa Solling).

C

D

standing between 1.61m and 1.85m tall, and two longer sections of the upper terrace wall on the southern side, including the famous curved wall, with its large inward facing niche. Apart from a short stub by the southern curve, the western wall is not visible.

The original size of the temple was suggested in the chronicles to have been much larger than the present area, defined by the first cloister. Excavations have located other lengths of the perimeter wall. For example, Oscar Ladron de Guevara (1967) dug a trench in the plaza next to the tower, discovering a 6m length of footings of the west wall, about 90cm in width, joined by a perpendicular internal wall. This finding is in line with the curved wall stub and observations by Max Uhle (1930), of about 12m of footings, perhaps with two doors within the church itself. This means that the northwest corner must have been demolished during church construction. Recent excavations in the second cloister have exposed the northeast corner of the *kancha* along Awaqpinta. It is estimated that the temple enclosure dimensions were north side, 74.3m (46r); west, 85.6m (53r); and east, 41.9m (26r). Rowe (1944: 26) suggested that the main entrance was probably the location of the church side door on Intipampa, while Béjar (1990: 107) deduced that it lay between buildings R-B and R-E (figure 7.14).

Kancha Buildings

There have been only three excavations to examine the stratigraphy of the surviving buildings in Qorikancha and a few more to locate vestiges of others (figure 7.16). These have been test pits and have encountered typical urban mixed deposits, in which modern and colonial ceramics, tiles, metals, and glass are found in the same stratigraphical layers as inka or even killke materials.

Raymundo Béjar (1990: 65–67) dug Pit 1 in R-2 against the right-hand jamb of its north door. He found that the threshold stone was set in a clay mortar at a depth of 47cm below the modern surface and that the adjacent inka floor consisted of compacted clay with small stones, hardened with dust from the *in situ* stone polishing. The footings were crudely finished and extended a further 80–90cm. Apart from wire and other later construction materials, this small pit revealed only 36 inka sherds, some llama bone, charcoal, and pieces of green diorite. The Lorenzo team also excavated in the northwest corner of the same building (Unit 4), finding only disturbed contexts with bricks, tiles, stones, and other materials used for the reconstruction, despite it being a typical location for offerings (Béjar 1990: 75).

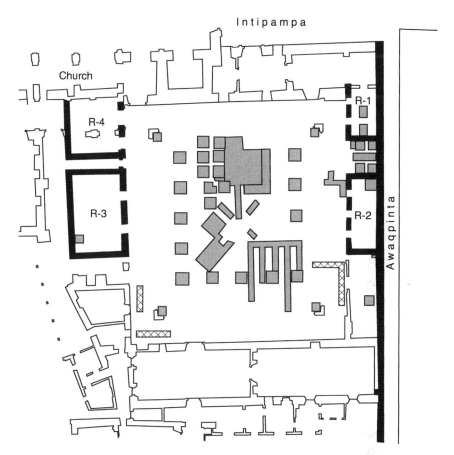

Figure 7.16. Location of the Qorikancha excavations, 1970–79 (after Béjar). *Black fill,* extant inka walls; *cross-hatched fill,* inka footings found in excavation; *gray fill,* excavation pits and trenches.

Béjar (1990: 68) excavated Pit 2 against the internal rear wall of R-3, near its southeastern corner, where he dug a 37cm thick upper layer of modern and colonial materials in a coarse sediment. Below this he found a floor, 18cm thick, consisting of a fine clay, compacted with gravel and andesite dust, and upon which were llama bones and a few killke and inka sherds. The footings were set into a loamy clay to a depth of 56cm.

Traces of other buildings were found by trench excavation that would conform with basic *kancha* planning. Clearly the footings, discovered by Ladron de Guevara, indicated a wall perpendicular to the perimeter wall and therefore at least one building, while Uhle's observations suggested the location of a second beyond the *kancha* on the western side. On the eastern side during the UNESCO conservation program, inka footings were found, similar to those of standing walls in width and orientation, suggesting that one or two buildings were located on that side. Recent excavations in the church itself have revealed some inka stonework in the crypt but no further evidence for structures (Oberti pers. comm.).

In the alcove between R-1 and R-2, an inka floor was noted with three surface holes through the enclosure wall to drain rainwater into the street below. Three separate excavations have revealed offerings at depths of 50 to 60cm in stratum II. For example, in Pit 3, against the wall of R-1, Béjar (1990: 69–71) found eleven fragments of llama lower mandible and ribs, one of which had been made into a weaving tool (*ruki*), and 21 inka and three killke sherds. Immediately below these were a 5cm tall spondylus llama and the grey limestone head of another at a depth of 55cm near R-1. In Pit 4 in the northwestern corner, Béjar (1990: 72) discovered an alpaca head carved in crystalline quartz and associated with forty fragments of human bone, eight fragments of llama ribs and long bones, a bone spoon, and a fossilized shell with killke and inka sherds. Later González dug Unit 2 in the center abutting R-2, finding at the same depth several blue sodalite beads and pieces of worked shell, associated with inka sherds and metal pins (Béjar 1990: 74).

The Patio

In the colonial patio, González excavated four units (96sqm), while the Lorenzo project dug five units (135sqm) in order to examine inka floors and ceremonial offerings and search for pre-inka structures and ancient canals (figure 7.17). While many of these showed signs of mixing with tiles, bricks, and reconstruction debris, at least ten discrete offering events were found in relatively undisturbed strata. There had been many others, indicated by typical offering artifacts, such as spondylus shell beads, cut pieces and figurines, gold and silver spangles and *tupu*, bronze bells, bars and *tupu*, as well as sculpted, polished stone objects, including stone *qonopa*, lapis lazuli, and turquoise beads, crystal quartz pendants, and inka and killke sherds (Béjar 1990; Barreda n.d.a., n.d.b.).

In the southwestern cloister corner in Unit II Square A-2, two pairs of similar offerings were located during the 1974 UNESCO-sponsored excavations (Béjar 1990: 77). At a depth of 30–40cm in stratum 2, a child's mandible was discovered, surrounded by three miniature silver *tupu* with their rounded heads touching the jaw. Immediately below this in stratum 3 (40–70cm), there was a similar find, but the focus objects were human

Figure 7.17. The Qorikancha patio excavations (photo by Raymundo Béjar 1990: no. 10).

milk teeth, surrounded by three miniature silver *tupu*. Elsewhere in stratum 3, a hollow silver female figurine was found standing upright, with five miniature silver *tupu*, one on either side of the head and the other three at different points around it (figure 7.18). Nearby and in the same layer, a gold male figurine lay on its back with two miniature silver *tupu* about its head and three gold ones radiating from its body. Inka pottery, spondylus beads, plaques, and quartz objects were associated with each of these. Whether these very specific finds represent a single offering event or several is unclear. However, the *tupu* arrangements around both a child's mandible and teeth and also around a figurine may suggest that this was a multiple event offering location. The different focus objects, human remains, and figurines may be thought to be equivalent and, by extension, represent a child sacrifice.

Other offerings included inka, killke, and lucre sherds, pieces of worked shell, a small gold sheet, and a sculpted limestone *qonopa* found adjacent to the north door of R-2; a collection of gold, silver, bronze, and shell beads, pendants, plaques, pins, and *tupu* on the west side in Unit III at the base of the second stratum (Béjar 1990: 77–78); and a 10cm high gold female figurine in a disturbed stratum at a depth of 70cm in Unit 1–17, immediately below a collection of spondylus shell beads and gold spangles (Béjar

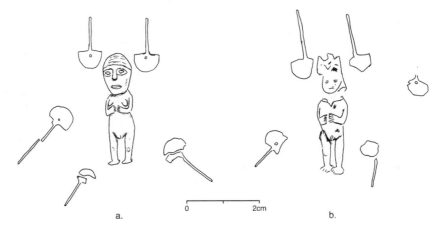

Figure 7.18. Figurine and *tupu* arrangements from Unit II square A-2 stratum 3 (II-A2–3) in Qorikancha patio. *A*, silver female figurine with five miniature silver *tupu*; *B*, a corroded gold male figurine with two miniature silver *tupu* at its head and three gold ones (drawn from two photographs by Raymundo Béjar).

1990: 74); three spondylus shells and two bronze *tupu* at a depth of 80cm in the patio (Barreda and Valencia 2007: 100–101). Spondylus shell beads were found throughout these excavations, as were several spondylus anthropomorphic and zoomorphic figurines, but their precise contexts have not been described. It is also known that a small gold female figurine and two silver females were found in the patio between 1.0m and 1.1m below the surface.

The quality of the excavated artifacts indicates both the importance of the rituals and the high status of the participants. For example, beautifully crafted turquoise and lapis lazuli beads from Chile, crystal quartz beads, spondylus llamas and beads, silver, gold, and copper anthropomorphic figurines, bells and *tupu*, and stone *qonopa*, possibly for grinding *vilka*,[18] were found in these deposits (Béjar 1990). The presence of killke sherds may support an earlier occupation of the site, and a crude wall found in patio excavations has been used to confirm it; however, such a conclusion is premature. It is possible that the wall is part of a construction cell for the building platform, and the killke pottery is simply fill.

The provision of water to the patio fountain and the temple in general was by stone-lined underground canal. For example, the chroniclers mention that water from the Hawkaypata *usnu* complex was directed into Qorikancha. In Unit III next to the patio fountain, several canals were found during excavation dating from the republican and colonial periods, including one at a depth of 1.2m that reused inka stones. Other canals have been found that drain the patio and R-3 toward the terraces.

Plazas and Open Spaces Surrounding Qorikancha

Formal plazas and other open spaces surround the temple, including the Qorikancha terraces and park to the south, Arrayan street to the southwest, Intipampa to the west, and the Canchón to the east of the Second Cloister. These have been investigated by rescue excavation.

The large area of the Qorikancha terraces and esplanade has been systematically dug by Raymundo Béjar (1998) in a series of small pits and long trenches, but there is only a preliminary report (figure 7.19). The stratigraphy was mixed as a result of both colonial and republican period building activities with few undisturbed prehispanic deposits. A number of sealed contexts in the western and central sectors discovered spondylus shell objects and a poorly preserved offering that consisted of llama *qonopa*, metal needles, *tupu*, spondylus, and animal bones. On the terraces, there were several offerings, including a human cranium with an arrangement of spondylus beads around it adjacent to the lower fountain and steps; several modeled jaguar plate handles adjacent to the upper fountain on the same staircase; a plate and a *maka* neck below the curved wall; a ceramic *qero* below foundations of the lowest terrace; and on the third terrace, a killke-style ceramic whistle, camelid in form, with about thirty small plates arranged in

Figure 7.19. Excavation trenches on the Qorikancha esplanade and terraces.

pairs. There were also numerous pieces of worked and unworked spondylus shell, metal *tupu*, needles, and a silver pectoral. Two figurines, a copper male and a bone female, were found in separate locations. Overall, 120,000 sherds were recovered, with many from various parts of Tawantinsuyu, including Lake Titiqaqa (Qolla and Chucuito), Chuquibamba (Arequipa), the Peruvian coast (Chincha and Chimú), and Ecuador (Heffernan pers. comm.), as well as local Killke vessels (Béjar 1998).

In excavations on the terraces directly below the curved wall, Arminda Gibaja (1990) found two inka fountains, one with two channels. Beneath one stone basin floor in a layer of fine sand, there was an offering of two spondylus llamitas, associated with five silver and bronze *tupu*, and covered with inka potsherds.

The terraces to the southwest of the temple were covered by the street, Arrayan. In 1991 an offering of an inka plate and a large *maka* neck was found adjacent to the street alongside the curved wall. Later, during trenching for urban utilities, a small rescue excavation was conducted after the discovery of a terrace wall at a depth of only 50cm (Zanabria 1997). It is of finely finished rectangular andesite and stands 2.90m tall and was associated with many sherds, ash, charcoal, and llama bones. In stratum III at a depth of 1.25m and close to the wall, there was a context that consisted of a compacted black sediment rich in organic matter, ash, and charcoal that had been heaped with animal bone and inka sherds to cover a deer antler and two beads, a typical burnt inka offering. Below this, there were several others, including a quartzite *qonopa* head associated with the cranium and small bones of a guinea pig; a stone bowl, a round *mutka* with two small *maka* necks, and llama and deer bone; an ash lens with calcined llama bones and sherds; and at 2.6m in depth, another guinea pig with sherds and charcoal.

These finds stimulated a larger excavation in 1997 to expose more terrace walls. Below the second terrace, there were the remains of an inka building with many associated offerings, including a carved stone puma and much pottery. Between the terraces and Qorikancha and at a depth of 3m, a ramp was located running down the terraces toward the river. Clearly, there are two inka levels of construction and occupation in this area. At a depth of 3.7m below street level, an inka stone-lined canal was found that probably brought water to the nearby fountain, while 50m to the west Oberti (pers. comm.) found inka and later canals, trending toward Qorikancha on the terraces at Avenida del Sol #200.

Several burials of both adults and children were found on the top terrace, in very disturbed contexts, some within only 10cm of the surface. On the second terrace at a depth of 4.7m, there were two tombs, both facing southeast: one, an adult male, was seated and flexed and associated with four plates, a large *maka*, a ceramic *qero* and other pottery, bronze *tupu* and beads; and the other, a youth, associated with turquoise and spondylus beads, metal *tupu*, a *maka*, plates, a pedestalled pot, and a chimú stirrup spout bottle, placed upside down. The remains of a sacrificed llama, with its head to the northwest, also was found. Elsewhere, a pair of plates, one inside the other, was found, a common arrangement for such objects in inka offerings.

In Intipampa, there have been several small-scale excavations. Luis Barreda (pers. comm.) has reported an offering, consisting of adult human teeth, associated with *tupu*, and llama and anthropomorphic figurines. In another trench, there was a pair of miniature loop handled plates, decorated with the maltese cross, as well as miniature *urpu*, *qero*, and lids.

The "canchón" was a garden yard of the Santo Domingo monastery, located about 90m southeast of the first cloister; it is now occupied by a school. Several test pits have been excavated by Rowe (1944), Béjar and by PER-39 (Béjar 1990) who found mixed deposits with large amounts of inka sherds as well as killke, colonial, and republican fragments but no footings. The only undisturbed context is a burial, reported by the monks, in the southeastern corner that contained a bird-handled plate, a jar, and two gold *tupu* (Rowe 1944: 46). Excavations in the Second Cloister produced some structural evidence, probably a second temple *kancha*, and a similar range of materials and offerings evidence (Béjar pers. comm.).

Discussion

This plan-seam therefore was separated into two areas and joined by a short street, Zetas. In the north it contained a large plaza, Limaqpampa, that stretched southeastward across the Tullumayu, with an *usnu* complex for public ceremonies and perhaps for certain reenactments for the people of Hurin Cusco. In the south, the principal Sun temple of Tawantinsuyu, Qorikancha, dominated the landscape and served as a cultural focus. Interesting offerings were made in its patio that have similarities to at least three recovered from patios at Tumibamba by Idrovo (2000), which were all in prepared pits, including one with a gold male figurine as a central focus.[19]

Numerous pilgrims must have come to Cusco from all over the empire to worship outside of the temple, to feed the Sun, drink with it, and deposit offerings in its honor in small pits surrounding the temple. These offerings were often small burnt piles of charcoal and ash that contained an important focus object, such as a bone, antler, a figurine, *qonopa,* and beads, a practice also observed at Tambokancha, and adorned with potsherds, perhaps even from their own homelands. These open areas around the temple also received human burials, generally accompanied by prestigious items. Who these people were is not known; some may have been sacrifices in honor of the Sun.

Kancha and Streets

The Residential Plan-Units

The three residential plan-units sit neatly, although unconformably, within the urban topography created by the important buildings and spaces of two plan-seams. They are organized about the main ridge axes, and each provides a network of well-planned streets, *kancha,* and compounds that offer a variety of living spaces. They conform to inka planning canons, as established by studies in Ollantaytambo and Calca and elsewhere in Tawantinsuyu (e.g., Bouchard 1976a). This chapter presents a basic analysis of the planning and architectural details for each unit, using both field observations and excavation data, measurements, and appropriate historical sources. A social interpretation of these areas is presented in chapter 9.

Plan-Unit I

Plan-unit I lies to the southeast of plan-seam B across the lower parts of the ridge, extending as one longitudinal street, Awaqpinta, from Zetas/ Intipampa to the steps above Avenida Garcilaso, where there are vestiges of a transverse wall (figure 8.1). This plan-unit extends to the north of Awaqpinta toward the Tullumayu river, while development to the south has been restricted by Qorikancha and its surrounding open spaces. This conclusion is confirmed by the Agurto (1980) architectural survey, which located more than twenty lengths of standing inka wall on the northern side (mz72, mz73, mzl77) but only two on the southern side (mz74, mzl76).

From Zetas, the first 60m of Awaqpinta is flanked on either side by original inka architecture, yielding a mean street width at ground level of 2.71m (1.675r). The north corner is made of finely finished, large green diorite blocks,[1] but beyond this the northern side displays a fairly intact polygonal

Figure 8.1. Plan-unit I. Awaqpinta. A, modern blocks and streets; B, inka blocks and streets.

a. Modern plan

b. Reconstructed inka plan

limestone wall, about 2.3m high, that is punctuated by modern doorways and an original lane entrance that is now a house door (figure 6.2a). The latter is located at 44.84m (27.75r) from Zetas and is marked by a change in stonework, for aesthetic purposes, to fourteen courses of relatively thin andesite blocks laid in sedimentary style, on footings of limestone blocks in clay mortar. The lane entrance is 1.93m (1.2r) wide at its base with a very steep inward batter, clearly separating one *kancha* from another. While the original limestone wall continues to the east, it gradually diminishes in height. At the left jamb of the second lane, at 93.65m (58r) from Zetas, it is only a few courses high. The right jamb has disappeared, but its location is marked by a property boundary; a standing wall indicates the width of this *kancha*. In the last twenty-five years, increased vehicular ownership has forced the repeated widening of both Intiqawarina (lane 3) and Awaqpinta southeast from this point as far as Pantipata (lane 6) and has systematically removed all traces of walls and footings.

The western façade of this plan-unit from the Zetas corner to Tullumayu is a mixture of original inka, transitional, and more recent walling. The earlier walls have been considered "transitional" in age because they only have 3.5% batter (Agurto 1980), and it is certain that such remodeling occurred to accommodate the insertion of new doors and windows. The walls are made of well-fitting rectangular andesite ashlars that stand 4.2m high with a width of 1.35m. Two building corners can be seen at roughly equidistant intervals from the survey origin point (44.58m, 44.84m) that suggest a row of three *kancha* (figure 8.1). In the wall facing Limaqpampa Chico, an original double jamb entrance has been rebuilt to accommodate a wooden door, but it has internal barholds in its inner jambs. It has three bas-relief serpents on its façade and a plain colonial shield on its lintel. There is a wall, 16.5m long, parallel to the façade that suggests a *kancha* building 13m in width.

There were certainly two lines of *kancha* within mz72 parallel to Awaqpinta. They were about 44.8m (27.75r) square with the inclusion of a laneway running from east to west on the northern side of each. There may have been a third line of *kancha* in mz72, but there is no structural evidence within the block. Property boundaries and two standing walls indicate the lane network and a *kancha* arrangement of four large or eight small buildings. At the eastern end of the street-block, a terraced wall separates the two lines of *kancha*. In the third *kancha* along Awaqpinta, a fine wall was recorded by Agurto (1980) separating the *kancha* and a parallel lane. It has a standard width of 80cm, but the style of stonework on its faces is different. Externally, its face is composed of limestone blocks in polygonal style, while internally it is made of medium-sized rectangular andesite blocks with eleven standard niches (Agurto 1980). It is capped with an adobe superstructure. The base of its niches is only 46cm above present ground surface, indicating about 1m of soil accumulation since 1533.

The full length of Awaqpinta is exactly 323m (200r) from Zetas to the wall above Avenida Garcilaso. Such an accurate measurement would indicate some planning. There is both field and property evidence for six lanes on the northern side, separating seven *kancha*. In mz72 beyond lanes 1 and 2, lane 3 (Intiqawarina) was indicated by two short lengths of inka wall and footings opposite each other,[2] while in mz73 there are several wall lengths and property boundaries which indicate that lanes 4 and 5 link up with two short passageways from Tullumayu. Only Pantipata (lane 6) has original standing walls with polygonal limestone stonework, now quite delapidated, on both sides of the street. It is located 278.16m (172.25r) from Zetas. There are vestiges of a door, at 21.78m (13.5r) as well as a northeast *kancha* corner at 44.84m (22.75r) and another at 89.2m (55.25r). On the eastern side of Pantipata, in mz177, there are wall remains and a lane entrance. On the southern side of Awaqpinta, the extension of Pantipata is flanked by an original wall of polygonal limestone but no evidence for any *kancha*. Entrance into each *kancha* would have been through doors on the eastern and western sides and not directly from Awaqpinta.

Along Awaqpinta the *kancha* lengths that can be measured range from 44.84 (27.75r) to 47m (29.1r), and the intermediate lane width is constant at 1.95m (1.2r). The original plan may have been to build seven *kancha*, each 44.41m (27.5r) in length, separated by a lane, each 2.02m (1.25r) wide to make up the 200 *rikra* distance; alternatively, the two measurements could have been 44.49m (27.55r) with lanes of 1.95m (1.2r). However, the field evidence shows that an error was made with the first measurement of the first *kancha* along Awaqpinta at 44.84m (27.75r). To maintain the *kancha* size required a lane width of 1 *rikra*. It seems that the mistake was not recognized, and the construction orders were not changed. The second *kancha* is only 46.62m (28.85r), and the seventh is 42m (26.0r).

A second line of *kancha* was constructed to the north of these, but these became reduced in size toward the east by the angle of the terrace. At the western end, they appear to be the same size, about 44.61m (27.625r) in width, including the lane. However, in row 2 the lane position is changed from one side of the *kancha* wall to the other, probably in order to rectify a surveying mistake and to place laneway along the top of a terrace wall.

At Intiqawarina #620, adjacent to Awaqpinta in mz73, excavations in 2004 and 2005 have revealed a typical urban stratigraphy with discrete structural evidence and a very mixed material culture. Several lengths of footings and wall were found at a depth of about 1.5m, in part associated with a compacted floor and an inka occupation (Arroyo 2005b). The footings comprise at least three courses of worked sandstone, diorite, andesite, and limestone blocks in a clay mortar and sitting in a trench cut into natural clay. The walls are polygonal limestone in style and plastered. They form two buildings at right angles to each other, separated by an open space. One has the lower part of a jamb of a trapezoidal doorway, and both face into an open patio. The dimensions of these buildings are not known. The northeastern one abuts the *kancha* enclosure wall and is about 8.1m wide; its length is not known. The façade of the western one is over 17m from the enclosure wall, implying that it must not have been keyed to it. Given the size of the *kancha* and the excavated building arrangement, there could have been four, six, or eight buildings surrounding a central patio (table 8.1).

Arroyo (2005b: 67) has claimed that these were killke buildings that had been reoccupied by the inkas. However, such a conclusion assumes that the different rock types in the footings and walls represent different phases, which is probably not the case, as killke ceramics are less than 10% of the total (Durand and Verastegui 2009). Where it has survived, the patio floor constituted a 10–15cm thick layer of compacted red clay and gravel. It was covered with broken inka pottery, camelid bone, ash, charcoal, and other items, including fragments of spondylus shell (Durand and Verastegui 2009). Another excavation at Zetas #390 revealed a wide green diorite footing that probably supported a very high inka wall (Farfán pers. comm.).

Plan-Unit II

Plan-unit II is the main residential sector of the city, located between Qorikancha and Hawkaypata, that is, between the two plan-seams (figure 8.2). It is organized perpendicular and parallel to the ridge street, San Agustín, which runs from Limaqpampa Chico for about 232.45m (144r) to the street, Triunfo/Hatunrumiyoq. As mentioned in chapter 6, the survey origin point was the southwest corner of San Agustín and Maruri. From this point, it is exactly 161.5m (100r) to Limaqpampa Chico and the same distance to Ancha Santa Catalina. There is also some regularity from north to south with the cross-street Cabrakancha-Maruri, which measures 323m (200r)

Table 8.1. *Kancha* dimensions in Cusco, Calca, and Ollantaytambo Qosqo Ayllu (in meters)

	Plan-unit	*Manzana*	W-E (m)	N-S (m)	Area (sqm)	Patio size (m)	No. of buildings	Relationship to enclosure wall
Awaqpinta	I	72	44.84	44.41	1,991.34	?	4	Separated
Sta Mónica–Cabrakancha	IIB	14, 15, 34	39.50	32.40	1,279.80	?	4?	Attached
Cabrakancha–Limaqpampa	IIC	35	39.40	37.95	1,495.23	?	4?	Not known
H. Libertador	IID	36 (1–3)	43.45	37.95	1,648.93	?	6?	Attached
		36 (4–5)	43.45	33.10	1,438.20		6	Attached
Kusikancha	IIE	37 (1–6)	43.33	48.30	2,092.84	29.0 × 26.8	8	Attached
Palacio–San Antonio Abad	III	13	64.46	39.00	2,513.94	?	6?	
Beaterio de las Nazarenas	III	12–1	64.40	38.00	2,447.20	23.0 × 23.0	6	Attached
Almirante	III	10	64.50	38.00	2,451.00	?	6?	Not known
Calca	—	IX, X	80.75	56.45	4,558.34	56.0 × 36.0	8	Attached
Calca	—	XVA, XVB	54.90	82.10	4,507.29	35.5 × 55.75	8	Attached
Qosqo Ayllu	—	1A, 1B, 2A, 2B, 3A, 3B	28.35	24.70	700.25	12.4 × 13.4	4	Attached
Qosqo Ayllu	—	10A, 10B	24.25	22.95	556.54	11.4 × 12.4	4	Attached
Qosqo Ayllu	—	12	39.95	45.50	1,817.73	21.6 × 21.6	4	Attached
Qosqo Ayllu	—	18	43.70	54.35	2,375.10	?	3	

Figure 8.2. Plan-unit II. *A*, modern blocks and streets; *B*, Inka blocks and streets.

from the Tullumayu entrance to the terrace by the Palacio de Justicia. This basic cross-like arrangement presented the inka planner with five distinct areas to urbanize: two to the north of San Agustín, and three to the south.

IIA Hatunkancha

According to eyewitness chroniclers, the compound called Hatunkancha lay on the eastern side of Hawkaypata. It had a single entrance and was surrounded by a very high fine stone wall and was thought to contain about 100 separate buildings. It was said to have been the residence of the temple priests, ministers, and the *aqllakuna*. It was divided into ten individual *solares* in 1534 (Rivera Serna 1965). By the mid-sixteenth century, the property of Diego Maldonado stretched from Triunfo to Ancha Santa Catalina. In its grounds, there were three *waka* that received sacrifices: two fountains, Canchapacha (CH-3:2), important because of certain legends, and Ticcicocha (CH-3:3), dedicated to Mama Ocllo; and a flat place, Puñui (CH-4:2), which was associated with sleep (Cobo 1990: 55, 56). Polo de Ondegardo (1990: 99) also reported the discovery of a shaft tomb on this property, which was "made of dressed stones . . . where the wife of the Inca was buried who came from the Yungas.[3] We found it to be very deep, three *estados* (5m), built with first-class stonework and about twelve feet (3.36m) square. They told us that the sand in the grave was from the coast and after we took it out, we only found below it a body in a cavity on one side of the grave."

From the historical documents, Hatunkancha contained the *aqllawasi*, situated between Loreto and Angosta Santa Catalina, and the Pukamarka quarter lay toward its eastern side. Garcilaso (1966: 427) confirmed that it faced onto the plaza and extended as far as a cross-street, beyond which there was a large housing block before reaching Qorikancha. He stated that it had a narrow passage, with many cells on either side and that there were also clay bins (*pirua*) of varying capacities in certain rooms for maize storage that had holes for easy and accurate dispensing. At the end of this lane lay the private *aqlla* quarters. Garcilaso (1966: 69) reported that Hernando de Segovia had dug part of a foundation within the *aqllawasi* and discovered a treasure worth 72,000 ducats.

The Enclosure

Hatunkancha extended from the Portal de Carrizos on Hawkaypata down Loreto street, along Maruri to San Agustín, where it turned left as far as

Table 8.2. Niche details for the Hatunkancha enclosure wall at Parillada Andina (formerly café Maruri) (in cm)

	Height	Bottom width	Top width	Spacing*
1	69.00	43.50	36.00	83.25**
2	69.05	42.70	35.80	84.50
3	69.30	43.40	37.30	83.20
4	69.10	43.80	36.30	83.90
5	69.30	43.40	36.20	84.10
Mean	69.15	43.36	36.32	83.79

* Spacing was measured from the bottom left corner of one niche to the bottom right of the next.
** The starting point is an angled stone block that suggests the location of another niche.

the rounded corner at Plazoleta Lambarrí, then in a straight line to the rounded corner with Portal de Belén at Triunfo, where it jagged back toward the Portal de Carrizos. It encloses an area of about 4 hectares.[4]

The enclosure wall is a magnificent freestanding construction made of rectangular andesite blocks laid in sedimentary courses, diminishing in size from bottom to top (figure 8.3a). Its external corners are distinguished by fine, rounded andesite blocks laid in sedimentary style (figure 8.3a); four are extant at Portal de Carrizos-Loreto (figure 8.3c), Maruri–San Agustín, San Agustín–Lambarrí, and Triunfo-Portal de Belén (figure 7.7). It has a considerable inward batter; on Maruri, at the Banco Wiese (Scotia bank), it stands fourteen courses high, about 4m, on top of five courses of limestone footings. Like that of Qasana, its internal face has regularly spaced, single-jamb niches placed eight courses, about 2.4m, above the floor. Such niches have been observed along Maruri in Banco Wiese #315–40 (16 niches) (figure 8.3d), Parillada Andina #355–61 (5), Disco 7 Boom's #363 (8) and the ex-ciné Maruri, as well in a restaurant in Maruri backing on to Loreto (6), in the second cloister of the Santa Catalina convent (29), and at the corner of Loreto with Portal de Carrizos (4). At Parillada Andina a line of five niches with stone lintels were recorded, demonstrating consistency in both size and spacing (table 8.2). To the top of the niche basal stone, they stood 2.34m above modern floor level. Observations in other locations along the perimeter wall indicate the same level of consistency.

The street façade from Loreto to Arequipa is devoid of any wall or footing evidence, a fact which Paredes (1999) has claimed is because the convent buildings, and therefore the *aqllawasi*, had originally extended into mz37. However, in a recent excavation, Rodríguez (2005) discovered a foundation trench parallel to Maruri, lined with red clay and small limestone blocks,

A

B

Figure 8.3. The Hatunkancha enclosure wall. *A*, external wall punctured by modern doors and windows in Maruri; *B*, enclosure wall footings at Triunfo #392; *C*, rounded corners at Loreto-Portal de Carrizos; *D*, internal niches at Banco Wiese (photo by Lisa Solling).

C

D

which continued under the footings of the modern façade in mz3. Since inka footings are considerably wider than modern ones, then it could be argued that these indicate that the enclosure wall had continued along this façade and that encroachment during the early colonial period had led to the closure of Maruri. This is supported by the fact that its lower courses and footings continue across Arequipa. This interpretation would mean that the enclosure wall had originally continued as far as Loreto, which implies that Apukamarca, the historical name for Arequipa, did not enter Maruri in inka times but was probably opened when Maruri itself was blocked.

At the Banco Wiese, the enclosure wall footings are made of andesite blocks (Maza 1995), and this is confirmed by excavations at Triunfo #392, where an 80cm wide wall and footing, comprising ten courses of rectangular andesite blocks, was found (figure 8.3b; Zanabria 1998a). Its total height is 1.4m with a widened footing in the lowest courses. Each stone block was well finished and measured 20–25cm in length and 15cm in height. These foundations lay in direct line between the rounded corners at Herrajes-Lambarrí and at Portal de Belén, and Yepes discovered another length at #338 Triunfo (Mormontoy pers. comm.). A 2009 excavation in Triunfo street revealed its width had been 2.8m in the early inka period, but a green diorite wall was subsequently dismantled (El Comercio 07/10/2009). The street was remodeled to form a wider assembly area, as indicated by the andesite alignment. Both excavations demonstrate that Hatunkancha itself lay on a lower level than the street.

No modern streets within Hatunkancha conform to the alignments of surrounding streets. Indeed, they have irregular widths and inconsistent orientations. For example, Ancha Santa Catalina curves northwards with no evidence of inka walling on its western side and only the façade of Casa Concha, an inka building, on its eastern side. Angosta Santa Catalina was widened illegally after the 1950 earthquake, exposing an inka wall that actually juts into it (Kubler 1952). There are no other vestiges on that side. In contrast, on the opposite side there is evidence of a rounded corner formed by a rectangular andesite wall, as well as several lengths of lower andesite courses with footings, and at the Banco de Interamericano de Finanzas (BIF), there is a tall wall on the western property boundary, perpendicular to the street, with four niches along its opposite face.

On the southern side of Arequipa street, there is a 12.75m long sedimentary, andesite wall, battered to the south, that ends at a magnificent rounded corner that turns into the convent. In contrast, on the opposite side there is no evidence of a continuous inka wall or footings, although some inka corners are visible in the lower courses with footings that indicate buildings and the spaces between them.

The internal streets therefore run between inka wall remnants. The single gate into Hatunkancha must have been in Ancha Santa Catalina in the gap between Gatos Supermarket and the Muki discotheque. However, other possible inka doorways can be found at Ciné Maruri, Banco Wiese, and along Loreto.

Buildings

None of the buildings in Hatunkancha were integrated into the enclosure wall and probably stood at least 5m from it. There are very few standing walls, footings, and excavated lengths within these street blocks (mz2, mz3, mz16), but their distribution does not indicate a system of *kancha*, as in mz37 and mz12. In contrast, these structures appear to be close together with little space for a patio in between, suggesting that this compound had a different arrangement of buildings within known inka planning canons.

As described in chapter 6, there are vestiges of two *kallanka* in the western half, at the Hotel Conquistador (mz2) and Casa Concha (mz16) (figure 8.4). They are similar in construction style, orientation, and probable number of doorways. Although there are many later structures in mz2 and Ancha Santa Catalina, no standing walls or excavated footings have been found between them. Therefore, these two buildings appear to face each other across a small plaza, about 55m (34r) wide. Excavations at Casa Concha have indicated that all four walls are built with rectangular andesite blocks in a fine clay mortar that rests upon similar footings that extend six courses to a sterile, red clay, just above the water table. A compacted red clay layer, 10cm thick, was found about 45cm below the modern floor, while the footings extended a further 85cm below the inka surface (Paz and Allcacontor 2002). Inka walls extend beyond this *kallanka* and define boundaries and other structures within the compound.

Twelve meters to the west of the Hotel Conquistador *kallanka* wall, there is another fine rectangular, sedimentary andesite wall, about 12m in length in Gatos Supermarket (mz2). This also faces east, and there is another one perpendicular to it on the southern side of the store. The former stands about 1.6m above the modern floor and has three wall segments, each about 3.9m (2.4r) long with a central-placed standard niche, separated by two trapezoidal doorways, each 2.44m (1.5r) wide (figure 8.5a). The southern wall is 5.61m long and about 2.7m high and is the internal side wall of the same building. At Triunfo #338, two wall lengths have been recorded that probably formed part of the western and northern walls of this structure, with a standard niche reported in the northern one. This building would have been about 38m (23.5r) by 7m (4.33r) with several doors, probably

A

B

Figure 8.4. The Hatunkancha *kallanka*. *A*, wall of *kallanka* at Hotel Conquistador juts out into Angosta Santa Catalina; *B*, the façade of the colonial Casa Concha *kallanka* (photo by Lisa Solling).

A

B

Figure 8.5. Remnant building walls in Hatunkancha. *A*, internal wall with sealed door and niche in Gatos supermarket; *B*, the front wall of an inka structure in Paititi Restaurant (photos by Lisa Solling).

another *kallanka*, that was only about 3.2m behind the other. Another wall with a north-facing internal niche is found in a shop at Triunfo #345.

Behind the Portal de Carrizos enclosure wall (mz3), there is some evidence for internal structures made of rectangular, sedimentary andesite blocks. For example, in restaurant Paititi, there is a long external wall of a building, 2.6m high, parallel to the remnant façade and separated from it by 5.68m (3.5r) (figure 8.5b). In the interior of the block, there is a tall internal wall in the Discoteca Muki with five standard niches facing onto the dance floor. This is about 9.7m (6r) behind and parallel to that in Paititi; they are probably part of the same building. Further east, there are several courses of a rounded corner, at a shop on Angosta Santa Catalina and a further 9.7m (6r) beyond it on the property boundary separating a shop and the BIF, there is a high wall with four standard niches on the internal western side. This again would demonstrate a building perpendicular to the street and 9.7m (6r) in width. The gap between the Muki wall and the rounded corner is about 5.7m (3.5r). Therefore, behind the enclosure wall in this location, there are two evenly spaced and equally sized parallel structures. Their length could have been about the width of the block, around 45m, or they may have been half, suggested by a property boundary, or even about quarter that size in a line across it.

Inside mz3 in the Santa Catalina Convent, there are the remains of two inka walls. One is visible, standing only a few centimeters above the modern wooden floor. It comprises a line of andesite blocks, protruding beneath the east-west chapel wall. It is about 5.5m in length and 80cm in width. Its southern side appears external to the structure. A north-south wall is found about 20m to the southwest of this. Elsewhere in the street-block, there is only the fine wall and corner along Arequipa, which would suggest a lane or a building corner. The Loreto enclosure wall has a double-jamb feature to the east of this location, while in the properties adjacent to Maruri, vestiges of the enclosure wall were found in excavation (Rodríguez 2005) and observed in a restaurant.[5]

On the north side of Arequipa (mz16), there is evidence of rounded corners, walls, and footings of relatively thin blocks of rectangular andesite (figure 8.6). One lies opposite the very fine wall in mz3 and represents a southwestern corner of a building. The walling to its west is modern, but to the east, at a distance of 19.32m (12r), there is a southeastern corner, while others occur in and near modern doorways at the following spacing: 2.5m, 6.5m, 2.5m, 7.4m. This suggests that there is a line of three buildings with west-east dimensions of 19.32m (12r), 6.5m (4r), and 7.4m (4.5r), separated

Figure 8.6. Building corners, walls, and footings in Arequipa street.

by a standard gap of 2.5m (1.5r). An inka wall reported on a property boundary about 9m to the west implies that this pattern continued in that direction as well (Agurto 1980). The property boundaries seem to indicate an arrangement of separate buildings, oriented perpendicular and parallel to Arequipa, and not a *kancha* pattern.

The Banco Wiese excavations revealed inka walls, footings, and compacted floors in several locations in the southeast, center, and northwest sectors of the first patio in association with a whole spondylus shell and some stone spindle whorls (Maza 1995). One remnant in the northwest sector was 90cm in width and formed a right-angled corner of a structure with inka ceramics on the remains of a prepared floor. These structural remains conform to the arrangement of individual buildings along Arequipa and would indicate that they were 15–16m in length. Some diorite and sandstone killke walls and footings were also located (Maza 1995).

Elsewhere in mz16, at the Museo El Quixote, #235 San Agustín, a colonial entrance has been inserted into the enclosure wall, and about 5m behind and parallel to it, there is a vestige of an andesite wall, three courses high and about 80cm wide, that is faced on both its northern and southern sides and is clearly a building remnant. In the interior, several short lengths of inka walls, footings, and part of a compacted red clay floor have been exposed during excavations inside and adjacent to the colonial chapel of

Casa Concha and elsewhere in that property (Paz and Allcacontor 2002) as well as in the property next door (García 2005). These finds appear to agree with the structural layout proposed for this block, and indeed the long parallel property boundaries perpendicular to San Agustín confirm such a hypothesis.

In mz2 the excavations at Triunfo #392 uncovered the façade and footings of an internal building and associated floor (Zanabria 1998a). It is located about 15m from San Agustín street and the same distance from the western enclosure wall. It faces south into the enclosure. It is made of polygonal limestone blocks set in a mud mortar, sitting on limestone and diorite footings. A compacted clay and stone inka floor remnant about 3sqm in extent was discovered adjacent to it, which was associated with inka potsherds, wall plaster, and charcoal. The wall survived because it had been the base of a republican adobe building, although the extent of damage to the site can be seen in the stratigraphy alongside the preserved floor, where a deep pit had been filled with an inka andesite lintel as well as tiles and later pottery. A parallel wall remnant from another building was found about 10m to the southwest.

Discussion

The field evidence for Hatunkancha indicates three critical urban features that distinguish it from other parts of the city (Farrington 2010b). First, it has a tall, freestanding, well-made enclosure wall, which concurs with Estete's observation. Second, its internal arrangement comprises rows of buildings, not *kancha*, that are located no closer than 5m from the enclosure wall. Third, it has an internal plaza flanked by at least two *kallanka*. Many of the recorded walls have been preserved on property boundaries, and interpretation of these presents an overall plan that should be further tested by excavation (figure 8.7a). The ethnohistorical evidence suggested that there was only one entrance to the compound and that it was probably situated in the northeast corner of the plaza, between Portal de Belén and Portal de Carrizos. Entry through it would have led the visitor between the Hotel Conquistador *kallanka* and the Muki and BIF buildings into the small plaza.

This plan is similar to that described by Morris (1971, 1974) for compound V-B-5 at Huánuco Pampa, which also has an enclosure wall with a single entry from the main plaza that leads into a small patio and then into a small plaza, which is about 47m (29r) by 57m (35.25r) (figure 8.7b). It is flanked on three sides by elongated, *kallanka*-like buildings that open onto

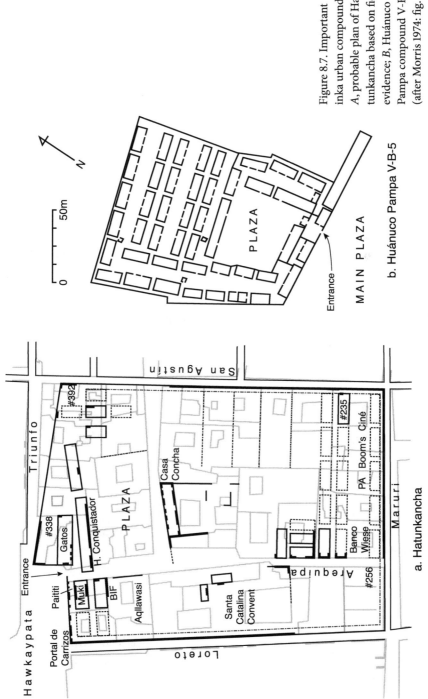

Figure 8.7. Important inka urban compounds. A, probable plan of Hatunkancha based on field evidence; B, Huánuco Pampa compound V-B-5 (after Morris 1974: fig. 2).

b. Huánuco Pampa V-B-5

MAIN PLAZA

PLAZA

Entrance

N

50m

a. Hatunkancha

Hawkaypata

Entrance

Triunfo

San Agustín

#392

#235

PLAZA

Casa Concha

PA   Boom's Ciné

Banco Wiese

H. Conquistador

#338

Gatos

Patiti

Muki

BIF

Aqllawasi

Santa Catalina Convent

Arequipa

#256

Portal de Carrizos

Loreto

Maruri

it and control access to the rest of the compound. The latter contains fifty rectangular buildings, of two different sizes, arranged in parallel rows and perpendicular lines. Each structure has only two doorways in its façade. From its archaeological signature, Morris (1971, 1974) deduced that this was an *aqllawasi* because of the high number of artifacts associated with textile making (spindle whorls, *ruki*) and *chicha* brewing (large pots) and because it is known that such tasks were carried out by the *aqllakuna* for both Sapa Inka and the Sun.

IIB Cabrakancha to Hatunrumiyoq Platform

This sub-unit measures 201.9m (125r) from the western corner of Ca brakancha to the similar point at the corner of the Hatunrumiyoq platform (figure 8.2). Today, it comprises three modern street blocks (mz34, mz15, part of mz14), but originally it was divided into two similar sized streetblocks and adjacent western lane at Santa Mónica street. Its width decreases progressively westward from 120.12m (74.38r) at Cabrakancha to 111.68m (69.15r) at Santa Mónica, to what would have been about 101m (62.5r) at Pasaje Inka Roca. Each lane runs relatively level from San Agustín for about 80m, then descends through terraces to Tullumayu.

There are very few standing inka walls recorded in this sub-unit. In mz34 there are external walls along San Agustín, Cabrakancha, Tullumayu, and Santa Mónica, while internally there is only a terrace remnant and two short lengths that belong to typical 8–10m wide buildings, parallel to San Agustín, suggesting a typical *kancha* arrangement. Excavations at San Agustín #239 (Novotel) provided little structural evidence, save some inka footings, the colonial reuse of inka elements, and a quantity of inka pottery (Mormontoy pers. comm.). Along San Agustín there is a corner and perpendicular wall at a distance of 32.4m (20r) from Cabrakancha. This is probably a north-south lane, which would suggest that this street-block had a line of three equal sized *kancha*, each with its own lane. On the west side of Cabrakancha, there is a blocked lane entrance at 79.0m (49r), that would have run along the top of the terrace, but there is no surviving evidence for an intermediate lane in either Cabrakancha and/or Santa Mónica. However, the property boundaries in mz34 suggest that there was a second line of *kancha*, and probably a third on the terrace below fronting on to Tullumayu.

The plan in mz15 to the west of Santa Mónica is thought to have been identical to mz34, but there are no standing internal walls and only short lengths of exterior inka walls and footings in mz15 along Santa Mónica (Agurto 1980). This original street-block has been completely altered, first by the sixteenth-century construction of the church and convent of San Agustín, its subsequent destruction in 1840, and later clearance to make the new street, Ruinas, in the late nineteenth century. Indeed, the extent of colonial alteration has been revealed by excavations amidst the convent ruins in mz15 during a controversial hotel project in 2009. There were no reported significant inka findings in the cloister and chapel area, but several inka walls, floors, and a canal were discovered in the northern part of the property beneath colonial fill that had been brought in to construct a building platform in the sixteenth century.

The main findings include a compacted lane surface with a central stone-lined canal perpendicular to Santa Mónica. It is bounded on the southern side by a well-fitted limestone wall in polygonal style, one length of which was 7.5m long and 1.2m high and was found about 5m below the surface (El Sol 04/18/2009). The archaeologist, Irwin Ferrándiz, also discovered the interior of a *kancha* building with wide footings, a floor with inka pottery and animal bones, and a burial of a 40- to 45-year-old male with grave goods beneath it at the level of the footings. There are also wall vestiges at right angles (Andina 10/14/2009). These walls and deposits have been cut by colonial and republican structures that lay above them. In the southeastern corner of the street-block, Ferrándiz also found a set of wide rectangular foundations in green diorite set in a clay mortar that probably date to the killke period.

IIC Cabrakancha to Limaqpampa Chico

This sub-unit extends from the eastern side of Cabrakancha as far as Limaqpampa Chico (mz35), a distance of 161.5m (100r) (figure 8.2). On the basis of both aerial photographs and the property map, there was probably a line of four identical *kancha* with intermediate lanes along San Agustín with another line to its north. When measured from like to like, the arrangement would have been lane (Cabrakancha) 1.5r, *kancha* 23.5r, lane 1.5r, *kancha* 23.5r, and so on.

There is some evidence for inka footings along San Agustín as well as walls along both Cabrakancha and Tullumayu, some terrace sections parallel to the river, and one wall as a property boundary at Tullumayu #350. There is a finely finished rectangular andesite lane entrance, 1.41m (0.875r) in width, in Cabrakancha at 39.42m (24.5r) from San Agustín, and the northern corner of a second, at 84.93m (52.5r) at the terrace top lane, Alianza. This implies that there were two lines of four *kancha*, with narrow lanes. The angled terrace would have ensured that the second row became progressively smaller from west to east. There has been no archaeological excavation in this block.

IID Hotel Libertador

In the area to the southeast of the survey origin point, there are two sub-units. The smaller (mz36) is separated from the larger (mz37) because of its greater length and different *kancha* arrangement. It is bounded by San Agustín, Romeritos, Maruri, and Zetas. It is 43.45m (26.9r) wide, or 46.03m (28.5r) including Romeritos. Its original length would have been 189.96m (119.6r), but this was reduced by the eighteenth-century widening of Maruri. While Vargas (2007: 227) has suggested that it had only four *kancha*, the aerial photographic and cadastral evidence suggests five, the first three of which conform to the distribution in sub-unit IIC, that is, with 1.5r wide lanes and 23.5r long *kancha*. The two eastern *kancha* are equal in length, 33.1m (20.5r) with no intermediate lane.

Few standing inka walls have been recorded for this block; there is an andesite sedimentary length along Romeritos and two shorter sets of footings with two wall courses on San Agustín. This block has had two excavation programs. The first occurred in 1962, when a trench was dug to fix a water leak in the first patio of the Casa de los Cuatro Bustos (Vargas 2007: 237–38), discovering a 1m length of inka andesite wall, 80cm in width, only 20cm below the surface. Its trajectory was from east to west, and there was a second parallel to it. These finds seem to be walls of adjacent structures in the first *kancha* of this sub-unit. Unfortunately, this excavation was not continued.

The second took place in 1980 in the eastern two *kancha* prior to hotel construction. José González (1981, 1984) reported that in his thirty trenches, more than 80% of the deposits had been disturbed by subsequent construction and the installation of reticulated water and sewer systems, leaving few sealed deposits (figure 8.8a). Nevertheless, he found many footings and walls of different periods. The earliest footings, dating to the killke period, were diorite and limestone pebbles and roughly worked blocks in a clay mortar. They were found at the base of the external *kancha* wall along Limaqpampa Chico and San Agustín and were connected to four similar perpendicular lengths, hinting at rectangular structure outlines. In the

Figure 8.8. Original plans of excavations and architectural studies in Cusco. *A*, plan of the 1981 Hotel Libertador excavations (González 1984); *B*, PER-39 plan of manzana 37, showing inka walls, property boundaries, and building cover (Agurto 1980).

a. Manzana 36

b. Manzana 37

patio, a 2.5m length of similar footings and wall was recorded on a different orientation. This was 80cm in width and was associated exclusively with killke ceramics.

González (1984) noted that these killke structures formed the foundations for sedimentary courses of inka rectangular andesite blocks laid in a clay mortar, particularly along San Agustín, where there is also an andesite door jamb for entry from Limaqpampa Chico. He recorded inka footings and lower courses of the enclosure wall in the internal corner of Zetas and Intipampa. In 1967, Ladron de Guevara, excavating in the street, found at a depth of 1.1m two courses of an inka foundation that ran parallel to the present external wall, perhaps for the whole length of Zetas (Vargas 2007: 230). This indicates that the original eastern wall had been dismantled to widen Zetas earlier in the twentieth century, and therefore that the inka *kancha* had been slightly longer.

Several architects have indicated that the enclosure wall along Romeritos, made of sedimentary laid rectangular andesite blocks, is inka in date (see Vargas 2007: 227–28). However, there are some problems with this attribution. For example, in places the lower wall is made of polygonal limestone, topped unevenly by sedimentary courses of andesite. This wall includes the outlines of four filled-in niches; however, such niches are rarely found externally and never in a street; it is clearly reassembled. González (1984) also challenged its authenticity and date as he dug a series of test pits. He found that the footings were different, consisting of four courses of andesite, diorite, and limestone blocks in mud mortar to a depth of 1m, while noting their association with a floor covered with ashy deposits, animal bone, and some inka-colonial sherds. He suggested a colonial date for the reconstruction of the wall. From the perspective of this broader analysis, these footings are not unusual and are similar to inka period foundations elsewhere in Cusco. This may suggest that it is largely a reconstructed wall on top of inka footings.

Inside the easternmost *kancha*, González (1984) discovered 80cm wide footings in rooms #2 and #3 that formed the rectangular outline of an inka building; these were associated with a compacted clay and gravel floor on which were many inka sherds and camelid bones. Other inka walls found in both patios suggest a series of perpendicular buildings, dividing the area into two *kancha*, with a total of six buildings in each. A well-made inka period stone-lined canal was found to trend across the eastern patio toward the doorway of San Agustín, while vestiges of a second similar canal were also detected between two southern structures in the adjacent *kancha*.

IIE Kusikancha

The fifth sub-unit is a large modern street block (mz37) defined by the streets Maruri, Pampa del Castillo, Intipampa, and Romeritos. It is clearly the residential area mentioned by Garcilaso (1966: 424), located between Hatunkancha and the temple. Its original name was probably Kusikancha, as this was also the first *waka* on the fifth *seqe* of Chinchaysuyu (CH-5:1), opposite Qorikancha (Cobo 1990: 57). It was also notable as the birthplace of Pachakuti Inka Yupanki, and members of Iñaca *panaqa* made sacrifices there.[6]

Since the late 1970s, it has been the focus of detailed study by both architects (Agurto 1980) (figure 8.8b) and archaeologists (Paredes 1999, 2001; Vargas 2007) because of its many standing walls (figure 8.9). At present, its block plan is a rough quadrilateral,[7] with the angled alignment of Pampa del Castillo, adjusted to the topography and terracing, disrupting a basic rectangular grid. However, as discussed in chapter 5, it has undergone several major changes since the 1530s, such as the widening of Maruri street by about 10m in the eighteenth century, its extension between Arequipa and Loreto in the late nineteenth century, and the widening of Romeritos by about 1m in the 1940s.

Kusikancha lost much of its inka, colonial, and republican architecture when its northern part functioned as a military barracks between 1940 and 1995. Yet it still retains the densest arrangement of inka standing architecture in the old city, which was recorded in detail by the PER-39 team (Agurto 1980) and by Mónica Paredes (1999). The stonework is exclusively rectangular andesite blocks, laid in a sedimentary style with a batter in the order of 12%. From the plan of inka walls, property boundaries, and building cover published by Agurto (1980), it is clear that a network of longitudinal (west-east) and transversal streets (north-south) divide it into nine *kancha*, of which six seem to be similar in size, and there is evidence for individual buildings within some. From measurement of an entrance on Intipampa, the longitudinal streets have the same width as Romeritos, 2.58m (1.6r), while the cross-streets are narrower at 2.1–2.2m (1.3–1.35r). Two enclosure walls of one *kancha* in the northeastern corner yield its external dimensions of 48.28m (30r) along Romeritos with a double-jamb doorway situated in the middle and 43.5m (27r) on Intipampa (figure 8.9c).

Additional wall lengths were reported by Paredes (1999), which enabled her to suggest a different plan. First, she described only eight *kancha*, of which only the three along Romeritos and one in the middle on Maruri

A

B

C

Figure 8.9. Inka walls in parts of mz37. A, a shop counter in Maruri; B, a shop display; C, double-jamb doorway in Romeritos to enter the *kancha* 6, the Hotel Libertadores—Palacio del Inka.

agreed with those of Agurto. The remainder were formed by a closer arrangement of streets along Pampa del Castillo. Second, she noted a lack of architectural evidence in the southwestern corner, which she claimed was because it was originally part of the *aqllawasi* and not an internal Kusikancha *kancha*. Certainly, there is a third transversal street which enters mz37 from Pampa del Castillo, dividing the second row *kancha* into two; it is uncertain how far this street continues into it.

In order to test this arrangement, there have been three small excavation programs at Pampa del Castillo #347 (Ardiles 1988) and Intipampa #263 (Rosell 2004; Tomayconsa and Pilco 1994) and a large one by a team from the INC-Cusco, who systematically excavated an area of 6,000sqm in the former barracks between 2001 and 2005 (Maza 2003; San Román et al. 2002, 2003; Vargas 2007). The latter has resulted in the conservation and some reconstruction of its ruins as a tourist park. It has also led to rehabilitation and partial reconstruction of the enclosure wall and doors along Romeritos and hence its re-narrowing.

The aims of the latter excavation were to examine the *kancha* that Agurto had indicated and to describe the urban milieu of the inka capital. The results uncovered the usual urban stratigraphy of footings, walls, floor, and pits and disturbed deposits, which ranged in date from killke to post-1950. Although this has made interpretation difficult, the large-scale open area excavations have enabled a much more comprehensive view of the extent and importance of each successive occupation. As a consequence, a better evaluation of the prehispanic period is possible, not only in terms of architectural and planning history but also through a social archaeological analysis of its inhabitants and activities. This large site extends through the street-block from Maruri to Intipampa and was divided into three rows, based on the predicted *kancha*: row 1 adjacent to Maruri, row 2 in the center, and row 3 adjacent to Intipampa (figure 8.10).

The lowest cultural levels were found in rows 1 and 2 and are characterized by stone footings, about 90cm in width, assembled from diorite, sandstone, and limestone in a clayey loam mortar and resting on top of a reddish-brown clay. The walls themselves are thought to have been made of polished andesite because there is a large amount of andesite dust present in the adjacent strata. They form rectangular outlines that are aligned differently in each row and contrast significantly with the overlying inka footings, floors, and *kancha*. Killke sherds have been found in association with these. A 40m length of stone-lined canal has been exposed in row 2, flowing from south to northeast. It is 90cm wide and 80cm high and is

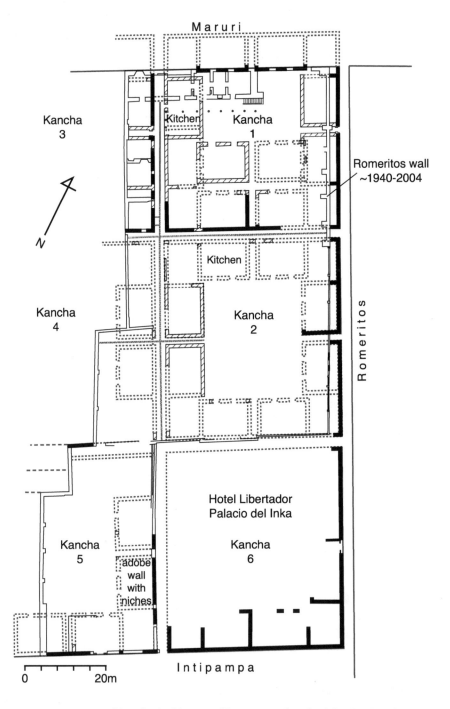

Figure 8.10. Excavated *kancha*, buildings, and lanes in Kusikancha (after San Román et al. 2002, 2003).

covered with diorite and sandstone slabs; its channel is large, 33cm wide and 40cm high. It had been constructed on top of a compacted red clay; it is associated with decorated killke potsherds.

The succeeding layer presents footings, walls, buildings, floors, streets, and canals that demonstrate that the inka *kancha* system represented a complete remodeling of the site. The predicted network of streets and *kancha* buildings was readily discovered, although in places there are gaps in footings as a result of colonial, republican, or even twentieth-century reconstructions, interventions, and installations. The standing wall lengths of *kancha* 3, parallel to inka foundations of *kancha* 1, are part of a longitudinal street that extends through row 2 as two lines of footings as far as the entrance on Intipampa. It averages about 2.6m (1.6r) in width, and its surface is a compacted clay and gravel matrix, 10–15cm thick, that slopes toward a stone-lined central channel that flows toward Intipampa. Two standing walls are also aligned with excavated footings to define two transverse streets, 2.2m (1.35r) wide, that also have traces of a central channel.

In excavation, the inka foundation walls are defined as a 90cm wide arrangement of quarried limestone blocks on a compacted clay bed. They generally have two or three courses and are set in reddish clay mortar. In some locations, there are adjacent horizontal layers of compacted red or yellow clay and gravel, probable inka floors, that have within their matrix both andesite dust and various stone artifacts, such as hammers and polishers, confirming that the walls were finished *in situ*. Some walls stand up to 2m in height, while in excavation others only display two courses above the original surface or simply footings. In 2004, excavations were extended into Romeritos, discovering the footings and lower courses of the *kancha* 1 and 2 enclosure wall, a double-jamb doorway in the center of each, like that extant in the third section, as well as the entrances to both transversal streets. Other specific excavations, beneath the façade of the colonial *casona* on Maruri, extended 2m into the street and revealed the lower eight courses of the front walls of two inka buildings that faced eastward into the *kancha* 1 patio. These had been used by eighteenth-century builders as stable footings for the new house façade (figure 8.11). The remainder of each structure was probably destroyed at that time. A 1m thick street formation has leveled up the road, burying the surviving wall stubs and protecting them from further destruction.

The evidence from *kancha* 1 and 2 and corroborated by excavation data from *kancha* 3 and 5 indicates that these are identical in form and size (figure 8.10). They are rectangular, 48.4m (30r) by 43.5m (27r), with double-jamb entrances in the center of both the northern and southern sides. They contain eight identical two-door structures, measuring 11.16m (7r) by 8.04m (5r) internally, arranged with two on each side of a central patio that measures 29m (18r) by 26.8m (16.5r). The pairs of northern and southern buildings are separated by a passage from the *kancha* entrances, while the eastern and western ones are separated by blind alleys. A lateral space characterizes each corner, measuring 9.62m (6r) by 7.44m (4.6r). In *kancha* 1 a stone-lined drain leads across this from the central patio to the street. Given the amount of destruction, it was believed that no original fabric had survived above the stone walls. However, as mentioned in chapter 5, during the cleaning of one wall above the stonework in *kancha* 5, five standard niches with wooden lintels were discovered in the adobe superstructure (figure 8.12), meaning that each building was made of andesite and adobe with nine niches in its rear wall.

Despite such planning, the inkas found it necessary to alter the layout of *kancha* 1 with the construction of two more buildings, each 12.90m (8r) by 8.40m (5.2r), in its central patio immediately in front of buildings 10 and 12 (figure 8.13). These were also built with limestone footings and andesite walls, although in some sections the stonework has been completely

Figure 8.11. The façade wall and portal of the colonial *casona* at Maruri #340 superimposed on the façade of *kancha* 1 buildings and doorway.

Figure 8.12. Standard niches in adobe on top of rectangular wall, inside building #8 of *kancha* #5, Kusikancha (photo by Lisa Solling).

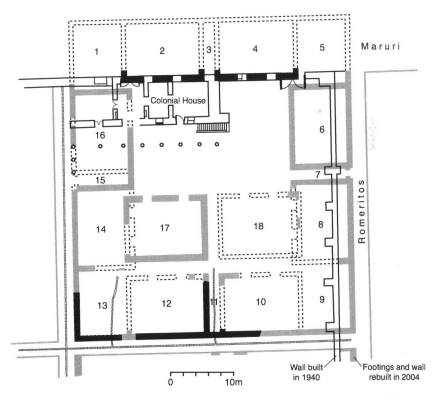

Figure 8.13. Remodeling of Kusikancha *kancha* 1 (after San Román et al. 2002, 2003).

removed, and its location could only be identified by a linear, clay-lined foundation trench. In the course of remodeling, two buildings were also destroyed by the demolition of the front and east walls of R-14 and R-8. Such redesign must have meant certain functional changes at this location. This arrangement of buildings, one behind the other, is found in other inka urban centers.

Plan-Unit III

Plan-unit III lies to the west of plan-seam A (figure 8.14). It was constructed about the continuation of San Agustín, known as Palacio and Pumacurco, as it ascends toward Sapantiana and Qolqampata. On the northern side, it is composed of a narrow band of terraces that descend to the river and its street, Choqechaka, in two modern street blocks (mz12, mz13). On the opposite side, it is confined by plan-seam A in mz1 but opens onto a broad leveled area in mz10 and mz11 as far as the terraced street of Waynapata. Further uphill, the slope is steeper and the terraces are narrower, but this probably remained a green area as far as Qolqampata. Overall, this plan-unit consists of rectilinear residential development, separated by narrow lanes, on either side of the main axis. The total height difference along the main artery through this area is 19m.

Theoretically, the survey origin point for this plan-unit should be located on the left-hand side of Pumacurco, at its junction with the cross-street, Tucuman–Siete Culebras; however, this point now lies in the Plazoleta Nazarenas and cannot be confirmed. Nevertheless, measurements from this point indicate that it may have been utilized for surveying purposes. For example, it is 124.2m (77r) along Pumacurco to the corner of Triunfo and 141.72m (87.75r) to the far side of Waynapata. The transversal street measures 227.77m (141r) from Ataúd to Choqechaka and is relatively level for about 200m as far as the terrace parallel to the river. This enabled a row of three street blocks, each 40r wide, separated by lanes, each 2.56m (1.58r) wide. In practice, there was some minor deviation from this plan because of the width of Pumacurco and the standard inka planning practice whereby measurements should be from like to like and that the common error is always a function of whether the street width has been included, a factor that probably explains the differences between mz10 and mz11.

There are many standing inka walls in mz1, mz12, and mz13, while only short lengths of the external walls survive in mz10 and mz11. The enclosure walls are made of sedimentary laid rectangular andesite, except for block

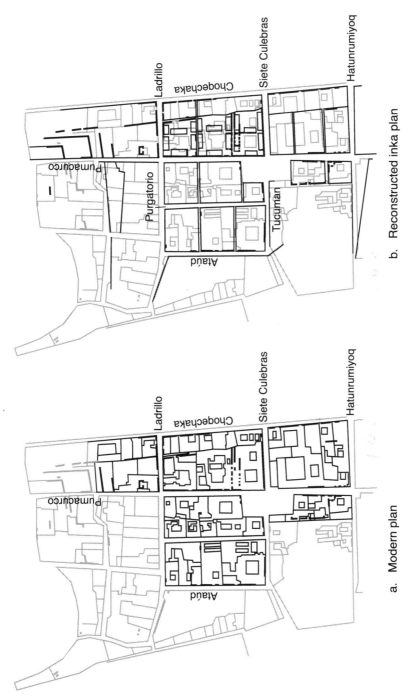

Figure 8.14. Plan-unit III. *A*, modern blocks and streets; *B*, inka blocks and streets.

mz1, where they are of polygonal style limestone. Judging by the wall data and relevant cartographic and cadastral information, each street-block is similar in size with the same basic internal plan and an average *kancha* length of 64.6m (40r) and each was divided into three equal *kancha*, separated by lanes. From the observed data alone, it is not possible to determine if each block was divided longitudinally to form six *kancha*. This may be resolved with reference to the excavation evidence from three archaeological programs: Casa del Almirante in mz10 (Zapata 1993), Casa Cabrera in mz11, and Beaterio de las Nazarenas in mz12 (Colque 2001).[8]

The first street-block (mz13) is 124.3m long (77r) from Hatunrumiyoq to the opposite side of Siete Culebras. Its enclosure wall has been largely reconstructed, although where it survives on Pumacurco, it is rectangular andesite. There is part of a doorway at about 33m from Hatunrumiyoq. Internally, in the southeast there are vestiges of cellular limestone walled buildings with adobe superstructure with, where visible, rows of standard niches (Paredes 2001:73). In contrast, the remainder has been severely altered by the construction of the chapel and monastery of San Antonio Abad, and few original walls have survived. A polygonal limestone terrace wall demarcates the edge of the building platform at about 64.4m along both Hatunrumiyoq and Siete Culebras. The present evidence would suggest that mz13 had consisted of three *kancha*, each 39m (24.15r) in length and 64.4m (40r) deep, separated by two transversal lanes. Along Choqechaka, the enclosure wall is of polygonal limestone, and at least one fine double-jamb door is extant. It is not known if this lower level was residential in inka times or a garden for the *kancha* above.

The second street-block (mz12) contains the architectural remains of the Beaterio de las Nazarenas, originally built in 1745 (Amado 2003). It measures 141.72m (87.75r) along Pumacurco and extends down to Choqechaka. Its southern and eastern enclosure walls were originally built of rectangular laid andesite on limestone footings, which has been reassembled in places to accommodate colonial doorways, windows, and a bell tower toward the southeastern corner. In contrast, on Choqechaka it is made of polygonal limestone, which is pierced by two double-jamb doorways (#286, #339), emphasized in rectangular andesite. A polygonal limestone terrace wall reduces the width of the upper building platform from 64.5m (40r) at Siete Culebras and to only 52.5m (32.5r) along Ladrillos.

In planning terms, this street-block has some similarities with mz13, but it has considerably more standing inka architecture. The internal distribution of walls, structures, and doors indicates that it was also divided transversally into three sections. In the Beaterio (*kancha* 1), there is the rear wall of a building with three standard niches and an inka-walled transverse street with a double-jamb door on its western side. There has been some debate regarding the dating of its external walls. For example, Agurto (1980) recorded many as inka transitional walls (figure 6.5), which the INC-Cusco architects have recently decided are colonial in date (Colque 2001). The basis for this seems to be the low angle of batter, a factor deemed to indicate colonial reconstruction, using inka blocks; however, the recorded angle is within the inka construction range, and in this book, such walls are regarded as inka. Another internal architectural survival is an adobe gable end with inka stone pegs of a two-story building at Casa de Cartagena (Pumacurco #336), parallel to the street in *kancha* 3 (figure 6.4; Paredes 2001).

In *kancha* 1 and 2 (5,200sqm), more than fifty trenches and pits were excavated inside rooms and patios for a total area of only 327sqm, about 6% (Colque 2001). These were up to 25m in length but rarely more than 1m in width. Such an excavation strategy has resulted in the opening of only "windows" into the disturbed republican, colonial, and inka occupation levels, which has meant that the pattern of inka footings, walls, canals, floors, and other deposits have been most difficult to distinguish and interpret. Both the narrowness of each trench and their dispersal across the site prevent a more accurate spatial evaluation of the remains. Nevertheless, some conclusions about its internal plan can be reached.

Numerous inka footings were located, comprising limestone blocks set in a clay mortar in trenches with a basal lining of red clay; variations included the occasional use of green diorite, sandstone, and even andesite. These foundations ranged in width from 83cm to over 1.1m and probably supported either a rectangular andesite or a polygonal limestone wall. Some inka footings have been stabilized during later periods with the use of mud and lime mortar. During 2009 more extensive excavations located more polygonal limestone walls, probably belonging to a *kancha* building, in section 2 (Andina 09/16/2009).

The excavations confirm that a lane, 1.99–2.01m (1.25r) in width, separated *kancha* 1 and 2; it is flanked by polygonal limestone walls on limestone footings set in clay mortar. Its republican period surface was paved with a central stone-lined drain, but at about 10cm below the level of the inka threshold a second paved floor was exposed that is probably inka in origin. It is clear that its original exit onto Pumacurco, about 38m (23.5r) from the corner of Siete Culebras, has been blocked by the construction of the chapel and the subsequent reconstruction of the enclosure wall. At a distance of 28.3m (17.5r) from Pumacurco, a double-jamb doorway gives access from this lane into *kancha* 2 via a short passage, 2.25m (1.4r) wide, between two polygonal limestone buildings. On the opposite side, the access into *kancha* 1 has been totally rebuilt to insert a colonial door, but its inka footings remain *in situ* and suggest a similar entrance. Elsewhere, the southern jamb of an identical door was found on the western edge of *kancha* 2. It is probable that the fine doorways on Choqechaka gave access not only to the lower level but also to the residential areas.

Using both architectural and archaeological evidence, the building on the western side of the first cloister has an internal width of about 5.8m (3.6r) and three niches in its rear wall. This dimension is in the same order as the building side walls in *kancha* 2, suggesting that in both the flanking buildings were similar, with perhaps an external width of 7.5m (4.5r). It seems appropriate that, on either side of the double-jamb door, there would have been identical buildings which, on the basis of Agurto's plans, would seem to be about 21m (13r) long externally. The width of the first cloister between extant walls with inka footings is about 23m (14.25r). Therefore, there would have been ample space in which to fit an equal sized structure at either end (figure 8.15). In addition, Agurto (1980) indicated an inka wall, delimiting the northern side of the first cloister. This might imply that the patio was divided, but there is no other archaeological information to support this assertion, although a stone-lined canal runs parallel to and 1m from it in typical inka fashion. This *kancha* contained buildings that were quite large, each with two or three doors, with empty corner spaces for domestic and other uses. The other two *kancha* have slightly different lengths along Pumacurco with different transverse widths, but it is presumed that a similar arrangement of buildings and streets was repeated in them.

On the opposite side of Pumacurco lies mz11, which would have been similar in size to mz12, about 140m by 64m, including the width of Purgatorio, although its area is reduced by Plaza Nazarenas. It is not known whether the plaza was original or a colonial development, removing one *kancha*. Only two external inka walls have been recorded: a polygonal limestone wall and footings in Tucuman and the façade of the *casona* Cabrera. The base of the latter structure has three or four courses of rectangular andesite blocks on limestone footings, including the remains of a double-jamb doorway about 14m (8.65r) from the corner with Pumacurco that would have been the entrance to *kancha* 2. The cadastral pattern suggests a similar transversal division of this block into *kancha*. However, in the

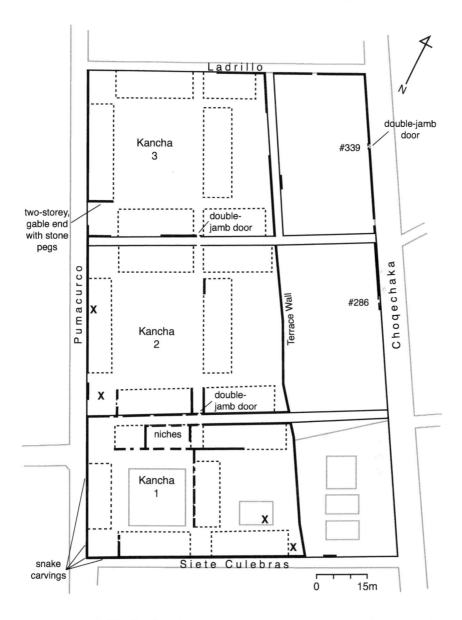

Figure 8.15. Probable inka plan of mz12, showing results of excavations in the Beaterio de las Nazarenas and the location of burials (after Agurto 1980 and Colque 2001).

absence of internal standing walls or further archaeological excavation, its internal layout cannot be described.

The adjacent street-block (mz10) between Purgatorio and Ataúd has similar dimensions to the others, 143m (88.5r) by 64.5m (40r), and it too was probably divided transversally into three. There are short lengths of enclosure wall extant on Purgatorio, Tucuman, Ataúd, and Waynapata, while on Ataúd there is an inka door, 2.07m wide, at about 52.5m (32.5r) from Tucuman. In contrast, only a single internal standing wall, running from north to south, is reported at Purgatorio #345 (Agurto 1980). In the southeastern corner is the Casa del Almirante, a colonial *casona*, which prior to its most recent restoration was subjected to an archaeological investigation (Zapata 1993). A total of 450sqm was dug as fifty excavation units in a relatively open garden, parallel to Purgatorio and therefore not in the main building or patio.[9] This consisted of two parallel 45m long trenches about 12.5m apart and two series of adjacent units, which were reported individually and not as an open area. The stratigraphy, to depths of 3.0m, was very disturbed with modern, republican, and colonial era pits, trenches, foundations, canals, drains, paths, pavements, and rubbish dumps with a mixed material culture. There is no definitive evidence for inka walls or buildings, although there are several foundation alignments that could be inka in origin, resting on layers of red clay, such as in unit N5-W5. In that location, quarried limestone blocks have been set in a clay mortar with a stone-lined canal running parallel to and in front of it. There are also many inka building blocks of limestone, andesite, and diorite that have been found loose in excavation or incorporated into later colonial or republican period structures and pavings. In terms of material culture, over 25,000 inka sherds were recovered, about 74% of the total number of ceramic fragments (Zapata 1993).

The other street-block (mz1) in this plan-unit also contains the cathedral with its side chapels facing onto Hawkaypata, which are part of plan-seam A. To the rear of both Triunfo church and the cathedral, there are vestiges of an inka lane parallel to Pumacurco, running between Triunfo and Plazoleta Nazarenas. A blocked transversal lane, 2.33m wide, is found in the enclosure wall along Pumacurco, 32.66m (20r) from the corner with Triunfo. Its side walls indicate that it joins the first and therefore divides this area into two *kancha*. The eastern one is about 32.5m (20r) square and contains the back and side walls of at least two internal buildings with standard niches. The second is larger, about 60m (37r) by 32.5m (20r), with a centrally placed double-jamb entrance on its southwest wall.

Discussion

The residential areas of the city were well planned and constructed to form plan-units, distinctive groups of similar structures in street grids that were strategically placed to serve the key religious, political, and administrative buildings in the plan-seams. Each plan-unit or sub-unit has a different *kancha* size and internal arrangement that may indicate differences in function or social composition.

In the majority of urban excavations, earlier pottery, including killke and lucre wares, occurs in small quantities; only in Qorikancha, Kusikancha, Hotel Libertador, and La Compañía have large amounts been recovered (see Covey 2003). However, it is premature to state that, since killke pottery has been found, this demonstrates evidence for an earlier occupation. It is always necessary to examine context and stratigraphy to establish any occupational sequence, and in typical mixed urban deposits, this needs to be a more systematic exercise. It is quite clear from several excavations that there are both extant footings and stratigraphical evidence to describe an earlier occupation in certain parts of the city. For example, in Kusikancha, footings have been found to be associated with killke potsherds and occupation levels. These are characterized by the use of green diorite in wall construction as well as its use with limestone and sandstone in footings. The results from Kusikancha and the Hotel Libertador indicate that killke footings form lines of separate rectilinear buildings, with a different orientation, about 30°, from the plan of plan-unit II (figure 8.16). In the former, they appear to be organized along streets and were associated with a stone-lined canal of the same era, while in the latter they were bounded by the alignment of San Agustín and a wall perpendicular to it (figure 8.16). The stratigraphical evidence demonstrates that these were dismantled prior to the construction of the inka *kancha* and streets, therefore confirming the chronicle evidence that Pachakuti Inka had removed the population before the new city was built. In contrast, other crude, irregular sub-surface walls of the same materials, not associated with occupation levels, such as at Qorikancha, were probably related to the construction cells for leveling-up to form stable building platforms by the inkas.

The architecture of inka Cusco is characterized by the use of two wall types—rectangular, finely finished andesite blocks; and polygonal, well-fitting limestone—and these in combination with adobe superstructures. Green diorite characterizes early inka construction and footings, but later it was used quite sparingly. However, it was used to highlight the corner

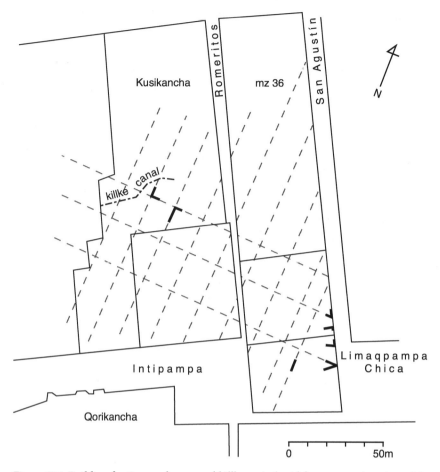

Figure 8.16. Building footings and proposed killke period grid from excavations in mz36 and mz37 (after González 1981 and San Román et al. 2002, 2003).

of Zetas and Awaqpinta alongside Qorikancha and the entrance from Tull-umayu into Cabrakancha. This indicates that the inka planners and architects may have either retained certain elements of the basic killke urban framework or, more probably reused such stones to give strength physically and metaphorically to these important locations.

Two other locations of green diorite construction in the city are in plan-seam A and relate to the alignment of Triunfo street. The massive rectangular green diorite Hatunrumiyoq platform was later covered in part with a veneer of polygonal limestone walling. Its alignment coincides exactly with that of a diorite wall discovered during excavations in Triunfo street (Andina 07/10/2009) and foundations in mz15. Other excavation data indicate that this street was widened by inka planners to create a small plaza at the junction with San Agustín, presumably for the gathering of processions prior to entry into Hawkaypata. A low stone platform has been found in Casa Concha with an associated stone canal and at least 250 sherds. It, too, is made of green diorite set in clay mortar, and the pottery is early, probably around AD 1200, either killke or qotakalle (Andina 10/03/2006).

Throughout the city, inka wall footings were generally made of limestone with some use of green diorite, sandstone, and andesite. Partially worked stones were invariably laid in a trench lined with thick red clay and laid in clay mortar for a height of two to five courses, 50cm to 1.2m. Similar mortar was also used for wall assembly. Inka floors were usually made of tamped earth and gravel, possibly colored red, white, or yellow. They can be distinguished as a compacted layer that also contains sherds and other objects. Stone paving in Cusco appears colonial or later in date and can be dated by its mortar and bedding, although there is some limited evidence from excavation of inka paved streets.

The question of "neo-inka" or transitional architecture cannot be resolved readily in this study. The dismantling and reconstruction of the city as a Spanish town after 1533 has led many to believe that any near vertical stone wall is not inka in origin, particularly if it has colonial doors and windows. Yet the batter of many of these lie within the inka range, and many are built with inka fabricated stones on top of inka footings. For example, at the Beaterio de las Nazarenas, the outer enclosure wall is regarded as transitional, while its footings exposed in excavation and its internal features are clearly inka in date (Colque 2001). Certainly, its external face has been remodeled by the insertion of Spanish features, including a bell tower, resulting in structural seams, not an inka trait, and the blocking of a lane. But was the entire wall rebuilt during the colonial period?

The plan-units, standing architecture, and excavation data enable a view that not only did the inka build basic *kancha* residential units of different sizes and configurations but that they had other enclosure types, such as at Hatunkancha, in which *kallanka*, a small plaza, and rows of buildings suggest a different urban pattern, known previously from Huánuco Pampa. The social meaning of such variations in urban residential plan will be discussed in the next chapter.

Urban Life

The city of Cusco, where their lords had their residences, was so large and so beautiful that it would be worthy to be seen even in Spain.

Sancho 1917: 192

The archaeological evidence from Cusco is very uneven in terms of both its quality and consistency. The excavation reports present basic stratigraphical data and material cultural finds in different ways, probably as a result of the amount of time allowed for analysis. Therefore, this prevents a robust comparative statistical analysis of the assemblages from across the city. By the same token, while there is general agreement on the forms and decorative styles of inka pottery, largely following Rowe (1944), these data are not always presented in the same manner. Any analysis is therefore not as comprehensive as it could be for each element of material culture, including animal bone. In many cases, only gross numbers of particular items are stated with no further description, while in others there is detail about specific finds but little on the majority. One factor that has dampened the enthusiasm for detailed interpretation is the lack of sealed deposits and the complicated, disturbed nature of the archaeological deposits. This has encouraged a prevailing logic that, if materials are mixed, then there is nothing that can be said with any certainty about the nature of the inka occupation. Such an attitude has made any comparative study difficult, but not impossible.

Despite these drawbacks, in this chapter I attempt to draw some general and, in places, specific conclusions toward a social interpretation of the finds and assemblages from the city. I consider three major topics: the nature of domestic life and the status of individuals and communities in different urban locations; the evidence of craft industry; and the disposal of the dead. Ceremony and ritual are considered in chapter 11. This should provide possibilities for some comparisons with the standard, historically derived social picture. One essential question concerns the relationship between building form and human activity: Is architectural difference a function of social practice?

Cusco Urban Society: The Chronicle Evidence

Everything written on inka society is derived from one or another of the chronicles, by either literal interpretation or anthropological analysis (e.g., D'Altroy 2002; Kendall 1973; McEwan 2006; Rowe 1946; Zuidema 1964). For Cusco, these sources have been used to discuss the nature of kingship, social organization, and economic obligation as well as ritual, religion, and worship in order to present a well-argued image of the capital city. To date, archaeology has contributed very little to this understanding because there has been a lack of detailed analysis and indeed a desire to remain confident in the veracity of the documentary sources.

For the inkas, their geographical space was called Tawantinsuyu, the four quarters (*suyu*), which they interpreted as existing at three levels: local, provincial, and state. Therefore, the inhabitants of the city belonged to one quarter or another, which gave them certain rights, privileges, and obligations. In a general sense, the *suyu* and the citizens were also organized into two moieties called Hanan (upper) and Hurin (lower) in which the former was dominant, comprising members of Chinchaysuyu and Antisuyu, whereas the latter was subordinate, containing those of Qollasuyu and Kuntisuyu. The *suyu* and moieties were also manifest spatially with Chinchaysuyu to the west and north of the city, Antisuyu to the north and east, Qollasuyu to the southeast, and Kuntisuyu to the south and southwest. The fundamental social groups were called *panaqa* for the nobility and *ayllu* for the ordinary people. These were endogamous, territorially based lineages that claimed descent from a mythical ancestor. In Cusco, there were ten of each, and each had a totemic or founding father. The three most important *panaqa* were part of Chinchaysuyu, including the royal *panaqa*, Qhapaq Ayllu, while there were two in Antisuyu, three in Qollasuyu, and two in Kuntisuyu—in other words, five in each moiety.

The king, Sapa Inka, was nominated by his father from among his legitimate male children, and although he founded his own *panaqa*, he also represented Qhapaq Ayllu for the purposes of government and ritual.[1] The king list and associated *panaqa* have been interpreted by many scholars as a historical dynastic sequence; however, the system of ten *panaqa* could also have been relatively permanent, and each new king always would have been attached to Qhapaq Ayllu.

One critical factor in this division was the *seqe* system of *waka* (shrines), which radiated from Qorikancha. Responsibility for the maintenance and veneration of each *seqe* and *waka* was held by the various *panaqa* and *ayllu* within each quarter. This system has been interpreted to describe various characteristics of inka society, such as hierarchy, obligations, marriage rules, and even territorial rights (e.g., Zuidema 1964, 1990).

The *panaqa* and *ayllu* were organized as territorially based kin groups, each with a founding or mythical ancestor, and were the basic social unit throughout the Andes. Andean society was also traditionally a dual system of opposing halves, such as Hanan and Hurin, each of which was divided into two. From the ethnohistorical documents, it is known that every *ayllu* and province had tribute obligations to the inkas in the form of *mita* (corvée labor), in which workers were assigned particular tasks for a certain period ranging from house building to military service; while in the home district each *ayllu* would also be responsible for cultivating, harvesting, and transporting the products of certain fields set aside for this purpose to state storerooms (*qolqa*). Tribute also was levied in goods on those communities that produced textiles, metal items, gold, coca, and other goods.

One particular form of social engineering was a policy of translocation, called *mitmaq*, in which whole *ayllu* were transferred from one area to another across Tawantinsuyu. This was done for various political and economic reasons, although they did move skilled metal workers and potters from Chimor and the central coast (Ischma) to work in the vicinity of Cusco and in other administrative centers (e.g., Espinosa Soriano 1970, 1983).

Outside of this system were groups of individuals who had been removed from their *ayllu* and village because of their skills, strength, or beauty and who were placed for life in the service of the Inka, the state, or the state religion. These were known as either *yanakuna*, men and women from various provinces who had been brought into service of the king or nobility to work their estates, maintain households, maintain mummies, or be praetorian guards, or *aqllakuna* (*mamakuna*), women selected as children to be educated to serve the Inka himself as concubines, cooks, brewers, servants, seamstresses, political brides for inka nobles or provincial leaders, and even for sacrifice.

It is known that only the nobility and their retainers, the *yanakuna* and *mamakuna*, lived in the city itself (Sancho 1917: 192), while provincial lords and other foreigners, ordinary local *ayllu* members, and *mitayoq* were housed beyond the physical bounds of the old city in peripheral settlements of various types (see chapter 10).

The historical data presents the archaeologist with a social understanding of the Cusco population as well as some notion about the various political, administrative, and religious functions that were performed throughout the city. For example, various palaces and other households functioned as elite residential units in which men and women dined, slept, and brought up families and in which retainers cooked, brewed beer, served food, made clothing, and perhaps even made pottery, metal goods, and other craft products. The temples, *waka,* and plazas were places of worship, offering, and ceremony, where *inter alia* copious quantities of food and drink were consumed. There were also *qolqa* in which the goods brought as tribute were stored around the city.

From the archaeological perspective, various questions can be asked. How can these people be identified? How did they live? Are the status differences between king and subjects, between *panaqa* and *ayllu,* and between Hanan and Hurin recognizable in the material culture and architecture of the city? Can the activities of food production and brewing be recognized and distinguished from the feasting and ceremonies in which they participated? Can various craft industries such as textile making, metal working, and potting be identified?

In inka archaeology there have been very few attempts to identify specific activities and functions, and the work of Morris (1974; Morris and Covey 2003) at Huánuco Pampa stands out in this regard. While the study of burials generally adopts a standard approach to explore social questions of the past (e.g., Parker-Pearson 1999), particularly with regard to status and ritual, inka archaeology lacks a comprehensive understanding of the range of burial practices and their meaning, and except for the work of Paredes (2003), Julien (2004), and Salazar (2006), there has been very little comparative study of data from the Cusco heartland.

As with any archaeological interpretation, the nature of the assemblage and its context are vital to understanding and interpretation. This becomes difficult when it is realized that the inka pottery assemblage is restricted with only fourteen basic forms (Meyers 1976), which were produced in a variety of sizes for different purposes, and this makes interpretation even more difficult. In the case of Cusco, such limitations are exacerbated by the disturbed and mixed deposits in which the materials are found, but these must be understood for successful analysis and interpretation.

Domestic Activities and Residential Life

Household archaeology is concerned with understanding the residues of domestic life in and around a residential structure, which is lived and slept in, and in which one might cook, eat, and work at some craft (Allison 1999). Inka domestic life has rarely been examined in the archaeological record, and although Silverblatt (1987) has examined the role of women in inka society using historical documents, there is nothing on the archaeology of women or childhood. Little has been written on the archaeology of cooking and cuisine, although Bray (2003a, 2003b) has considered the culinary functions of inka pottery as cooking, storage, or serving vessels, using the principles of "vessel performance" (table 9.1). Nevertheless, this does not mean that the miniature versions of these pots actually performed the same function, as they were more symbolic and representative of the larger vessel, according to the andean concept of *ekeko*. Another domestic chore was the brewing of *aqha* (maize beer or *chicha*), which was also produced on a larger scale to cater for state festivals (Morris 1979).

The Cusco diet was primarily vegetarian with a great emphasis on tubers, such as potatoes (*Solanum tuberosum*), oca (*Oxalis tuberosa*), ulluco (*Ullucus tuberosus*), and añu (*Tropaeolum tuberosum*), on pulses, including beans (*Phaseolus vulgaris, P. sieva*) and tarwi (*Lupinus mutabilis*), several pseudo-cereals, such as quinoa (*Chenopodium quinoa*), and fruits. Maize (*Zea mays*) was culturally the most important crop, particularly among the elite (Murra 1960). It was grown in quantity and was used mainly for beer production, but also consumed boiled (*mote*), toasted, and as popcorn (*kancha*). Potatoes and other tubers were eaten freshly boiled or baked, but were also freeze-dried as *chuñu* and *moraya*, or simply dried and ground into flour. Meat constituted only a small part of the diet; domesticated guinea pigs (*Cavia porcellus*) and camelids (*Lama* spp) were commonly eaten on special occasions, while wild white-tailed deer (*Odocoileus virginianus*), taruka (*Hippocamelus antisensis*), and vicuña (*Lama vicugna*) were regularly exploited. Water birds and freshwater fish were also consumed, while dried and fresh fish was even brought from the coast (Cobo 1979: 230). Spices and flavorings included chili or *uchu* (*Capsicum frutescens*), salt, and herbs, such as *wakatay* (*Tagetes minuta*). Apart from baked roots, toasted maize, beans, and roasted meat, stews, such as *rokro*,[2] were also made using vegetables, meats, chili, herbs, and salt (Cobo 1990: 199).

Food preparation is an essential task that requires a basic set of tools for chopping, cutting, and grinding, a water supply, fire or stove, vessels

Table 9.1. Inka pottery forms and functions

Meyers no.	Pottery type	Quechua name	Cooking	Serving, Consuming	Storage	Transport
1	*Maka* (aryballo)	*maka*		Serving liquids	*Chicha*, dry goods	Yes
2	Narrow necked, flat bottomed bottle	*aisana*		Serving liquids	*Chicha*	
3	Face-neck jar	*puiñu*		Serving liquids	*Chicha*	
4	Jar with loop handle	*aisana*		Serving liquids	*Chicha*	
5	Jar with loop handle	*puchuela*		Drinking	*Chicha*	
6	Wide-mouthed jar with two handles	*rajchi*		Serving liquids		
7	Wide-mouthed jug with loop handle	*rajchi*		Serving liquids		
8	Large wide-mouthed container	*urpu*	Fermentation, boiling		Dry goods	
9	Large wide-mouthed container	*raki*	Fermentation, boiling		Dry goods	
10	Pedestalled pot	*manka*	Boiling, stewing, toasting			
11	Casserole [deep] dish	*manka*		Serving food		
12	Flat-bottomed bowl, everted walls, and two strap handles	*puku*		Serving food		
13	Shallow plate with lugs and/or handles	*puku*		Serving food		
14	Qero	*qero*		Drinking		
	Open-mouthed tripod or tetrapod	*jankjana*	Toasting			
	Small jar with loop handle	*qocha*		Serving liquids		
	Tall, narrow necked, flat bottomed bottle	*tticachurana*		Serving liquids		

Sources: Bray 2003a, 2003b; Meyers 1975; Pardo 1957.

for cooking, and, of course, stores of food. The archaeological evidence indicates that flaked stone knives and scrapers as well as metal knives must have been used as cutting, chopping, and scraping tools, while large tabular grindstones (*maran*) with a round hand stone (*tunaw*) served to grind seeds and tubers to flour, although small polished stone vessels (*mutka*) may have been used for more delicate grinding of small seeds, herbs, medicines, and hallucinogens.

Cooking was accomplished using two basic methods. In one, food was boiled and toasted in ceramic pots on small open fires. These fires were often unenclosed on a house floor, where pots could be placed in the hot embers and cuts of meat roasted. A more sophisticated method involved the construction of low clay structures, 10–15cm high, with a fire-box and one or more small holes in which to rest a pot (Cobo 1990: 195). The typical inka vessels used for this were the pedestalled pot with a lid, the pointed based *urpu* or *raki,* and the open-mouthed tripod. Direct evidence for cooking occurs as sooting and carbon residue on the lower exterior of a pot and/or as charred food fragments or a residue in the interior. Various types of ceramic and wooden plates and bowls were used to serve food, while the two-handled casserole dish was used to serve *rokro* and soups.

The other technique is the earth oven (*watiya*),[3] which was used to bake tubers and roast meat and now is mainly practiced in fields at harvest time. However, it was probably also common in urban Cusco. It involves digging a small pit, lining it with firewood, clay, and stones, and then lighting a fire to heat the clay and stones. When hot, the stones are moved to one side and the food arranged in the center, and the whole is covered with grass and earth. When cooked, the contents are removed and the oven is filled in and never used again. If this method was also practiced in urban kitchens, then one would expect the resultant stratigraphy to show evidence of much digging and churning of deposits with both restricted and scattered lenses of fire-reddened stones, nodules of fire-baked clay, charcoal, ash, carbonized grass, and wood.

Throughout Cusco, the stratigraphy is exceptionally disturbed, and direct evidence for cooking areas is difficult to find. However, in 2002, on the interior floor of two structures at Kusikancha, the excavators found the remains of several circular and sub-circular baked clay objects, some of which stood on rectangular, low clay platforms (figure 9.1). There are twenty-six in *kancha* 1 R-16 and more than twenty in *kancha* 2 R-2. They range in height, diameter, and thickness, and their internal form is either conical or cylindrical. One contained the sherds of a pointed vessel base

A

B

Figure 9.1. Kusikancha kitchens. *A, Kancha* 1 building 16; *B, Kancha* 2 building 2.

that fitted perfectly. It was initially thought that these features had functioned as crucibles for metal processing or as molds in pottery making.
However, both contexts have fire-reddened floors with patches of ash, charcoal, burnt grass, and charred wood as well as potsherds, lids, stone knives,
metal tools, and worked camelid bone as well as broken animal bone, some
of which was charred and calcined. It is suggested that they represent stands
for holding pots with round or pointed bases, such as *maka, urpu,* and *raki.*
These were also low, square clay platforms with holes in which pedestalled
pots or *urpu* could have been placed over a low flame. The ash and charcoal patches were the result of open fires in which cooking pots had been
placed. It can be concluded, therefore, that these two rooms functioned as
kitchens for the preparation and storage of food and beer.

This is confirmed with reference to finds at Huánuco Pampa and at four
locations near Cusco. Craig Morris (1974: 53) reported clay molds that he
deduced were jar supports from several parts of Huánuco Pampa, including Unit V-B-5. Julinho Zapata (1983) dug in building #3 of the Qatawasi
sector near the main entrance of Machu Picchu in which he found several
similar baked clay objects as well as sherds from at least twenty-four *olla,*
seven *maka,* eight *raki* with eight lids, fifteen large plates, and a grindstone
(*maran*). He concluded that vast quantities of food and drink had been
prepared there. In more recent INC-Cusco excavations, more than thirty
similar clay stands were found associated with many inka potsherds in a
large room at Espíritu Pampa, while two have been found in a room adjacent to the carved rock at Urqo (Candia 2008). At Tambokancha, excavations in structure 5 in the prestigious Sector A revealed a kitchen with
similar finds (Farrington and Zapata 2003). Each end of that building had
an area, defined by a low clay wall, the floor of which was severely reddened
by fire. It had been covered with ash and charcoal, and within these patches
were several circular baked clay pot stands. This site had been deliberately
destroyed by the inkas, immediately prior to the conquest, indicated by the
scatter of smashed clay stands, cooking, storage, and serving vessels as well
as carbonized food remains that were strewn thickly across the kitchen
and adjacent corridor. The latter included maize, *tarwi,* two types of beans,
potato, *oca,* and chili peppers as well as camelid and guinea pig bones and
even a whale rib bone.

The remains of a clay oven were found in structure 2 at Intiqawarina
#620, associated with extensive ash and charcoal lenses, camelid bone, and
inka pottery (Durand and Verastegui 2009). Immediately to the north of

this building, the prepared inka floor of the corner patio was covered with a kitchen midden, comprising a 20cm thick layer of ash, charcoal, animal bones, and inka pottery. The disturbed strata, discovered in most urban excavations, can still indicate that cooking had occurred within a household, particularly if charcoal and ash lenses are found associated with baked clay nodules, reddened clay surfaces, burnt and calcined bones, and/or carbonized food remains. The associated pot forms can also be examined for soot or food residues. Using these criteria, problematical stratigraphy can be interpreted, particularly if it is associated with inka structural features, such as walls and doors. For example, fire-reddened inka floors with charcoal and ash deposits and with sherds from cooking, storage, and serving pots have been noted at Plateros #348 in Qasana (Castillo 1999), at Triunfo #392 in Hatunkancha (Zanabria 1998a), and at several other locations in *kancha* 1 and 2 at Kusikancha (San Román et al. 2003), while fired clay lumps, charcoal, and utilitarian pottery have been found in the Canchón (Béjar 1990). Two large urns were found against the rear wall of structure F in a rear *kancha* of Amarukancha, a typical location for kitchen storage (Cumpa 2000). *Maran, tunaw,* and *mutka,* used for specialized grinding, have been discovered at Triunfo #392, made of red porphyry (Zanabria 1998a), and at Nazarenas, made of green diorite, sandstone, and andesite (Colque 2001), while in *kancha* 1 R-8 at Kusikancha, a broken *tunaw* made of andesite has also been found.

Animal bones have been found in abundance in excavations throughout the city. Camelids predominate, with small amounts of guinea pig and deer, but their frequency declines significantly with the advent of cattle, sheep, and pigs. Camelid and guinea pig bones and classic inka pottery have been found scattered over inka floors at San Agustín, Casa Concha, Hotel Libertador, and Kusikancha, while calcined bones, mixed with charcoal and ash, occur at several sites, including Beaterio de las Nazarenas, La Compañía, and Hotel Libertador. To date, no carbonized plant remains have been reported from any excavation.

Aqha was the principal inka beverage, as it is among modern-day andean peasants (Nicholson 1960). It was consumed regularly by all household members, was a major component of the food and drink supplied on labor projects, and was a vital ingredient of ceremonial life. It became sacred, a drink that was shared with the Sun, other deities, and ancestors (Guaman Poma 1980: 246 [248], 287 [289]) at many ceremonies, when it was consumed by pouring it into an *urpu* or directly into the *usnu* hole.

On all ceremonial occasions, the inkas drank it in copious quantities and, according to Cobo (1979: 28), "the principal activity is to drink until they cannot stand up," while Estete (1924) noted that during major festivals the imbibing participants would also urinate directly into the *usnu* hole, implying the beer's sacred character as an offering continued after consumption. The drink could also be flavored with ground seeds from the pepper tree (*Schinus molle*), and on occasion ground *vilka* seeds (*Anadenanthera* spp) could also be added to give it not only alcoholic but also hallucinogenic qualities (Cobo 1990: 169; Polo de Ondegardo 1965).

It takes about five days to prepare, and it needs to be consumed within a few days as it quickly turns sour, although some finer varieties are known to have been kept for up to a month. Its production requires a large amount of dried maize,[4] space for germination, a *maran* and *tunaw*, a nearby source of water, a source of heat to start fermentation, and several large, wide-mouthed *urpu* or *raki* and several large narrow-mouthed *maka* for fermentation and storage, and clay stands. It is generally served from smaller *maka*, jugs, or gourds and drunk from a wooden *qero*, although the inkas also used ceramic, gold, and silver ones on specific occasions.

It would be expected that every household would have been self-sufficient in *aqha* and would have a *maran* and the appropriate pots for brewing available in their kitchens and patios. However, its production for ritual feasting and ceremonies would have required a much larger area and more equipment, and as we have noted, this task fell upon the *aqllakuna*, who would be required to produce such large quantities. Several archaeologists (e.g., Moore 1989; Moseley et al. 2005) have excavated such large-scale beer-making sites, dating to various prehispanic periods, and discussed the processes, tools, and ceramics used in mass production. For the inkas, Morris (1979) has described the archaeological assemblages he found in Huánuco Pampa in the enclosure V-B-5 and in the *kallanka* surrounding two large internal plazas, II-B-2 and II-B-3, of the royal group, in which he considered the distribution of large vessels, such as *raki* and *urpu* and grindstones, as indicative of such preparation. He also noted the presence of several round clay stands for *maka* and *urpu*. The consumption of maize, and therefore *aqha*, has been studied at Machu Picchu and Jauja, using an isotopic analysis of human bone (Burger et al. 2003; Hastorf and Johannessen 1993). These results indicate that it formed a considerable portion of the diet, as maize was mainly drunk as a highly prestigious ritual beer in copious quantity at all festivals and ceremonies.

In the two kitchen areas of Kusikancha, described above, the large, thick pots and clay stands may indicate that *aqha* was made in them as well. It is not known if these kitchens and brewing facilities provided only for domestic consumption or for large festive occasions as well.

Other aspects of residential and domestic life demonstrate that garbage was probably disposed of by burning and/or dumping it in pits in *kancha* corners, such as at Intiqawarina #620. Low sleeping benches have been recorded at some sites, such as Tambokancha, where they generally stand about 20cm above floor level with a width of about 180cm at the narrow end of a building. In Cusco, its later urban history has led to such a massive loss of the inka residential fabric that such structures have generally not survived, although one, with an earth body encased by a stone retaining wall, has been reported against the north wall of Casa Concha (Colque 2001). There has been no study comparing households from different plan-units in Cusco to assess details of status and family makeup.

Craft Activities

Craft industry was vital to the well-being, opulence, and redistributive activities of many ancient states, including Tawantinsuyu; production was generally managed by the state through the control of labor. The state, religious, and individual requirements for manufactured goods were critical for the required display of power and authority. For example, the Sapa Inka was dressed every day in new clothing; he ate from gold and silver plates and drank from gold and silver *qero*. Likewise, the nobility displayed the insignias of rank that also required ready access to craft products, while the state used fine textiles, gold and silver vessels, and other items as gifts to provincial governors and local chiefs. Such goods were also offered in sacrifice to *waka* as displays of faith and reverence. In order to achieve such access and control, the inkas required the raw materials and the finished product as tribute from various communities throughout Tawantinsuyu. For example, the provinces of Huánuco and Lupaqa were required to supply fine *qumpi* cloth and other textiles, clothing, sandals, featherworks, wooden bowls and *qero*, and even pottery as tribute, most of which was transported to Cusco (Julien 1982; Murra 1982). Alternatively, whole provincial craft *ayllu* were settled in Cusco as *mitmaqkuna* to work exclusively for the state or the Sapa Inka in the manufacture of various items. For example, a community of silversmiths was translocated to Cusco from

Ischma on the central coast (Espinosa Soriano 1983), and another moved from the mining town of Curamba to live in the suburb of Carmenqa; they were awarded farmland near Zurite.

The archaeological evidence for craft production has focused on the implements used in production, such as spindle whorls for spinning wool and cotton, shuttles (*ruki*) for weaving, and crucibles and molds for metalworking and pottery, as well as the waste products, such as wasters, broken molds, charcoal, ash, and slag. Lapidary working is indicated by stone flakes, chips, dust, and half-finished or broken objects. Such materials generally have a restricted distribution, either in a single workshop or a compound that may also contain evidence of kilns (e.g., Topic 1990, 2009).

There is considerable evidence of inka provincial pottery making facilities from the Chimú valleys of Jequetepeque (Donnan 1997) and Leche (Hayashida 1999), northern Lake Titiqaqa (Spurling 1992), and Argentina (Lorandi 1984). These have been identified by the presence of wasters, molds, sherd scrapers, stone burnishers, fired floors, and piles of unfired clay in close proximity. In Cusco and its hinterland, no manufacturing sites have been seriously investigated; only two are known, and others are postulated. For example, on a hillside about 400m from Tambokancha, there is a dense scatter of overfired, underfired, and other misshapen wasters, of which many are decorated among the remains of probable open kilns (Farrington field notes, 2004). At the palace of Quispeguanca, a large pile of wasters was found in the excavation of the royal residential sector, but no fire-reddened surfaces have been identified to locate the production site (Heffernan pers. comm.).

Textile production has been studied from the archaeological record by Craig Morris (1974) at Huánuco Pampa. He concluded that, since there were between 200 and 300 spindle whorls in compound V-B-5 and since this area had also showed evidence of extensive beer making, then this must be the *aqllawasi* of that city. In contrast, Spurling (1992) discussed the extensive documentary evidence for a large-scale facility of *mitmaqkuna*, making *qumpi* cloth and feathered items at Milliraya in the northern Titiqaqa basin, yet his surface surveys yielded only three spindle whorls. Closer to Cusco, documents have indicated the presence of a sixteenth-century *obraje* at Quispeguanca and fifty *yanakuna*, who maintained the mummy of Wayna Qhapaq.[5] This information encouraged the conclusion that textiles had been made at that site, despite the discovery of only a few spindle whorls (Farrington 1995). At Machu Picchu, camelid bone *ruki*, spindle whorls, and needles have been found in graves and elsewhere in the city to indicate textile production, certainly at household level (Eaton 1916). Miller (2003: 53) has suggested that bone spindle whorls were probably used for finer threads, such as vicuña, from which *qumpi* cloth is made.

Other craft manufacturing sites have also not been studied in depth. At Machu Picchu, a metal workshop has been identified in structure 16 of sector 18, where the floor was partially covered by sheets of silver scoria and there was a clay mold set into the floor with droplets of molten bronze around it (Mormontoy pers. comm.). Helsley-Marchbanks (2004) has reported another metal manufacturing site at Muyuntasita near Chayanta in Bolivia, where she found fire-reddened earth floors, baked clay *tupu* molds, deformed artifacts, metal droplets, and charcoal. A lapidary workshop has also been described near the Snake Rock at Machu Picchu containing large quantities of stone hammers, polishers, pieces of schist and jasper, stone bowls, and grindstones (Mormontoy pers. comm.).

The evidence from the rural palaces of Quispeguanca and Tambokancha, as well as a revision of finds from another at Chinchero, leads to a conclusion that they were places of royal residence, administration, and ceremony, and these activities were sustained by in-house craft production. Therefore, it can be postulated that the Cusco royal palaces should have considerable evidence of a range of craft industries.

However, the Cusco urban excavations have provided little evidence for specific workshops, although there is some for craft activity. The small trench and pit nature of the archaeology and the mixed character of the deposits have prevented a broad understanding of the distribution of critical artifacts. For example, the evidence for textile production is equivocal. Ceramic, stone, and bone spindle whorls have been found in small numbers in residential *kancha*, including Intiqawarina #620 (mz73), Kusikancha (mz37), Casa del Almirante (mz10), Nazarenas (mz12), Triunfo #392 (mz2), and Banco Wiese (mz16), and some among the deposits near Qorikancha, but none on the terraces immediately adjacent (Béjar 1998). There are also few *ruki,* and their distribution is similar. The examples are made on camelid bone, but there is one from deer antler found on the Qorikancha terraces. Zanabria (1998a) discovered an elaborately carved *ruki* on a llama long bone at Triunfo #392 (mz2) that had been shaped into a feline head at one end and notched with claws at the other. Bronze and copper needles, probably used in textile production, have been found at Casa del Almirante and the Qorikancha terraces and park. Textile manufacturing equipment has not been discovered in profusion in any one location to suggest a major cloth making facility, but its widespread distribution must indicate that small-scale production was carried out in most residential areas.

With regard to pottery production, the only evidence is a single ceramic mold of a lizard attachment for a cooking pot or *qero*, which was found in Tullumayu near Limaqpampa in the 1930s. This could imply that mz35 had a pot making facility, but more excavation is required in that area. In most excavations, there has been little detailed analysis of the ceramics to identify sherd scrapers and polishers used in manufacturing, nor are there any reports of wasters within the old city. Likewise, there is no evidence for metal working, shell cutting, lapidary work, or other types of craft manufacture.

Death in the City

There has never been a comprehensive study of inka burial practices (Kaulicke 2000), although there have been investigations of tombs in Cusco (Paredes 2003) and Tumibamba (Idrovo 2000) and a review of earlier finds in the Cusco area (Julien 2004). In addition, there have been some comparative skeletal studies concerning health, cranial deformation, and trepanation practices during the inka period (Andrushko 2007; Andrushko and Verano 2008; Verano 2003). In excavations in Cusco, at least fifty-five burials and several disturbed concentrations of human bone have been found as well as a further twenty-four in the immediate suburban area. In order to interpret these, it is necessary to determine patterns in the disposal of the dead across the city and compare these with other burials from Tawantinsuyu. In this section, burial location, the type of tomb, the range and placement of grave goods, the sex and age at death, and any other biological traits are examined.

The standard practice of disposal of the dead in Cusco was to place a wrapped corpse, seated with its knees drawn to the chest in a secluded place, such as a cave (*machay*), under a rock, in a *chullpa* tower, or even in an abandoned building. The body was furnished with pottery, personal ornaments, work tools, and food to accompany it to the afterlife. Subsequently, this type of resting place was walled up. Murúa (1987: 415) described this practice by commenting that the burials of commoners were mainly in high places in the countryside, in "fresh air." Such graves were visited by kin members from time to time and celebrated with more food and drink. The looted remains of these tombs can be seen on many cliff faces and in cavities under boulders throughout the Cusco valley (e.g., at Mesa Redonda, Inkilltambo, and Rumiwasi) and in the Sacred Valley between Pisaq and Machu Picchu (Eaton 1916; MacCurdy 1923). The most important individuals, such as the kings and other royalty, were also kept in this way in special "houses" in and around Cusco, where they were furnished with elaborate goods and food and generally looked after (Pizarro 1986: 100–101). Their mummies were brought to the plaza on occasion in order to participate in ceremonial proceedings and to be consulted as revered ancestors about matters of state.

Therefore, among the inkas for reasons of ancestor worship, interment per se was not a common practice, either for the ordinary person or for royalty. However, there were other forms of disposal, noted in the archaeological and ethnohistorical records, that do include burial, such as in a prepared pit, a clay capsule, inside a large urn, and in a deep shaft. All types have been recorded in locations in and surrounding the city and appear contemporary. Therefore, it could be argued that for the inkas each type must have had a different meaning that, to some extent, might be indicated by their location or grave goods.

Prior to discussing the urban finds, some observations about the inka practices of interment can be derived from other studies. For example, about thirty burials in prepared pits have been described in an elite residential area and temple patio at Tumibamba (Idrovo 2000), where each tomb was roughly circular, 1.25m deep, and the body was seated with goods placed in front of it and to either side. The tomb itself was filled with distinct layers of earth, stones, and gravel and invariably capped with a large stone. These were found in several locations: inside buildings, in corners, or against walls, in *kancha* patios, and in corner spaces. A most interesting observation from Tumibamba is that there was a mean sex ratio of about 3.2 females to each male (Idrovo 2000). Excavations in the Suchuna and Muyuqmarka sections of Saqsaywaman have revealed another technique in which the seated body was placed initially in a dried clay bowl on the ground surface with its grave goods in front and then fully enclosed in a clay capsule (Paredes 2003). These were arranged in lines and groups. Earth was piled over each capsule to bury it completely. Paredes (2003) noted that these were placed at different levels, suggesting several phases of burial activity. The third type, burial within a large pot, such as an *urpu*, has been described in many locations, including at Yucay (Silva 1982) and at Cutimbo (Tantalean and Pérez 2000). In this, the body was placed seated in a wide-mouthed vessel with its grave goods and buried in a prepared pit. It was also covered either with a stone slab or another pot. The fourth method, in a deep shaft tomb, is described in the ethnohistorical literature, such as the sacrifice of Tanta Carwa (Zuidema 1978), but no purely inka shaft tombs have been dug scientifically, although discoveries on Awsangati (Pardo 1941) and at Kancha Kancha near Pisaq are probable examples.

Kancha Graves

In the extensive excavations at Kusikancha, twenty-two burials, containing twenty-four individuals, were found in quite shallow but prepared oval pits (San Román et al. 2002, 2003). One double grave contained an adult female and infant (CF23), and another held an adult female with another adult (CF18). In general, all were between 10 and 20cm below inka floor levels, with a mean diameter of 65cm and a mean depth of 80cm in order to accommodate the seated corpse. Sixteen have been found within *kancha* buildings, seven mainly against one wall, four in a corner, with five in the center, while another five were located in the central patio, of which one was against a front wall and two were in an entrance to a blind passage between two buildings[6] (figure 9.2). The remaining two were located in the corner patio between buildings 12 and 14 in *kancha* 1. Two of the graves date from the early inka (killke) period, while the remainder are inka, of which two were associated with the second building phase of *kancha* 1. A number of round pits were found empty in *kancha* 5; one was adjacent to a 50cm long bronze bar which was probably part of the looted grave goods (Maza pers. comm.).

At Kusikancha, both groundwater and the proximity to inka floor levels have caused deterioration of the grave contents. According to Andrushko (2007: 96), there are fourteen females, two males, and five adults that cannot be sexed in this collection. She also listed an infant (CF23), a 6- or 7-year-old child (CF11), and an adolescent between 15 and 16. She has commented that this skewed sex ratio implies "an artificially created population of women," such as the *mamakuna*. There are few young adults (18–25 years), but half the group were over 25 and a further quarter were over 45. In terms of health status, none had suffered malnutrition or anemia because there are no cases of linear enamel hypoplasia or cribra orbitalia nor has anyone been subjected to cranial trauma. Only one individual had an annular oblique cranial vault modification, perhaps suggesting a Titiqaqa origin, while another had suffered from osteoarthritis (Andrushko 2007).

While the construction of tombs is quite standard and their locations

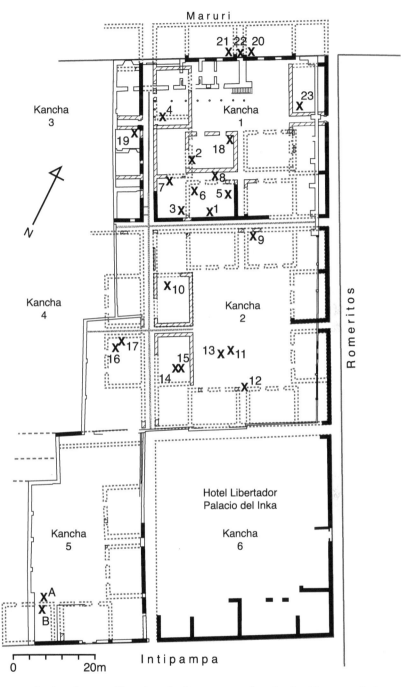

Figure 9.2. The distribution of burials and offerings in Kusikancha. Burials are marked with crosses, while the adjacent numbers refer to table 9.1. Other finds adjacent to round pits include *A*, a bronze bar; *B*, a silver male figurine.

Table 9.2. The Kusikancha graves

Grave no.	*Kancha* and building/space	Sex/age class	Orientation	Number and types of ceramics	Other goods
1	*Kancha* 1 R-12	?/A	W	None	Bronze *tupu*, two spondylus pendants, turquoise bead, lapis lazuli bead, five spondylus beads
2	*Kancha* 1 R-17	?/A	S	None	None
3	*Kancha* 1 R-13 lateral patio	?/A	—	To R: a small jar; to L: a jar	Two silver *tupu*, silver *aqorasi*, metal ball, seven round silex stones
4	*Kancha* 1 R-16 near wall	?/A	E	One decorated *tticachurana* at feet, one casserole pot on head	None
5	*Kancha* 1 R-12	?/A	SE	None	None
6	*Kancha* 1 R-12 corner	?	—	Head covered by an inka sherd	None
7	*Kancha* 1 R-13 lateral patio	?/A	S	In front: small pot, small pedestalled pot, miniature *urpu*; to L: miniature casserole pot, three pairs of small plates with painted llamas	Brown flaked knife
8	*Kancha* 1 patio	F/A	W	Miniature *urpu* and pedestalled pot	Metal *tupu*
9	*Kancha* 2 R-4 corner	F/A	S	None	Bone knife or awl
10	*Kancha* 2 R-16	F/A	SE	Small decorated pot, black pot with convex base	None
11	*Kancha* 2 patio	?/C (~12y)	S	Small decorated killke jar	Two metal *tupu*, small metal *tumi*, tweezers, spondylus valve
12	*Kancha* 2 R-11 passage between R-10 and R-12	?/A	—	Inka and killke sherds	None

13	*Kancha* 2 patio	?/A	NE	None	None
14	*Kancha* 2 R-16	M/A	NE	Killke sherds	Two metal *tupu*
15	*Kancha* 2 R-16	?	—	Killke dish	None
16	*Kancha* 4 R-8	?	—	None	None
17	*Kancha* 4 R-8	?/A	E	Decorated casserole pot, *qero* on top	None
18	*Kancha* 1 R-17	F/A(25y); ?/A	E	two inka sherds	*Jiwaya*
			S	None	None
19	*Kancha* 3 R-8	F/A(50y)	SE	Monochrome *maka* by head, sherds	None
20	*Kancha* 1 R-4	?	S	None	None
21	*Kancha* 1 R-2	M/A	N	Sherds	Dog
22	*Kancha* 1 R-3, passage between R-2 and R-4	Dog		None	None
23	*Kancha* 1 R-6 corner	F?/A; C/ neonate	E	Two *maka*, a monochrome inka bird-handled plate, bird-handled plate decorated with chilis, a broken plate,	Sandstone fragments cover the adult female with slate underneath; a bronze *tupu*, fragmented *maran*

Source: San Román 2002, 2003.

Note: Key to sex and age class: M, male; F, female; A, adult; C, child.

seem to follow basic principles, such as against the footings of walls, in building corners, and in patios, in order to understand the population of Kusikancha better, it is also necessary to examine the grave goods (table 9.2). From this, it becomes possible to consider the nature of funerary rituals. At death, people do not appear to have been treated in the same way. For example, in terms of personal items, only seven had a *tupu* for pinning the clothing of which only one (CF3) can be considered rich with two silver ones. That same individual also had a silver *aqorasi*, a metal ball, and some round stones. Of the remainder, five had a bronze *tupu*, while another (CF9) had one made from bone. One of those with a bronze *tupu* (CF1) also had an array of lapis lazuli, turquoise, and spondylus shell beads. One adult male (CF21) had a dog buried with him (figure 9.3), while nearby there was a similar grave (CF22) with only a dog.

Figure 9.3. Grave #21 at Kusikancha. A man buried with his dog.

Ten graves had ceramic offerings, of which only two had more than two vessels. CF7 contained an adult female who was seated facing east, and on her left-hand side there were eight miniatures, including a globular pot, a pedestalled pot, a *raki,* and a small decorated casserole dish with horizontal handles, a pair of plates with a decorated border of stylized camelids, a pair of brown polychrome plates, and a brown obsidian knife. It was located in the corner space between buildings R-12 and R-14 in *kancha* 1. The other, CF23, was situated in the southeast internal corner of R-6, also in *kancha* 1. It was slightly larger, 1.20m by 65cm, and contained two individuals, an adult female with the remains of an infant cranium and two long bones on the right side of her pelvis. The top of the grave was ringed by a circle of stones, including pieces of a broken *maran,* and was covered with slate flags, 20 to 30cm square. Below these were fragments of seven large pottery vessels, including *urpu, maka,* and dishes. A broken copper *tupu* shaft was found beside her mandible. Two regular sized bird-handled plates, one plain and the other painted with red and brown chilis on a cream background, were discovered by the upper body and a broken plate lay by her pelvis. The body was also sitting on a slate layer. This grave had a stone capping, and objects were placed at different heights during its filling. However, there is no mention of whether there were any textural or color changes in the fill. In two other graves (CF4, CF6), the head was covered by a large sherd. In contrast, there were five graves (CF2, CF5, CF13, CF16, CF20) that had no personal items or grave goods.

Each grave contained some ash and charcoal, suggesting that something had been burned and probably food prepared for the funeral ritual and to accompany the dead, but the general lack of pottery means that wooden vessels or gourds must have been used. It is not known whether the number and type of grave goods at Kusikancha reflects a scale of social status within the community, and while this is a tempting conclusion, it cannot be proven. More burials in similar circumstances are required.

At Intiqawarina #620, the remains of five burials (six individuals) were found (Durand and Verastegui 2009). They include two primary burials, one of a woman and child interred in the patio and the other, an unsexed adult, inside a building, while there are three accumulations of human bone, probable secondary burials, all of which were found in the patio. The grave goods were relatively poor with both types, ranging from a few sherds and a spindle whorl to nothing. At the San Agustín hotel site (mz15), an adult male has been found buried in or adjacent to a *kancha* building in the northeastern corner. He was associated with inka pottery, including a decorated *maka*, two polychrome jars, a bronze *tumi*, and four stone tools, while a human maxilla was found nearby (El Comercio 10/11/09; Andina 10/14/2009).

The excavations in the Beaterio de las Nazarenas (mz12) uncovered only two burials, both located in corner spaces between *kancha* buildings (Colque 2001). These were an infant in the northeast corner of *kancha* 1 and an older child in the southeastern space of *kancha* 2 (figure 8.15). In addition, there were two other concentrations of human bone: a small group in the second patio of *kancha* 1, and the upper maxilla and teeth of an adult against the rear wall of a structure on the western side of *kancha* 2. All four were missing several bones, and their state of conservation was poor. Given that these are locations similar to those at Kusikancha and Tumibamba and that the patio sediments had been considerably disturbed, it can be concluded that all were probably burials. The two children were associated with similar grave goods, including potsherds, spondylus shell, and a metal object, as well as charcoal and ash, although the infant also had a quartz scraper, a slate polisher, and a bone spindle whorl (Colque 2001). The adult had fragments of a corroded copper needle and a piece of textile, stained green by a copper *tupu*.

The excavations in Casa del Almirante (mz10) yielded no identifiable graves, merely a collection of sixty-eight human bones, scattered through the mixed stratigraphy of several excavation units (Zapata 1993). Two clusters of human bone can be recognized. One was a minor grouping of seven bones in adjacent squares in Trench 4, while the other was a group of forty-one bones found in two contexts of three adjacent units toward the eastern side of the block. A number of walls and footings made of inka worked stones were located in these units but were considered to be colonial constructions or modifications. While the *kancha* plan is not known precisely, this location could be considered a corner space, if the distribution of colonial buildings reflected the original inka arrangement and had reutilized inka footings. These excavations yielded 4,500 inka plain and decorated sherds, over 87% of the total, as well as a *mutka*.

Elsewhere in the residential sectors, two other burials merit attention. There was a prepared 1.5m deep pit burial found in the patio of Amargura #107, directly behind Qasana (mz8). It contained the remains of an adult with a *maka*, three plates, and a pedestalled pot (Zanabria 1998b). In recent excavations in Hotel El Arqueológico on the corner of Pumacurco and Ladrillos (mz28), inka walls of a probable *kancha* building were found associated with a pot burial, consisting of a large *urpu*, with the remains of a male child with some metal goods and a small *urpu* (Farfán pers. comm.).

This evidence demonstrates that men, women, and children were buried in similar ways in most residential areas. The assemblage patterns suggest similar funeral rituals for the people who lived and worked in these areas, while none can be considered elaborate or rich. These seem to be ordinary people who were buried near where they had lived and worked, with few personal possessions and some offerings. The evidence confirms a burial ritual in which they were carefully dressed and prepared in the usual inka sitting position with knees drawn up to the chest and placed in a small round pit. From the charcoal and ash deposits, food was probably prepared for the guests at the grave side and was also placed in the grave for the deceased. Finally, the grave was ritually filled, perhaps in distinctive layers, and grave goods were carefully placed on the tomb floor and at appropriate levels during this process. The tomb was capped with something solid, such as a sherd or a stone, and the floor was repaired.

Hatunkancha Graves

As argued earlier, Hatunkancha was an important residential compound for the inka elite and *aqllakuna*. It is known that a deep shaft tomb of an Inka queen (*Qoya*) was found on the property of Diego Maldonado during the sixteenth century. However, its major excavations have yielded only two graves with no other references to finds of human bone. These tombs were both found in Casa Concha in 2006 and have not yet been published. The first is that of an adult male, who was found in a seated position with an arrangement of fourteen classic inka pots and a single chimú vessel among the grave goods. In terms of the quality of the decoration and iconography as well as their placement around the front of the body, Luis Cuba, the excavation director, suggested that this was the grave of an inka noble (Andina 07/19/2006).

The second included the skeletal remains of a 2-year-old alongside the remains of a young woman (Andina 09/10/2006) (figure 9.4). A total of twenty-six objects were carefully arranged as offerings in the tomb in front of the two seated individuals, including ceramics, such as *maka*, plates, and a pedestalled pot, of which there were four pairs of small items and

Figure 9.4. Grave found in Casa Concha (photo by Andina).

two pairs of wooden vessels (plates and *qero*). Bronze *tupu* had pinned their clothing together. According to Cuba, the quality of the goods associated with the child implies membership of the inka nobility, accompanied by either its mother or nanny, as the adult's status cannot be determined. He added that the child's elevated social status was confirmed because the grave was in Hatunkancha.

Both graves are more elaborate than any found in Kusikancha, and again it is tempting to consider the possibility that they are those of the elite. However, more needs to be published and comparisons made with Tumibamba and other locations.

Burials in Significant Locations

A number of interesting burials have been found in culturally important places within the city, such as the area surrounding Qorikancha; the two plazas with *usnu* complexes; on terraces overlooking Hawkaypata and the city; and adjacent to other known shrines and ritual locations. This section will consider whether these were standard urban burials or whether they were ritual offerings as part of the ceremonial landscape of the city.

Qorikancha was the most significant place in the city, and it had become a destination for pilgrims from throughout Tawantinsuyu. Excavations within it have yielded at least one collection of forty fragments of human bone in Pit 4 in the northwestern corner of the alcove (Béjar 1990: 72). This is a standard urban burial location, but it was not recorded as such because of the disturbed deposits and the disposition of the bones themselves. Yet it was associated with killke and inka potsherds, an alpaca head carved from crystal quartz, some camelid bones, a bone spoon, and a fossilized shell, all of which can be considered as offerings or grave goods. Other contexts in the temple patio there are offerings, formal ritualized arrangements of material, associated with selected human skeletal elements (see chapter 11).

In the immediate temple environs, several burials and a large number of offerings have been dug, including ceremonial placements of human bones and artifacts on the terraces on the southern side and in Intipampa to the west. Burials have been discovered in two locations. One was dug by Dominican monks in the southeast corner of the Canchón to the east of Qorikancha. It contained a bird-handled plate, a jar, and two gold *tupu* as grave goods (Rowe 1944: 46). On the Arrayan terraces to the southwest, a number of burials were found in the 1990s, including adults and children. For example, there was a child's grave on the upper terrace. while on the second level at a depth of 4.7m there were two tombs, displaying similar orientations, facing southeast (Fernández pers. comm.). One contained the remains of an adult male with a bronze *tupu* and bone beads who was accompanied by four plates, a large *maka*, a ceramic *qero*, and other pottery. The second was an adolescent with turquoise and spondylus beads and metal *tupu*, who was interred with a *maka*, several plates, a pedestalled pot, and a chimú stirrup spout bottle, placed upside down.

Although the two plazas and *usnu* complexes were very important locations for public ceremony and offering, neither the excavations in Hawkaypata nor in Limaqpampa yielded any human remains. However, on their peripheries, there have been some discoveries. For example, near Hawkaypata, two child crania were found in the *kancha* area of Amarukancha, and at least one tomb was discovered in San Juan de Dios adjacent to Kusipata (Zapata pers. comm.). In addition, a probable inka gravelot was discovered in Casa Trelles (mz18), which, when acquired by the museum in the 1930s, contained four *maka* and two pedestalled pots but no human remains (Museo Inka Inventory 61/1849–54).

At least two burials have been found in the vicinity of Limaqpampa. The first came from a property in Abracitos and included a human cranium, a small *urpu*, two miniature bowls, and the base of a pedestalled pot (Museo Inka Inventory 65/1895–1900), while the other was dug during construction of the Estadio Universitario. The second was rather rich with several personal items, including three bronze and two silver *tupu*, some bronze needle shafts, a pair of bronze *aqorasi,* and a trapezoidal spondylus shell bead as well as eight complete pots: a decorated face neck jar, a *maka* without its neck and rim, a neckless bottle, and five plates, with miscellaneous sherds and some decorated necks (Museo Inka Inventory 60/1731–36, 60/1743–53).

In 2009 during excavations in Triunfo street, Carlos Rosell discovered a disturbed funerary context, containing three crania and many post-cranial bones, 65cm below the modern street surface (Andina 07/16/2009). It is not known what grave goods, if any, were found.

The slopes surrounding the city to the north, west, and southwest were extensively terraced in inka times. Such flights were not for agriculture but for aesthetic reasons, serving to domesticate the abrupt, savage landscape and place the city within a well-managed human environment. As we shall see, in several places suburban villages and storerooms were built on them, while one significant trait is that several inka tombs and offerings were also deposited in them, as if to look over the city as symbolic defenders.

One of these was a burial found at Waynapata, the major terrace above and to the northwest of Hawkaypata. In September 1957, municipal workmen, digging a trench to install a water pipe, discovered a tomb at a depth of 1.5m below street level. Luis Pardo (1959) oversaw its rescue excavation. It was particularly rich, consisting of an adult skeleton, probably male, with personal items and many grave goods. Beside the skull was a finely decorated *raki* with modeled feline handles, and between it and the cranium were a *maka* and a pedestalled pot, while at the foot were two plates and a miniature jar (*aysana*), a lid, and a ceramic spindle whorl as well as numerous sherds from bird-handled plates. Other finds included the remains of a wooden *qero*, a wooden spoon, two bone spoons, two *ruki*, and other worked bone. Among the personal items there were fragments of brown woolen textile, a silver *tupu*, several bronze items, including five *tupu*, many shaft fragments, two *aqorasi*, three small cylinders, three copper *tumi*, and a stone knife. There were also the remains of a necklace with a stone pendant and both round and trapezoidal spondylus beads and fourteen small fish carved in spondylus. Food had been placed on one plate, as it was full of cockroaches.

The inka city contained numerous venerated *waka*. They included natural features, such as springs, fountains, stones, carved rocks, and elements of the built environment, including *usnu* platforms, its erect rocks, the Qasana doorway, the plaza itself, and places where important individuals had slept, rested, or had some association. One such location was Pumaqchupan, the narrow ridge of land between the two rivers near the confluence at the southeastern end of the city. It had a hut in which the remains of all burnt offerings and ashes from every sacrifice were stored until shortly after the December solstice, when these were ritually thrown into the river during the Mayucati ceremony (Molina 1989: 114–17).

In 1942, during leveling and soil removal works at Pumaqchupan prior to urbanization, three tombs and various offerings were found, only 200m from the entrance to the railway station (Llanos 1943). There were two urn burials. An infant had been interred at a depth of 70cm in a small, polished, dark red-brown and cream pot with handles covered by a stone slab, but without grave goods. The second was a large neckless *maka* that contained an adult cranium with tabular oblique deformation and no grave goods. The third grave was described as intrusive because the body position was horizontal, not an inka trait, but it was associated with an inka pot and sherds from an incised black vessel from the Chincha valley. As this was not a scientific excavation, Llanos had to rely on a witness description for body position, and given its location and grave goods, it could be an inka burial in which the body had simply fallen backwards during burial. This was found with a cache of many prestigious objects, including silver banners thought to have been used in inka processions.

At the northwestern end of the city alongside the river Tullumayu, there is a large carved limestone outcrop called Sapantiana, which has been substantially defaced over the centuries. It was originally surrounded by a limestone wall, zigzagged on its southwestern side, and with two small structures on its summit. In the 1930s during conservation work, some human remains, perhaps from a looted tomb, were found (Valcárcel 1935: 5).

Burials and Society

For many archaeological sites, cultures, or periods, burial analyses have traditionally provided the archaeologist with opportunities to evaluate the varied nature of the tomb, the body, its personal possessions, and grave goods in order to offer some understanding of local social organization. While these attempts have had varied interpretative success, one must always be cautious about the extent to which such conclusions should be taken (e.g., Parker-Pearson 1999). Many assumptions are made about the quality, quantity, and size of tomb architecture, personal dress, and grave goods, believing these, as in our own society, to be indicative of the wealth and social status of the dead person. However, they make this exercise fraught with difficulties.

Inka society was not driven by the imperatives of western economics and the accumulation of private wealth. Social position was a function of proximity to the main line descent. How status was gained or manifest, while generally understood from the documents, is not subtle enough to permit confidence in the results of burial analysis. The study of inka burials is therefore notorious because many members of the society were never interred per se. As described earlier, the Sapa Inka, his Qoya, and other nobles were not buried in the ground but "mummified" and kept "alive" in an ancestral "house," where they continued to participate in many aspects of life. The bulk of the population in Cusco and the inka heartland likewise were not buried but simply placed in a *machay* or *chullpa*. Therefore, for the archaeologist, both the upper echelon of inka society as well as its peasantry were never buried and would be missing from any analysis, unless there were sufficient recordings of such "open air" locations.

Yet, as we have seen, there is evidence from the city that some people were buried, while the results from Tumibamba, Saqsaywaman, and other places provide a limited comparative set of graves. The questions of who those people were and why they were buried, while much of the population was not, need to be resolved prior to any social assessment. In order to establish some motivation for burial, we need to consider several basic parameters, such as location, tomb architecture, and content.

In Inka society, the basic social groupings were the *ayllu* and the *panaqa*. These institutions gave all members rights to land and resources as well as obligations of communal duty, tribute, and labor. Almost certainly, membership also granted them rights to be placed with their ancestors in their group's "cemetery," that is, in caves, overhangs, boulders, and *chullpa* in their own territory. Those people, who were brought to Cusco as *yanakuna* or *aqllakuna* in the service of the Inka and the Sun, had been removed from their homelands and *ayllu*. They had lost all connection with their ancestors, *ayllu,* and lands and therefore upon death they probably were disposed in the places where they lived and worked because they had no rights in Cusco. In the urban residential *kancha*, the simple pit burials followed a set of basic rituals in acceptable places chosen among the houses. While this pattern is echoed at Tumibamba and to some extent at Qosqo Ayllu but not at Patallaqta or Machu Picchu, the reasons for such discrepancy could be practical, such as a lack of suitable cliffs, rocks, or overhangs, but more probably a lack of cultural access to such areas.

In order for inka society and government to function efficiently, the inkas also made offerings to their deities of men, women, and children. Such sacrifices were often made and buried in prominent natural places, on terraces, adjacent to temples and to *waka*. These individuals could have been buried with an array of high status goods or none at all, depending on the nature of the ritual.

The archaeology from Kusikancha demonstrates a society with a majority of females, perhaps a workforce of *yanakuna*, who worked for the state in a social group in which everyone was treated more or less the same. A similar picture emerges from Tumibamba, where in the sector Aqllawasi Oriental, the sex ratio was ten females to each male (Idrovo 2000). The type of personal items and grave goods interred with each individual may reflect their positions in the work hierarchy or simply gifts they may have received. Indeed, both Kusikancha and Tumibamba have graves that, in proportion, display a similar distribution of materials. In both over half were buried without any ceramics, and the remainder were accompanied by up to nine vessels, although at Tumibamba there was only one elaborate grave. In both sites, those identified as males consistently have few or no ceramics, although the one in Tumibamba has various gold items (Idrovo 2000).[7]

Despite the imbalanced sex ratio, there seem to have been some sort of family life at Kusikancha, where children from neonates to teenagers were found as well as a restricted number of adult males with proportionally more grave goods. This pattern is partly confirmed by the evidence from Nazarenas. The keeping and burial of pet dogs adds to an understanding of such a way of life.

It has been argued that the two burials in Casa Concha indicate a status difference between those who resided in Hatunkancha and those from the *kancha,* because the former had many more pots as grave goods. This may confirm the assumption, derived from the chronicles, that this was an elite compound. However, one interesting feature is that the most elaborate burial from either Hatunkancha and Kusikancha is an adult female with child. The excavator commented that most of the artifacts seemed to be associated with the child, who was therefore born into a high status position. There may be other plausible explanations, but more research is necessary.

Elsewhere in the city, burials have been found in a variety of tomb forms and also in nonresidential locations adjacent to important places, such as Qorikancha, the plazas, *waka,* and the city in general. While the range of grave goods remained similar and their quantity and quality is not significantly different, it is only their location that distinguishes them from those buried in the *kancha.* Therefore, it can be concluded that these burials must represent some form of offering and veneration. There is no specific evidence from any of these to suggest that they had been sacrificed for this purpose, but it is a possibility, although ordinary individuals who had recently died could have been used for this purpose. More careful archaeology is needed to resolve these issues.

Discussion

The excavations in the city have provided a few glimpses into certain aspects of the daily life of its inhabitants. This is particularly true where housing stock is more or less standardized and arranged in *kancha.* These units housed mainly communities of women, but there were some men, children, and their dogs to indicate that for some there was a family life. The *kancha* were used for all aspects of life from the domestic arrangements of sleeping and cooking to local level entertainment, ritual, and burial. From the limited evidence to date, each *kancha* appears to have had at least one kitchen where food and *aqha* were prepared. Who these people were is not clear, but it seems that they made textiles and may have been engaged in other productive activities on behalf of the Inka or the state, not the least of which may have been the large-scale production of food and beer for various ceremonies. Therefore, it is probable that they were *yanakuna* or *aqllakuna*. This conclusion might explain why they were buried in the *kancha,* because their status means that they had lost connections to their own *ayllu* and therefore to community burial locations. On the basis of the excavated assemblages, it is clear that Kusikancha, Nazarenas, Casa del Almirante, Intiqawarina, and San Agustín were similar in activities and perhaps social makeup as well.

The evidence for craft activity remains equivocal. To date, no extensive areas have been found that would suggest large-scale textile production, potting, metal working, shell working, or lapidary making. There is some evidence that textiles were made at a household level, but whether or not this was coordinated is not known. The evidence for extensive food production and brewing to service ceremonies and rituals is not available, although the kitchens in Kusikancha could be viewed as part of a larger system.

The assemblages from Hatunkancha are not substantially different from those of the *kancha.* This was also an area of residence and craft activity, but by a different social group, and judging by the two burials at Casa Concha, it included men and women of higher status, although their identity remains unclear. It is possible that they belonged to the inka nobility, and there is documentary evidence that the *aqllawasi* also inhabited part of this compound. Hatunkancha was certainly different because it was a system of individual buildings, not a *kancha*-like arrangement, and it contained its own small plaza, flanked by two *kallanka.* The makeup of its population must await further detailed excavation in this area.

There has been too little excavation to detail the activities and social arrangements in the palaces of Qasana, Amarukancha, and Uchullo and the houses of Waskar, or even in the large halls that flanked them. Only the small excavations in Plateros and Procuradores and the few finds from the Compañía church indicate activities much like those described for Kusikancha, with some child burials in the very damaged stratigraphy of the church.

The documents clearly indicate a social division of the city into Hanan and Hurin, and there have been several attempts to indicate how much of the city belonged to either of these moieties. It is commonly divided at Hawkaypata to demonstrate that Hanan lay above the line of the street, Triunfo-Hatunrumiyoq, meaning plan-seam A, although it is more likely that the division was plan-seam B, with most of the city being allocated to Hanan and only the blocks to the southeast, plan-unit I, to Hurin. In terms of the archaeology, neither the architectural appearance nor the assemblages support any moiety division. There are variations in both across the city, but neither presents a definite boundary between one and the other. It is suggested that only the elite and their retainers, *yanakuna* and *aqllakuna*, lived in the city itself, while noble foreigners, ordinary local *ayllu* members, and *mitayoq* lived beyond the physical bounds of closed urban space in peripheral settlements of various types.

Hundreds of thousands of inka sherds have been found in Cusco, and it would be expected that certain vessel types or designs were found exclusively in particular areas. However, this is clearly not the case, for even comparatively rare pots decorated with figurative designs are found in most assemblages, indicating that the whole city was of a higher status than elsewhere in the heartland.

The *kancha* of three plan-units can be regarded as similar but distinct urban neighborhoods (Smith 2010), whereas Hatunkancha was organized quite differently architecturally and socially. How they functioned to support the palaces and temples is not known archeologically.

10

Suburbs and the Inner Heartland

The hinterland of Cusco, like that of other cities, was critical for supplying food and other resources to the capital, while its landscape features sustained the rituals and cultural hegemony of inka rule. Its role was manifold. It can be defined as the upper Watanay basin, covering an area of about 270 sqkm, that extends to the southeast as far as the Angostura, where the valley floor narrows to just 300m with abrupt slopes to the north and south (figure 10.1). Culturally, it is the area covered by the *seqe* system, also termed the Inner Heartland (Bauer 1998; Farrington 1992). It is presumed that this was the area remodeled by Pachakuti Inka Yupanki in order to redefine the relationship between the city and its hinterland (Betanzos 1996: 50–58). In the rural districts, this program involved two phases: the depopulation of an area of two leagues, 11km, around the city to allow the construction of new agricultural infrastructure, and the channelization of the rivers to control floods and create new agricultural lands through drainage. New canals, reservoirs, and terracing schemes were built, and swampy and seasonally wet ground was drained, particularly on the valley floor (Betanzos 1996: 50–55). New storehouses were erected, and it seems likely that new rural settlements were built. These lands were then allocated to the urban *panaqa* and *ayllu* as *chapa*, that is, long narrow tracts to be used for irrigation agriculture, dry farming, and pastures, in order that each group had access to a range of sustainable food and wool resources (Zuidema 1990).

The system of 328 *waka*, arranged along forty-one lines or *seqe* that radiated from Qorikancha, can be used to provide a spatial division of the Inner Heartland (Farrington 1992). Although both Niles (1987) and Bauer (1998) have argued that the individual *seqe* were not straight, neither has established a precise location for every shrine or shrine toponym nor the original place-name of each carved rock to deny the veracity of Cobo's and Molina's statements about straightness.[1] Indeed, the boundaries of the four quarters can be delimited as straight and that the alignment of certain *seqe* can also be used to identify the irrigation districts of Hanan Cusco because they often intersect with an intake, spring, or other significant point along a canal system (Sherbondy 1982; Zuidema 1986, 1990). The responsibility for the maintenance of certain *seqe* and shrines logically indicates who had access to particular land and water resources. On the basis of her analyses of the lands and waters of both Sucsu and Aucaille *panaqa* in Antisuyu and the boundary between them, Jeanette Sherbondy (1982: 85–92) has laid down principles by which the lands of each *panaqa* can be identified by mapping its first and last *seqe*.

In the next two chapters, I explore the relationship between the city and its social groups with the hinterland. First, I present evidence for different settlement types that were important for the functioning of the city, capital, and state, and the distribution of land resources. Second, I examine the incorporation of that landscape into the ritual sphere of the city by the examination of shrines (*waka*) and origin places (*paqarina*).

In 1982, the INC-Catastro researchers completed an archaeological field survey of the valley, recording and mapping a large number of inka and earlier sites, including terraces, channelization schemes, canals, reservoirs, carved rocks, *kancha*, isolated buildings, small towns (*llaqta*), storerooms (*qolqa*) and tombs (Orellana pers. comm.). In recent years, Brian Bauer (2004) has also conducted an intensive site survey, finding evidence of buildings and sherd scatters for 114 inka period settlements larger than 0.25ha, many of which also yielded killke sherds. He recorded 16 large sites with a surface area of between 5ha and 10ha, 23 medium sites (1ha to 5ha), and 75 small sites (0.25ha to 1ha). While it has become standard practice for archaeologists to use such areal measurements to determine site hierarchy, it masks the range of site types that they themselves might differ in cultural importance from the "bigger is more important" logic. This is particularly so, when it is remembered that the inkas were not organized, according to the laws of western economics, but that there were other priorities for the state, its king, nobility, and general population that laid cultural emphasis on particular places in landscape, not just those that were extensive. Perceiving what those priorities were and how they were manifest is addressed, but not solved, in this and subsequent chapters.

Previously I have argued that there must have been important cultural motives for the distribution of different types of site and settlement in the Inner Heartland and that this is a function of the territorial division between the four *suyu*, their social groupings, and their cultural obligations

(Farrington 1992). For example, village settlement is highly localized with very little in Chinchaysuyu, where sites are mainly of a ritual nature, although there are several planned villages further downvalley in both Antisuyu and Qollasuyu and another close to the city in Kuntisuyu (Niles 1987). Similarly, all carved rocks are found in the *suyu* of Hanan on the north side of the river, yet none at all in Hurin, although the distribution of stone *waka* were roughly equal in both areas.

Suburban Villages

The suburban villages lie just outside the built-up area of the old city and were separated from it by terraces, fields, and rivers (figure 10.1). They were rapidly absorbed into the colonial urban sprawl of Cusco and details of their extent have been lost. For example, Qolqampata is located only a short distance above Waynapata, while rivers and terraces divide Toqokachi and Qoripata from the city. Despite such spatial separation, the city was integrated with these settlements that serviced its institutions and those of the state. The inkas seem to have permitted those who served them in the city to occupy these villages. Their inhabitants probably included some *panaqa* members, local non-inka *ayllu*, such as the original inhabitants, inkas-by-privilege from the nearby heartland, as well as foreign dignitaries, who had come from the provinces to pay homage to the Sapa Inka, to worship at Qorikancha, and to participate in the daily, calendrical, and other ceremonies held in Hawkaypata. However, during certain festivals, such as *sitwa*, all foreigners were required to leave the city. What this means is uncertain, but I suspect that it probably refers only to what I have called the old city. If so, then foreigners would have needed only to retreat to their suburban houses until that ceremony had been completed.

Garcilaso (1966: Bk. 7 ch. VIII) listed twelve such settlements, which were located up to 1,000 paces from the city, including Carmenqa (Santa Ana), Wakapunku, Qolqampata-Chocopata (San Cristóbal), Toqokachi (San Blas), Munaysenqa (Recoleta), Cayaokachi (Belén), Chakillchaka (Santiago), and Picchu (see Chávez 1970; Rowe 1968). These places survived the Spanish invasion and remained integral to urban life, providing the labor force during much of the sixteenth century. They also became the focus of the native parish policy, when churches were built in 1559 and 1572 (Julien 1998).

The ethnohistorical documents record that craft *mitmaqkuna* from the Chinchaysuyu provinces were housed in Carmenqa after their arrival in

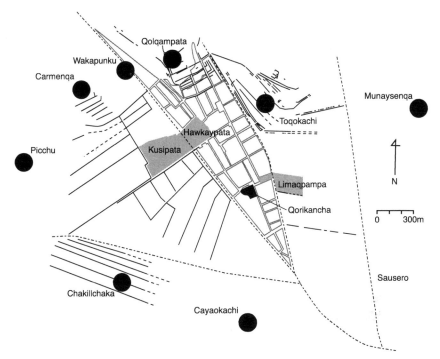

Figure 10.1. The suburban villages and terraces.

Cusco. In other words, they lived and worked in a suburb in the *suyu* of which they were native and close to the main *qhapaq ñan* from that quarter.[2] Following this principle, then it could be argued that those from Antisuyu settled in San Blas and Recoleta, from Qollasuyu in San Sebastián, and from Kuntisuyu in Cayaokachi and Chakillchaka as well as in Choqo and Cachona.

Qolqampata (San Cristóbal)

Qolqampata is situated about 25m above the city on several broad terraces where the gradient is less steep (figure 10.2). It was separated from both Waynapata below and Saqsaywaman above by narrow terraces but is now integrated into the urban area. In inka times, this prominent location, overlooking the city, became a royal suburb. Bauer (2004: 136) noted that it was associated with the conquest period kings—Manqo II, Paullu Inka, and Carlos Inka—but it probably had a much longer history. The palace contained the smallest of the large halls, reported by Garcilaso (1966: 320–21). Other chronicle evidence states that it housed the fourth *waka* on

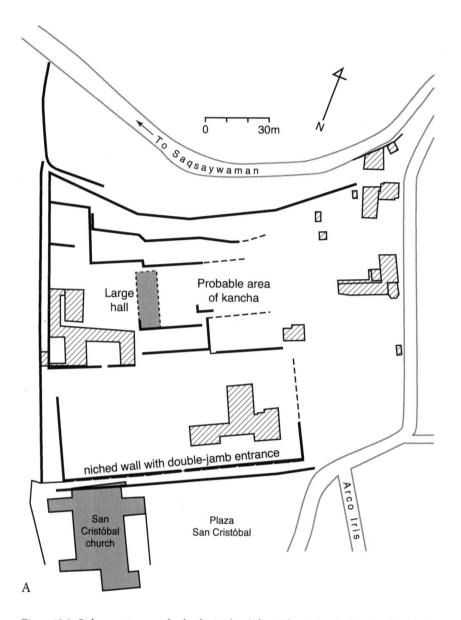

Figure 10.2. Qolqampata, a royal suburb. *A*, plan (after Valencia 1984: plano 2); *B*, niched wall and entrance; *C*, large hall façade.

B

C

the fourth *seqe* of Chinchaysuyu (CH-4:4), a stone, which was ordered to be worshipped by Pachakuti Inka (Cobo 1990: 56), while Sarmiento (2007: 187) wrote that the palace had been built by Waskar.

The site stretches upslope in a flight of terraces with three broad open level areas. The original retaining wall for the lowest level has been destroyed by road construction, although it is upon this that the church of

San Cristóbal was built by Paullu Inka in the 1540s. Behind this, there is a narrow retaining terrace, entered via a ramp on its north end, and a monumental wall. The latter is made of polygonal limestone, stands 3.65m high, and is divided into two equal lengths of 52.5m (32.5r) by a double-jamb doorway with six full-length, double-jamb niches, equidistantly placed, in each half (Agurto 1980). Such a wall with outward facing niches is typical of rural palace complexes in the Yucay area (Farrington 1995). It also has side walls that define the complex width. A ramp leads from the doorway to the middle terrace level, which is devoid of structures (Valencia 1984). The next terrace wall has a segmented form close to the center with a colonial hacienda building to its south, while it is only 10m in front of another wall that supports the final level upon which there are major structural remains. Its only standing architecture is a magnificent rectangular andesite façade of a large hall. It comprises the southern part of a single wall, 3.6m tall, erected on limestone footings. Its southern corner is intact, and between it and a double-jamb doorway there is a standard trapezoidal window. The wall continues for only about 1.5m beyond the door; however, examination of the footings indicates that the building had a width of 9.7m (6r), which means that the door was exactly in the center and that, using the inka principles of symmetry, there would have been another window on the northern side. Such a façade is typical of the large halls that recorded elsewhere (Farrington 1995; see chapter 3). Given that this terrace is only 27.5m wide, the hall must have been quite small, probably only about 25.85m (16r) in length; it is similar in size and vista to the one found at Canchispuqyo (table 2.7).

In 1974, as part of PER-39, Alfredo Valencia (1984) conducted a limited excavation program in which only 62sqm were dug in eight trenches, in order to gather architectural and cultural information. He found the footings of the eastern wall of the main building around 9.6m from the western wall and also footings parallel to the façade, but only a few meters from it. The latter, if supporting a wall, would have made the building too small for such a façade; it was probably the wall of a construction cell that provided the stable building platform. There were no excavations to determine the actual building length. Valencia (1984) also discovered wall footings and a corner to the north, which indicate that, like rural palace locations, several structures lay alongside this large hall, perhaps in a *kancha*. The finds consisted of much inka pottery, but also some qotakalli period sherds, three bronze *tupu*, camelid bone *ruki* and a bone bead.

Beyond the palace area there have been several other excavation programs. In the church, Martín-Rubio, excavating a crypt beneath the altar, recovered the remains of an adult male whom she believed to be Paullu Inka, a young woman, two older women, and two small children, lying on their backs, facing southeast, and hands crossed on the chest (Andina 09/13/2007). Only two inka traits can be observed: the women were surrounded by a circle of stones, and there was a dog skull accompanying them.

Julinho Zapata (1998a) excavated four trenches in a steeply sloping vacant lot below the church and road (mz9C). While this had been used as a dump for a long time, republican period terrace walls were found that reused inka stone blocks. There was only one short length of well-fitting limestone wall set in a mud mortar, which was an original terrace, but there was no evidence for any inka buildings. It seems that inka walls had been dismantled and the blocks reused during later periods for retention terraces. The material culture was very mixed, containing thousands of fragments of colonial and modern tiles as well as many inka potsherds and a few killke ones. The inka assemblage included decorated fragments of jars, *maka, qero,* and *urpu,* with not only geometric but also figurative designs.

In excavations at Teqseqocha #256 (mz25), Italo Oberti (2002) also demonstrated that four polygonal limestone terraces on the southern side were not occupied by structures during the inka period but remained green space, separating Qasana from Qolqampata. In the early colonial period, they were simply built over for housing as streets and gardens were formed. While he found lucre, killke and inka pottery, mixed with materials of later periods, the total amount was very small in contrast to that exposed by Zapata (1998a).

Above and to the southwest of Qolqampata lies the Colegio Salesiano, a school first built in that location, known as Choqopata, in 1905. The suburb probably extended over its terraces. Construction of school buildings and infrastructure required archaeological intervention in 1998, 2000, and 2002 (Aguilar 2002). Each project demonstrated mixed deposits, ranging from killke through to modern, and each also defined inka terrace walls, made from pillowed limestone blocks laid in a polygonal style on limestone footings. House footings were also found. The first stage of the site formation sequence was the dismantling of any inka standing structures and the upper terrace courses, which allowed slopewash to bury the remains. Second, retention walls were built occasionally over the next 400 years on top of this fill, leaving the inka vestiges deeply buried. Aguilar (2002) found an inka burial against terrace footings in T-RA at a depth of 2.88m, containing a male and a female, both aged between 50 and 60 years, and seated side by side, facing west. The grave goods included inka potsherds, five copper *tupu*, some rectangular beads, spondylus shell, and an obsidian flake associated with the person on the left; the other had no grave goods. In 2000, Zanabria noted that among the ceramics were provincial sherds, including chimú, taraco, and chucuito, that had perhaps been placed in offerings to overlook the city (Aguilar 2002).

Wakapunku

The suburb of Wakapunku was located on either side of the Saphi river between the rear wall of Qasana and the road to Carmenqa and Chinchaysuyu, but its full extent is not known. According to Garcilaso (1966: 425), it was associated with the place of learning, *yachaywasi*, and it extended over the terraces as far as Qolqampata and Choqopata. In 1534, some Spaniards took property in this area.

There have been only three archaeological excavations in this area, and none have produced inka structural evidence. The first was in association with the restoration of Casa Tigre on the corner of Tigre and Saphi (Zapata 1992), which encountered very mixed deposits. There was evidence for an intensive inka occupation, with many potsherds from *maka*, jars, *urpu*, plates, and bowls, identified in the three decorative styles (A, B, C), as well as animal bone in charcoal and ash lenses and at least one piece of spondylus. While no specific inka structural evidence was found, two footings and a stone-lined canal have inka characteristics but have alignments different from the standing colonial building.

The second was conducted by Zanabria (1998b) and Mormontoy in the rooms and patio of a colonial house at Amargura #107. They encountered a disturbed inka occupation, revealing no structural evidence but more than 500 sherds, mainly Inka A and B, with only one killke fragment and animal bones. A chimú blackware two-handled dish was found, probably part of an offering, and in the patio, an adult cranium with long bones was discovered in an unlined 1.5m deep pit, with grave goods including a *maka*, three plates, and a pedestalled pot.

In 1996, about 500m further up Saphi on inka terraces, Claudio Cumpa excavated an elaborate tomb that contained a seated adult male with his legs stretched in front. Among the grave goods were several fine ceramics, including a decorated *maka* and a pedestalled pot, beads, and several metal items (Gunduz pers. comm.).

Carmenqa (Santa Ana)

Carmenqa lies on a bluff above Kusipata and the Saphi river, at a point where the road from Chinchaysuyu descends toward Wakapunku. According to several sixteenth-century documents, it was the location where craftsmen and their families from Chinchaysuyu provinces, such as Chimú, Chachapoyas, and Ischma, were settled by the inkas (e.g., Espinosa Soriano 1983). The church of Santa Ana was constructed in 1560, probably on top of an important *waka*, probably Marcatampu (CH-7:3), which had only round stones (Cobo 1990: 59).

There have been several excavations in the vicinity of the church. First, Valencia discovered that it stands on a platform, surrounded by limestone polygonal terraced walls, and in 1993, work in the plazuela revealed inka pottery as well as animal and human bones (Bustinza 2008). At least two inka burials were discovered among many colonial interments: an adult female placed in a large *urpu* with a gold *tupu* and turquoise and shell beads, and a child, also in an *urpu* (Paredes pers. comm.). Recent excavations, both outside and inside the church, have revealed a dense layer of inka pottery, associated with charcoal, ash, calcined animal bones, and spondylus shell, that had been perforated many times by colonial burials (Bustinza 2008). Stratigraphical analysis has revealed that an original inka foundation trench had been robbed to build the church; it was associated with an inka floor, clay oven, camelid bone, and sherds. It had also been cut by the construction of the church and the subsequent burials. The suburban extent along the ridge has not been determined, although there is inka ceramic and architectural evidence in mz55.

Above Carmenqa, adjacent to the inka road, two offerings have been found that overlook the city, Saqsaywaman, and the Saphi valley. First, Alfredo Valencia (1979: 13–14) reported the discovery of a 25cm long bronze bar, an item occasionally associated with an inka burial or offering, in a road cutting at Chanapata in 1969. Second, during the digging foundation trenches for a house at Tica Tica in 1998, an important offering was encountered in an unlined pit, about 1.5m below the surface (Miranda pers. comm.). It included a spondylus anthropomorphic figurine, a gold llama figurine, two bronze *tupu* over 20cm in length and a miniature one, four bronze needles, a bronze *tumi* with llama bone handle, a miniature polished stone bowl, a miniature ceramic plate and bowl, two whole spondylus valves, and an unfinished brown woolen textile with several balls of wool.

Toqokachi (San Blas)

San Blas lies on inka terraces on the north side of the Tullumayu and stretches upslope toward Qenqo. It includes an area called Kantupata, which Chávez (1970: 9) listed as a separate suburb to the west. The area around the church was probably the location of the Inti Illapa shrine (CH-2:3), a temple where the Thunder god was venerated and children were sacrificed (Cobo 1990: 54), and it was where the mummy of Pachakuti Inka Yupanki was found (Sarmiento 2007: 155). Unfortunately, there is no evidence for any inka buildings, although there are carved rocks further east at Mesa Redonda and Titiqaqa. Both the Morris (1967) survey and the recent one by Paredes (1999) have revealed surface ceramics across this area, but it is impossible to gauge their meaning.

There have been few excavations, although some archaeological finds have been made. The most notable is the burial of an adult male, found on an inka terrace, in Suytuqhato behind the church, during trenching for house foundations. Raymundo Béjar (1976) reported that it was indicated by a circle of pebbles and limestone pieces, 3.9m in diameter with a large green diorite rock (1.1 × 0.9m) in the middle. The latter covered a 1.2m deep pit, containing the seated skeleton of a 30-year-old male, facing north. He was accompanied by only two pots: a finely decorated, flat-bottomed bottle placed on the left-hand side and a decorated *maka* about 45cm in front. Another significant find is a 2.3cm high bronze figurine of a male blowing a trumpet at La Calera above San Blas (Museo Inka Inventory 33/929).

Munaysenqa (Recoleta)

Inka roads from Antisuyu entered the valley from the northeast and descended toward the Recoleta monastery and hacienda, where the village of Munaysenqa was probably located. It is situated on an alluvial fan at the foot of a steep slope and immediately below the carved rock, Titiqaqa. In the 1960s this area still contained the remains of stone structures and inka sherd scatters and its slopes were part of Morris's probable *qolqa* zone; however, it has been significantly urbanized in recent years. In 1905 Max Uhle excavated in this vicinity, and while there is no report, his finds included a *maka* decorated with maize plants, a decorated loop handled pot, three bronze *tupu* and a large needle, a flaked silex knife, and two marine shells (Valencia 1979). These are largely complete and must have been recovered from a grave or an offering, but context is not known.

Cayaokachi (Belén)

Cayaokachi was located in the modern hilltop suburb of Qoripata and was the location of the first Belén church (Rowe 2003a). It was also where the mummy and *wawki* of the fourth Inka, Mayta Qhapaq, were found in 1559 (Cobo 1979: 120).[3] Although this was a significant inka suburban village, prior to recent urbanization, there are few architectural traces but only a dense sherd scatter (Cumpa 1988). It has been investigated several times, mainly in rescue excavations, since the 1940s.

Rowe (1944: 43–44) dug a test pit near the fallen church tower, finding cultural deposits to a depth of 1.5m, but noting no clear stratigraphy. Nevertheless, he recovered over 8,600 sherds, of which the majority were inka. He also examined two child burials that had been badly damaged by road construction. In 1976–77 Miguel Cornejo and Percy Paz excavated in the El Olivo area, where they found sealed burial contexts and architecture (Cumpa 1988). This provoked the INC to declare Qoripata a "heritage reserve" in order to protect the undisturbed strata. However, ten years later when Santiago District Council leveled part for a football field, several burials, pots, and architectural remains were destroyed and many objects were looted. As a consequence, surface surveys were made from a 5,000sqm area, collecting more than 6,400 sherds, 60 lithic artifacts, and some worked bone, including *ruki* and spindle whorls (Cumpa 1988). Elements from the entire valley sequence were found, although killke, lucre, and inka sherds dominated.

In 1987, Wilfredo Yépez excavated in the southwestern area near the Guardia Civil post, where a kindergarten was under construction, discovering some architecture and an inka burial (Cumpa 1988). Finally, during works by Seda Qosqo along Francisco Bolognesi street, Zanabria (1997) did some rescue excavations. A 150m long trench had been cut through several funerary contexts, rubbish dumps, and pre-inka and inka structures. He expanded it in one location and at 75cm below the surface he found an adult interred in a large *urpu*. It was covered with a large sherd from the base of another *urpu*. The burial pot was broken, but contained ash, pieces of charcoal, a black sediment, and human bones of a seated individual, with a small polished stone bowl placed to its right.

All architectural remains in Qoripata are sub-surface and have been noted only in road cuttings or archaeological excavations. Three wall construction styles have been noted: *pirka* with either pebbles or quarried sandstone blocks in a mud mortar, and well-fitted polygonal limestone blocks. The hard clay sediment covering this area suggests that these structures had been topped with adobe brick, which has decayed *in situ*, burying the lower walls. Unfortunately, no individual buildings can be described.

Chakillchaka (Santiago)

This suburb also lay across the Chunchulmayu river, about 1km from the plaza and adjacent to the road from Kuntisuyu. It remained a focus for people of that *suyu*, becoming the location of a parish church in 1572. Covey (2009: 251) reported that it contained silversmiths from the "lowlands" who had been brought to Cusco by Wayna Qhapaq. It ceased to be a separate settlement in the late sixteenth century. There is no standing prehistoric architecture, and there are few records of discoveries. However, during 2009 the digging of trenches for a new Public Health Center in Tambopata, Urb. Dignidad Nacional, revealed and partly destroyed a fine rectangular inka wall of a building, 3m below the surface (El Sol 06/16/2009).

Picchu

With the expansion of the city to the southwest, in the late 1980s, a chapel was built on a hilltop to service the new Picchu suburb. Many archaeological finds were made during its construction, but unfortunately there is no record of their detailed context. Among the discoveries was a large decorated *urpu*, containing the skeleton of an adult male, associated with two small, finely decorated *maka*, five copper-silver *tupu* (two miniature and three regular), two figurines, a gold female, and a gold llama were also found in the foundation trenches for this chapel (Mormontoy pers. comm.).

Workers' Villages (*Llaqta*)

The workers' villages are located further out from Cusco at distances ranging from 2km to 13km; they are mainly downvalley with only two relatively close to the city (figure 10.3). These are generally well planned with a number of individual stone and adobe houses; they usually have a small

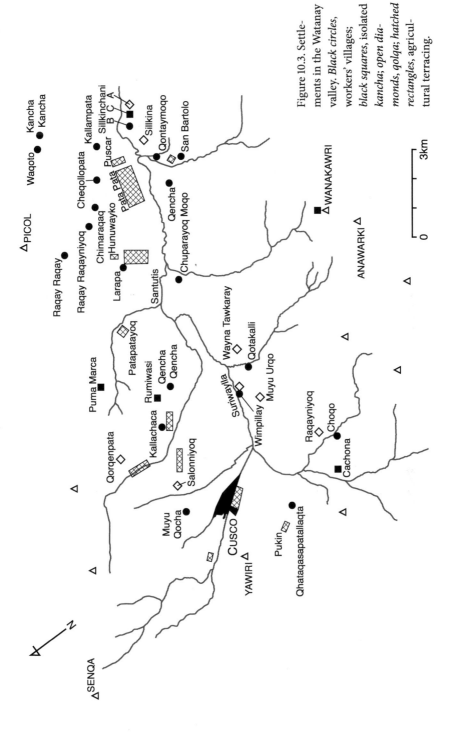

Figure 10.3. Settlements in the Watanay valley. *Black circles, workers' villages; black squares, isolated kancha; open diamonds, qolqa; hatched rectangles, agricultural terracing.*

plaza and, in some cases, a small *usnu* complex. The buildings are standard sizes, with a single door, and are arranged either in lines and rows with intervening streets or more randomly about paths on convenient slopes and terraces, with the door facing downhill. They are not surrounded by walls, such as the large urban enclosures and *kancha*. It seems probable that they housed either local *ayllu* or *mitayoq*, tribute laborers from provinces, such as Huánuco and Lupaqa, who were brought to Cusco to farm the lands of the Inka, *panaqa,* and the state, to herd their llamas and alpacas, and to quarry and transport building stone for the city. They were almost certainly allocated lands on which to cultivate their own foods.

The *llaqta* are not evenly distributed throughout the hinterland because of landownership and usufruct difficulties. On the northern side, the main ones are located in the foothills, adjacent to streams and alluvial fans between San Sebastián and the Angostura, and associated with the terraces of Choqekiraw, Larapa, and Pata Pata (table 10.1a). There are also several settlements in and around the andesite quarries at Waqoto and at Muyu Qocha, respectively. The geography of the southern side has many small streams and narrow valleys and therefore lacks major terrace schemes, but there are many small villages, overlooking the main and tributary valleys, and two larger ones, Qotakalli and Qhataqasapatallaqta (Claros and Mormontoy 1992) (table 10.1b). Their site catchments indicate that each was involved in intensive agriculture and grazing.[4]

Muyu Qocha

This 5ha village extends over two hilltops, close to Saqsaywaman and large limestone quarries. Rowe (1944: 50) reported the remains of many rectangular buildings that had been destroyed to make fields and that the surface was littered with inka sherds, while Bauer (2004: 104–5), in his site survey, confirmed its dense, exclusively inka occupation. Aerial photographs show a rectilinear plan with streets and at least 40 house locations (Servicio Aerofotográfico Nacional 21-6-1956: photo no. 8485-436); Bauer 2004: photo 9.9).

Raqay-Raqayniyoq

This village is located at an altitude of 3,480m in Hatun Wayqo above and 1km east of the Larapa Chico terraces (figure 10.4a). It comprises at least

Table 10.1a. Settlements in the north side of the Cusco valley

Site	Alt (m)	Type	Architecture (area)
Muyu Qocha	3,650	Village	40+ structures (5ha)
Raqay Raqay	3,650	Village	16 structures, plaza (2.3ha)
Raqay Raqayniyoq	3,480	Village	51 structures (3.5ha)
Chimaraqay	3,450	Village	23 structures (2.85ha)
Cheqollopata [PCZ-6–73]	3,370	Village	43 structures, 3 patios (3ha)
Kallampata	3,450	Village	19 structures, terraces (1.5ha)
Waqʼoto	4,000–4,140	Village, *kancha*, quarry	(5–10ha)
Kancha Kancha	4,100	Village, quarry	6 structures
Qencha Qencha [Rum-6]	3,470	Village, terraces	6 structures (3ha)
Larapa NW	3,440	artifact scatter	(5–10ha)
Patapatayoq	3,450	Terraces	21 terraces (10.5ha)
Larapa andenes	3,440	Terraces	35 terraces (650ha)
Hunu Wayku	3,425	Terraces	13 terraces (3ha)
Pata Pata	3,240	Terraces	30 terraces (715ha)
Puscar	3,370	Terraces	20 terraces (3.5ha)
Pumamarka	3,460	*Kancha*, temple	5 structures (1ha)
Rumiwasi [Rum-1]	3,450	Ancestral house, *kancha*	3 structures on rock, tunnel, niched walls, 2 structures and curved wall patio below
Rumiwasi-2	3,498	Isolated buildings	3 structures
Rumiwasi-3	3,560	Buildings	2 structures
Arkawasi [Rum-4]	3,568	*Kancha*	4 structures (1ha)
Kusikallanka [Rum-5]	3,570	*Kallanka* on platform; carved rock	2 structures
Qencha [Rum-6]	3,470	*Kancha*	6 structures
Qorqenpata	3,743	*Qolqa*	11 structures

fifty-one rectangular, gabled buildings that average 9.68m (6r) by 5.35m (3.3r), each with a single door on the southern side (Niles 1987: 31–37). They are built of quarried sandstone blocks set in a mud mortar, *pirka* style, up to 1.50m, with adobe bricks and internal trapezoidal niches on top. It was planned and constructed with no definite streets, as the houses are

Table 10.1b. Settlements in south side of the Cusco valley

Site	Alt (m)	Type	Architecture (area)
Qencha	3,270	Village	10 structures (1.5ha)
Roqueyoc Moqo or Sillkincha	3,200	Village, terraces	3 structures, terraces
San Bartolomé	3,280	Village	5+ structures
Qontaymoqo	3,200	Village	9 structures
Sillkinchani B	3,200	Village	5 structures
Cabra Q'asa	3,530	Artifact scatter	
Peqokaypata		Artifact scatter	(0.5ha)
Chuparayoq Moqo	3,270	Village, artifact scatter, cemetery	16 structures
Qotakalli	3,344	Village	83 structures (7.7ha)
Wimpillay	3,350	Village, artifact scatter	Some structures (6ha)
Qhataqasapatallaqta	3,510	Village	65 structures (20ha)
Cachona	3,550	Village, artifact scatter	Several structures (5ha)
Choqo	3,530	Artifact scatter	(5ha)
Pillawa	3,200	Cemetery	—
Rumitaqayoq	3,400	Terraces	23 terraces
Mesapata	3,350	Terraces	10 terraces
Churumoqo-Chacoyoc	3,400	Terraces	8 terraces, 1 structure (0.55ha)
Pukin	3,625	Terraces	9 terraces
Sillkinchani C	3,190	Kancha	6 structures, patio
Wanakawri	4,030	Kancha	7 structures, patio
Pukakancha	3,350	Kancha	3 structures, patio
Sillkinchani A	3,250	Qolqa	9 structures
Sillkina	3,400	Qolqa	10+ structures
Wayna Tawqaray	3,350	Qolqa	8 structures
Muyu Urqo	3,350	Qolqa	Structures
Pukinkancha	3,680	Temple	Not known

arranged in short rows on terraces (figure 10.4a). A small stream divides it into two sectors, while a reservoir and canal provided drinking water and irrigation. There has been no excavation, but surface ceramics are mainly inka with a few killke and lucre sherds (Claros and Mormontoy 1992). It is a planned agricultural community to house workers with homogeneous social status.

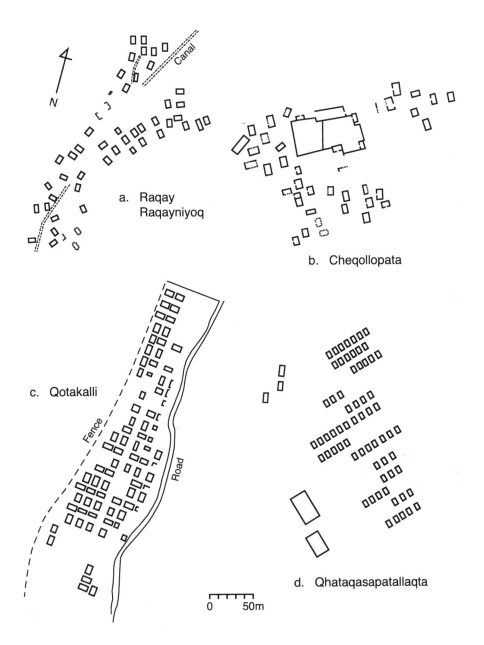

Figure 10.4. Plans of selected workers' villages (*llaqta*). *A*, Cheqollopata (after Claros and Mormontoy 1992); *B*, Raqay-Raqayniyoq (after Claros and Mormontoy 1992); *C*, Qotakalli (after Zapata 2002); *D*, Qhataqasapatallaqta (after Candia 1992b).

Chimaraqay

About 500m to the southeast of Raqay-Raqayniyoq lies Chimaraqay (3,450m), which consists of at least twenty-three similar rectangular, stone, and adobe structures, arranged in two clusters with some degree of grid planning. Recently, Bustinza excavated several houses, confirming an inka domestic occupation, and found a number of sub-floor burials (Torres 2011). This was a farming settlement adjacent to a stream for water supply and overlooking fields for cultivation.

Cheqollopata

Cheqollopata also lies on the lower mountain slopes at 3,370m on the flat-tish part of a colluvial fan, about 40m above the Pata Pata terraces. It is situated about 1,100m southeast of Chimaraqay and the same distance north-west of Kallampata. It is 3ha in extent and comprises forty-two rectangular buildings, surrounding a group of three interconnected walled patios on different levels, to the north, east, and south, while to the west there is a small quebrada (figure 10.4b). There are no formal streets, but most houses are facing southwest. The buildings are structurally and morphologically similar, built of sandstone blocks set in a mud mortar up to a height of 1.5m with adobe bricks on top. Each has a single door and internal trapezoidal niches. The largest is 16.40m (10r) by 7.40m 4.5r), and the smallest is 6.40m (4r) by 2.80m (1.75r) (Claros and Mormontoy 1992). In the center, the three patios, each surrounded by *pirka* perimeter walls, abut each other on differ-ent levels. Patio A (35m × 30m) is rectilinear; patio B (40m × 30m) is above A with salients on two sides; patio C (27m × 10m) lies to the north of B and is rectangular with a northeastern entrance. Each has associated buildings, within or adjacent to it.

The site has been heavily looted to the extent that Claros and Mormon-toy (1992) selected three looters' pits in different structures to section and record stratigraphy. R-22 is a large building, 16.4m (10.2r) by 7.4m (4.6r), with three archaeological layers. An inka floor was found at a depth of between 0.85m and 1.10m, comprising a compacted layer of clay and small stones with some charcoal and inka pottery embedded in it. Its surface was slightly undulating, indicating use, and it overlay sterile sediments. The sec-ond test pit in R-40 in the upper part of the site yielded a similar floor and ceramics. The third was dug in the southeast corner of patio B and exposed the internal faces of two walls of a rectangular building, while at a depth of

1.75m, they found a 4cm thick ash layer with charcoal and potsherds on top of the inka floor. Clearly, this patio had an internal building that probably had administrative and/or ritual functions.

Torres (2011) excavated in several houses near the patios, confirming an inka domestic occupation. He discovered two sub-floor burials in circular pits in hut corners. Both had been seated on a stone slab with associated grave goods: one with two casserole dishes and a small plate, and the other with a small decorated *maka*, two small bird handled plates with bird decoration, and two bone beads. In another hut there was a large circular pit containing the dispersed remains of at least five individuals, including at least an adult and two children. They were accompanied only by a single piece of copper. Another disarticulated skeleton was placed within the body of a wall. It had also been placed on a slab. Among the bones were some pieces of worked spondylus shell and some metal *tupu*, carbonized maize kernels, and some sherds.

Waqoto

The andesite quarries of Waqoto are located on Urqo Wiraqocha mountain at an altitude between 4,100m and 4,240m on the northeastern rim of the basin, 15km from Cusco. They cover an area of about 1.5sqkm and have been extensively exploited from the inka period through to the present. They have been the focus of two archaeological studies that have located three settlements peripheral to the quarry (Miranda and Zanabria 1994; Tovar 1996). In the southwest near Waqoto village, there are several platforms, llama corrals, an extensive artifact scatter, and many structural remains, mainly quadrangular and subcircular in form. There is also an unfinished flight of twelve irrigated terraces and a reservoir to provide both drinking and irrigation water. The second settlement, Kancha Kancha, lies on the southeastern edge and consists of platforms, rectangular and subcircular structures, dry-stone walled corrals, and a reservoir. Along the inka road between them, Challwanayoq is a small settlement of two rectangular buildings, arranged around a patio, adjacent to two well-made inka terraces. While in the quarry area itself, there are extraction pits, working platforms, ramps, worked and unworked stones, and about sixty small workers' huts with domed roofs.

In the Hatun Kancha area near the village, there have been nine excavations to investigate walls and structures and another in similar buildings at Kancha Kancha as well as in the quarry. The typical structure is a small subrectangular or subcircular hut with a tamped clay and gravel floor augmented by andesite flagstones and a corbelled roof. It has a single entrance with the jambs and lintels made from worked andesite, and its internal walls have small trapezoidal niches. Most huts had the remains of a clay and rock stove, or firepit, associated with charcoal, ash, and calcined animal bone, mainly llama. The pottery is mainly inka, indicating domestic activities with sherds of large storage *urpu*, cooking pots, and serving dishes, including jars, plates, and *maka*. Each hut had evidence of stone working, including several finished architectural blocks, including roof pegs and a lintel, as well as numerous hammerstones, polishers, and knives. A llama sacrifice was found in one hut, associated with plate sherds and a *peska* die[5] (Miranda and Zanabria 1994: 126), and a guinea pig offering was found in another (Tovar 1996: 179). Tovar (1996: 161–62) discovered the burial of an adult male in a third, sitting on three andesite flagstones, with a decorated *maka* in front.

Two larger rectangular structures, built of quarried andesite rectangular blocks, laid in sedimentary style, were investigated at Kancha Kancha, where Tovar found paved andesite floors set into a layer of compacted clay. The ceramics were exclusively inka, including a fragmented large *urpu* resting in a hole against one wall. There was little evidence for cooking and none for stone working, suggesting that these were only occasionally occupied, perhaps by administrators. At Challwanayoq, a small trench was placed in the corner of a large building (15m by 6m), with a central doorway, revealing a compacted red clay floor, but no cultural materials were found. Miranda and Zanabria (1994: 128–30) suggest this had an administrative function.

Unlike the agricultural villages, the quarry settlements lack the formal planning of houses and streets. They are workers' huts, which have been provided with a farming and pastoral infrastructure and a water supply. Close to the working areas, there are inka-style rectangular buildings with trapezoidal doorways, presumably to manage production.

Qontaymoqo

Qontaymoqo is located on a small ridge at 3,200m near the Angostura, where there are nine rectangular structures with rounded internal corners and constructed with quarried sandstone blocks set in a mud mortar. The walls are 70cm wide but only stand about 50cm high; they have a 5% batter and are plastered. Each has a single doorway. The site is associated with terraces, prehispanic middens, platforms, and roads. A surface collection produced many sherds, mainly killke with some qotakalli and inka, as well as animal bones, lithic implements, and andesite fragments (Claros and Mormontoy 1992).

Three buildings were excavated, generally finding a compacted clay and gravel floor, covered with a scattering of ash, charcoal, killke and inka sherds, camelid bones, and andesite flakes and dust (Claros and Mormontoy 1992). However, the excavation in the largest house (R-1) proved quite different. It is 11.5m (7.1r) by 6.5m (4r) and stands up to 2.7m high at the prominent southern end. They dug a total of 5sqm, finding evidence for a qotakalli period occupation floor but also an upper one, characterized by many killke and inka sherds, camelid bones, charcoal, and ash. A trench in the doorway revealed andesite door jambs and a stepped threshold, made from quarried sandstone slabs. Below this, a decorated bird-handled plate, turned upside down, was uncovered that overlay an arrangement of camelid bones and the skeleton of a dog with its head resting on a stone. It was also associated with the bones of an adult and two juvenile rodents, probably guinea pigs.

Chuparayoq Moqo (Lucerinas)

This site is situated on a hill on the valley floor close to the south bank of the river about 8km from Cusco. Claros and Mormontoy (1992) reported sixteen structures, an artifact scatter, and a cemetery. Domingo Farfán (2009) conducted rescue excavations in twelve vacant lots after urbanization had destroyed much of the site, discovering several rectangular sandstone huts, smaller in size than those in other villages. On various occupation floors he found lucre, killke, and inka pottery, as well as spindle whorls, *ruki*, grindstones, *kurpana* (clod-breaker), and carbonized maize kernels. Several subfloor burials were discovered, two in house corners and three disturbed graves associated with wall foundations. One of the house corner burials was associated with a killke plate and another with an inka pedestalled pot, a miniature jar, fragments of a wooden *qero*, a bronze *tumi*, and guinea pig bones. This village clearly had had a local late period occupation, but it is not known if its population had been replaced by *mitayoq* workers.

Qotakalli

This large site is located on a relatively flat natural terrace between two very deep gullies on its western and eastern sides. It has eighty-three separate rectangular houses in an area of 7.7ha (figure 10.4c). These were built in *pirka* style with sandstone blocks and river pebbles set in a mud mortar. The settlement is very well planned with the buildings arranged in twenty-two east-west rows, separated by three wide north-south streets. Generally, the building axis alternates between rows of east-west houses and those north-south. In the northern sector, the houses maintain similar axes, but it is not as well organized.

House dimensions vary slightly from 9.0m (5.6r) by 4.6m (2.85r) to 11.11m (6.9r) by 6.48m (4r), while the separation between them averages about 8.0m (5r). Zapata (2002) recognized six types of dwelling according to the number of internal rooms and the location of the door, usually on the east, south, or west sides. One structure seems to be a public building, probably an *usnu* platform, 6m by 8m. It has an internal stone altar, and its paved floor stands on a raised earthen platform about 1.8m high. It faces west.

There have been three excavation projects at Qotakalli. In 1972, José González dug a building on the western side, concluding an inka date for its construction.[6] Julinho Zapata (2002) and his students excavated four further structures, and in 2003 the INC-Cusco extended this work with excavation of five more and site conservation works (Benavides 2003; Bustinza 2004).

The house excavations indicate that each had been constructed initially as a single room that was later subdivided in order to create private areas for specific functions, such as storage, cooking, and sleeping, and that rooms were added when more space was required. There was considerable evidence for food preparation, such as carbonized potatoes and maize, calcined camelid, guinea pig and bird bones, clay stoves, cooking pots, large storage jars, both *maran* and *tunaw* grindstones, flaked stone knives, and scrapers. The pot sherds were from plates and cups for serving as well as *urpu* and *maka* for brewing and transporting *chicha* to the fields. Later excavations confirmed such activities with intact pots *in situ* on floors, such as a large *urpu*, a casserole dish, and a narrow-necked jar. Zapata (2002) noted that in the two-roomed houses, the room by the door was the kitchen and dormitory, while the inner room was a pantry and storeroom.

A total of thirteen subfloor human burials were found in three houses (Zapata 2002). In R-19, there was an adult female in the northwest corner, in a seated flexed position, leaning against the north wall footings and looking into the room, while in R-54, an infant was found in a pit in the southeast corner of room B. In room R-20A, there was an adult buried in the northwest corner, one in the northeast corner, and two placed side by side in the southeastern corner. All were seated and flexed, leaning against the footings and looking into the room. In room B there were single adult burials in all four corners, except in the northwestern corner, where three individuals had been superimposed on top of each other; the lowest one was seated flexed and remained articulated, like the top one, whereas the one in the middle had been disarticulated and arranged like a secondary burial. In addition, a sub-adult was placed on the eastern side of this group. The grave goods were modest, mainly potsherds, such as *maka* bases, placed on the head. The only exceptions were two copper *tupu* with the female in R-19 and a quartz knife on the head of a sub-adult in R-20B. A further sixteen individuals were found in similar locations in 2003 and 2004, confirming the custom of burying the dead within the house, below the floor, in the corners of interior rooms and against the footings.

An 80cm diameter, stone-lined pit was also found in the center of R-20B, containing burnt offerings, which had been filled with stones to the original floor level. It is thought that this had been buried in honor of the seven interments in the house and immediately afterwards the house was abandoned and the door walled up (Zapata 2002). Burnt offerings were uncovered in houses R-2, R-11, R-12, and R-53, and at their thresholds, where household goods such as *maka*, *maran*, and *tunaw* had been smashed as part of closing rituals. A typical offering object was the detached *maka* neck.

A dog was found in a deep pit in the southwest corner of R-19 and another in the northeast corner of R-54. These articulated skeletons were arranged, lying on one side and surrounded by guinea pig bones; they appear to be ritual offerings for the initial occupation of a house. In one funerary *urpu*, stone beads were found, including six carved felines and nine carved miniature *urpu*.

A most significant find was in house R-75, which contained 344 disarticulated and mixed sets of skeletal remains (Andrushko 2007). These had been removed from their original graves and hastily reburied in this structure. It seems that shallow pits were dug, and several skeletons were thrown into each and covered with only about 20cm of sediment. During reburial, these became disarticulated, and many small bones were lost. There were very few accompanying items; the common finds were metal *tupu*, needles, and spindle whorls (Benavides 2003), but it is uncertain whether these relate to the original occupation or the subsequent burials. At the end of this ritual, the building was also ceremonially sealed. It is thought that this happened during the sixteenth century, although radiocarbon dates from two skeletons indicate that death may have occurred a century before the conquest.[7]

Males form the majority (54%), while, like Kusikancha, the age range displays 53.25% over twenty-five years, but there are proportionally more infants (14.72%) and more children and juveniles (24.67%) (Andrushko 2007). In contrast to the urban populations, they had higher incidences of dietary stress disorders and anemia, and many had suffered cranial trauma and trepanation (Andrushko 2007). The majority had unmodified skulls, although six (3.7%) had tabular erect deformation and seventeen (10.5%) had annular oblique, which would suggest that the population of Qotakalli was diverse and included people from the Titiqaqa area, the local region, and possibly from the central or northern coast.

Qhataqasapatallaqta

Qhataqasapatallaqta is located on Mikay Urqo, a hill 2.5km south of Hawkaypata at an altitude of 3,510m. Thirteen lines of rectangular buildings, running downslope, overlook the city, and a plaza on the summit to the southwest contains an *usnu* platform and several larger buildings (figure 10.4d). It has an area of about 1.5ha and has been recently protected from urban sprawl. There have been several archaeological investigations at the site, particularly since 1990.

Rowe (1944: 51) reported that its houses were small and poorly constructed, merely foundations, and that the site had been severely looted. Yet Candia (1992a, 1992b) recorded sixty-five houses of sandstone *pirka* masonry set in a mud mortar. They have similar dimensions: 11.2m (7r) by 6.4m (4r) and a standard wall width of 80cm, which increases to about 1m on the northern and eastern downhill sides. The walls are quite low with no indication of doors, niches, or gable ends (Candia 1992a, 1992b). The spaces between them form parallel streets, 10m wide, with narrower perpendicular lanes. On the ridge top, there are two rectangular structures in a poor state of conservation; one is quite large, 28m by 19m, while the other measures 10m by 8m.

Surface surveys by Rowe (1944) and Barreda (1973) noted materials of the qotakalli, lucre, killke, and inka styles. The first excavation in 1972 saw José González and Dean Arnold dig some structures, reporting a large number of inka storage vessels and a carved turquoise figurine. Later, Wilfredo Yépez conducted salvage excavations during road construction at its eastern and northern margins, where he found two very small buildings of imperial inka architecture, associated with decorated inka pottery as well as lucre and killke sherds (Candia 1992a).

Candia (1992a) mapped the site, noting in a pit dug for an electricity pole that hut walls had originally been plastered. In the northern part, he examined in detail three killke structures, built of sandstone river pebbles in a mud mortar, that had clay and gravel floors, one with a low clay stove. He also excavated an inka structure, A-3 with a later partition wall. He determined that its foundations extended 1m in depth to bedrock and that the inka floor was a red compacted clay with gravel, 10cm thick, with an undulating, ash-covered surface. At its base against the north wall, he found a round red stone, about 20cm in diameter, that covered a semicircular, stone-lined burial pit. The poor state of conservation meant that only the cranium and upper arms of an adult female were recovered. The skull was inverted with the lower mandible nearby and orientated to the east. Accompanying the bones were a decorated bone spoon, a bronze *tupu,* and an andesite polisher. The ceramics included a miniature *urpu,* placed in front of the skull, parts of two pedestalled pots, and a bone spindle whorl.

In 2002–2003 the INC excavated more buildings, each about 9.0m (5.6r) by 6.0m (3.7r) (Bustinza 2003; Pilares 2002). These had clay floors, strewn with ash and charcoal, with camelid bones and carbonized maize kernels, potatoes and peanuts, as well as low clay stoves. There were many serving vessel sherds, such as plates and bowls, as well as large numbers of thick-walled *urpu* for food storage and brewing. There were also spindle whorls and *ruki* for spinning and weaving. Some storerooms with ventilation shafts were also exposed, containing significant numbers of large vessels, such as *urpu* and *maka* (80–90 cm in height). Domestic offerings included dog burials, burnt camelids, and *maka* necks (Bustinza 2003). In addition, a stone-faced *usnu* platform was investigated that was the focus of a small plaza area, and twenty-eight burials were found within several inka buildings. The majority of burials were in pits in internal corners,

Figure 10.5. Excavations at Qhataqasapatallaqta (photo by Andina).

while a number were also discovered in large *urpu* in similar locations. Andrushko (2007) reported that the population was healthy with only one case of cribra orbitalia and none of linear enamel hypoplasia. There was no cranial deformation, although two had suffered cranial trauma. The sex ratio was equal, while the age distribution was similar to that of Kusikancha.

Carmen Concha has directed two further seasons of archaeological research at this large village site. In 2009, she excavated twelve houses, finding grindstones, stone hammers, spindle whorls, metal knives and bars, killke and inka ceramics, and twelve more burials (figure 10.5) (Andina 10/07/2009). Among the architectural finds were a house with an internal stone altar, as well as patios, passages, and steps, while each structure also had a small storeroom. Of the burials, most were found inside buildings in corners and against walls, although there were some associated with peripheral areas, such as patios and steps. The most unusual was that of a 60-year-old, who was found seated in a large *urpu* inside a house, associated with ten metal, ceramic, and stone objects. Adjacent to the pot were found the remains of three children, probably sacrifices, and an adult female, as well as a stone fireplace.

In 2010, she dug in the southwestern sector of the site, including a building, measuring 10m by 8m, originally mapped by Candia. She found that this had two levels and had been divided into four rooms, including a patio with clay pot supports, a kitchen with clay stove, broken plates, cooking pots, and *maka*, a storeroom with ventilation ducts and clay bins, and a room with a 3m long bench (Concha 2011). Within the latter, there was a cist burial containing a juvenile (15–17 years) with a *maka*, a pedestalled pot, three pairs of small plates, three *tupu*, and a die. The skeleton of a 1-year-old was found in a tall decorated jar, only 1.5m from the cist. Within the storeroom, a multiple burial was discovered, comprising six crania and some other poorly preserved postcranial bones. These are thought to be secondary burials of family members.

Qhataqasapatallaqta was a planned village with a small *usnu* complex and a limited number of storage facilities. Its inhabitants were certainly users of killke and inka pottery and may have been local. They practiced similar rituals of burial and offering to those described for other Cusco villages. It probably functioned as a source of labor for the city itself and for agriculture.

Discussion

While the plan of each *llaqta* is different, they do appear to have been built to a set of broad planning principles and are not like those of Late Intermediate period settlements in and around Cusco (cf. Kendall). The houses are all built of quarried sandstone laid up in *pirka* style, and they are remarkably consistent in size within each site. Each has a single entry and stands in rows and lines and not in *kancha*. Modifications in the form of subdivision and addition have occurred in many houses throughout these villages, which would suggest permanency. Public plazas and even *usnu* platforms have been provided. The material culture found in each village is itself quite consistent in form and decoration, mainly inka in date, although killke and lucre sherds have been found in some settlements. The presence of the latter would suggest that these housed local farmers, but is this true for all of the villages described?

Indeed the funerary corpus shows that the occupants buried their dead within the house, below the floor in the corners of interior rooms and against the wall footings. Such a practice expresses the nature of a family cult that maintained harmony between the household and the spirits of dead ancestors, who became through this act the protectors of the house, a tradition that is not essentially inka or local. It could be argued that these *llaqta* were occupied by *mitayoq* who had been brought into Cusco to farm the fields for the *panaqa* as part of tribute on behalf of their own *ayllu* or province and also to quarry and build the city for the Inka. Answers to these questions may be seen in the relationship between these settlements and the following two settlement types: isolated *kancha* and *qolqa*.

Isolated *Kancha*

The isolated *kancha* is a distinctive characteristic of inka rural settlement planning. It is found in the planned rural areas of the lower Vilcanota valley, generally associated with channelization and terrace schemes. It consists of a walled compound with a single entrance with three to six buildings and a central patio, although variations do exist. Examples include Durazni-yoq and Chaullaraqay near Ollantaytambo, Tunasmoqo and Kiswarpata in Cusichaca, and Torontoy, Chachabamba, and Palkay near Machu Picchu. It is thought that these may have been elite residences with permanent or temporary inhabitants, who supervised farming or other work. They may have had a small shrine for state agricultural rituals. This role was also carried out by isolated buildings, such as *kallanka*, flanking an unwalled patio. For example, in the Rumiqolqa andesite quarries, Ives Béjar (2003) has recorded a patio, flanked by two *kallanka*, as the administrative focus for that location.

In the Cusco valley, this pattern is repeated with several isolated *kancha*, located near agricultural lands, *qolqa* and planned villages, and in which various *panaqa* members may have lived to supervise the rural estates (figure 10.3). Three are described—Pukakancha, Sillkinchani and Wimpillay—but several others may be considered, including Arkawasi, Pumamarka, and Bobedayoq, while another on the northern flank of Wanakawri must have played some role during the ceremonial events on that mountain (Claros and Mormontoy 1992; Rowe 1944).

Pukakancha

This is a poorly preserved *kancha* on the western slopes of Tawkaray hill, only 250m from the storerooms, overlooking Qotakalli (Bauer and Jones 2003). It is located in a small field with a dense pottery scatter of inka and earlier sherds, covering an area about 100m square. There are three rectangular buildings facing a patio[8] (figure 10.6a).

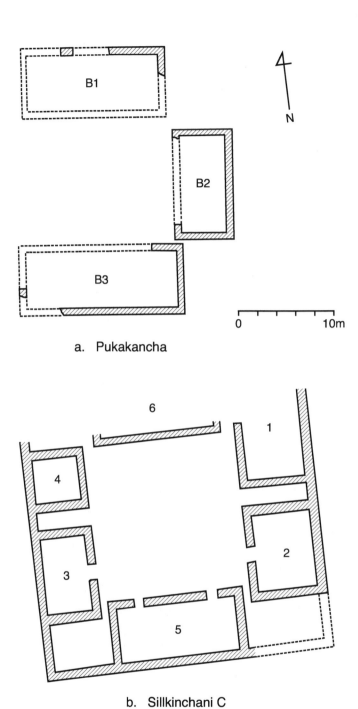

a. Pukakancha

b. Sillkinchani C

Figure 10.6. Isolated *kancha*. *A*, Pukakancha (after Bauer and Jones 2003: 7); *B*, Sillkin-chani C (after Mormontoy 2000).

Bauer and Jones (2003) excavated six small pits in and around these buildings. They determined that B-2 had been constructed on top of a Middle Horizon occupation, whereas B-1 had been built on sterile soil. They noted that the walls had been constructed by digging a foundation trench to a depth of at least 50cm and a little wider than the footings. These were assembled with large stones in a clay mortar and the trench filled with alternating layers of different colored clays. In B-2, an earth mound had been built up on the outside of the wall to give it additional support. The floor was constructed by dumping a white, chalky deposit (*qontay*) to raise the level, and covering it with a 5cm layer of red clay. Finally, the walls were plastered. The interior excavations in B-1 and B-2 yielded both decorated and undecorated inka sherds and some animal bone fragments on the inka floor, which had been well maintained and kept relatively clean. A bronze celt was also found in B-1. A wood charcoal sample collected from B-1 has yielded a calibrated radiocarbon date of early fifteenth century.[9]

Sillkinchani C

The Sillkinchani C walled *kancha* is situated near the Angostura on the southern side of the valley. It is close to the storerooms but 50m below them. It is poorly preserved with most walls only surviving up to 40cm above ground level and several not visible on the surface (Mormontoy 2000). It comprises six rectangular buildings, arranged in pairs on the west (R-4, R-5) and east (R-1, R-2) sides, and single structures on the northern (R-6) and southern (R-3) sides (figure 10.6b). The eastern and western pairs are of different sizes: the northerly ones are about 6.5m (4r) square, while the southerly pair have external measurements of 8.1m (5r) by 6.4m (4r) and a centrally placed doorway. Each pair is separated by a blind corridor, 1.7m (1r) in width. The northern and southern structures are 13.4m (8.25r) by 5.6m (3.5m) with two doors. There are four lateral patios, of which only three survive. The southwestern corner lateral patio has two small holes in its west wall to drain the upper part of the *kancha*.

The buildings are made of sandstone blocks in a clay mortar on top of 70cm deep footings, while the corners and door jambs are well-worked rectangular andesite. Floor preparation consists of a layer of stones 10–15cm thick upon which a 10cm layer of earth was compacted.

Mormontoy (2000) dug seventeen excavation units, several of which were contiguous but recorded separately. Over 20,250 potsherds were recovered, of which all but 235 were inka. These were both everyday plain wares and decorated ceremonial ones. Other finds include granite and grey andesite round *mutka* and rectangular *maran* grinding stones, quartz and other stone knives, a variety of stone and ceramic polishers for working pottery, and considerable quantities of animal bone (camelid, rodent, dog, and bird), some of which was burnt. These represent both a domestic occupation, craft activities, and the performance of some rituals. This was confirmed by the discovery of several human burials and various offering contexts.

A primary burial of a young female was found in a semicircular pit, 70cm in diameter, and lined with small stones and clay in the blind corridor between R-1 and R-2 (Mormontoy 2000). She was in a seated, flexed position, facing north, but in a poor state of conservation. There were two bronze *tupu* on her sternum and on her right there was a black pot, with fire blackening, two inka polychrome casserole dishes, and a sewing basket. There were several other offering pits in this corridor, four of which contained deteriorated human remains with inka vessels or simply necks and rims. One held two plates that covered a human long bone, metatarsals, rib and maxilla, and a lower pit with more bones and a miniature pot. Another contained a deformed cranium with a single long bone, a pedestalled pot, and eight miniature plates. It is thought that these are secondary burials (Mormontoy 2000). In R-1, a pit was found against the south wall footings, containing a cranium and several postcranial bones with six plates and fragments of *qero*, casserole dish, and *maka*. There was also a secondary burial interred with a *maka* neck. Other offering pits in R-1 and the blind corridor had mainly potsherds, worked stone and charcoal.

In R-3 there were also two offering pits. One contained worked quartz, spondylus shell, a pearl, a metal spangle, a bronze bell, three stone spindle whorls, four worked bones, and stone ceramic polishers, and the other contained a globular vessel, a broken plate, and a lump of hematite, which may have been used both as a pigment and for its curative qualities. In 1998, some offerings were found in the southwest corner space, including two guinea pig burials, a dog burial, and five large *maka*, while Mormontoy (2000) also uncovered the lower mandible and part of the maxilla of a dog in the southwestern lateral patio.

Sillkinchani C probably housed a permanent elite population that buried their dead under the floors and conducted various ritual offerings, including secondary human burials, dogs, and guinea pigs. It is possible that these reflect both dedicatory offerings and continuing ritual activity. There were both male and female residents who were engaged in fabricating pottery, making textiles, and perhaps even lapidary work. The location, close to *qolqa* and villages, indicates that this was a small administrative site. It was deliberately abandoned, and its doorways were sealed with narrow sandstone walls before the arrival of the Spaniards.

Wimpillay

This settlement lies on a low rounded hill between the Watanay river and the base of Muyu Urqo, about 4km from the city. Three *seqe waka* lay within it: Membilla Pukyo (QO-5:2), a spring of drinking water that received offerings of sea shells; a group of stones called Mamacolca (QO-6:2), and a house called Acoywasi (QO-6:3), where the mummy of Sinchi Roca was kept (Cobo 1990: 73–74). Indeed, the mummies of both Sinchi Roca and his father, Manqo Qhapaq, were found in Wimpillay in 1559 by Polo de Ondegardo (Sarmiento 2007: 76–78). The former was seated between copper bars.

This prestigious location on the south side of the valley had been occupied continuously since late Formative times (Barreda 1973). It is terraced with open spaces, lines of rectangular houses, *qolqa,* and a cemetery. There have been many archaeological investigations, particularly as the area is becoming increasingly more urbanized. Alfredo Valencia dug an inka *kancha,* consisting of eight good quality buildings in the western part of the site. Between 1987 and 1989, the INC conducted excavations on the eastern side, also finding some fine architecture, human burials, and offerings. The material culture discovered included high quality inka polychrome pottery, spindle whorls, *ruki, tupu,* and agricultural tools, such as *kurpana* (Farfán 2011).

Discussion

In the Cusco valley, the isolated *kancha,* except for the one near the summit of Wanakawri, were closely associated with irrigated or drained agricultural lands and were close to both workers' villages and storehouses. They were inhabited by an inka elite whose role may have been to administer labor, production, and storage. They were also the scene of many dedicatory offerings and continued ritual activity.

Qolqa

The chroniclers Sancho (1917: 195) and Pizarro (1986: 99) stated that there were numerous storerooms on the slopes surrounding the city, which were full of blankets, clothing, sandals, weapons, metal goods, wooden beams, and foodstuffs. There was even one that held 100,000 dried birds for featherworking. On the basis of many studies (e.g., LeVine 1992; Morris 1967), hillsides overlooking inka towns or agricultural lands were the ideal location for state *qolqa*. Following this logic, Morris (1967: 159) conducted brief surveys on the slopes above the city, and from his observations of footings, *qolqa*-like floors, and thick-walled sherds, he concluded that there had been *qolqa* in a zone that extended from near San Cristóbal eastward for a distance of about 3km as far as the university. He urged that there should be excavation to verify this, but unfortunately this zone became rapidly urbanized in the 1970s and 1980s without further investigation. About 5km below the city, Morris did record the site of Tawkaray, which had two flights of eight *pirka* storehouses that were architecturally different from those at Huánuco Pampa, Hatun Xauxa, or in the Cochabamba valley. These are long, narrow structures, built on two levels, with several doors with entry from the front, sides, and behind. He examined similar buildings in the Vilcanota valley and agreed with Nuñez del Prado that these were *qolqa*. In his classification, Morris (1967: 196–99) termed them "Qollqa-Ollantaytampu rectangular (QOR)" storerooms. Since then, archaeology has confirmed their function, and other locations have been investigated (Huaycochea 1994; Zecenarro 2001) (figure 10.3; table 10.2). Bauer (2004: 98, map 9.2) has recorded nineteen storage sites in the urban hinterland.

Wayna Tawkaray

This site lies on the northwest slopes of Tawkaray and has sixteen large QOR storehouses, made of *pirka* (Morris 1967: 162–63). It is arranged in two flights of four side-by-side pairs, about 200m apart, and one above the other. Each pair is separated by a 1.8m staircase with a central canal. The main size is 30m by 4.9m with a 35cm high walled platform, made from finely cut, pillowed limestone blocks, dividing it lengthwise (Pilco 2004). A second building size is 17.3m by 4.9m. Excavations have revealed that the 1m wide platform contained a series of stone-lined ventilation ducts, 14 in R-1 and 25 in R-2, and that on its upper surface there had been a succession of rectangular clay bins (*taqe*) (Pilco 2004). Ash, charcoal, and some inka

Table 10.2. *Qolqa* in the Cusco valley

	No. of buildings	Size (m)	No. in row	Spacing in row (m)	No. of doors	Internal platform	Clay bins	Ventilation ducts
Wayna Tawqaray A	8	30.0 × 4.9	4	2.0	4	yes	yes	yes
Wayna Tawqaray B	8	17.3 × 4.9	4	1.4	3	yes	yes	yes
Muyu Orqo	4	31.5 × 5.5	4	5.0	4	yes	24	yes
Sillkinchani A	9	25.6 × 5.7	3	2.15	6	no	none	none
Salonniyoq	2	15.75 × 4.9	2	1.1	3	yes	13	12
Qorqenpata	11	25–30 × 3.1	2–3	2–2.5	4	yes	not known	—
Chingana Grande	1	16.0 × 5.0	1	—	—	yes	not known	—
Sillkina	81	3 × 3	27	1.2	none	no	not known	not known

potsherds were also found. In a better preserved building, there were small trapezoidal niches. The only significant finds were a decorated jar, a cup with a painted maize plant, and a male anthropomorphic figurine sculpted in camelid bone.

Further excavations have revealed a *maran*, stone blades, *ruki*, spindle whorls, charcoal, and calcined animal bones in R-2 and R-3 (El Sol 01/09/2009; Benavente 2011). A simple burial of an adult female was found in R-2, associated with a broken quartzite *qonopa*, while in R-3 there was another burial, consisting of a seated individual and three other crania. An offering of six broken *maka* was found in the floor of R-6 covered in red clay and charcoal.

Muyu Urqo

This is a prominent dome-shaped hill that rises 70m above the river on the south side of the valley close to the airport and Wimpillay. Excavations on its summit have located a Formative sunken temple, and it served as a sacred mountain from then until the inka times (Zapata 1998b). Its original inka name was Tampuvilka. On its western flanks, José Pilares (2008) has recorded a row of *qolqa*, curving around the contour, built of sandstone in a clay mortar with plastered walls. Each has four wide doorways and two interior benches, one against the rear wall and the other along the front wall. The average dimensions are 31.5m by 5.5m. He excavated R-3 and noted that its rear bench is 80cm wide and was divided by 10cm thick clay walls into twenty-four regularly spaced individual bins, each 85–90cm by 65–70cm. In the stone-faced platform under each bin was a ventilation shaft. The other bench is about 1m wide and is also divided into bins but without ventilation shafts. It is clear that the bins had been subjected to fire, because they contain ash. Several fragmented pots were found *in situ*, including tall, decorated, two-handled jars, a large *maka*, and casserole dishes (Pilares 2008).

Wimpillay

Recent excavations have exposed four *qolqa*, each 16.4m by 4.65m (Farfán 2011). They have two entrances, face north, and are aligned in pairs. The floor deposits contained *ruki* and spindle whorls as well as a *kurpana*. *Qolqa* 1 contained a sub-floor burial of a seated adult accompanied by a *maka*, plate, and two cooking pots, a pedestalled pot, and a double-chambered chimú vessel with a modeled monkey attachment.

Sillkinchani Sector A

This site is located on the northwest slope of Aq'oyoc Moq'o near the Angostura. It is a complex of nine identical rectangular buildings, arranged in ascending rows of three buildings (figure 10.7). Each is 25.6m by 5.7m with six trapezoidal doors in the façade, each 1.3m wide (Mormontoy 1994). The rear walls of each building are thick to aid slope retention and reach a height of 4.50m. The lower part of each wall is built of sandstone blocks, 70cm thick, and stands up to 2.80m with adobe courses on top; all are coated with red plaster. The adobe gable ends have trapezoidal windows for ventilation and light. Each building is separated by an open space, 2.15m wide. There is no evidence of any internal bench.

Claros and Mormontoy (1992) dug test pits in R-2 and R-9. One in the northeast corner of R-2 exposed a 20cm thick, semicompacted sediment with small stones as the inka floor, covered with 150 inka sherds. Below this, there were killke sherds, a human bone, and five camelid bones. A similar picture emerged from the southeast corner of R-9 with a floor surface embedded with inka sherds and charcoal pieces.

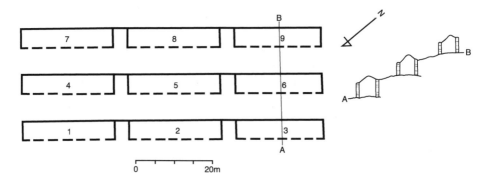

Figure 10.7. The Sillkinchani A storerooms (after Mormontoy 1994).

Salonniyoq

The remains of two similar *pirka* buildings, arranged side by side, were re-cently excavated on the northeastern flank of Salonniyoq, the carved rock complex of Lakko (Guillén 2008, 2009). They are both 15.75m long and 4.90m wide with three façade doors, oriented to the east, with a low plat-form running lengthwise in which were arranged 12 stone-lined ventilation shafts. There were also several clay bins on top of the platform, and carbon-ized maize kernels were found on the floor. Recently, a similar structure with ventilation ducts and large *urpu* was found to the southwest of the carved rock at Chingana Grande (Socualaya 2008).

Qorqenpata

This is a group of eleven similar buildings of *pirka* and adobe on the sum-mit and slopes of Qorqenpata to the southwest of Yuncaypata. The site plan is not formal, but they are scattered in rows of two or three across the hill-side. Ten of them face south and one east (Zecenarro 2001). They are in a poor state of conservation and are between 25m and 30m in length and about 3.1m in width. They have been set into the slope with a strong back retaining wall and were probably two stories high with doors on each level.

Sillkina

A second type of *qolqa* has been identified at Sillkina on the southern side of the valley. It has two parallel terraced walls, about 15m apart and 106m long (Claros and Mormontoy 1992). On the terrace, there are three lines of identical buildings, each 3m square, separated from each other by about 1.2m, and built with quarried sandstone in a mud mortar. There are probably twenty-seven structures in each line, and although several stand over 1.5m tall, the remaining walls are usually no more than 50cm high; there are no apparent doorways, although small openings and steps have been noted. Excavations have been inconclusive, yielding only a handful of inka sherds. However, on the basis of the planned nature of the site, the standard small size of the structures and the lack of entrances, it is suggested that these are storerooms but for a commodity different from that stored in the QOR.

A similar site, Raqayniyoq, has been recorded at 3,490m in the Choqo valley (Rueda and Gonzales 2004). It is located on a terrace with the remains of thirteen identical rectangular structures (4.1m × 3.5m), with a line of small stone bins in front and several larger buildings.

Discussion

The elongated QOR type of *qolqa* predominates in the valley, although variations in length, number of doorways, and the presence or absence of bins and ventilation ducts may indicate that different products were stored in them. A second type has been recognized but not intensively investigated. What is clear is that both types are state planned, constructed, and operated. Like the isolated *kancha*, they also received dedicatory burials and offerings.

Agricultural Landscape

At 3,450m in altitude, Cusco lies toward the upper limits for successful maize cultivation. The rolling farmlands above the city favor the cultivation of andean root crops, such as potato, ulluco, and oca as well as quinoa and tarwi, and there are also extensive pastures. The slopes and valley floor lands, and even the wetter lands on the plateaux, were either too steep, too wet, or flood prone for successful harvests without some form of agricultural engineering. Therefore, their remodeling was critical to produce abundant harvests for the large amounts of feasting required for the ceremonial round. This necessitated the channelization, not only of the Saphi and Tullumayu streams but also other tributaries and indeed the main Watanay river itself, as well as the reconstruction of canal systems and terrace construction to develop new productive lands (figure 10.1). The ethnohistorical accounts attribute these changes to Pachakuti Inka Yupanki, but whether every terrace scheme can be dated to his influence is not clear.

River channelization is a complex engineering achievement for which the inkas are famous (Farrington 1984a). For example, in opening up the Vilcanota valley floor for successful cultivation, they controlled and straightened a 50m wide, swift-flowing mountain river. Several schemes, each a few kilometers in length, can be seen still functioning at Pisaq, Calca, Yucay, Pachar, and a 7km stretch at Tanqaq below Ollantaytambo. Such engineering works confined the flow between strong walled banks and prevented devastating annual floods and erosion. Another advantage is that each scheme would also have drained adjacent flats and made them available for cultivation. Not only did the inkas engineer large rivers, they used their skills to control smaller streams and drain the adjacent lands (Farrington 1984a). In Cusco, as we have seen, the channelization of the two rivers was essential for urban planning by reducing floods and erosion, particularly at Hawkaypata and for those buildings adjacent to the stream. It was clear that such environmental control also served to domesticate the landscape with man-made straight channels. According to Betanzos (1996: 54–57), Pachakuti Inka intended to reclaim the flood plain as far as Muyna, although very little survives of that project, if it was ever completed. Just below Cusco, there are remnant stone-walled river banks at Suriwaylla and at Santutis, which reclaimed the lands of Oscullo and Sanobamba.[10] Tributaries, such as the Cachimayu at Inkilltambo, were also channelized. In the Urbanización Kennedy, on the Watanay floodplain, Ardiles (1986) excavated a network of small stone-lined drainage channels at various depths, which would have effectively drained that area for maize cultivation. Overall, such reclamation schemes would have increased maize production significantly.

The inkas were also skilled stone-walled terrace builders, for both farming and landscaping purposes, such as on the southern and eastern flanks of Saqsaywaman and San Blas. Inka terraces have particularly identifiable features, including canals, wall drains, and various types of staircase (Heffernan 1990, 1996a). In the Watanay valley, there are two extensive areas of terracing on the northern lower slopes near San Jerónimo, where both the Larapa and Pata Pata flights display few of the classic inka features and probably predated the reform of the city. Other terrace schemes are smaller and found mainly on the slopes of the northern plateaux and in narrow valleys of the southern flank. In field survey, wall-steps and drains have been noted on irrigated terraces, such as at Inkilltambo, whereas recessed parallel staircases (RPS), characteristic of royal estates (Heffernan 1990), have only been noted in two locations: Machaybamba in upper Chakan and Avenida Qollasuyu near the university campus. This is confirmed by a mid-sixteenth-century document in which inka nobles claimed very few lands in Cusco, focusing on unterraced fields and pastures to the north and salt pans near San Sebastián.

The agricultural resources and landscapes of the four *suyu* are different. For example, in Chinchaysuyu, the main Chakan canals and reservoirs provided irrigation to large areas of Hatun Ayllu, particularly at Llaullipata and Fortaleza (Sherbondy 1982). In contrast, the lands of Qhapaq Ayllu, south of Saphi, were on relatively poor and unstable slopes, watered by a canal from a spring on *seqe* CH-3 and augmented by a longer one from outside the basin (Sherbondy 1986b: 43). Indeed, the settlement pattern and geography in this sector is more characteristic of Kuntisuyu (Farrington 1992). Nevertheless, its most important terracing must have been the large area, now urbanized, adjacent to the city, between *seqe* CH-1 and CU-14. The difference in quality between these lands probably reflects the relative size and importance of the two *panaqa*. Qhapaq Ayllu, the king's lineage, would have been smaller than that of Hatun Ayllu and would not have required such an extensive tract of local land with good water supplies, as did Hatun Ayllu. The main royal estate lay further west at Zurite and Limatambo (Farrington 1992; Heffernan 1996a).

The agricultural landscape of Antisuyu contains some extensive, but separate, terracing schemes between San Sebastián and San Jerónimo. In contrast, in Qollasuyu and Kuntisuyu, although subdivided and assigned by the inkas in the same manner, the valleys are narrower with few large-scale schemes, except for a flight of broad inka terraces at Killke. Probably the best farmland in the hinterland was the newly reclaimed floor of the Watanay valley. Yet even these were not private royal lands, nor did they belong to the main *panaqa* but probably to non-royal *ayllu* of Antisuyu and Qollasuyu or to the state.

The articulation of the city with its hinterland follows some general principles and is also associated with some very particular cultural aspects of the inka world. The suburban villages, except for Qolqampata, were located along the *qhapaq ñan*, which approached the city from all four *suyu*. It is natural that suburbs would develop in such places, particularly given the specific and exclusive qualities of the city itself. It would imply, therefore, that these were true suburbs, housing both the foreigners and the non-elite, who were vital for the well-being of Cusco by working in the city and producing craft goods for it. Essentially, these villages should be considered part of the urban area, while Qolqampata, with its palace focus, presents a different role, an urban extension, which may indeed be a relatively late establishment. Further stratigraphical work to establish its antiquity is necessary.

Following basic geographical principles, the distribution of the other site types throughout the Inner Heartland is not even but skewed for cultural reasons. In general, the plateau area above Cusco, nominally Chinchaysuyu and Antisuyu, does not seem to contain many of these site types, and these lands must have been regarded differently. However, lower down the valley in Antisuyu, Qollasuyu, and Kuntisuyu, the rural settlement pattern is quite clear, with each place lying adjacent to resources vital to the city and the state. For example, the planned workers' villages are situated within 1–3km of productive inka farmland, on which their inhabitants must have worked for either the state or the religion, and also close to other lands that they probably tilled for their own subsistence. In some cases, these lands are in association with state *qolqa*. The same is true of the hamlets in the vicinity of the andesite quarry at Waqoto, where workers lived and farmed as well as quarried and transported stone, and at Muyu Qocha, where the workers also quarried the limestone to build Saqsaywaman.

The isolated *kancha* provide a contrasting form of settlement but in similar locations. As very formal inka urban nodes within the hinterland, and invariably close to storerooms and planned villages, they presumably oversaw production and managed storage. Several are also associated with inka ritual practices, including the ancestor cult, which means that the articulation of the rural landscape with the urban center needs to be further investigated.

As far as the material culture is understood, the inhabitants of all rural settlements appear very similar to each other and also like their urban *kancha* counterparts. They used mainly inka style pottery, including some contemporary local killke and lucre wares. They prepared similar foods and *chicha*, buried their dead, and made offerings in ways very much like those living in the urban *kancha*. However, not all burials occurred under house floors because there are numerous *machay* locations, particularly in the north and northeast, and a large hilltop inka cemetery has also been excavated at Pillawa in the lower valley (Raymundo Béjar pers. comm. 2000). It contained 155 graves, with pottery, metal objects, stone knives, and worked bone tools among the grave goods. The meaning of these different burial practices in the rural sector requires further investigation.

I have considered these settlements to be inhabited by both local *ayllu* and provincial *mitayoq*, but all must have been provided with inka equipment for their official and daily tasks. They may have been perhaps confronted with various bylaws about how to live in these settlements, which has made them more homogeneous archaeologically.

Conclusions

Therefore, the relationship between the city and its hinterland can be seen in various ways. First, it provided vital irrigable and dry farmland, pastures, drinking water, stone quarries, timber, and other resources that were vital for sustaining the population of the city. Second, suburban villages were established close to the city for the housing of indigenous groups and *yanakuna* craftsmen brought from distant provinces to produce the paraphernalia used in ceremonies and also for use by prestigious provincial visitors. Third, it provided space for planned villages (*llaqta*) that were established more distant from the city for use by *mitayoq*, the construction workers, who had been brought to Cusco under provincial tribute obligations. These settlements and workers were overseen from isolated state *kancha* and the resulting produce stored in state *qolqa*. Fourth, its lands were allocated to the royal *panaqa* and *ayllu* of the city, not only for economic production but also for social production. Fifth, as we shall see in the next chapter, it provided vital cultural space for a network of *waka* and the *paqarina* of the royal *panaqa*, thus integrating it into the city.

11

Ceremony and Ritual

In any traditional city, politics, social activities, economic life, and the practice of ritual, ceremony, and religion were intimately interwoven. It is often difficult for the archaeologist to separate these functions, and it is easy to allow one to dominate interpretation. Inka archaeology is no different. As we have seen in previous chapters, while it is possible to separate the sacred from the profane, every aspect of inka public and private life was controlled by cultural mores and practices. These ensured that the sun would rise each day, that the ancestors, gods, and spirits were fed, and that they were consulted before state or private decisions of a political, economic, and social nature could be made. In other words, for the inkas, the sacred and the practice of ritual were vital for the well-being of the Sapa Inka, the state, the *panaqa,* and their own identity.

In this chapter, I consider inka ceremonies and rituals through the chronicle accounts, and I explore the relationship between Cusco and its hinterland through the *seqe* system and the role of its landscape in the origins, history, and ceremony. I also examine the archaeological record from both the urban and rural sectors to attempt to piece together certain rituals.

Ceremonial and Ritual Practice

Ceremonies were held in Cusco each day, each month, and each year in a calendrical cycle. Inka ritual and ceremonial activities on the state and private levels have been widely reported in the chronicles (Cobo 1990; Molina 1989). According to Cobo (1990: 110), such ceremonies were practiced without change in the order, form, location, sacrifices, offerings, orations, music, dances, or personnel. They were concerned with many things, such as matters of origins, dynasty, and succession, including royal birth, the inauguration of Sapa Inka, royal funeral (*purucaya*), and the health of the

Inka. There were also matters of religion and supernatural phenomena involving communication with Wiraqocha, the Sun, and the ancestral kings *inter alia*, the initiation of young boys, the solstices, the diplomacy and exchanges of meeting with visitors, the receipt of tribute, and the agricultural cycle of field preparation, planting, irrigation, harvest, the cleaning of the city, and victories in battle. There was also a ceremony, *itu raymi*, that could be called at any time in order to mitigate environmental disasters, such as earthquake, flood, drought, or plague.

The most basic ritual was the daily sacrifice to the Sun of a llama that took place at first light in Hawkaypata (Cobo 1990: 113). The animal, called a *napa*, was draped in a red mantle; its throat was slit, blood was drawn, and then the carcass was burned with coca leaves. Every month there was a larger sacrifice of 100 identical llamas or alpacas, which had been assembled from the flocks of the Inka or the Sun; for each month, this ritual required a different animal coat color or markings.

Most public ceremonies were conducted in Hawkaypata, around the *usnu* complex. They were generally attended by the statues of the major deities, including Punchaw (the Sun), Wiraqocha (the Creator), and Inti-Illapa (Thunder), accompanied by their priests, the mummies of previous Inkas and their wives, with their carers, the Sapa Inka himself and his court, as well as the members of the *panaqa* and *ayllu* of Hanan and Hurin Cusco. Each had their own seat in a precise location, according to status, around the *usnu*. Occasionally the statue of Wanakawri was present, as were the images of the provincial *waka* kept in Cusco. For some ceremonies, such as *sitwa*, all foreigners, those with "broken ears,"[1] and the deformed could not attend and were asked to leave the city. Dogs, too, were removed on certain occasions to prevent them from howling and desecrating the event.

Other locations, where major feasts occurred, included Qorikancha itself, Intipampa, and Limaqpampa. In the most fundamental ceremony, *qhapaq hucha*, when Qorikancha was dedicated, the major sacrifice occurred in front of the image of Punchaw in the temple, but because so few people could witness or participate in it, it was transferred to Hawkaypata for more general appreciation (Betanzos 1996: 48). As a result, this linked the religious center with the political, and it developed into the ceremony that was used to bind Cusco ritually to the provinces.

In Limaqpampa the maize harvest festival was celebrated in May (Cobo 1990: 71). This had been instigated by Pachakuti Inka Yupanki and was attended by the nobility dressed in long red cloaks. Great sacrifices were made, including the burning of llamas, clothing, and food and the burial of gold and silver objects (Betanzos 1996: 66). Similarly dressed people attended the *yawayra* ceremony in July to beseech the Sun and Thunder with sacrifices of white llamas, feathers, seashells, coca, and maize to grant them a productive year (Molina 1873: 20). Cobo (1990: 154) explained that the inauguration ceremony of a new Inka was held in Limaqpampa before the images of Punchaw and other gods, during which sacrifices were made of 200 children and 1,000 llamas. Llama figurines and gold and silver *qero* were buried, and cumbi cloth, seashells, and feathers were burned. Sarmiento (2007: 173) added that the inauguration of Wayna Qhapaq took place in Qorikancha, while he was presented to the people in Limaqpampa. Pumaqchupan, at the confluence of the two rivers, held one important ceremony, *mayucati*, when the ashes of the year's sacrifices were thrown into the river.

Procession and movement through the landscape, in the city, the heartland, and the more distant provinces, characterized several ceremonies (Moore 2005: 151–57; Zuidema 1999). These involved not only the carriage of the Sapa Inka, ancestral mummies, and deity images on litters, but also *panaqa* and *ayllu* members and soldiers marching in appropriate costumes and carrying colorful banners, as well as dancers, drummers, flautists, and conch-shell trumpeters. The street or road was cleaned in front of Sapa Inka and strewn with important things, such as ground shell and coca leaves, while llamas selected for sacrifice were also driven. During particular events various dances and processions wound their way through the streets between Qorikancha and Hawkaypata.

Many ceremonies linked the city to the rural hinterland, while others were associated with the worship of individual *seqe waka*. For example, the major *raymi* events were held at Sun temples for the June solstice on Mantucalla hill and for the December solstice at Pukinkancha. During the *warachiquy* initiation festival in the month of Qhapaq raymi, the novices had to visit Wanakawri on two occasions for sacrifices, race down from Anawarki, visit the summit of Yawiri, collect straw from Chakan Wanakawri, and visit Qalispukio. While the ceremony began in Qorikancha, they gathered each day before dawn in Hawkaypata to toast the Sun as it rose, and it was there that it culminated. The *sitwa* festival in September was used to drive out sickness, and it began when 400 warriors from the four urban *suyu* left the *usnu* in a relay into their own quarter as far as either the Vilcanota or Apurimaq rivers, where they ritually bathed. As a consequence, the boundary of the Inner Heartland was ritually defined as the place where the urban runners handed over to those from the Outer

Heartland. One other major ceremony, the inauguration of Sapa Inka, moved in procession from the hill of Quispikancha near Tipón in the east to Limaqpampa, where the investiture took place.

The Inka, nobles, and people who attended these ceremonies were provided with copious amounts of *chicha* and fine foods. On some occasions special maize dough cakes, prepared with the sacrificed llama blood called *sanku*, were served to guests on golden platters. The idols of the gods and the mummies of the Inka kings and queens were fed by burning the food in front of them and by pouring their *chicha* onto the ground in front or into a ceremonial urn and the *usnu* hole.

In these ceremonies, the common offerings form two types, those that were burned and those that were buried. Sacrificed llamas as well as foodstuffs, clothing, and carved wooden figurines were generally burned, and the residual charcoal and all unburned materials were ground up. In contrast, children, gold and silver objects, figurines, and sea shells were buried. For example, gold figurines were buried in sets around the *usnu* complex, each representing the social groups of the city (Betanzos 1996: 48). On certain occasions, sacrificed camelids, dogs, and guinea pigs were buried. Some offerings were thrown into a stream or pool or slung toward an inaccessible mountain, while others were simply blown on the wind.

A Cultural Landscape of Shrines

The nature of inka religion and its belief system meant that gods, ancestors, and oracles were maintained and consulted, as living beings, about different aspects of life, such as state affairs and private decisions. In addition, different physical phenomena were venerated, not only the Sun but also the Moon, thunder, lightning, wind, and hail as well as landscape features, including mountains, caves, cliffs, rocks, water features, and trees. The chroniclers estimated the number of shrines and sacred places in Cusco from 328 to over 450. These included six sacred mountains, Wanakawri, Anawarki, Yawiri, Senqa, Picol, and Pachatusan, which fringed the southern, western, and northeastern horizons of the city (Sarmiento 2007: 119) (figure 11.1), while snow-capped Awsangati was another important sacred place, dominating the downvalley skyline in the southeast, 80km away (Guaman Poma 1980: 275 [277], 280 [282]).

In the city, suburbs, and Inner Heartland, many natural and man-made places were dedicated as *waka*. These included mountains, hills, passes, rocks, caves, and water features or constructions that were tall or appeared

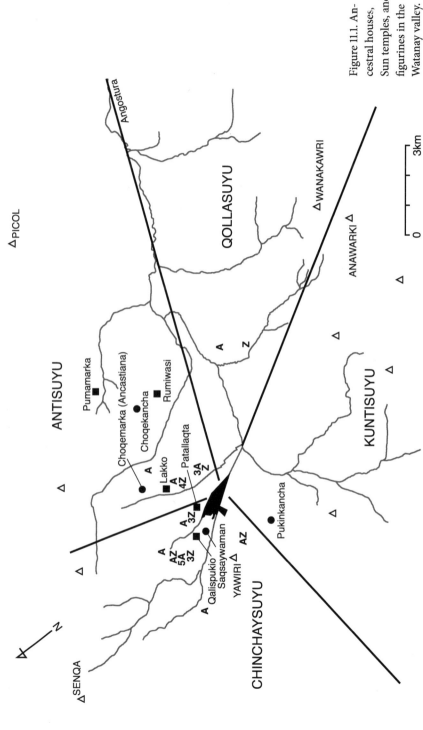

Figure 11.1. Ancestral houses, Sun temples, and figurines in the Watanay valley.

△PICOL

ANTISUYU

Pumamarka ■

Choqemarka (Ancastiana)
● Choqekancha
Rumiwasi ■

△
A
■ Lakko
A
4Z
Patallaqta
3A
Z

3Z ■
A

△
AZ
5A
3Z

A Qalispukio
Saqsaywaman ●
■

YAWIRI △

AZ

A Z

QOLLASUYU

△WANAKAWRI

ANAWARKI △

△

△

KUNTISUYU

△

● Pukinkancha

△

CHINCHAYSUYU

△SENQA
△
↗N

△WANAKAWRI

0   3km

Table 11.1. Physical types of *seqe waka*

Types	Chinchaysuyu	Antisuyu	Qollasuyu	Kuntisuyu	Total
Structures	15	10	7	8	40
Water features	22	32	26	22	102
Cave	1	1	0	2	4
Hill/mountain	14	14	22	24	74
Pass	3	2	0	3	8
Stone(s)	26	26	32	24	108
Quarry	1	3	0	0	4
Flat ground	13	8	17	7	45
Tomb	2	0	2	5	9
Trees	2	0	0	0	2
Idols	2	2	1	1	6
Road	1	0	0	1	2
Waka	0	1	1	0	2
Total observations	102	99	108	97	406
Total *waka*	85	78	85	80	328

Source: Cobo 1990: 51–84.

to enter the earth (Albornoz 1989). Any unusual feature, its color, shape, or sound, such as a rise in a flat plain, a rock in a cave, or even a bulge in a terrace wall, could have been the reason why one place became *waka* and a similar feature did not. There were also places with significant cultural associations, such as where the Inka had slept, or where a mythical ancestor had turned to stone, or where something had occurred in the myths of origin, ancestors, and defense of the city. Another class was the pass, where the traveler first glimpsed or lost sight of Cusco. At each place, specific rituals were performed and offerings made (Cobo 1990: 51–84).

One well-known grouping of shrines, known as the *seqe* system, was an orderly array of forty-one lines on which were located 328 *waka* that radiated from Qorikancha across the Inner Heartland, thus binding both the city and the rural districts irrevocably to the center (Cobo 1990; Bauer 1998; Zuidema 1964, 1990). The shrines were distributed more or less evenly between the four *suyu* and included a range of natural and man-made places, of which stones and water features (springs, etc.) were the most important with more than 100 examples each, followed by hills, buildings, and flat places (table 11.1). No one *suyu* dominated in any one particular class of shrine. As previously explained, this system also conveyed obligations for maintenance of both *waka* and *seqe* upon the various urban social groups and gave them rights to the adjacent territory. Each *waka* received its standard offerings, listed by Cobo (1990: 51–84) (table 11.2). However,

Table 11.2. Offerings at *seqe waka*

Type of offering	CH	AN	QO	CU	Total
Children	7	6	12	9	34
Gold	4	3	5	0	12
Silver	2	1	5	0	8
Figurines	2	3	2	0	7
Clothing	4	9	6	1	20
Shells	8	18	14	1	41
Llamas	4	7	1	0	12
Coca	0	2	1	1	4
Dust	1	0	0	0	1
Other things	1	0	0	0	1
Sacrifices	21	3	3	1	28
Ordinary sacrifice	4	0	0	0	4
Universal sacrifices	5	1	0	0	6
Universal sacrifices—no children	0	1	0	0	1
Usual sacrifices	0	5	4	0	9
Usual sacrifices, including children	0	0	0	1	1
Usual sacrifices—no children	0	0	3	0	3
Solemn sacrifices	3	2	0	0	5
Great sacrifices	2	0	0	0	2
All things in sacrifice	2	7	2	0	11
All things in sacrifice—no children	0	2	1	0	3
Everything else	3	0	3	2	8
Offerings	1	2	2	2	7
Eaten	0	1	0	0	1
Consumed	1	0	0	0	1
Venerated	13	5	3	0	21
Buried	2	0	0	0	2
Burned	3	2	0	0	5
Festivals	0	0	2	0	2
No information	25	21	39	65	150
Total	118	101	108	83	410
Number of *waka*	85	78	85	80	328

Source: Cobo 1990: 51–84.

no information was presented for 150 of them, while a further 88 received some form of "sacrifice" or "offering." There were 34 places where children were sacrificed and 41 that received various sea shells, while others were given clothing, gold and silver objects, and figurines.

Urban *Waka*

There are 53 places listed as *seqe waka* in the old city, in addition to Qori-kancha itself (Cobo 1990). In terms of offerings, described by Cobo, the urban and rural *waka* received the same kinds of gifts, including children.

Naturally, there is a cluster in and around the temple, with at least four shrines inside it (CH-2:1, CH-3:1, CU-1:1, CU-5:1) and a further fifteen adjacent to it, including four named Tampukancha (QO-3:1; QO-6:1; QO-9:1; CU-5:1) (table 12.2c). As expected, the *waka* that were houses of the siblings of the origin myth were also located next to the temple (QO-6:1, QO-8:1, QO-9:1, CU-5-1, CU-7:1), whereas others owned by, or associated with, a particular Sapa Inka were found in the city to the west of Qorikancha. For example, Pachakuti Inka Yupanki had a house, Condorcancha (CH-3:4), his birthplace at Kusikancha (CH-5:1), and the place where he slept Qora Qora (CH-5:5), while the worship of a stone (CH-4:4) at Qolqampata was instigated by him. There were also nine *pururauca waka* that had served him by defending the city during the Chanka war. Similarly, Wayna Qhapaq had his house of Pumacurco (CH-3:5), his palace at Qasana (CH-6:5), and the place where he slept at Cugitallis (CH-8:4). Surprisingly, Thupaq Inka Yupanki was not associated with an urban *waka*, only some in the hinterland, although Albornoz indicated that he had been born in Kusikancha (Duviols 1967: 26). Two *Qoya* were also venerated in the city, Mama Ocllo at a fountain called Tiqsicocha (CH-3:3), and Curi Ocllo, whose house was at Qolqampata (CH-4:3).

There were urban shrines devoted to the principal deities. For example, Wiraqocha Pachayachachiq was venerated at the house called Pukamarka (CH-6:2), while his *wawki*, a round stone (AN-1:2), stood next to Qorikancha. Illapa/Chuquilla was worshipped at Pukamarka (CH-5:2), while his priests bathed in Aucaypata paccha (CH-8:3). Wanakawri had also a shrine, dedicated to him in the city, a garden called Mancochuqui (CH-8:2), overlooking the Saphi river.

As noted in previous chapters, elsewhere in the city, *waka* were in all plazas (CH-5:4; CH-8:3; AN-5:1; QO-2:1), some streets (CH-5:3; CH-6:3), and most of the principal buildings and compounds, where there was either one (e.g., Kusikancha CH-5:1) or several in critical locations within it, such as Hatunkancha (CH-3:2; CH-3:3; CH-4:2), Qasana (CH-6-4; CH-6:5), and Pukamarka (CH-5:2; CH-6:2).

Rural *Waka*

The remaining *seqe waka* were located in the suburban villages and rural areas. It is tempting to consider that each carved rock or fountain must have been one, but this does not seem to have been the case; they may simply have been shrines within another system. While unsuccessful attempts have been made to identify each *waka* (e.g., Bauer 1998),[2] it is perhaps more profitable to examine patterns of cultural meaning that manifest in the field evidence and provide connection between the written description, the physical site, and its archaeological record. I have isolated two categories, ancestral "houses" and Sun temples, that merit further exploration (figure 11.1).

In the previous chapter, it was mentioned that there were important differences in the settlement and agricultural patterns between parts of Chinchaysuyu and the closer zones of Antisuyu, when compared with the rest of the Inner Heartland. In explanation, we can note that the prominent *panaqa* of Hanan Cusco were allocated the area to the west and north of the city and therefore claimed the most significant, but not necessarily the most productive, lands and resources. This encompassed the upper basin, including mountains, plateaux and the important Chakan canals. This area has many eroded limestone outcrops, some of which were carved, and naturally contained caves and springs, which became culturally important as *waka* and burial *machay*, and which, in turn, promoted the establishment of temples and royal tombs, drawing the ancestors into the daily life of the city by way of the provision of water. Terraced farming and herding took place in this area, conducted on behalf of these *panaqa*, probably by people from the workers' villages of Muyu Qocha and Choqekiraw and supported from the city itself.

Ancestral Houses (*Paqarina*)

Among the *seqe waka*, Cobo (1990: 51, 55) listed two places as "house of the Inka," namely, Patallaqta (CH-1:2), belonging to Pachakuti Inka Yupanki, and Qalispukio (CH-3:7), belonging to Thupaq Inka Yupanki. These were the places where the mummy and *wawki* of the dead Inka were kept and maintained along with its other possessions.[3] Pedro Pizarro (1986: 100–101) probably described one such location, a cave in which there was a golden effigy of a king as well as gold sandals, life-sized gold and silver llamas, and pottery. In the field, they have been identified as site clusters, surrounding the famous carved rock of Qenqo (Sherbondy 1982) and around the Qocha to the northern part of Saqsaywaman, respectively (Fernández 2001). Essentially these locations include a series of spatially related sites, which hitherto have been dealt with separately. Fieldwork by Farrington (2010c) and Farfán (2002) has demonstrated that each involves one or more carved rocks with tunnels and benches on which to sit a mummy, a curved niched wall that encloses a patio or plaza, channelized springs and pools, and at least one carved image of a feline (figure 11.1).

The Qocha is a large walled subcircular amphitheater, about 100m in diameter, with full-length niches on its southern side, that received water from nearby springs and reservoirs. Suchuna lies on its western side (figure 11.2). It has a series of terraces, a zigzag wall, a smaller niched subcircular feature with small limestone outcrops within it, carved rocks, and a larger limestone block with the remains of a tunnel.[4] The area to the north comprises some structures, a low limestone outcrop, carvings, and springs, while about 80m further north is the famous Tired Stone or Chingana Grande, a carved rock with the remains of a cave and associated with terraces and some structures. On its eastern side is Chingana Chico, a low limestone outcrop with extensive tunnels and internal carvings, including an altar. There is a zigzag wall on its eastern side, overlooking a valley that flows south into the city. This complex is thought to have been Qalispukio, the burial "house" of Thupaq Inka Yupanki, and almost certainly therefore the *paqarina* (origin place) of Hatun Ayllu (Fernández 2001).

Much of this complex has only been revealed in excavation since the mid-1980s. There are several buildings on the north side, including a niched courtyard adjacent to Chingana Grande, as well as terraces, a bath complex, and a *qolqa* (Socualaya 2008). Significant burials with grave goods have been recorded adjacent to the Qocha itself and Chingana Grande, while others can be seen eroding from the surface to the north. On the Suchuna terraces, over ninety burials, arranged in rows, have been excavated (Paredes 2003; Solis 1999; Torres 2001). All faced east or southeast toward the sacred mountains, Awsangati and Wanakawri. The majority were buried in clay capsules at different levels. This unusual technique would have required much preparation, because each capsule was placed on the surface and then covered with fill to level the terrace. Therefore, they must be more or less contemporary burials. Each has comparatively few grave goods, while several have none at all. These may have been part of Thupaq Inka Yupanki's retinue who chose to accompany him in death.

The Patallaqta complex is focused on the carved rock of Qenqo and has several limestone outcrops, caves, structures, and springs. It is thought to be not only the resting place of Pachakuti Inka's mummy but also the *paqarina* of Vicaquirao *panaqa*. Qenqo itself is a large carved limestone massif with feline and bird carvings, a tunnel, internal room, and altar. There is a semicircular patio on its northern side with a niched wall, fountain, and subsidiary structures that focus upon an upright stone, probably

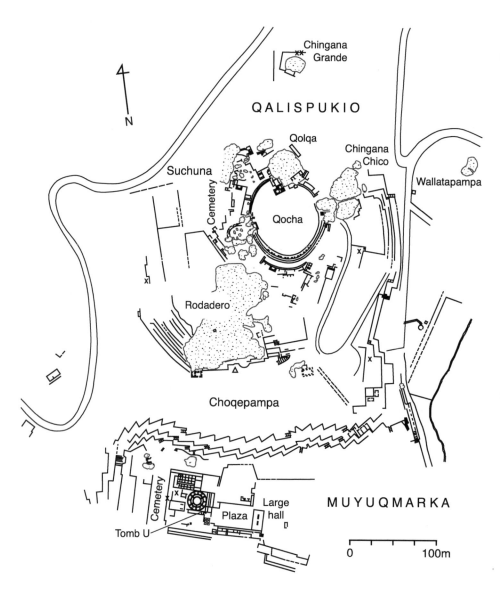

Figure 11.2. The ancestral house (*paqarina*) of Qalispukio and the Sun temple of Muyuq-marka at Saqsaywaman (after Vargas 2007). The crosses mark the location of burials, and the triangle marks the location of a cache of broken figurines and other miniature sculptures.

representing a puma, standing on a platform in front of the rock (Paternosto 1989: 66–77). There are some smaller carved rocks and caves to the north and terraces to the east. About 150m to the west is another large limestone outcrop with an overhang that overlooks Qenqo itself. It is associated with some structures, terraces, and a carved seat and continues to receive offerings. Below the main site to the south is Lower Qenqo, a low hill, which is walled in polygonal style with a zigzag section on its southern side. Its summit has carved rocks, vestiges of structures, and a patio.

There have been few excavations in this complex since the 1930s, when ten sets of human remains, one associated with three silver *tupu* and another with a decorated inka plate, were found during conservation work (Franco 1935), perhaps suggesting the burial of at least one elaborately dressed individual. Recently, the INC-Cusco has dug in the vicinity of the large western outcrop, revealing a large rectangular structure in the northwest sector with a complex of eleven small rooms, internally arranged around the perimeter, each with triple-jambed niches, and a group of five rectangular structures and a fountain in the southeast (Zegarra 2008). An offering in this sector included small baked clay llama feet, associated with a metal knife in the form of a llama mandible, decorated plates and *urpu*, and a bone *ruki* and needle. There was also a stone-lined tomb, containing a seated adult looking west with grave goods, including an *aqorasi*, tweezers, and spondylus beads. One room in another sector contained a collection of textile making equipment, such as spindle whorls, *ruki,* and palettes that had been burned when the building caught fire.

About 1km to the east lies a third complex that in many respects resembles the first two. It is focused on the limestone hill, known as Salonniyoq or Lakko, which has been elaborately carved on its summit and southern face, where there are also two short tunnels with altars and niches, one with a pair of carved felines and a snake at its entrance (Franco 1937). On the summit, there is a carving of felines, birds, and a snake (van de Guchte 1990). Aveni (1981) recorded an alignment for the June solstice sunset from a carved vertical plane to Waynaqorqor. Lakko overlooks other sites that are considered part of this complex, including several carved rocks and *machay* in the Chispayoq valley to the north, a reservoir to the south, and about 300m further south the carved rock, cave, and buildings of Kusilluchayoq, which also has a feline carving. As a result of its similar attributes, Farrington and Farfán (2002) have suggested that this complex could have been the "house" of Viracocha Inka and the *paqarina* of Sucsu *panaqa*.

Recent excavations around the base have revealed the importance of Lakko (Guillén 2008). On the southern side in front of the tunnel entrances, a series of buildings, patios, a passageway, and a zigzag wall have been discovered alongside the rock. One large rectangular structure, 14.6m (9r) by 6.6m (4r), has two doors and an interior dividing wall. There are two large, polished and shaped limestone blocks against its façade that must have served as altars, while in the interior, a polished limestone donut-shaped object was found that is about 45cm in diameter and about 20cm tall. A puma, lying on its right side, has been carved in the round on half of its rim. It is thought to be a portable rim for an *usnu* hole for the receipt of libations. Three spondylus llama figurines and a gold male figurine were also found near this building.

On the rock itself, 2.5m in front of this building, two double-jamb carved niches have been exposed, preserving red, blue, and white painted plaster. Among the finds are finely decorated inka *maka*, casserole dishes and plates with animal and human designs, bronze *tupu*, needles, *lauraki* with bird and anthropomorphic figures, *tumi*, a bone llama figurine, animal bone *ruki*, spatulae, and flute, and some spondylus flat beads. A gold bracelet and a bronze *tumi* were buried inside one cave, while eight funerary contexts have been discovered in stone-lined chambers. On the northeastern side of the hill, two *qolqa* were excavated with ventilation ducts and associated with carbonized maize and the remains of large, domestic storage vessels. At nearby Kusilluchayoq, investigations by Torres (pers. comm.) exposed more fully the structures adjacent to the carved outcrop, revealing a series of rooms, spaces, and niches as well as the tomb of an adult with two finely decorated *maka*. These excavations suggest that this complex was an important *paqarina* as well as the location of many rituals.

Rumiwasi

Farrington and Farfán (2002) have claimed that this site complex was also a "house" of an Inka, probably Yawar Waqaq, and the *paqarina* of Aucaille *panaqa*. It is situated on the hillside above the modern town of San Sebastián and has seven structural sectors. The lowest, Sector I, is a walled limestone outcrop that has a short tunnel with an internal niche through it and three narrow, *chullpa*-like entrances in the wall beneath it that give access to small chambers. This is the focal point for a curved, terraced patio with two buildings and a probable fountain within it. On top of the rock, there is a rectangular building with an external niche on either side of its main door, facing southwest, and another on the eastern side, facing southeast toward Awsangati. The hillside above has large limestone boulders with *machay* containing human bones and several other building groups. For example, Sector V is a carved rock in a patio with two *kallanka* and a spring from which a canal flows through terraces toward Rumiwasi itself. Sector VII is the uppermost and is a walled rectangular platform, 48m by 9.5m, with at least one looted grave, inka sherds, and burnt llama bone.

Small-scale excavations have uncovered much fine elaborate inka pottery as well as decorated lucre vessels, inka in form and to some extent in decoration (Diáz and Farfán 2000). Sector I is the most distinctive with decorated *maka*, plates, and *qero* and two unusual lidded jars. Other finds include a bronze *tumi* and *tupu*, camelid bone *ruki*, some brown textile fragments, a stone bowl, and fine pieces of shaped mica. The other sectors have fewer *maka* and plates but contain *urpu* and cooking pots.

Other "Houses"

Cobo (1990: 63, 67) named two other locations as "houses" of important inkas. One is Amarumarkawasi (AN-1:7), which he stated belonged to Amaru Thupaq Inka. This is a large limestone massif to the north of Qenqo, called Lanlakuyoq. It has several tunnels and structures within its northwestern corner as well as several walls (van de Guchte 1990). It has some carvings, particularly of niches, but no felines. On its southern side, there is a short zigzag wall. It lies on the boundary between Chinchaysuyu and Antisuyu on the watershed of the Puqru and Amaru streams. Amaru Thupaq Inka was the brother of Thupaq Inka Yupanki, who governed the city when the king was absent; hence his "house" has a liminal position between two *suyu*. It probably held his mummy.

The second is Pumamarka, a *waka* (AN-6:6), where the mummy of the wife of Pachakuti Inka Yupanki, Mama Anawarki, was kept and received "children and other things" (Cobo 1990: 67). It is a complex site with a limestone outcrop located to the north from which issues a perennial spring. Below this a colonial hacienda occupies at least two fine inka buildings, built of rectangular coursed andesite ashlars, which are separated by a double-jamb doorway and passage. Each is about 13.0m by 6.2m with two doors facing south, while the interiors have standard niches. Excavations in one revealed two burials, of which one is of a 35-year-old female, who was accompanied by a *maka*, some plates, and a pedestalled pot (El Comercio 09/06/08). On the eastern side, there is a wall with several full-length niches facing north.

The excavations have also demonstrated that the patio had been built up in colonial times, because at a depth of about 3m below the level of the inka buildings, the top of a fine andesite wall was found, itself about 3m tall. A substantial curved walled structure at this level has also been found, which has led the archaeologists to consider its similarities to Qorikancha and suggest that it was probably a temple (El Comercio 09/06/08).

Wimpillay and the Ancestors of Hurin Cusco

At Wimpillay there was an ancestral house for the mummies of earlier kings, which were kept secluded and worshipped in special locations in Hurin Cusco and brought out for particular celebrations in Qorikancha, Hawkaypata, and Wanakawri. In 1559, Polo de Ondegardo discovered the stone image of Manqo Qhapaq in Wimpillay, and the mummy of his son, Sinchi Roca, was found in a house called Aqoywasi in the same village. The stone image was described as one *vara* (83.5cm) tall, "dressed and properly adorned" (Cobo 1979: 111–12; Sarmiento 2007: 74–75) and his *wawki* was a carved stone bird called Inti. The mummy was wrapped in a coarse maguey cloth bundle that lay between some copper bars and beside his *wawki*, a stone carved in the shape of a fish called Wanachiri Amaru (Cobo 1979: 114; Sarmiento 2007: 78). Despite its importance, the archaeology of inka Wimpillay remains unpublished, although the excavations reported in chapter 10 discovered fine architecture, human burials, and offerings. The nature of the *paqarina* remains unknown.

Sun Temples

In the rural hinterland, Sarmiento (2007: 145) reported that Pachakuti had four Sun temples built and furnished with golden idols, *waka*, and servants in order that they could be walked between like the "stations of the cross." Cobo (1990: 65, 67, 82) named three *seqe waka* as peripheral Sun temples, two to the north at Choqemarka (AN-3:4) and Choqekancha (AN-6:3) and Pukinkancha (CU-10:2) in the south, that participated in rituals during the June solstice and December solstice, respectively. Cieza de León (1959: 153–55) described the fourth at Saqsaywaman (figure 11.1).

Choqemarka

Choqemarka was described as a *waka* (AN-3:4) and a Sun temple located on Mantocallas hill, itself a *waka* (AN-3:6), and there were two others, both fountains, on its flanks.[5] Cobo (1990: 65) stated that it was "where the Sun descended many times to sleep" and that it was offered children. The

Mantocallas *waka* was venerated for the celebration of the maize harvest in the presence of the Inka, who remained there until the June solstice. Cobo added that these were the focus of drunken feasts with offerings of carved and dressed wooden figurines and the burning of llamas. Although the Sun temple and hill were in the same location, neither toponym has survived.

On the basis of archaeoastronomical measurements, Aveni (1981) and Zuidema (1981) deduced that, since the June solstice sun could be seen setting behind Waynaqorqor from a carved feature on the summit of Lakko, then that site must have been Choqemarka. However, that place was probably only a *paqarina*; it was not large enough for other functions. In contrast, Bauer and Dearborn (1995: 87) have suggested that Mantocallas must be the hill across the Chuspiyoq valley, now known as Ancastiana, which is higher and more massive than Lakko. There are rectangular compounds on its summit, and from there they have achieved similar observations of the June solstice sun setting behind Waynaqorqor. Ancastiana is partially terraced, and at its base on the western side there is a fine wall with outward facing niches, certainly an architectural symbol for an important building complex. Neither the enclosures nor the lower finely niched terrace have been excavated.

Choqekancha

According to Molina (1989: 123), this was an important hill above San Sebastián that received human sacrifices to the Sun during the *qhapaq hucha* ceremony. Cobo (1990: 67) described it as a hill (AN-6:3) and a Sun "house," and it received a solemn sacrifice "to gladden the Sun." At the end of the June festivals of *inti raymi*, it was a subsidiary place to Choqemarka, a destination for half of the Cayo dancers,[6] while it shared six llamas for sacrifice with another hill, Paucarkancha (Cobo 1990: 142).

While no hill above San Sebastián has retained the name, three authors have placed it in three different locations.[7] It is probable that none is correct and that it may have been a rounded hill to the west of Kallachaka and north of Rumiwasi, which is currently being farmed and on which is located an ancient reservoir on the Suqsu-Aucaille canal. There is a scatter of inka sherds in the fields over this hilltop but no surviving architecture.

Pukinkancha

This *waka* (CU-10:2) was described by Cobo (1990: 82) as a "house of the Sun" on the hill above Cayaokachi that received child sacrifices. Molina (1989: 49, 110) remarked that it housed painted boards that related inka history and that the statue of the Sun, Wayna Punchaw, was taken there on the 23rd day of *qhapaq raymi*, to witness sacrifices to the gods in order for all nations and peoples to prosper and multiply. It was then returned to Cusco, preceded by the *sunturpaucar* and a gold and silver llama. Other *waka* included its upper enclosure wall, called Kancha (CU-10:3), which also received offerings, and a fountain, Pukinpukyo (CU-11:3), that had none specified (Cobo 1990: 82).

Zuidema (1982: 63–65) claimed that the Inka had watched the December solstice sunrise over Mutu mountain from this temple. Although Bauer and Dearborn (1995: 91–92) have indicated that their observations disprove such a hypothesis, Zuidema (2003) continues to doubt their judgment. Nevertheless, it was a Sun temple that was visited at the December solstice, probably to view the sunrise.

In 1990, with urbanization colonizing the slopes of Pukin, many worked andesite blocks were uncovered in digging house foundations. As a result, Justo Torres conducted some rescue excavations for the INC-Cusco. He found a foundation wall, more blocks, and several offerings, including pottery and some flat gold pieces (Bauer 1998). Later, Merma (2001) excavated more than 160sqm in advance of the construction of a sports field. Under a thick overburden, she found a 12.5m rectangular andesite wall and its footings that had been part of a *kancha* building, as well as a prepared floor, several charcoal and ash lenses with burnt animal bone, and inka pottery. Beneath the floor, there were five burials with six individuals, including an elaborate double burial of an adult couple with twenty-one vessels, while an adult female had twelve, although the remainder only had three, one, and none. These were all discovered inside sealed clay capsules, probably placed as offerings on the original surface prior to the construction of the inka temple. A further investigation in 2003 by Pilares exposed similar finds and graves (Villacorta 2011).

Saqsaywaman

Since the 1530s, this impressive site to the northwest of the city has been invariably described as a fortress (e.g., Sancho 1917: 193) because of its hilltop location, its three monumental zigzag walls, and the role it played during the uprising of 1536. Both Sancho (1917: 194) and Pizarro (1986: 104) noted its many storerooms, which contained clothing and weapons. However, Cieza de León (1959: 153–55) remarked that the inkas regarded it as a "house of the Sun," and although some of its structures were *waka* in the *seqe* system, unlike other temples, it was not part of that system. Betanzos

(1996: 155) claimed that it had been planned by Thupaq Inka Yupanki and constructed over a six-year period.

Saqsaywaman occupies a long ridge that overlooks the city to the southeast, and it is flanked on the north by three parallel, zigzag terraced walls, made of cyclopean limestone blocks, that are adjacent to a large plaza called Choqepampa. It is known from the chronicles that there were three towers, of which one, called Muyuqmarka, was round and stood at the western end, adjacent to a rocky outcrop. The second and third towers remain ill-defined along the ridge line. On the southern side, there are terraces, some niched, and at the eastern end of the ridge at Cruz Moqo is a fountain. The whole site was systematically dismantled during the sixteenth century for its building blocks (Dean 1998).

Archaeological work commenced with investigations by Uhle in 1905, who dug on the uppermost zigzag terrace and discovered a probable offering of several bronze objects, including a 50–60cm long bar with both ends doubled, a conical plumb bob, a chisel and tweezers, as well as eight camelid bone *ruki*, many pierced animal teeth for a necklace, a feline incisor, a ceramic disc, quartz knives, and a piece of crystalline quartz (Valencia 1979). Conservation and restoration excavations under Valcárcel (1934, 1935) took place on the zigzag terraces and at the western end of the ridge, exposing the drains and circular footings of the Muyuqmarka tower and some rectangular building outlines. A large hall with a central line of rectangular column footings was exposed on the eastern side of a small plaza as well as a series of buildings adjacent to a terrace wall on its southern side (Valcárcel 1934: 4–8). Although these excavations produced exceptional discoveries, no notes survive on archaeological context. In terms of individual finds, there are two female silver figurines, a spondylus male one, a pair of feet from another spondylus one, and the head of a ceramic figurine. He also found one gold and two spondylus llama figurines and the head of another in limestone. The inventory listed many spondylus beads and pendants, some stone carved maize cobs and kernels, several pairs of plates, miniature *maka* and other items of pottery, as well as several stone *qonopa* and other stone and bone objects. While the remains of at least fifty individuals were found as well as three other boxes of human skeletal material, Julien (2004) has only pieced together twelve burials and their grave goods; unfortunately, their precise discovery location remains unknown.

During further conservation work in 1982, Fidel Ramos discovered eleven adult male burials behind segment #26 of the third wall near the western gate (Barreda and Valencia 2007: 122). Each was seated and covered with clay.[8] They contained a series of bronze objects, such as bracelets, an *aqorasi,* and a six-pointed mace head, while other finds included *ruki,* spindle whorls, a bone tube, a vicuña wool textile fragment, a decorated killke plate, and small ceramic disks.

The Muyuqmarka tower has three concentric walls and buttress footings and drains within a 22.6m (14r) square structure. Its central room is only 9.35m (5.8r) in diameter and was entered from the northern side. It was surrounded by several rectangular buildings and patios. In the northeastern corner of the southern rectangular structure, a rich burial was found in Tomb U, while the remains of another were discovered in the northwestern corner (Franco and Llanos 1940). Excavations in the late 1990s uncovered more structures, including a large rectangular building with a grid of 1.6m square footings, probably for storage bins, to the north, and a large hall with wide walls and two lines of rectangular column footings to the west. These also revealed several major offerings in the area to the west of the tower, including the burial of an adult male, associated with a *tupu* and a piece of malachite, and the disturbed tomb of a young female. On the southern side, eight buildings were found in 2004 containing a wide range of potsherds of inka, killke, chimú, and tiwanaku as well as gold and silver spangles and ear spools, precious stone, spondylus shell, and cut bone. The excavators, Gloria Choque and Sabino Quispe, considered these workshops for fabricating ceremonial miniature objects, including figurines (Xinhua News Agency, 11/16/2004).

On the western terrace edge, the tomb of a seated male was found with a *maka*, a pair of plates, and a small *urpu* with silver bells and *tupu* (Bonnett 2003), while on the terrace below, Paredes (2003) discovered a line of fourteen tombs, some quite shallow, one covered by an *urpu* and two in clay capsules. The associated goods and offerings are very similar to those reported by Julien (2004), suggesting that the latter were also from a terrace, perhaps the zigzag walls.

Elsewhere in the site, both Pardo (1970) and Valencia (1970a) reported graves on the northern side of the plaza, while Valencia (1970b) has also found a layer of deliberately broken figurines and other stone micro-sculptures of humans, animals, and plants in Choqepampa itself. Bauer and Dearborn (1995: 88) have noted that at the June solstice the sun can be viewed setting behind Waynaqorqor from the Choqepampa plaza.

From an archaeological perspective, the temple characteristics that this site displays are its massive zigzag walls, its niched wall on the southern side overlooking the city, its round tower, and the quality of its architecture.

Its burials and offerings in structures and on terraces seem to be dedicatory in nature, perhaps for the inauguration of the temple. While the finds from the 1930s suggest many ritual offerings, it is quite difficult to associate these together spatially and stratigraphically or even to any specific events.

Other Shrines and Offerings

There are other rural places that may have been shrines. For example, excavations near some limestone outcrops, carved rocks, and fountains, including Wallatapampa (Guevara 2008), Inkilltambo (Andina 09/21/2008, 12/17/2008), *waka* Pachakuti (Uscachi 2009), and Titiqaqa (Prada 1986) have revealed offerings as evidence for veneration. Yet none can be identified within the *seqe* system.

The Archaeology of Ritual and Ceremony

As discussed, most inka ceremonies and rituals involved much oration, procession, music, singing, and dancing as well as feasting, drinking, and making offerings and sacrifices. The archaeologist has a difficult task to identify the signature of such activities in the general accumulation of deposits. The public places, where such major events took place, can be investigated systematically, but ritual at the household level, which used ordinary artifacts, animals, and plants, becomes difficult to distinguish from domestic discard. Nevertheless, archaeologists have noted patterns in such assemblages that might suggest some kind of formalized ritual behavior. Therefore, it is not only the type and number of items that are important markers of such activity but also their disposition relative to each other and their surroundings, their archaeological context, and the general geographic location. One example from England demonstrates that so-called domestic debris found in ditches at the early Neolithic site of Windmill Hill in England was similar both in content and method of disposal, to suggest some kind of ritual feasting and drinking (Whittle et al. 1999). In Mexico, Elson and Smith (2001) have been able to establish patterned deposits at Aztec sites, particularly houses, and have equated these with documentary descriptions of the New Fire Ceremony. However, the latter example is rare, as most archaeology does not have such good historical accounts to assist it.

The documentation for inka calendrical and other festivals and rituals does not appear to be comprehensive enough to observe distinguishing features in the assemblages that enable the archaeologist to state that a particular context derives from a particular ceremony. Nevertheless, Reinhard (2005) and Ceruti (2004) *inter alia* have argued that the human sacrifices on high mountain tops in Qollasuyu and Kuntisuyu with their associated assemblages of pottery, figurines, and other artifacts are indicative of the *qhapaq hucha* ceremony. While they may be right, Molina (1989: 123) stated that the Inka's instructions for this ceremony were that children were to be strangled and buried with "gold and silver figures of humans and silver ones of llamas, and they burned camelids, clothing and little baskets of coca." However, there is nothing specific in this assemblage that exclusively links it with that particular ritual. For example, Cobo (1990: chaps. 13–16) reported that such artifacts were also offered at *waka* in other contexts in Cusco. What Reinhard and Ceruti have found is a patterned assemblage that is repeated at other types of site in Tawantinsuyu, such as La Plata island off the Ecuadorian coast and at Pachacamac on the central coast.

In the majority of inka ceremonies, most offerings were either buried, burned in a brazier or on the ground, poured into an *usnu* basin or river, or consumed by the participants. In most cases, the resultant debris was collected and stored in Pumaqchupan, from where it would be dumped into the river at the start of *mayucati*. Therefore, very little would have survived for the archaeological record, and if it did, it would be exceedingly difficult to distinguish whether animal bones, plant remains, charcoal, and ash were the product of domestic discard or ritual disposal. Cobo (1990: 110) wrote that inka ritual practice was "very orderly and careful" and unchanging, but the offerings were different according to the gods, shrines, and purpose. Therefore, the archaeologist should be able to determine patterns in the location, the nature and number of objects, and their placement relative to each other in order to be able to consider potential meaning for any deposit.

For example, assemblages of burnt animal bones, charcoal, and ash found in lenses at Qorikancha and Hawkaypata must be the product of ritual action, not domestic discard. At Tambokancha, many piles of burnt remains have been found associated with beads, broken pottery, and other artifacts, suggesting that dressed wooden effigies were burned as focus objects, such as Cobo (1990: 65) recorded for Mantocallas, or that other objects, such as *tumi* and stone knives, performed that role. The overall context of these deposits suggests that pottery was also ritually smashed, tomb contents were removed, doorways were sealed, walls were pulled down, and roofs were deliberately burned and collapsed over these floors. This indicates a ritual of "house" abandonment that appears to have had a long history in the Andes (e.g., Moseley et al. 2005). It might be suggested that this had been Manqo II's reason for the burning of Cusco in 1536, which destroyed many urban structures.

There are several specific artifact patterns observed in excavations in Cusco that point to either a complete ritual or part of one. Most offerings, including burials, are arranged in deliberately dug pits or placed in large vessels that are located in specific places and that may indicate the same meaning or two different ones. In many cases, these have been capped by a flat rock, pot, or piece of plaster or flooring. In the burials at special places, such as at Suchuna, Muyuqmarka, and Pukinkancha, a third form of placement is the construction of a clay capsule, which itself is buried by piling earth around and over it.

An example of an offering in a large *urpu*, 96cm in diameter, was found in an inka building in the Banco Wiese (mz16) by Julio Maza (1995). It was set 1.75m below floor level and contained eleven fine pottery items with a large tetrapod pot as the central focus, flanked on either side by two pairs of plates, each cream with a red central spot and placed on edge, with a red and cream jar in front and a bowl and a small pot positioned behind. This collection of pots, arranged within the *urpu*, is distinctive, but its meaning has been lost. It was associated with camelid bones, textile fragments, and some ash. Nearby, there was a second offering in a pit that contained a circular bronze *aqorasi* as a focus with a silver *tumi*, a bronze *tumi*, various silver and bronze *tupu* and shafts, and a round *maran* and *tunaw* made of granite.

Most offerings appear to have a focus artifact, such as a *maka*, figurine, human body, or even a single human bone. Other objects are usually placed to one side or another, but rarely behind, the focus. In addition, objects may be placed at different heights in a pit. For example, at Waynapata, a significant feline-handled pot was placed at head height and other artifacts at the feet. In many cases, pairs of objects identical in size and decoration are found adjacent to each other, either right side up, inverted, or on edge. This is often considered to be representative of the andean concept of duality, displaying a balance between social groupings or other forces, but the variations in placement mean that there may be other more subtle meanings. The placement of pottery and wooden and metal vessels in an offering or burial also was part of the provision of food, either to a deity, specifically to Pachamama, or to the deceased for its journey to the afterlife. It should be noted that specific cooking vessels, such as pedestalled pots, are characteristically found fire-blackened, suggesting that cooking took place as part of the ritual, while other vessels probably contained food and *chicha*, such as at Waynapata.

The direction in which an object is facing in the arrangement may also be critical. For example, the burials at Suchuna, facing southeast, are thought to be looking toward Wanakawri or Awsangati. Similarly, the nubbin on a *maka* or *urpu* or even the decoration panel may have been deliberately oriented when the offering was made to look toward something significant.

Another characteristic is that many objects occur in such contexts as miniature versions of basic ceramic, wooden, metal, or textile forms, including vessels, figurines and effigies, clothing, tools, and houses. Both Sillar (1994) and Meddens (1994) have considered these as aspects of communication with the deities, citing the role that children play in such matters, and that the miniature, called *illa* or *ekeko*, contains the essence of the full-sized object and represents it in an offering to the ancestors and gods, even though it is tiny and nonfunctional.

This principle can be seen in the common practice of burying anthropomorphic and/or zoomorphic figurines, made of gold, silver, copper, or spondylus, as a focus object or as an accompaniment to one. These are generally only 2.5cm to 10cm tall, although larger ones were used in specific ceremonies. The anthropomorphic figurines are commonly associated with miniature *tupu*, implying that they were dressed with mantles and headdresses, such as those on the high mountain tops. If these objects are thought to contain the "essence" of what they represent, then they must be substitute humans and llamas and therefore can be interpreted as surrogate sacrifices. Among the *seqe waka*, there were three locations that specifically received anthropomorphic figurines and wooden effigies, and three more that received zoomorphic ones, while eight received miniature clothing (Cobo 1990).[9] It should be noted that at three of these locations, children were also sacrificed.

Figurines have been found in several places in the old city as well as in the rural hinterland (table 11.3). Anthropomorphic figurines have been recovered from archaeological deposits in three important ritual places in the city: Qorikancha,[10] the Qorikancha esplanade and park, and at Pumaqchupan, while a fourth is from a *kancha* patio in Kusikancha (figure 11.3). Others have been found casually in the grounds of Qasana palace (mz8) and in Pumacurco (mz28). In the rural areas, they have been excavated at several important sites, including the Sun temple complex of Muyuqmarka, where a figurine workshop was found,[11] and elsewhere in Saqsaywaman

Table 11.3a. Anthropomorphic figurines from the city and the inner heartland

Location and excavation	Plan-unit/ seam	Material	Sex	Context, Museo Inka cat no.	Description, height
URBAN					
Qorikancha cloister	B	Silver hollow	F	Cala II A-2 stratum 3: arranged with minia-ture *tupu* (2 silver; 3 gold)	Standing
Qorikancha cloister	B	Gold-silver	M	Cala II A-2, stratum 3: arranged with minia-ture *tupu* (5 silver)	Standing
Qorikancha cloister	B	Gold	F	Unit I-17, depth 70cm	Standing, 10.0cm
Qorikancha cloister	B	Gold	F	At a depth of 1.0–1.1m	Standing, 3.0cm
Qorikancha cloister	B	Silver, laminated	F, F	At a depth of 1.0–1.1m	2 standing, 6.0cm, 7.0cm
Qorikancha cloister	B	Silver	F	Cala II	Standing, 12.0cm
Qorikancha cloister	B	Spondylus	M, F	1972 cala, but not described	Several standing
Qorikancha park and esplanade	B	Copper Bone	M F	Square C'-25, stratum 2	Standing Standing
Intipampa	B	?	?	In excavation	?
Pumaqchupan	—	Silver	F	Offering, context un-known; 57/1627	Standing, missing feet, 14.5cm
Kusikancha (sector III)	IIA	Silver	M	In excavation; sector V in *kancha* patio	Standing, 11.0
Pumacurco	III	Gold, laminated	F	Casual excavation	Standing, 2.8cm
Pumacurco	III	Gold, laminated	F	Casual excavation	Standing, 2.8cm
Pumacurco	III	Gold, laminated	F	Casual excavation	Standing, 2.8cm
Pumacurco	III	Gold, laminated	M	Casual excavation	Standing, 2.8cm
Pumacurco	III	Gold, laminated	F	Casual excavation	Standing, 5.0cm
Qasana	A	Metal?	M, F	Casual excavation	~2 standing
SUBURBAN-RURAL	Site type				
La Calera, San Blas	Terrace	Bronze, hollow	M	Context unknown, 33–929	Standing, blowing a trumpet, 2.3cm

continued

Table 11.3a—*Continued*

SUBURBAN-RURAL	Site type	Material	Sex	Context, Museo Inka cat no.	Description, height
Saqsaywaman Muyuqmarka	Sun temple	Silver, hollow	F, F	Excavation, context unknown; 1–381, 1–382	2 standing, 5.8cm, 5.8cm
Saqsaywaman Muyuqmarka	Sun temple	Spondylus	M	Excavation, context unknown; 1–427	Standing, 4.8cm
Saqsaywaman Muyuqmarka	Sun temple	Spondylus	?	Excavation context unknown	Standing, not known
Saqsaywaman Muyuqmarka	Sun temple	Gold, silver, spondylus	M, F	In excavation of eight buildings to S of tower	Not known
Saqsaywaman Paucarmarka	Sun temple	Coral	F	Excavation context, depth 30cm	Standing, not known
Saqsaywaman Cruz Moqo	Temple	Gold	?	Excavation, offering context	Standing, 2cm, sitting, 8mm
Saqsaywaman Choqepampa	Plaza	Calcite	M, F	In upper 60–80cm with other broken miniature objects	~11, broken
Chingana Grande	Ancestral house	Silver	F	Context unknown beside carved rock	Walking, 3.5cm
Wallatapampa	Carved rock	Spondylus	M	In room beside carved rock, associated with line of four llamas	Standing
Lakko	Ancestral house	Gold	M	Beside carved rock and structure R-03	Standing, missing left ear, 3.42cm
Titiqaqa	Carved rock	Baked clay	F	Excavation, context unknown beside carved rock	Standing
Titiqaqa	Carved rock	Baked clay	F	Excavation, context unknown beside carved rock, 2–414	Standing holding *qero*, 6.0cm
Titiqaqa	Carved rock	Spondylus	?	Excavation, context unknown beside carved rock, 2–158	98 body parts
Titiqaqa	Carved rock	Spondylus	—	Excavation, context unknown beside carved rock, 2–17	Feet only
Picchu chapel	Summit	Gold	F	In foundation trench	Standing
Tiqa Tiqa Carmenqa	Hillside	Spondylus	M	Pit in foundation trench	Standing
Wayna Tawqaray	Hillside	Camelid bone	M	Excavation in *qolqa*	Standing

* Barreda noted that tens of anthropomorphic and zoomorphic figurines, carved from spondylus, as well as several in bronze, were recovered from the Qorikancha cloister in 1972.

Table 11.3b. Zoomorphic figurines from Cusco and the inner heartland

Location and Excavation	Plan-unit / seam	Material	Animal	Context	Description
URBAN					
Qorikancha alcove between R1 and R2	B	Spondylus Limestone Crystal quartz	Llama Llama Alpaca	Pit 3 strat-2, depth 55cm " Pit 4 strat-2	Standing Head only Head only
Qorikancha alcove between R1 and R2	B	Spondylus	Llama	—	Head only
Qorikancha cloister	B	Silver/gold	Llama	Depth 1.10m	Standing
Qorikancha cloister	B	Gold	Llama	Depth 1.10m	Standing
Qorikancha cloister	B	Spondylus	Llama	1972 cala	Several standing
Qorikancha fountain	B	Spondylus	Llama	In fine sand beneath stone floor of fountain, covered with inka sherds	2 standing
Intipampa	B	Metal?	Llama	Not known	Standing
Hawkaypata	A	Gold Silver Spondylus	Llama Llama Llama	Line of four lla-mas beside *usnu* platform	Standing 2 standing Standing
Qasana	A	Metal?	Llama	Casual excavation	~2 standing
Almirante	A	Copper	Llama	Casual excavation	Standing
Pumaqchupan		Spondylus	Llama		Standing
Pumacurco	III	Gold Gold	Llama Puma	Casual excavation	Standing 2 standing
SUBURBAN-RURAL	Site type				
Saqsaywaman Muyuqmarka	Sun temple	Spondylus	Llama Llama	Excavation, context unknown: 1–2, 1–3, 1–4	2 standing Head only
Saqsaywaman Muyuqmarka	Sun temple	Gold, silver, spondylus	Llama	In excavation of 8 buildings to S of tower	Not known
Saqsyawaman Choqepampa	Plaza	Calcite	Llama, fish, bird	In upper 60–80cm with other broken miniature objects	~13 broken
Wallatapampa	Carved rock	Gold Silver Spondylus Copper	Llama Llama Llama Copper	Line of four in room beside carved rock with a spondylus male figurine	Standing Standing Standing Standing

continued

Table 11.3b—*Continued*

SUBURBAN-RURAL	Site type	Material	Animal	Context	Description
Lakko	Ancestral house	Spondylus	Llama	Beside carved rock and structure R-03	3 standing
Lakko	Ancestral house	Limestone	Llama	In excavation unit SW UE3-B1–3	Standing
Titiqaqa	Carved rock	Gold	Llama	Beside carved rock, 2–237	Standing
Picchu chapel	Summit	Gold	Llama	In foundation trench	Standing
Tiqa Tiqa, Carmenqa	Hillside	Gold	Llama	Offering in house foundation trench	Standing
San Sebastián	Not known	Gold	Llama	Casual excavation	Standing
San Sebastián	Not known	Bronze/silver	Llama	Casual excavation	Standing
San Sebastián	Not known	Bone or spondylus	Llama	Casual excavation	Standing
Peqoypata	Isolated *kancha*	Spondylus	Llama	Excavated offering, with killke jar and carved stone	Standing

(Andina 09/09/2008; Valcárcel 1934; Valencia 1970b), at the Lakko *paqarina* complex, at the carved rocks of Titiqaqa and Wallatapampa, and on slopes overlooking the city at La Calera, Picchu, and Tiqatiqa (figure 11.1).

One particular arrangement is demonstrated in the Qorikancha patio in which a figurine forms the focus of an array of miniature *tupu*, which was also replicated with foci of human milk teeth and a child's mandible. Similar contexts have been found near the temple, where almost identical offerings were noted on the esplanade and in Intipampa. The interchangeability of the central focus between figurine and child cranial bones and teeth confirm the *ekeko* principle, and both items probably represent a child sacrifice. This point raises the issue that in some graves there are only partial skeletons deposited with objects; for example, one extensive offering from Tipón contained only a few bones from two individuals inside a large *maka* (Delgado 1998). In most cases, this cannot be attributed to poor bone preservation because several of the thicker, more robust long bones are generally missing. Therefore, there is a deliberate use of a human bone to represent a complete individual.

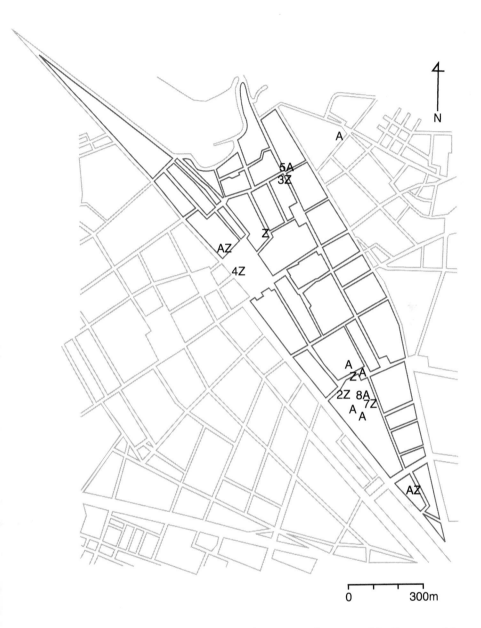

Figure 11.3. The distribution of figurines in the city. *A*, anthropomorphic; *Z*, zoomorphic.

The distribution of zoomorphic, mainly llama, figurines is similar (figures 11.1, 11.3). Several, including broken ones, have been found in archaeological contexts in the city at critically important ritual places such as the Qorikancha, the fountain alongside the Sun temple, at Hawkaypata, and at Pumaqchupan. They have also been found in Qasana and in mz9A, the location of Waskar's palace, and along Pumacurco. In the rural hinterland, they have been discovered at Muyuqmarka Sun temple and other parts of its complex, the Lakko *paqarina* complex, the Wallatapampa and Titiqaqa carved rocks, the Picchu hilltop chapel and Tiqatiqa, overlooking the city, and lower down the valley near San Sebastián and Peqoypata. While they were discovered in ones and twos in specific contexts, one arrangement stands out: a line of four llama figurines, found alongside the Hawkaypata *usnu* platform; another has been recently excavated at Wallatapampa with the addition of a spondylus male figurine (Guevara 2008). This pattern has been previously recorded on high mountain tops, such as Llullaillaco (Ceruti 2003) and Misti (Reinhard 2005). It is thought to represent the male activity of herding or driving llamas, perhaps leading them to sacrifice. Betanzos (1996: 48–49) reported that figurines were buried around the Hawkaypata *usnu* complex to represent the lords and lineages of Cusco, describing them as "squadrons" being offered to the Sun, presumably as surrogate sacrifices. Nevertheless, both locations also demonstrate significant llama burials and burnings.

At a citywide level, there may be some significance in the finding that the figurines and other materials in Pumaqchupan in Hurin Cusco were made of silver, while similar finds from Pumacurco in Hanan Cusco were of gold, but whether this is the result of the lack of archaeology, chance, or a reflection of a real pattern will require much more research.

Over 400 broken anthropomorphic and zoomorphic figurines and other small objects, such as maize cobs, kernels, fish, small vessels, and fragments of beads and fossils, were found in excavation on the north side of Choqepampa, the main plaza at Saqsaywaman (Valencia 1970b). These were fabricated from various materials, including bone, shell, calcite, quartz, and serpentine, and appear to have been deliberately broken and scattered in a ritual within a public place. Similar objects were found intact in the Muyuqmarka excavations of the 1930s. The calcite anthropomorphic pieces represent both males and females and include eleven heads, a face, and a headdress, seven torsos, and two sets of legs and feet (Valencia 1970b: 162–66). Likewise there were thirteen llama heads, several bodies, legs, and feet. This cache of deliberately broken objects must represent another inka ritual.

None of the offerings and burials equates specifically with any known ceremonies, and we can only glimpse the overall nature of offering and sacrifice. For example, in Qorikancha there is certainly patterned evidence that would suggest major llama sacrifices and the ritual sacrifice of figurines as surrogate children, despite the generally disturbed stratigraphy and broad range of artifacts. Each excavation from the areas surrounding the Sun temple confirms its absolute importance with the replication of some rituals externally as well as several burials with grave goods and imported pottery in disturbed strata, suggesting that individuals had traveled to Cusco to worship and make offerings outside the temple walls. Likewise, the range of pottery found in Hawkaypata and in the vicinity of the Muyuqmarka Sun temple suggests similar pilgrimage activities.

Burial rituals for the urban *kancha* and outlying villages have been seen as normal practice for inhabitants who were working for the Inka, Sun, state, or *panaqa*. In contrast, the burials around Qorikancha and the rural Sun temples of Saqsaywaman Muyuqmarka and Pukinkancha, at the *paqarina* complexes of Suchuna, Qenqo, and Lakko, and at Waynapata overlooking Hawkaypata seem to represent a different type of interment that perhaps is not related to the burial of ordinary inhabitants. These individuals seem to have been especially selected to be offerings, even human sacrifices, in these special locations in honor of the Sun, a particular Inka ancestor, or another deity to mark the inauguration of a building or temple or simply to serve the Inka on his journey to the afterlife. The different forms of tomb and grave goods may indicate special circumstances of death and offering. The elaborate burials found in Casa Concha (mz16) in Hatunkancha and the ethnohistorically recorded tomb of Mama Ocllo may simply be other examples of the latter grouping, but full publication of these finds is awaited.

Another particular pattern is the burial of dogs. These have been recorded in Kusikancha and in several rural villages. In only one case in Kusikancha is the dog part of a human grave and considered a pet. In the others, they are generally buried within the locations of typical household graves, but they contain a complete dog skeleton associated with llama and guinea pig bones. One was even covered by an inverted plate and interred at the threshold of a house in Qontaymoqo, obviously as a household protector. These rituals were probably concerned with the perceived role that the dog played in the underworld; for example, many chroniclers reported that black dogs were often sacrificed as *apurucu* (Polo de Ondegardo 1965; Santillan 1968: 138).

Discussion

Ritual activity and the processes of offering and sacrifice that accompanied it are highly symbolic, stylized, and repeated events that are recognizable in the archaeological record if the appropriate detailed stratigraphy and inventory of finds are available. The offering represents a cache of nondomestic goods, often valuable and unused, or sacrifices of humans or animals buried alongside or within a sacred place or in some other important location. Therefore, it has been possible to identify some offering types, according to the inventory and disposition of all excavated goods and organic materials, the type of pit, the location of the find within or adjacent to a site, the orientation of the offering, and the general location of the site.

This is merely a first attempt to accumulate what is known about inka ritual behavior, but while it can be confirmed that the major places experienced ritual activity, none of the deposits can be attributed specifically to any particular ceremony. As far as can be seen, the archaeological record confirms that there were specific rituals held within the household, both urban and rural, that can be generally understood but not specified as to which particular ceremony they represent.

12

The Navel of the World

In his study of ancient Chinese cities and ancient urbanism in general, Paul Wheatley (1971: chap. 5) emphasized four issues critical to understanding urban symbolism: geomantic precautions, cardinal orientation and alignment, the symbolism of the center, and the parallelism between the macrocosmos and microcosmos. He demonstrated the connection between the political and the sacred for each realm of ancient urbanism, as the political ruler and his decisions were sanctioned by traditional religious norms and by his own legitimacy as the embodiment of the deity. His analysis of cities in China, India, and Southwest Asia relied heavily on the written document, supported by architectural and archaeological information. For the inka world, the written documents are of much lesser value; they provide hints about the symbolism of Cusco but need to be evaluated more carefully to support our understanding of the architectural and archaeological record. Nevertheless, these four topics can be considered.

Our knowledge of inka history suggests that mythological and symbolic elements were developed locally without much interaction with earlier cultures from elsewhere in the central Andes and that, as Sabine MacCormack (2001b) has cogently argued, such traditions eventually were projected onto the diverse cultures and provinces that constituted Tawantinsuyu. Indeed, Cusco mythology and legend aggrandizes the inkas in their struggle for local hegemony. It links them to the previous glory of Tiwanaku, and it acknowledges the role and subordinate nature of pre-existing local peoples through the maintenance of their *waka* within the inka tradition. While these stories and inka culture itself are essentially andean in nature, and therefore widely understood across the southern and central Andes, local traditions, toponyms, and myths were utilized effectively in the expansion of the new state and its transmission of the urban concept.

This chapter is concerned with the symbolic aspects of the urban to-pography of Cusco and its perceived role as the navel of the world. First, I examine the geomantic myths of urban foundation and the meaning of the toponym, as well as others around the city. Second, I consider the issue of orientation and the symbolism of the center, dealing in particular with the *axis mundi* and its appropriate ceremonies. Third, I address the inka worldview and the notion that Cusco was "the city of the puma," as inter-preted from certain historical texts, and propose an alternative celestial archetype. Finally, I deal with the concept of *cusco*, as the city became the quintessential template for new imperial settlements that were constructed to administer the provinces as new or other *cusco*.

Geomantic Myths for the Establishment of the City

The foundation of Cusco is described in mytho-geomantic accounts in which the original ancestors were seeking a propitious place where they could establish themselves in perpetuity. It is linked to two cycles of origin myth that were current in the south central Andes prior to the Spanish conquest (Urbano 1981). One described the creation of the world on the Island of the Sun in Lake Titiqaqa; while the other was concerned with the emergence of local peoples from their own origin places. For the inkas, these were interlinked and they paid particular attention to their own as-sociation with Titiqaqa and Tiwanaku and, of course, to their ancestors' journeys to found Cusco, which they believed privileged them and their settlement at the expense of everyone else.

While there are several different chronicle accounts (Urbano 1981), most commentators accept the one compiled by Sarmiento de Gamboa for Vice-roy Toledo in 1572 (e.g., Urton 1990). The inkas believed that the world, in-cluding the Sun, Moon, and stars, had been created and put in motion by a supreme deity, called Tiqsi Wiraqocha Pachayachachiq, during a dramatic event at the Sacred Rock on the Island of the Sun in Lake Titiqaqa. Fol-lowing this, he created men and women as wooden, clay, or stone images at the nearby city of Tiwanaku, giving them specific identities with names, language, songs, and dress as well as crops and animals for their subsis-tence. Later he and his assistants traveled throughout the region, calling for each group of figures to travel underground to a specific location from which they were to seek a homeland and establish their community. While on a pilgrimage to the Sacred Rock, Thupaq Inka Yupanki saw a cat with flashing eyes walking upon it (Ramos 1976). Given the quechua translation of the place-name, *titiqaqa*, as the "cat on the rock" and the fact that this animal was common in Tiwanaku iconography, the puma perhaps became a totem for the inkas as a memory of their origins.

Tiqsi Wiraqocha Pachayachachiq then journeyed to Cusco, where he created a lord called Alcaviza as his local representative, and commanded the inka figures he had made to emerge from a mountain with three caves in Paqariqtambo, called Tambo T'oqo (Urton 1990). The four Ayar brothers and four sisters came through the central cave, while the founders of other social groups appeared from the others. Their journey to found Cusco and establish their dynasty was from south to north, but en route the siblings stayed in various locations for short periods, cultivating and examining the qualities of each settlement (see Bauer 1992a; Urton 1990).

A golden staff, called a *tupayauri*, an andean symbol of authority, was their main geomantic tool. It was carried by Manqo Qhapaq (Sarmiento 2007: 63), and according to Cobo (1979: 105), they had received the staff directly from the Sun himself with instructions to test the earth at every stop on their journey. When they found a place where it sank easily into the ground, that place would become the location of their settlement. Sarmiento (2007: 69) noted then they even smelled the soil as an added precaution. These are very practical tests of the depth, friability, and drainage of a soil and for the potential productivity of a location.

Sarmiento (2007: 68–69) also noted differences in the accounts by relating two versions of its successful penetration of the earth at Wanaypata: first, that it was one of two staffs thrown by Mama Waqo from Matawa, and second, that it was Manqo Qhapaq himself who actually thrust it into the ground. Santa Cruz Pachacuti Yamqui (1992: 187) added that this location was endowed with good water from the HananChakan and HurinChakan springs. These acts thus provided them with farmland and water.

The second task was to establish a settlement. Sarmiento (2007: 66) stated that the siblings had gained their first sight of Cusco from Wanakawri, when they saw the mountain and the upper valley framed by the arch of a rainbow, which they took to be a good sign "that the world will never again be destroyed by water." Murúa (1987: 50) added that this occurred in the rainy season. In order to view such a rainbow from Wanakawri, it would mean that it was shortly after sunrise on a day close to the December solstice.[1] One traditional prehistoric andean motif of authority depicts a human, standing under such an arch, that is commonly interpreted as a rainbow or the Milky Way (e.g., Bourget 1995). Indeed, this is conjured in these accounts, placing Manqo Qhapaq, Wanakawri, and Cusco at the very center of authority and of the world.[2]

Betanzos (1996: chap. 4) related that, while on Wanakawri, one brother, Ayar Uchu, acted as intermediary between the siblings and the Sun. On his return he stated that their father had proclaimed his brother to be the ruler, calling him Manqo Qhapaq, and that they were to settle in the valley below. Later, his mission completed, Ayar Uchu turned to stone on the summit to become the most important inka *waka*. According to Cobo (1979: 106) in a different story, the golden staff readily entered the ground on top of the mountain, and in so doing it gave them rights to the valley below, whereas yet another version (Cobo 1979: 104) told that one of the brothers used his sling to hurl stones to the four corners of the earth as an act of gaining possession of the valley. Each of these events underpinned the symbolic importance of Wanakawri and its role in the foundation story, confirming it as an important shrine, a sacred mountain, that defined their territory.

The final act of possession was the seizure by Ayar Awka of a brilliant, glittering stone outcrop and boundary marker called *cozco*,[3] which was located on a high spot, probably within the curved wall of Qorikancha (Sarmiento 2007: 69). On behalf of his siblings, he flew onto it and promptly turned to stone, becoming part of its form and thereby gaining possession. This rock, containing an inka ancestor, therefore legitimized their right to the surrounding fields of Wanaypata. It became their settlement focus; the first Sun temple, Intikancha, was built there and the town established around it.

These geomantic precautions, critical signs, and mythical events led to the successful founding of Cusco and the inka dynasty by Manqo Qhapaq. The places, mentioned in these myths, became revered by the inkas, who set about establishing themselves in the valley and vying for power with neighboring groups.

A critical time in Cusco mytho-history was the Chanka invasion and defeat, which resulted in the elevation of Pachakuti Inka Yupanki to Sapa Inka and his reconstruction of the city and its hinterland. Indeed, the legendary defense of the city and the role played by the army of stones[4] that became *waka* represent another "foundation" that established further memorial events and places. At least two other *waka* (CH-9:7, CH-9:9) were significant places of the final battle against the Chanka, while other victories were commemorated at CH-2:2 and CH-7:4. These were events that changed the landscape of Cusco and its political fortunes. Therefore, Cusco had a set of founding ancestors and a re-foundation under the great king,

Pachakuti Inka Yupanki, that marked the landscape with *waka* that needed to be remembered, worshipped, fed, and maintained.

The Meaning of Cusco

The Spaniards first heard about El Cusco in 1532 during their march and subsequent stay in Cajamarca. Their initial understanding was that this title referred to the ruler of the land, the Sapa Inka, who they eventually discovered was called Waskar. They also heard that El Cusco Viejo was his father, the recently deceased king, Wayna Qhapaq, and that there was a city where El Cusco resided (e.g., Mena 1967; Sancho 1917: 129; Xerez 1985: 121). Susan Ramírez (2005: chap.1) has noted that initially this term exclusively referred to the person of the king and only later did it become the name of the capital. Following Garcilaso and Cieza de León, she argued that it was considered inappropriate to utter the name of the king, and therefore he was only addressed with this broad epithet (Ramírez 2005: 20). However, once personal names had been learned, then the practice of using El Cusco to refer to the kings ceased.

Many have considered the toponym *cusco* and its meaning. Among the chroniclers, both Garcilaso (1966) and Guaman Poma (1980) suggested that it meant the "navel [of the world]," while Sarmiento (2007: 69) noted its use as the name of a stone boundary marker in the foundation myth. Murúa (1987: 499) thought it was the name of the person who first established the city, literally Cusco guanca, while Montesinos (2007: 107) thought it meant a pile of stones, also in reference to the myth. The lexicographer González Holguin (1989: 58) used it in phrases in his dictionary, such as "to level out or flatten" and "to be fair in passing judgment and in negotiation." Modern scholars have used the chronicles to indicate other meanings, such as "swampy ground" (from Betanzos's description) and "a levelled rocky place" (Espinoza 1979: 160–61). In modern quechua, Beyersdorff (1998) has translated its stem, found in certain *waka* names, as meaning "in the middle." It can be concluded from these translations that *el cusco* really means the center about which everything in the world revolves and from which all is governed; it therefore can be both an individual and a place. As Tom Zuidema (1973: 21) noted, "the living king was the center of the universe," while Ramírez (2005: 21–23), in reviewing the term *new cusco*, argued that the inka court, and therefore El Cusco, was where the Sapa Inka resided and that it was probably peripatetic. As a consequence, Cusco could refer to many places, as Guaman Poma (1980: 161–62) implied.

Other Important Toponyms

Other toponyms in the vicinity of Cusco also lend weight to its symbolic importance and meaning. For example, the city lay between two rivers that flowed from northwest to southeast, counter to the passage of the sun, as if tracing its course through the night. The Saphi flows from the slopes of Senqa, a sacred mountain, and then passes Chakan Wanakawri, a *waka*, and under the Chakan natural bridge, where, in legend, Inka Roca had discovered water for irrigation and drinking (Cieza de León 1959: 202–203). The Tullumayu flows from the Qalispukio, the "house" of Thupaq Inka Yupanki, where his mummy was kept and venerated.

In Quechua, *sapi* means a tree root, and a *waka* (CH-6:7) of this name was described as a root of one of the gnarled, long-lived trees, the *q'euña* (*Polyepsis racemosa*), native to the area (Cobo 1990: 58).[5] The inkas made sacrifices to it for the preservation of the city, and their shamans believed that it was the ontological connection to the earth deity, Pachamama, who had founded the city. It was of fundamental and symbolic importance. Nearby there was another shrine, Sapipacchan (CH-6:6), the pool of the tree root, where the Inka used to bathe and where prayers were made to maintain water quality and thereby the strength of Sapa Inka himself, and Quisco (CH-6:8) on top of Saphi hill, which received sacrifices for the same reasons as the tree root. This river therefore had links to Pachamama and to an earlier Inka and was considered vital for the well-being of the Inka and the city. The name of the second river, Tullumayu, is made up of two words, *tullu* (bones) and *mayu* (river) and can be literally translated as "bone river." Its significance is that it flows from an important location for the worship of an inka ancestor, Qalispukio, where Hatun Ayllu maintained the "house" and the mummy of Thupaq Inka Yupanki; it is therefore "the river of the ancestors."

Whereas most place-names can be translated, particularly those from the *waka* list (see Beyersdorff 1998), and appropriate meaning can be developed with regard to enhancing the symbolism of the city, only a few need be considered. These include places mentioned in the foundation myth and initiation rituals, sacred mountains as well as plazas, palaces, and temples in the city, and places where specific events were commemorated (table 12.1). For example, among the sacred mountains, Wanakawri means "the royal scepter,"[6] Yawiri, "the dead lord" and Pachatusan, "the stanchion of the world." In the city, many places had significant and appropriate toponyms. For example, Hawkaypata has often been translated as

Table 12.1. The meaning of selected Cusco toponyms

Toponym	Feature	Meaning
Cusco	City	The center or navel of the world
Wanakawri	Sacred mountain	Royal scepter of atonement or offering
Anawarki	Sacred mountain	Exquisite wavy hawk
Yawiri	Sacred mountain	The (dead) great lord
Senqa	Sacred mountain	The nose
Picol (Pillco)	Sacred mountain	Multicolored bird; hummingbird
Pachatusan	Sacred mountain	Stanchion of the world
Hawkaypata	Plaza	Terrace of tranquility; open terrace
Kusipata	Plaza	Terrace of happiness
Limaqpampa	Plaza	Place where he speaks
Intipampa	Plazuela	Place of the Sun
Qorikancha	Sun temple	Golden enclosure
Kiswarkancha	Temple of Wiraqocha	*Kiswar* enclosure
Qasana	Palace	Place of ice; panel of four squares on an *unku*; house with four identical parts
Amarukancha	Palace	Snake enclosure
Hatunkancha	Enclosure	Big enclosure
Tambokancha	Enclosure	Lodge enclosure; walled residence
Qora Qora	Large hall	Field of weeds
(A)Pukamarka	Enclosure or district	Red enclosure; lord's enclosure
Pumaqchupan	River confluence	Puma's tail
Pumacurco	Street	Puma's spine or puma roar
Wakapunku	Entrance to city on Saphi	Gate to the shrine or sanctuary; sacred gate
Saphi	River and *waka*	Tree root; ancestor river
Tullumayu	River	Bone river

Source: Beyersdorff 1998: 179–96.

the "terrace of tranquility," but more likely it was simply "the open terrace," Limaqpampa is "the place where he speaks"; Qorikancha, "the golden enclosure," was partly clad in gold panels; and Kiswarkancha, a place associated with Wiraqocha Pachayachachiq, referred to the long-lived *kiswar* tree (*Buddleia longifolia*), which also had special ancestral qualities as *mallki* (Sherbondy 1986a).

Certain toponyms must have been exceptionally important for the inkas because they are repeated in the landscape. For example, Wanakawri, the

Table 12.2a. Wanakawri place-names in Cusco

Suyu	Toponym	Seqe code	Type	Offering
Chinchaysuyu	Chakan wanakawri	CH-5:7	Small hill	—
	Churuncana, Churucani wanakawri	CH-7:7 Albornoz #17	Round hill with stones above Carmenqa	All kinds of things and children
Antisuyu	Machay wanakawri	AN-4:7	Stone shaped like Wanakawri mountain	All kinds of things
	Ata wanakawri	AN-9:5	Stones next to hill	Usual things
Qollasuyu	Omoto urqo,	QO-5:10	Small hill in puna with three stones	Sacrifices
	Omoto yanakawri	Molina	Station on way to Vilcanota	
	Wanakawri	QO-6:7	Sacred moun- tain with stone	Llamas, gold, silver, small gar- ments, children
Kuntisuyu	Cumpu wanakawri	CU-5:5	Hill with ten stones near Choqo	—

Sources: Cobo 1990; Albornoz 1989; Molina 1989.

sacred mountain associated with the origin myth and an important *waka* in its own right, is found in the name of six locations in the valley (Cobo 1990: 51–84), each described as a hill with at least one stone upon it (table 12.2a). Apart from Wanakawri itself, these subsidiary ones are distributed with two each in both Hanan *suyu* (Chinchaysuyu and Antisuyu) and one each in both Hurin (Qollasuyu and Kuntisuyu). Albornoz (1989: 180) also listed six in Jaquijahuana and two more in Calca, while one in Cusco he called Churucani wanakawri (Duviols 1967: 26), which Cobo (1990: 59) had listed simply as Churuncana (CH-7:7). The latter is another toponym that also occurs as a *waka* name in all four *suyu* (table 12.2b). Molina (1989: 75) noted that Churucalla was also the Kuntisuyu handover point for the *sitwa* shouts and weapons. These four locations were described as stones on a hill, and three of them received child sacrifices as part of their offerings. Its meaning is obscure, but it probably means "the son of an important man or ancestor,"[7] particularly as Cobo (1990: 59) related that the sacrifices on Churuncana (CH-7:7) were dedicated to Wiraqocha Pachayachachiq. An

Table 12.2b. Churuncana place-names in Cusco

Suyu	Toponym	Seqe code	Type	Offering
Chinchaysuyu	Churucani wanakawri	CH-7:7	Round hill with stones above Carmenqa	All kinds of things and children
	Churuncana	Albornoz #17	Large stone surrounded by many small ones	
Antisuyu	Churuncana	AN-9:4	Stone on top of a hill	—
Qollasuyu	Churuncana	QO-1:3	Small, round hill with three stones on top	Usual things and children
Kuntisuyu	Churuncana	CU-4:4	Large stone on a hill next to Anawarki	Children
	Churicalla		*Sitwa* boundary point	

Sources: Cobo 1990; Albornoz 1989; Molina 1989.

alternative explanation perhaps relates to the buildings of a royal palace of which the storerooms were labeled *churakuna* (Guaman Poma 1980: 329 [331]). The toponym Tambokancha, meaning "the walled residence," is used for four *waka* close to Qorikancha itself (table 12.2c), three of which are associated with kings of the origin myth, and it is also the name of a royal settlement near Zurite. The place-name Atpitan probably means "the seat of a great lord" (Beyersdorff 1998: 180). Four *waka* with this name are associated with sacrifices during the June solstice, and they are also found in all *suyu* (Zuidema 2003; table 12.d).

Table 12.2c. Tambokancha place-names in Cusco

Suyu	Toponym	Seqe code	Type	Offering
Qollasuyu	Tampucancha	QO-3:1	Three stones	Worshiped as idols
	Tampukancha	QO-6:1	Hut, residence of Manco Qhapaq Inka	Usual things, except children
	Tampukancha	QO-9:1	Seat of Mayta Qhapaq	Venerated
Kuntisuyu	Caritampukancha	CU-5:1	Small plaza in Santo Domingo	Everything and children

Source: Cobo 1990.

Table 12.2d. Atpitan place-names in Cusco

Suyu	Toponym	*Seqe* code	Type	Offering
Chinchaysuyu	Alpitan	Molina *waka*	Hill (Senqa or Quiancalla)	Llama sacrifice at June solstice sunset
	Senqa/Cinca	CH-5:9	Hill—outcrop in valley; Ayamarca *paqarina*	—
Antisuyu	Autvit urco	AN-1:4	Large cave in ravine, Hualla *paqarina*	Sprinkle llama blood
Qollasuyu	Atpitan	QO-1:6	Stones in a ravine, where one loses sight of Wanakawri; Sons of Wanakawri	—
	Apitay	Murúa *waka*	Wanakawri stone, where Ayar Uchu turned to stone	Llama sacrifice at June solstice sunrise
Kuntisuyu	Apian	CU-6:1	Round stone in Sto Domingo (*pururauca*)	Llama sacrifice at June solstice noon
	Acpita	—	Community 2km west of Wanakawri	

Sources: Cobo 1990; Murúa 1987.

City as Cosmogram: "The City of the Puma"

Cusco is often regarded as the "city of the puma," but the original meaning of this phrase has recently been manipulated into something that was not intended by either Pachakuti Inka Yupanki, who conceived the city plan, or by later rulers, who enhanced it. In this section, I examine this concept from the perspective of puma iconography and myth to establish that the feline was never intended to be a physical manifestation in the city plan; it was a term used to identify the inkas themselves.

This popular belief stems from the writings of two chroniclers: Betanzos and Sarmiento de Gamboa. In his account of the reconstruction of Cusco, Betanzos (1996: 74) wrote: "After [Pachakuti] Inca Yupanque divided up the city of Cusco . . . he named all the places and lots. He named the whole city lion's body, saying that the residents of it were limbs of that lion. He personally was the head of the lion." He was careful in his use of this metaphor, suggesting that the puma was really a metaphysical under-standing of Inka identity. In contrast, Sarmiento (2007: 151) misinterpreted it, crudely assuming that it had physical and therefore visible attributes: "[Thupaq Inka Yupanki] remembered that his father, Pachakuti, had called the city of Cusco the lion city. He said that the tail was where the two riv-ers unite which flow through it; that the body was the great square and the houses around it, and that the head was wanting. It would be for some son of his to put it on. The Inca discussed this question with the orejones, who said that the best head would be to make a fortress on a high plateau to the north of the city."

Several twentieth-century authors have taken Sarmiento's statement lit-erally. For example, John Rowe (1968), following work by Manuel Chávez Ballón, assumed that the urban plan had been laid out in the form of a puma and that its outline could be seen in the layout of inka walls and streets, in which the head was the fortress, Saqsaywaman, the tail was the confluence of the two rivers, the body was the city itself, and the plaza lay between the front and back legs. Other versions have been published with the puma in various positions on the street plan, surviving walls, and ter-races (e.g., Agurto 1980, 1987; Gasparini and Margolies 1980: 48) (figure 12.1). Similar interpretations have been drawn on the plan of inka Tumi-bamba, modern Cuenca in Ecuador, making it another "city of the puma" (Idrovo 2000: 86–88; Lozano 1991: 143–47). These were also encouraged by the similarity of disposition and orientation of the Tumibamba river and the Watana stream as well as the use of the toponyms, such as Pumapungo and Wanakawri. While these plans have become popular images of ancient Cusco, they do not represent what Betanzos was careful to enunciate: that the puma was a metaphor and not a two-dimensional ground image.

Some scholars have sought to review the role played by the puma in inka society. For example, Zuidema (1983) analyzed Betanzos's statement, inter-preting that "puma" had been used to mean the inka "body politic" and that the people were its limbs, while the Sapa Inka was its head. In other words, he argued that they used the puma metaphor, a fierce and respected animal with which they were very familiar, to convey the identity and power of themselves and their ruler.

In a speculative paper, the anthropologist Bill Isbell (1978), proposed that the plan of Hawkaypata and its surrounding buildings symbolically resembled an inverted U, a feature that had characterized the plans of early andean ceremonial centers, such as Garagay and Chavín de Huantar. He considered therefore that there had been no fundamental change in belief

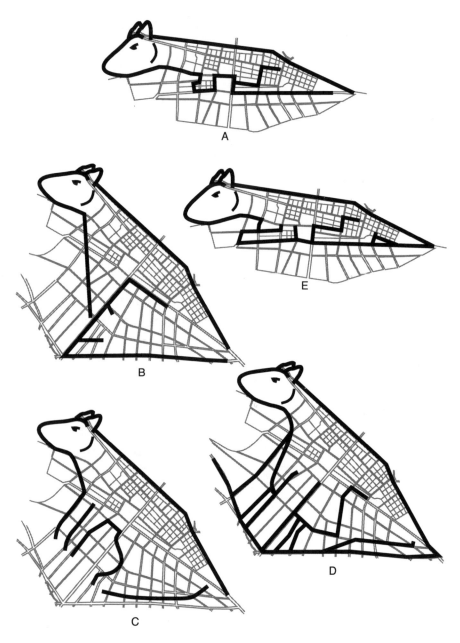

Figure 12.1. Puma plans of the city. *A–C*, (after Gasparini and Margolies 1980: fig. 37); *D–E*, (after Agurto 1980).

systems and their manifestation in urban planning over 3,000 years. Using the ethnographic analogy of a Desana long house and famous cosmological diagram of Santacruz Pachacuti Yamqui, Isbell concluded that this was a basic amerindian trait. The left-hand side buildings of Qora Qora and Qasana represented the royal line of descent and were essentially masculine and that those to the right, the *aqllawasi* and Amarukancha, were associated with feminine roles. He added that the base of the U was the northern side, containing the Temple of Kiswarkancha and Uchullo palace, which were associated with the creator and formed the body and stomach of the puma. While this idea may be persuasive in some respects, it does not work as an inka model because the topography and functions of the plaza are considered differently now than in the 1970s. The location of Kiswarkancha is no longer thought to have been on the plaza. The plaza became an integral part of the concept of *cusco*, which required very little in the arrangement of surrounding buildings.

While Barnes and Slive (1993) considered the feline model to be a European introduction to the Andes, it is clear from my own studies of the sacred landscape and iconography that the puma had become a powerful symbol, a totem, for the inkas (Farrington 2002). For example, puma skin cloaks were described in visions experienced by Wiraqocha Pachayachachiq before the Chanka war and they were worn by men at important ceremonies in Hawkaypata. Another significant event in inka legendary history was that undertaken by Thupaq Inka Yupanki as a pilgrimage to the place where Wiraqocha had made the world begin, the Sacred Rock on the Island of the Sun. There he witnessed a cat walking on the rock, breathing fire and radiating light (Ramos 1976). The quechua translation of *titiqaqa* is the "cat on the rock." It is also surmised that the name of the mythical creature protecting the rock, the *khoa*, was confused with the mythical feline in the Cusco region, the *qoa*. It is possible that the puma became a totem for the inkas as a memory of their origins and links to Titiqaqa, and as a result a pair of pumas were carved in stone on top of the inka origin mountain, now called Puma Urqo (Bauer 1992b). As a consequence, felines were also carved at the ancestral "houses" and *paqarina* of the Hanan Cusco hinterland (Farrington 2010c). It should be noted that, in contrast to the llama, the feline was rarely used in inka iconography, and its occurrence on pottery vessels was largely restricted to the nubbin on classic *maka* and *urpu* within the classic geometric design that Bray (2000) has described as a depiction of the origin myth. From this evidence, it can be argued that the inkas identified themselves with this feline and that they perceived themselves as descendants of Tiwanaku, whose own iconography was regaled with pumas.

The puma therefore came to symbolize the people, Sapa Inka, and the city. This was derived from not only the physical prowess of the feline but also its associations with the places of the creation of the world and of humans in Titiqaqa and Tiwanaku and carved subsequently at the place of the origin of the inkas themselves. It became the symbol of inka identity but not the physical outline of the city.

A Celestial Archetype

Wheatley (1971) observed that many ancient urban civilizations of the northern hemisphere viewed their *axes mundi* as being directly beneath the pole star, which they perceived to be the center of the upper world. Sacred mountains, such as Mount Meru and Elburz, lay in this position, as did the great cities of Chang'an, Beijing, Jerusalem, and Mecca. The plane of the heavens therefore was copied on earth as a celestial archetype for the plan and functions of the capital city as it was the pivot of the world about which everything revolved, just as the pole star was the heavenly pivot about which all other stars revolved. The inkas, in the southern hemisphere, where there is no obvious reference star for the South Pole, looked to other aspects of their cosmological relationship with the heavens.

They viewed the Milky Way, the great celestial river (*mayu*), and the constellations within and around it as the cosmological mirror of their world (*kay pacha*) (Urton 1978). In andean ethnography, the hydraulic cycle—the movement of water through the three cosmic planes, the landscape, and the human body—plays a significant role in understanding local cosmology. On the basis of his ethnographic work, Urton (1978, 1982: 59–62) noted the belief that the earth floats on the cosmic ocean beyond the horizon and that the two streams of the Milky Way are filled with water when its northern end lies below the horizon and flow toward the confluence in the south. Near where the two rivers meet is the brightest star closest to the South Pole, Alpha Crucis, which could be considered a pivot of the southern heavens.

Urton (1978) has commented that in Cusco at the time of both solstices, sunrise is coincident with the angle of the Milky Way across the sky. In June, the sun rises through it, as it is oriented from northeast to southwest, conducting the celestial waters toward the southwest. Similarly in December, it is angled from northwest to southeast, and the sun was seen to rise through it on the southeastern horizon. The flow of heavenly water toward the confluence mirrored in part the river flow in Cusco from the northeast.

It is proposed that Cusco, likewise located between two rivers, could have had the center of the Milky Way and Alpha Crucis as its celestial archetype. To illustrate this, Starry Night Backyard v4.0.5, a planetarium program, was used to simulate the year 1500. Just before dawn on the morning of the December solstice, as the sun began to rise through the Milky Way on a bearing of 114°, Alpha Crucis was at its highest point in the southern sky and directly on the meridian, 180°. At this critical time, Alpha Crucis, situated between the two heavenly rivers and around which the other stars circled, represented Cusco, the center of the inka world. All observers would have been reminded of their origins. First, they would have recalled Wiraqocha's creation of the world at Titiqaqa, as the sun emerged from the mountains of Awsangati and Urcos Viracochan; the latter is a dome-shaped eminence, associated in myth with Wiraqocha himself. Second, by turning to the south, they would have seen the arch of the Milky Way with Alpha Crucis at its zenith, in the same direction as their own *paqarina*, Tambo Toqo, and therefore they would have been reminded of their origin cave. But as the sun climbed, these elements would have been lost in the growing brightness of the day.

Therefore, both solstices represented for the inkas important symbolic times because their world, the Milky Way, and the sun converged at the center, Cusco (Urton 1978: 166). The December solstice had the additional memory of origin, as they observed their own deity, the Sun, signifying their own intimate association with its creation, that of the world and of themselves.

Magli (2005) proposed that the Cusco celestial archetype was a dark cloud constellation, located in the Milky Way between Cygnus and Vulpecula, at the confluence of its two rivers, which he termed the puma. Although there is merit in his basic observation, the name is problematical. It is not grounded in contemporary folk astronomy nor in our documentary knowledge of inka astronomy (Urton 1982).

Orientation and Cardinal Directions

The question of building orientation and planning axes have been regarded as fundamental to understanding the symbolic properties of any ancient city. For the ancient planner, orientation can be achieved by erecting a

Table 12.3. Astronomical observations from the city

Date	Event	Rise / set	Observation point	Horizon point
22 December	December solstice	Rise	Hawkaypata	Awsangati
			Pukinkancha	Mutu mtn
			Limaqpampa	Awsangati
			Muyuqmarka	Awsangati
22 December	December solstice	Set	Hawkaypata	Llamakancha
			Qorikancha passage between R-3/R-4	Killke mtn
				Killke mtn
			Intipampa	Killke mtn W shoulder
			Limaqpampa	Picchu
			Lakko	Picchu
			Muyuqmarka	
13–14 February / 30 October	Passage of sun through zenith	Rise	Hawkaypata	Tipón
			Qorikancha	Tipón
			Picchu	Tipón
			Limaqpampa	
	Passage of sun through zenith	Set	Hawkaypata	
21 March / 22 September	Equinox	Rise	Hawkaypata	Pachatusan
			Muyuqmarka	Pachatusan
21 March / 22 September	Equinox	Set	Hawkaypata	South of Picchu
26 April / 18 August	Passage of sun through anti-zenith	Rise		
	Passage of sun through anti-zenith	Set	Hawkaypata	Picchu
			Tipón	Picchu
			Tipón	Mama Simona
14 May / 1 August		Set	Hawkaypata	Picchu stone foundation (*sukanka*)
23 May / 23 July		Set	Limaqpampa	Picchu stone foundation (*sukanka*)
21 June	June solstice	Rise	Qorikancha R-3-R-4 passage	Hill to north
21 June	June solstice	Set	Qorikancha patio	Picchu stone foundation (*sukanka*)
			Lakko	
			Ancastiana	Waynaqorqor
			[Choqemarka]	Waynaqorqor
21–24 June	Pleiades	Heliacal rise	Qorikancha R-3-R-4 passage	Hill to north

Sources: Aveni 1981; Bauer and Dearborn 1995; Zawaski and Melville 2007; Zuidema 1981, 1982.

building facing a major landmark or monument, a major sunrise or sunset,[8] or true north or another cardinal direction. Cusco is oriented specifically to observe on distant horizons both the December solstice sunrise, from behind the sacred mountain of Awsangati, as well as the December solstice sunset on the hills of Pukin and Killke. Both can be viewed from Qorikancha and Hawkaypata as well as from other locations in the city (Bauer and Dearborn 1995). Other solar observations, such as sunrise and sunset at the June solstice and on the day the sun passes through zenith could also have been made from these locations to much closer horizons, which would compromise viewing accuracy, or from other places on the valley flanks beyond the city (table 12.3).

The division of the hinterland into four quarters implies extensive spatial knowledge, although no *suyu* boundary conforms with the cardinal directions, and only one to the southeast, between Antisuyu and Qollasuyu, aligns with a major solar event. It appears at first glance that nothing is known about the inka understanding of the cardinal points. However, on a broader scale, the spatial relationship between certain important places in the Outer Heartland and Cusco does suggest that some knowledge of cardinality. For example, Heffernan (1996b) noted that important inka sites lay along a line extending due west from the city that mirrors, in part, the flight of Wiraqocha to the coast. The line due south leads to the sites of Mawqa Llaqta and Puma Urqo and hence to the *paqarina* of Tambo Toqo, while due north and east of the city were located significant mountains, Sawasiray-Pitusiray and Pachatusan, respectively (table 12.4). At the level of individual buildings and structural groups, cardinal orientation played some role, such as the *usnu* platform at Vilkaswamán, but its impact is to be seen more broadly in the plans of new *cusco*, such as El Shincal and Huánuco Pampa.

Therefore, although the daily movements of the sun and the moon from east to west were vital to the inka understanding of their cosmology, as was the observation of important sunrises and sunsets, cardinality was not strongly marked in their architecture, but it underlay critical links to important places in the Outer Heartland. Nevertheless, it was understood and was used in places throughout Tawantinsuyu, but in Cusco it was a concept that became subverted by the establishment of the *suyu* and their geographical distribution.

Table 12.4. Prominent places located in cardinal directions from Cusco

Cardinal direction	Name	Type	Importance of place
North	Sawasiray-Pitusiray	Sacred mountain	First *waka* of Antisuyu
East	Pachatusan	Sacred mountain	Ata wanakawri
	Sinakara	Sacred mountain	Location of *Qoyllor riti* ceremony
South	Puma Urqo (Tambo toqo, Paqariqtambo)	Origin mountain	Inka origin place
West	Tilka	Sacred mountain	*Sitwa* terminus mountain
	Saywite	Carved rock	Sacred place from where one first sees the Cusco heartland
	Vilkaswamán	City	City with Sun temple
	La Centinela	City	Inka palace and temple

Symbolism of the Center

Cusco was the *axis mundi* of the inka world, as both ruler and city. As a place it was the center, the navel, about which everything revolved. It was the capital in the true sense of the word in that it contained the two most important buildings, the Sun temple, Qorikancha, and the royal palace, Qasana. It was also surrounded by critical places, where major events had taken place during the history of the city. These included places associated with foundation where ancestors had turned to stone, where the upper valley was first sighted and where others had lived and died. There were also places with which later ancestors were associated, including Chakan, the site of battles, the *pururauca* warriors, and places where an Inka had slept, rested, bathed, or died or the "house" where an Inka mummy was kept. In short, Cusco was surrounded by places of critical memory that were revered and ennobled in the histories of the people.

Qorikancha, built on a rock called *cusco*, that contained the petrified body of a founding brother, became not only the place where the golden statue of the Sun was kept and worshipped but also where the images of the other deities were held and to which the ancestral mummies and the images of provincial *waka* were brought periodically for major celebrations. It controlled the local practice of worship as the center from which the *seqe* system radiated. As suggested by Zuidema (1977), each *seqe* and shrine was worshipped in calendrical turn from this central focus. It therefore served to divide the hinterland into lands for the different *panaqa* and *ayllu* and to divide the empire into its four *suyu*. Its basic architecture comprised a high walled enclosure with a *kancha*, while its buildings, clad with gold panels, would have glistened and shone, as if the Sun dwelt in each of them, enhancing the experience and dazzling visitors, both those in the inner sanctum and those who came merely to gaze upon it and its golden garden. The southern outer wall with its unusual curved form that enclosed the sacred rock looked out across the valley toward the December solstice sunset, indicating the cultural importance of that time of the year.

Observed from the southern esplanade, Qorikancha stands like a large stepped pyramid on the high ridge line with lower terraces and the tall vertical face of its upper terrace and curved wall. There was at least one cave in or below the rock that was entered from a terrace below the curved wall, just as at Machu Picchu and Tumibamba. It commanded as the center of *Kay Pacha* and facilitated communication with the other two realms, *Hanan pacha*, the upper world, and *Uqhu Pacha*, the underworld.

Betanzos (1996: ch.11) described the dedication ceremony of Qorikancha after its rebuilding by Pachakuti that involved the Inka himself and important nobles. Their faces were painted from ear to ear with lines of sacrificed llama blood, as were the walls of the temple. This culminated in the burial alive of a young boy and girl, as *qhapaq hucha*, in its patio in front of the newly erected golden statue of the Sun, Punchaw. An archaeological manifestation of such events may be observed in the arrangements of figurines or child cranial materials surrounded by miniature *tupu* (Farrington 1998).

Although within the urban core, its location in a plan-seam meant that Qorikancha was almost completely surrounded by open space with a small plaza to its west, terraces on its southern side, and open ground to the east. Naturally, Intipampa became the focus of ceremony and assembly, as it was located adjacent to the temple gate, while the other spaces became places where pilgrims could perform rituals and sacrifices and make offerings. The archaeology of these locations demonstrates that offerings were made that imitated those in the temple itself, as well as human burials, perhaps sacrifices, but also the ritual killing of llamas, and the offerings of objects, including figurines, *qonopa*, and pottery vessels from all over Tawantinsuyu.

Qorikancha was the *axis mundi* of Cusco. It held the images of the Sun god and the other deities, and entertained in religious festivals the Inka king, nobles, ancestors, and of course the *waka* of Cusco and the provinces.

It attracted people from the city, the hinterland, and the empire to worship at its eminence and brilliance. Yet few could gain entry into its holy sanctuary and witness its ceremonies.

Shortly after Punchaw had been inaugurated, a stone shaped like a sugar-loaf and sheathed with gold was erected in the *usnu* complex in the middle of Hawkaypata, as a Sun image for everyone to see and worship (Betanzos 1996: 48–49). It too would have shone and dazzled from its location on top of the platform beside the libation hole. It became the public focus of ceremony in Cusco, as such rituals were repeated for all to see in the main plaza. As part of these ceremonies, the Punchaw statue was placed in a litter and carried around the city, blessing both Cusco and its inhabitants (Betanzos 1996: 48), a circumambulation that would have demarcated its extent as sacred space. Its dedication ceremony took place before the golden statue of Punchaw, brought there for this special occasion, the ancestral mummies, and the Inka himself. A large hole was dug for offerings and filled. It continued with the construction of a stone font, adjacent to the platform, around which occurred the ritual burying of figurines and llamas as well as large-scale llama sacrifices, drinking, and great feasting. Such a ritual suggests a symbolic replication of *qhapaq hucha* in the plaza for all to witness. As such, the *usnu* platform, with its upright stone and terraces, stretching upward like a sacred mountain, and its libation hole, as an opening into the underworld, represent another *axis mundi*, one that does not usurp the primacy of Qorikancha but represents it publically and therefore politically. Cusco had become not only the person and the center but also the Sun itself, whose worship was now so vital. It was this concept of *cusco* that was taken to the rest of the empire.

Hawkaypata therefore represented a more secular center, flanked by three palaces and large halls and by Hatunkancha. The Sapa Inka, El Cusco, lived in Qasana and used his position as son of the Sun politically to legitimate his own actions and decisions, using both the ancestors and *waka* as oracles that could foretell the fate of everything, from the rains and harvest to the well-being of the realm.

Its geographical position at the head of the valley assisted its spatial confinement and reinforced it as an ideal location in their worldview. From Hawkaypata and Qorikancha, sacred mountains can be observed, particularly those to the east (Pachatusan) and southeast (Awsangati, Wanakawri, and Anawarki), which would have reinforced their belief in who they were and how they had gained their strength and political greatness. For example, Wanakawri and Anawarki were *waka* eulogized in the foundation myth and, as we have seen, the former was an essential location in the inka psyche, a place from which the city was founded. The important December solstice sun could be seen rising out of Awsangati, a mountain that absorbs the shape of the closer dome-shaped hill, associated with Wiraqocha, and that metaphorically implies that the Sun came from Lake Titiqaqa itself, its birthplace. The memorials to their origins, to Wiraqocha and to their father, the Sun, embrace this southeastern horizon. Cusco was confined by its position between the two rivers, a meeting place of waters, a middle place, a navel that reinforced their view, just as the water that nourished the city also came from their mythical ancestors.

The city was not walled, and there were no gates to shield it from entry or gaze, but clearly a strict code of practice must have restricted entry at certain times from even the closest suburbs. This is underlined by the name of the last suburb on the road from Chinchaysuyu, Wakapunku, immediately adjacent to the Qasana rear wall, which can be translated as "the gate to the sanctuary [of Cusco]" or "the sacred gate." Observation of the city, its temples, plazas, and palaces from afar must have been important and presumably encouraged. It was, after all, the center of the world. The Inner Heartland was defined physically by the upper basin and culturally by the extent of the *seqe* system but also by the ceremonies and legendary events that determined specific boundary places (Farrington 1992).

The Concept of Cusco

In an earlier paper, I argued that the symbolism of Cusco, the navel of the world, needed to be repeated in all provincial places to reinforce and display the power and authority of inka rule (Farrington 1998). This required that the origin story be repeated and the calendrical ceremonies in honor of the Sun and harvest as well as the *sitwa* and initiation rituals reenacted in a settlement and landscape that was conceptually Cusco, whether it be on the Peruvian coast, in the highlands of Ecuador, or in the valleys of Argentina and Chile. In other words, the concept of *cusco*, the concept of the center, the ideal city, needed to be replayed with all of its *cusqueño* references. This meant that places were called new *cusco* or other *cusco*, and other toponyms from the capital and its legendary historical narrative and mythology were transferred onto alien landscapes as a means of domesticating and dominating them and making them inka.

One ceremony in particular became an important factor in this process. According to Betanzos (1996: ch.11), *qhapaq hucha* was first enacted at the dedication ceremony for Qorikancha, attended by Pachakuti Inka Yupanki himself and his nobles, and it involved llama sacrifice, the painting in blood of lines on the faces of those present and the temple walls, and the burying alive of a young boy and girl at the foot of the golden statue of Punchaw. A short while later, this ceremony was repeated for the ordinary people in Hawkaypata, when another statue of the Sun was revealed, an upright stone with a gold sheath, erected in association with the *usnu* complex. More llamas were sacrificed, and figurines representing the lineages of Cusco were ritually buried around the platform. It was the worship of the Sun that characterized both of these ceremonies. It is significant that the two most important aspects of *qhapaq hucha* were the sacrifice of children, who were dressed finely as "children of the Sun," and of llamas from the flocks of the Sun in Cusco, which were driven with the procession and whose blood was such a vital ritual liquid.

The promotion of this ceremony by Pachakuti, as Tawantinsuyu expanded, led to the development of a ritualized redistribution system that formally handled tribute brought to Cusco from the provinces. Once in the city, the Inka made decisions that would retain some of it, return some to its originating province, or divert it to other provinces in special processions for sacrifice and offering. According to Molina (1989: 120–21), children, clothing, llamas, and figurines were brought from the provinces and presented to the Inka in Hawkaypata, where they were walked twice around the statues and *usnu* complex and then divided. The redistributed materials, children, and llamas were eventually carried in procession to the *sitwa* border stations of the Inner Heartland and progressively transported to their destination. *Qhapaq hucha*, dedicated to the Sun, became a ritualized political device that bound the distant provinces and their rulers to the center of the world.

Qhapaq hucha processions and ceremonies have been mentioned in the historical literature. For example, a procession en route to Quito was seen passing through Pumpu in the central highlands (Rostworowski 1988: 65–66); the Chacalla people acquired a *qhapaq hucha* from the inkas at Hatun Xauxa (MacCormack 1991: 153); the famous sacrifices at Ocros and Cajatambo were of this type (Duviols 1976; Zuidema 1978); while the people from Lupaqa and other provinces recalled that they had had to give children to the Inka for sacrifice in Cusco, Quito, and even Huánuco (Mac-Cormack 1991: 150).

If this ceremony was instrumental in transferring inka rituals and the worship of the Sun to the provinces, then it could be argued that it must have taken place in a *cusco*, a location with its attributes and toponyms that became Cusco for the event. Using the quechua concept of *ntin*, Jerry Moore (1996: 797) has indicated that "(such) massive public gatherings . . . were related to the well-established inka notion of correlating spatial and social centers as representations of transformed wholeness." In my earlier paper, I argued that three planning features were required to achieve this (Farrington 1998). First, there must be a plaza, or open space, in which people could assemble to view the spectacle, worship, and make the appropriate offerings and libations. Second, there had to be an *usnu* complex, including a platform, hill, or rock that could be interpreted as the image of the Sun and that provided both an upper component for the congregation to look at and a pit, basin, grave, or canal that enabled entry of objects or liquids into the ground. Therefore, the Sun and other sky and underworld gods could be communicated with and fed. The third component was a rectangular structure that could serve as a watch-house for the guardian and storeroom for the ceremonial paraphernalia.

More recently, these ideas have been touched upon by other researchers. For example, Coben (2006) considered that new *cusco* needed to be theaters in which inka calendrical rituals took place. He identified eight architectural similarities between Inkallaqta and Cusco of which plaza and *usnu* platform were central to the notion of replication. However, he recognized that more specific work was needed at each site to understand these variables. Christie (2007) presented several site descriptions to argue that a plaza, a *kallanka*, and a foregrounded rock, not an *usnu* complex, was used to publicize inka state ideology.

"Oh Sun! . . . Let There Be Cusco and Tampu"

The expansion of Tawantinsuyu, beginning in the reign of Pachakuti Inka Yupanki, presented the inkas with a serious problem: how to keep the nations they had conquered loyal. Various strategies were adopted to enable success, such as the translocation of peoples, as *mitmaqkuna*, from rebellious provinces to more benign locations and their replacement by others more loyal to inka goals. The establishment of an urban network was another, which enabled the inkas to feel comfortable in these new environments, constructing many new *cusco* from which to govern and control each province. These not only housed a permanent population of inka elite and their servants but were also capable of maintaining the royal court and its entourage during its peregrinations about the empire. These places served, like Cusco itself, with accommodation, storerooms, plaza, and an *usnu* complex for festivals. This means that along the roads to the northern and southern frontiers, there would have been a hierarchy of settlements, some large and very important and others smaller to provide short-term overnight accommodation (Hyslop 1984). The critical factor for each settlement was that it was "in the image of *cusco*" and that at times was Cusco itself.

The term *cusco* was used as a settlement type in some chronicles, but these do not provide a comprehensive list of all such towns in Tawantinsuyu. For example, Cieza de León (1959: 339) wrote that Thupaq Inka Yupanki had built a new *cusco* in Huarco, now identified as Inkawasi in the Cañete valley (Hyslop 1985), expanding the theme with the comment that the streets, plaza, and surrounding hills were named after places in Cusco itself. Guaman Poma (1980: 185 [187]) mentioned five other *cusco*, three to the north of the capital (Quito, Tumibamba, Huánuco Pampa) and two to the south (Hatunqolla, Charcas) (table 12.5). Other chronicle evidence indicates that important inka buildings were located in particular towns, including the aforementioned *cusco*. For example, there were at least ten places with a Sun temple from Caranqui in the north to the Island of the Sun. Indeed, Francisco de Xerez (1985: 104), an eyewitness to the conquest, after describing the one at Cajamarca, noted that such temples were located in every town. Guaman Poma (1980: 1085 [1095], 1090 [1100]) named seven towns with houses that had belonged to a particular Inka, and other early descriptions also indicate settlements with an *usnu* platform and others with an *aqllawasi*. Cieza de León (1959: 165–66) even listed the administrative centers of several inka provinces. Clearly, this evidence produces a distribution of *cusco* and *cusco*-like settlements, with imperial functions, mainly to the north of Cusco and along the coast, but almost none to the south. In fact, Cieza added to his list by saying "and others as far as Chile." This spatial bias simply reflects the route of conquest and the interests of the first settlers because there are almost as many inka towns and settlements existing to the south as to the north of the capital (see Hyslop 1990; Raffino 1981, 1988, 1993).

Apart from the use of the term *cusco*, other toponyms were grafted onto provincial townscapes and landscapes, thereby linking those places symbolically with the space and functions of Cusco itself. They include such names as *wanakawri, anawarki, hawkaypata, qorikancha, tambokancha,* and *qenqo*. For example, mountains called Wanakawri have been located around several important centers, including Quito (Burgos 1995: 264),

Table 12.5. Documentary evidence for new *cusco*

North	New / other *cusco*	Houses of Sapa Inka	Temple of Sun	*Usnu* platform	*Aqllawasi*	Wanakawri	Head of province
Caranqui			X		X		X
Quito	X	X				X	X
Mucha		X					
Latacunga							X
Tumibamba	X	X	X	X	X	2	X
Caxas					X		
Huancabamba			X		X		X
Tumbez					X		
Cajamarca			X	X	X		X
Wamachuco		X					
Wari		X					
Huánuco Pampa	X	X	X	X	X	X	
Pumpu		X					X
Hatun Xauxa		X		X			X
Vilkaswamán		X	X	X	X	2	X
Pachacamac		X			X		
Huarco-Inkawasi	X					X	
South							
Hatuncana							X
Ayavire							X
Pucará				X			
Hatunqolla	X						X
Chucuito							X
Isla del Sol		X	X		X		
Tiwanaku				X			
Chuquiabo							X
Charcas	X						
Paria							X

Sources: Albornoz 1989: 176; Cabello Valboa 2011: 433–34; Cieza de León 1959: 70, 92, 109, 114, 126, 165–66, 333, 334, 336, 339; Cobo 1990: 85, 91; Estete 1924; Guaman Poma 1980: 185 [187], 1085–90 [1095–1100]; Xerez 1985: 104.

Ingapirka (Rojas 2006: 34), Tumibamba (Idrovo 2000), Cajamarka, Huánuco Pampa, Vilkaswamán (Santillana 2001), and Inkawasi (Hyslop 1985).
Around the royal palaces of Chinchero and Tambokancha to the west of
Cusco, there were six hills with *waka* called Wanakawri as well as other
shrines called Anawarki, Qorikancha, and Tambokancha (Albornoz 1989).
Indeed, Santillana (2001: chap. 5) has drawn attention to a probable system
of inka shrines, many using names of Cusco *waka*, that are found in the
landscape about the inka center of Vilkaswamán. These include two hills
called Wanakawri and others named Anawarki, Saywa, Killke, and Amaru,
as well as a spring, Qhapaq pukyo, Kantupata, and a quarry, Choqebamba.
Other toponyms in the vicinity include Pumawanka and Pumaqocha.
There is certainly much documentary and ethnographic work that could
be done around many of these towns to evaluate the long-term impact of
such toponymic transfer.

One further trait that may be used to signify a *cusco* is a *seqe* system
of shrines around other centers. Polo de Ondegardo (1990: 46–47), who
had recorded the Cusco *seqe waka*, claimed that there were 100 towns with
similar systems, but he named only one, Pocona in Bolivia. He understood
these to be in the image of Cusco but knew they were not carbon copies,
merely in a similar setting. Nevertheless, this knowledge has been lost, despite some contemporary ethnographic examples.

Important archaeological investigations have taken place at these new
and other *cusco*, such as Huánuco Pampa (Morris and Thompson 1985),
Pumpu (Brown 1992; Matos 1994), Tumibamba (Idrovo 2000), and Inkawasi (Hyslop 1985), but except for studies around Hatun Xauxa (D'Altroy
1992), their hinterlands rarely have been investigated. Essentially, those
centers and many others, including Ingapirka, Ayapate, Machu Picchu,
Inkallaqta, El Shincal, Chilecito, and Viña del Cerro, are conceptually similar, although their plans at first glance seem radically different from each
other and from Cusco itself. They contain the same elements, focused upon
a plaza and an *usnu* complex within or adjacent to it. The latter invariably is a platform, but it may also include a stone, hole, canal, or river. The
plaza may be flanked by at least one, if not several, *kallanka*-style buildings with many doorways opening onto the open space. Another desirable
item from Cusco that was to be used in the new *cusco* was the use of its
favorite building stone, andesite. As we have seen, the core of Pachakuti's
city was built using andesite for all important structures, but the discovery
of more than 450 well-dressed blocks of Rumiqolqa andesite in southern

Ecuador (Ogburn 2004a, 2004b) suggests that we need to reevaluate the traits transferred from the capital to its new centers.

Many types of site have these attributes. For example, the plaza of the palace of Wayna Qhapaq at Quispeguanca was flanked by some *kallanka*-like buildings and had a large unworked stone in its center with an adjacent canal (Farrington 1995). Other non-urban sites also have a plaza, *usnu* complex, and at least one rectangular *kallanka*-like building, such as Tunsukancha, Nevados de Aconquija, and Turi. In Ecuador, the Pilaloma sector of Ingapirka has an upright stone and a tomb as *usnu* in the center of a small patio within a *kancha* (Fresco 1983). Several mountain top sanctuaries also display these attributes, albeit on a very reduced scale. For example, at the *sitwa* ceremony terminus hilltops around Cusco, there are platform plazas and rectangular structures; Heffernan (1996a) has described a series of plazas and terraces on the summit of Tilka with several rock outcrops and a pair of buildings immediately below. Even many of the famous high altitude sanctuaries have a small open space and platform with a small rectangular structure, such as on the pre-summit of Quehuar (6,100m) and the summit of Licancabur (5,921m) (Beorchia 1984; Ceruti 2001). On the flank and summit of Cerro Mercedario (6,250m) in Argentina (Beorchia 1984: 129) and the summit of Cerro San Miguel (3,000m) near Machu Picchu (Reinhard 1991: 67), there is a small upright stone in the middle of a hilltop platform, while at Mirador de Mollepongo (3,200m), a ceremonial site overlooking the Gulf of Guayas, there is a group of platforms, terraced rocks, structures, and a fountain (Odaira 1998). Meddens and his colleagues (2010) have discovered ninepin-shaped stones buried in a rural mountain top *usnu* platform in Ayacucho. In other words, the architectural components, which seem to be the physical essence of *cusco*, are present in a variety of site types, not just urban centers, and many have evidence of important ceremonies. Many well-known examples could be selected to illustrate new *cusco* and the essentiality of inka planning in both a physical and conceptual sense, but I have only selected one which has many but not all of these required attributes.

El Shincal de Quimivíl: A New *Cusco*

Tawantinsuyu stretched from Pasto in southern Colombia as far south as Cerro La Compañía in central Chile, and throughout its length and breadth, there were many places that served as new *cusco*. South of Lake

Titiqaqa in the provinces of Qollasuyu, inka architecture can be described as more rustic than that in Cusco or even in the centers along the road to Chinchaysuyu, where high quality rectangular laid walls can be found. In the southern region, inka buildings are characterized by *pirka* walls set in a mud mortar with adobe brick superstructures, all of which was covered with thick, painted plaster. Studies of inka urbanism in this region have demonstrated that there were many imperial plantations with a unique style of urbanism, comprising plazas, *kallanka*, *usnu* platforms, *qolqa*, and walled *kancha* that are very different from those in the heartland (Raffino 1981, 1993).

El Shincal is a large inka center in Catamarca province in northwestern Argentina, situated on *qhapaq ñan* between Hualfín to the northeast and Watungasta to the west (Raffino et al. 1983–85). It is located in a thorn forest at an altitude of 1,240m on an alluvial fan between the rivers Hondo and Quimivíl; there are foothills on three sides and open views to the south. It has a square plaza, a platform, and several *kallanka* with nine other groups of buildings, as well as two small groups of *qolqa* (figure 12.2). Rodolfo Raffino (2004) has described and conserved the site, while he has extensively excavated its sectors and hinterland. Its importance within Tawantinsuyu was such that it remained a viable focal point and became the location of the second Spanish town foundation in Argentina in 1558, as Londres.[9] Therefore, El Shincal must have been a very significant new *cusco* in Qollasuyu.

In this section, I examine this hypothesis, using several approaches, including its urban planning, architecture, and the use of the inka measurement system, its archaeology, symbolism, and indeed its setting within the landscape (Farrington 1999). Hyslop (1990: 91) described El Shincal as a radially planned town with a large plaza and scattered compounds. However, it is not like those in Peru, such as Huánuco Pampa or Pumpu, because it lacks a dense urban network of compounds, structures, streets, and patios.

Its plaza is large, walled, and relatively square, about 175.22m (108.50r) a side, despite the difficulty in the construction of right angles and a slight misalignment of the southern wall, which was corrected by a zigzag. It is laid out cardinally, diverging only 1.5° from magnetic north. There is an entrance in the southwestern corner through which passes a stone-lined canal. It contains a platform, about 16.15m (10r) square, that stands more than 2.0m high and is approached by a 3.63m (2.25r) wide staircase in the center of its western façade, which faces about 265° magnetic; therefore,

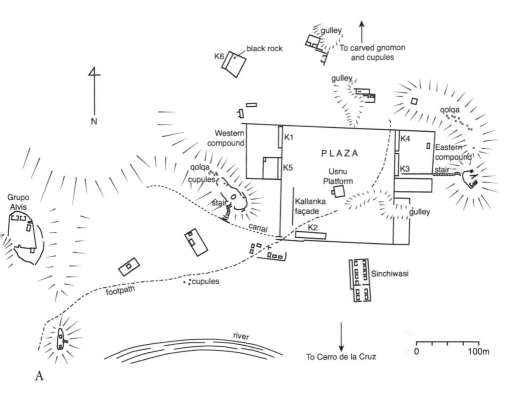

Figure 12.2. El Shincal de Quimivíl. *A*, urban plan; *B*, the walled plaza looking east with the *usnu* platform in the center left, *kallanka* (k1) to the right and an unfinished *kallanka* façade in the foreground.

it is orientated slightly differently to the plaza itself (figure 2.5). A canal alignment passes close by to suggest that this was part of an *usnu* complex.

There is a four door *kallanka* (K2), parallel to the south wall, and the incomplete façade of another, parallel to the west wall, both within the southwest corner of the plaza. At the northern end on both the eastern and western sides, there is a compound containing a pair of identical three-door *kallanka* that face inward to a patio. To the north, there are several isolated compounds with various structures, including one with a *kallanka* and a large black granite *wanka*. To the south, there is a walled compound of twelve separate structures that Raffino (2004) has termed *sinchiwasi*, with an external, elongated structure on its western side. There are several other groups to the southwest, including a terraced hilltop with two identical structures facing each other, a form characteristic of Cusco heartland, and the Grupo Alvis, a large walled compound containing several structures. On the flood plain to the west extend irrigated fields in which there are several sherd scatters, perhaps indicating suburbs, some flat rocks with cupules, the largest associated with the remains of a *chicha* making facility (Giovannetti 2009), an inka shaft tomb, and other graves (Salceda and Raffino 2004).

Cartographic analysis and the measurements of buildings, patios, walls, and doorways reveal that the plan of El Shincal was conceived and executed using the inka unit of linear measurement, the *rikra* (Farrington 1999). The plaza and *usnu* platform were carefully laid out, along with every building and compound. Despite this, as in parts of Cusco, some errors were made that were generally corrected by the builders in the field. For example, the southern plaza wall must have been constructed by two different work gangs who commenced from either end but on different trajectories; this was an error adjusted simply by adding a zigzag behind the K2 *kallanka*.

As stated earlier, symmetry was a key to good inka architectural design. At El Shincal this principle was applied in the construction of the eastern and western compounds, which were symmetrically arranged with regard to the plaza and the main internal structures. Symmetry and equal spacing were also design traits for wall features, such as doors, niches, and windows. While the positioning of doorways was symmetrical in most *kallanka*, one structure, K2, was erected probably by two construction gangs, as its four façade doors were placed incorrectly (Farrington 1999); this mistake was not corrected. Nevertheless, these were minor errors that were easily minimized and did not detract from the type of settlement envisaged for this location. Only in K1 are there trapezoidal niches remaining on its four internal façade walls, each of which has four small niches with an equal spacing of 1.16m (0.72r). Therefore, El Shincal was a carefully planned inka center, despite the fact that its appearance bore little resemblance to Cusco itself. This conclusion is enhanced when the excavation results are examined.

Raffino (2004) has excavated in three important locations to examine the nature of the inka occupation. The *usnu* platform consists of a rubble and earth mass, retained by *pirka* walls that stretch to over 2m above the plaza surface. Like the Huánuco Pampa platform, its outer wall extends above floor height and prevents, to some extent, a view of events taking place on the summit. Raffino et al. (1997) dug several excavation units and determined that its center had originally been paved and that there was a 60cm high stone bench adjacent to the north wall. However, a large ceremonial fire pit, dug during the colonial period, perforated the floor, destroying much of its integrity, while displaying a massive indigenous celebration, attributed to the period of a rebellion in the late sixteenth or early seventeenth century. On and within the inka floor itself, he also found significant evidence of inka ceremonial activity, including charcoal, ash lenses, and a scatter of artifacts: the most significant are human vertebrae and molars, a bronze *tumi*, an Inka Provincial *maka* rim and bird handle from a plate, antler, burned camelid bone, and carbonized plant remains, including coca leaves.[10] This would suggest some form of offering had taken place that may have been concerned with a burial and the sacrifice and burning of adult camelids, ceremonies not unlike those performed at the *usnu* in Hawkaypata in Cusco as *qhapaq hucha*.

The second excavation occurred in *kallanka* K1 in the western compound, which, like the platform, had a significant hispano-indigenous occupation (Raffino 2004). At the southern end, there were two cooking pits, each about 30cm in diameter and full of charcoal, that were associated with Inka Provincial *maka*, bowls, and some local late pottery styles, such as Belén white-on-red and Fambalasto white-on-red. There were also a few sherds from the Titiqaqa basin, such as Inka Pacajes. Two large local *chicha* jars were also found. Other finds included bone spoons and awls, quartzite and obsidian blades, stone and ceramic spindle whorls, and bone and shell beads. The carbonized plant remains included maize, beans, and algarrobo (*Prosopis* sp.) seeds, with much evidence for seed processing and the preparation of alcoholic drinks (Capparelli 2011).[11] Among the animal bones were camelids, guinea pigs, *suri*, several local mammals, and birds. This evidence suggests a permanent occupation with a focus of domestic activities and spinning.

The third excavation was in the so-called *sinchiwasi* compound in which some internal structures and patios were dug as well as some units in the external building (Raffino 2004). This enclosure had been divided into two by a low wall with buildings in each sector that are basically identical in size (6–8m by 5m) with a single entrance from the central patio. The two sectors proved similar in content and therefore function. Each hut comprised a central floor with a low bench on either side. The floor held a large fire pit for cooking, associated with charcoal, food remains, and broken pottery, whereas the benches were hard, compacted clay tops with little material culture, that were probably used for sleeping, although some did have an isolated burned patch. Overall, these results are quite different from the other two structures. The pottery is cruder, with many more local wares and no Inka Provincial pots. The carbonized plant remains indicate a greater dietary reliance on Prosopis flour or bread (Capparelli 2011).[12] The range of animal bones is not very different from that in the other two structures. Raffino (2004) has noted that this compound provided housing for local groups from the Yocavil and Santa María valleys and the Hualfín district, who had probably been brought to serve as *mitayoq* for the state settlement, perhaps as farmers or herders.

The excavation results demonstrate a range of activities that are expected at a provincial inka center, a new *cusco*, such as ceremony, elite residences, and textile making. They also indicate different classes of people, elite in the central area and the lower ranked who lived close to the center but who probably farmed, herded, and performed menial tasks to maintain El Shincal as an important provincial center. The symbolism derived from its architecture and enacted in its ceremony is also enhanced by a consideration of its landscape setting.

Although cardinal orientation was not significant in the planning of Cusco, several provincial sites, such as Calca, were planned in this way or have certain structural elements that face a cardinal direction. The El Shincal plaza and its adjacent compounds are virtually oriented to the cardinal points, and although the *usnu* platform is aligned slightly differently, it is still within 5° of due west. On both the eastern and western sides of the plaza and immediately behind the compounds, there is a steep hill with an artificially flattened summit (figure 12.2). Each stands about 25m above the plaza floor and is terraced. The eastern hill is approached directly from the plaza by a street and staircase that must have passed through a gateway; on the summit, there are the footings of a rectangular structure at the southern end. The western hill is more irregular in shape, and a stone staircase ascends it not directly from the plaza but from the southwest near a small compound. It has no summit structure, but there are several smooth rock outcrops that have been modified, one of which contains a pair of cupules, each about 20cm in diameter and 20cm deep. Their function must be ceremonial because of their hilltop location. Similar features have been recorded at several sites in Qollasuyu and elsewhere, such as at Chena in Chile and Samaipata in eastern Bolivia. These two hills constrict the plaza on both sides, and their critical summit locations are on a line passing cardinally through the *usnu* platform.

At a distance of 460m due north of the *usnu* platform, there is a craggy outcrop of coarse red granite that extends eastwards from the inka road to a cliff top overlooking Quebrada Hondo. On this ridge there is a flat outcrop, about 1.7m long and 0.85m wide, which has a round gnomon, 15–20cm high and 30cm in diameter, shaped into it, and nearby there are several other slabs with worked cupules. In the Cusco area and elsewhere in Tawantinsuyu, such as Colluctor in Ecuador, there are similar sized and shaped gnomons and cupules. This carved rock is the furthest south in the empire, and although its function is not known, it must have some ritual meaning.

From the plaza and *usnu* platform there are wide open views across the fan for many kilometers to the south. At a distance of about 1.5km due south of the platform is Cerro de La Cruz, a small range with two main peaks. Both summits are walled and terraced, and both have been leveled and display cupules and vestiges of structures; one has a building with an interior niche. Low on the southwestern side, facing away from El Shincal, there is a cave known locally as a *salamanca*.[13] It is formed by a large boulder on a scree slope above the uppermost canal. It is only about 12m deep and about 6m wide with a narrow vertical chimney at the rear through which the wind howls. According to local tradition, this place is taboo; no one will enter because it "sings." Inside there is no surface evidence of inka activity, but its cardinal location, its hilltop modification, structures, and hillside cave are reminiscent of Puma Urqu, the hill with the origin cave of Tambo Toqo, found due south of Cusco.

Up to a distance of several kilometers from the plaza, there are hilltops and rocky outcrops with cupules as well as cliffs and caves to suggest that El Shincal may have been surrounded by a series of shrines. For example, a short distance to the southwest there is a steep hill, cerro Divisadero, with a narrow rocky peak summit that stands 46m above the plaza level, and on its very top there is a single cupule, 30cm deep, worked into a slab. It has no functional explanation other than to suggest it is a possible shrine in a culturally marked landscape.

The cardinally located hills fringing the site create a significant cultural microcosm, which focused on the *usnu* platform and plaza within this expansive landscape. Each has significant features, such as buildings, cupules, a gnomon, and unworked large boulders on the summit, while Cerro de la Cruz also has a cave that sings to remind people of inka origins and the underworld.

The symbolism of this center, the re-creation of the inka origin myth within its landscape, 1,500km from the capital, and the reenactment of ceremonies and deposition of offerings that are reminiscent of those in Cusco suggest that, even without the characteristic toponyms, El Shincal is indeed a new *cusco* and one of the most important places in this region of Qollasuyu. In other words, the landscape of El Shincal, the center and its surrounds, reproduces the symbolism of Cusco and the idealized notion of the inka city. Detailed hinterland fieldwork, mapping, and excavation around this and other centers throughout Tawantinsuyu will enable us to consider more clearly the concept of *cusco* as a means by which the inkas transformed places into ideal images of their own civilized landscape: Cusco, the sacred city in its hinterland.

13

Cusco

Toward an Understanding of Inka Urbanism

The inka capital, Cusco, was a permanent, fairly densely populated urban center that displayed the characteristics of a central place with both religious and secular monumental architecture, palaces, and residential neighborhoods. Although the urban core was small, limited to the space between the two rivers, it was surrounded closely by a group of suburban villages, and its influence further extended through the productive hinterland of the valley and upper basin through settlement nodes, including *llaqta* (workers' villages), isolated *kancha*, *qolqa*, temples, and *waka*. How it was defined seems to have varied. For example, in the *seqe* system, Cusco covered the entire upper basin from its focus in Qorikancha, but it was also identified as the urban core when it was last glimpsed. Such flexibility of definition could be noted when foreigners and others were compelled to leave during certain ceremonies. Where did they go? Where was the boundary separating the city from the hinterland? For the purposes of this book, the city was initially defined as the well planned central area, and its boundary lay in the unbuilt spaces on terraces beyond the rivers and outside the plazas. Hence the name of the last suburban village on the road from Chinchaysuyu was Wakapunku, "the gate to the sanctuary." Later I extended the boundary to include its hinterland, an area Pachakuti Inka Yupanki also replanned and delimited by the *seqe* system.

Our understanding of inka Cusco has been enhanced through this systematic analysis of the available historical, architectural, and archaeological data, and for the first time we have a comprehensive view of the city, its rural hinterland, and the role of urbanism in inka life. Yet this work remains only a first step, because more needs to be done, particularly the publication of archaeological results from many excavations, followed by the design and execution of more survey and excavation in the city and surrounding areas. Its conclusions should not be seen as an end in themselves but as the basis for future research. In these endeavors no single set of data should be privileged, but all should be brought to bear on the rigorous testing of such hypotheses.

Therefore, this study has made some contributions and speculations to the understanding of the canons of inka urban planning and the nature of the Cusco town plan; the urban functions of the various plan-units and plan-seams; the social and economic status and activities of the residential population; the nature of ceremony and ritual; burial and the disposal of the dead; and the relationships with, and the planning of, the hinterland settlements—suburban villages, *llaqta*, isolated *kancha* and *qolqa*, the symbolism of the city, and the concept of *cusco* as an idealized city to provincial Tawantinsuyu.

The Canons of Inka Urban Planning in Cusco

In order to analyze the field evidence for inka urban planning, much background information was required to deal with the disparate evidence. For example, knowledge of the construction materials, methods, and standing buildings in technical and functional detail provided an interpretative potential for remnants of walls, footings, foundation trenches, floors, and entrances found in archaeological excavation. Similarly, knowledge of the inka surveying and measurement system and its practice in laying out small towns enabled an evaluation of how the plan of Cusco was conceived and executed in the field. By the same token, the location of basic building types, functional associations, and proximity to each other and open spaces was also vital for understanding the canons of planning. Furthermore, the two analytical techniques—town plan analysis and urban archaeology—required a detailed understanding of historical land use and property information, architectural surveys, and the use of archaeological reports in order to develop a clear picture of historical changes to the original inka street, plaza, and plot patterns as well as of the formation processes creating the archaeological stratigraphy.

The results indicate that inka Cusco can be divided logically into five basic planned areas, including three integrated plan-units, that is, grids of residential properties and streets that separated and surrounded two more irregular but equally well planned plan-seams that contained open spaces, palaces, and temples. Beyond the urban core there was green open space in the form of terraces that separated the city from the nearby suburban villages. The whole was woven together about the axis of the ridge along which ran two consecutive long streets. Only the plazas stretched beyond the urban space between the two rivers. This would suggest that the whole plan was conceived and constructed at one time during the inka period and that, although there were some precolonial modifications to streets, *kancha,* and individual buildings, it remained largely intact until the conquest. It had been built over an earlier grid, as witnessed by regular hut outlines with occupation floors in Kusikancha and Hotel Libertador, but not all so-called killke walls were habitations. Many lack occupation floors and can be described as the retaining walls of construction cells to create a leveled surface prior to building.

The execution of the plan relied on accurate measurement with the two lengths of the main axis being whole numbers of *rikra.* For example, Awaqpinta from plan-seam B at Zetas to the end terrace is 323m (200r) and San Agustín from Limaqpampa Chico at Zetas to the terrace wall at Ese is 807.84m (~500r), with certain plan-units being 161.5m (100r) and 201.9m (125r). Along these were then laid out *kancha* and lanes equidistantly with the basic whole unit measurement being from the corner of one *kancha* to the identical corner in the next, including both the *kancha* and the lane-way. For each of the three plan-units a survey origin point can be identified about which the grid was laid out. The principal cross-street, Maruri-Cabrakancha, in plan-unit II measures 323m (100r) from terrace to terrace, although the survey origin point is not central but on San Agustín, 125.15m (77.5r) from the Tullumayu entrance. The main cross-street in plan-seam A is Triunfo-Hatunrumiyoq. It marks the boundary between plan-units II and III and is 220.35m (136.5r) long from the plaza to Choqechaka and crosses San Agustín–Pumacurco at 262.47m (162.5r) from Limaqpampa at Zetas.

Plan-units I and III were both simple grids of *kancha* and lanes, while plan-unit II was different. It was planned as a single grid, but within it five different sub-units were erected of which four were *kancha* and lanes and the fifth was a large enclosure, Hatunkancha, with rows of separate buildings and a plaza flanked by two *kallanka.* In these areas *kancha* sizes ranged from 1,280sqm to over 2,500sqm, and the number of houses per *kancha* was between four and eight but was internally consistent in each.

The main public buildings lay in and around the two plazas in plan-seams A and B, which ran from southwest to northeast between the two rivers and beyond. In plan-seam A the large plaza on the north side of the river, Hawkaypata, was surrounded on three sides by royal palaces that had walled enclosures containing patios and *kancha* and their adjacent large halls, while a fourth palace was constructed on a terraced hill in the northwest corner of the plaza. The architectural knowledge of these constructions is limited, but the pattern, as seen in the extant walls, excavations, and street plan for each, compares with rural palaces, such as at Chinchero and Quispeguanca *inter alia*. There were buildings on at least two sides of the Kusipata plaza, one with a double jamb doorway, but too little data is available to discern the function of these structures. Likewise the buildings that may have surrounded Limaqpampa, both within the city and on the other side of the Tullumayu, are not known, although there are wall footings, some reconstructed walls, and at least one double jamb doorway in Zetas in mz74, but no excavations have taken place.

Each plaza contained an *usnu* complex, including a platform, an erect stone, and a hole associated with a canal or river. These had been mentioned in the chronicle literature, but were only discovered by excavation in 1996 (Hawkaypata) and 2008 (Limaqpampa). Each has a long retaining wall made in polygonal style, running northwest to southeast, with a higher occupation floor situated behind it. The former had evidence that it had been reclad in rectangular andesite, while the latter had a lower wall and a staircase. The dimensions of neither platform are known, but it is thought that they would have been among the largest in Tawantinsuyu.

The most important building in plan-seam B was Qorikancha, the Sun temple, reconstructed by Pachakuti. It was an enclosure, built in fine rectangular andesite, with a curved wall overlooking the open spaces of southern terraces and esplanade. It contained a *kancha*, patio, and some other buildings. One canal brought water from the plaza through this patio and down onto the esplanade, while others approached it through the town and along the terraces. It housed the golden statue of Punchaw, while images of other deities were also venerated. It was also the center of the *seqe* system and housed many *waka*.

The Nature of Ceremony and Ritual

The historical documents present fairly rich descriptions of many inka ceremonies and rituals, conducted in the city, such as the daily sacrifice of a llama in Hawkaypata, the monthly rituals of killing a hundred llamas, as well as annual ceremonies such as *inti raymi, qhapaq raymi, sitwa,* and *mayucati* and others held infrequently, such as *qhapaq hucha, itu,* royal inauguration, and royal funeral (*purucaya*). Such ceremonies were held at specific times and for specific reasons in various important places, particularly in Hawkaypata, Limaqpampa, or Qorikancha, as well as in palace patios and large halls and at other places throughout the hinterland. It is known they were attended by senior officials, including the Sapa Inka, the royal household, the royal mummies, and the images of the deities who were seated in a set order near the *usnu* complex in the center of the plaza as well as by the local *panaqa* and *ayllu* members and even foreigners from the provinces. However, for certain ceremonies the latter had to leave Cusco for the duration of the event.

In Qorikancha the Sun was worshiped as well as other deities. Its patio provided limited space for ceremonial activities, and as mentioned, Pachakuti ensured that the important rituals, such as *qhapaq hucha*, were replicated in Hawkayata to enable the general population to witness and to take part. The open spaces surrounding the temple were also the scene of ritual and prayer for those who could not enter.

Hawkaypata was where the Sapa Inka made royal proclamations and consulted his ancestors before the assembled noble *panaqa,* ancestral mummies, and other images of the gods. The space surrounding the *usnu* complex would have made certain that those assembled within 25m of it could have heard all speeches and orations and observed the rituals and sacrifices before it (Moore 1996). There was adequate space beyond them for the processions, parades, bands, and dancers symbolically to circle the center, the *usnu* complex, the king, and the ancestors. Limaqpampa with its own *usnu* complex provided the scene for certain specific public events, including those associated with the agricultural year and the inauguration of the Sapa Inka.

In general, inka ceremony involved a variety of activities, including dancing, music, singing, chanting, oration, procession, prayer, offerings, and sacrifices for specific purposes. Such events were accompanied by much feasting and copious drinking, and both food and toasts were offered to the Sun, other deities, and the ancestors. These were poured into the *usnu* hole, onto the ground, or burned in braziers and the ashes were poured into the same receptacle.

Procession was a vital part of inka ceremony in the city, in the hinterland, and at large in the empire. Depending on the occasion, it involved the carriage of the Sapa Inka, mummies, and statues on litters, as well as the marching of officials, lineages, dancers, and musicians. In the city, the widest streets linked Qorikancha, Limaqpampa, and Hawkaypata and also connected with the roads from the *suyu*. Therefore, streets such as Triunfo, Loreto, and Procuradores as well as the bridge from Kuntisuyu via Kusipata served as *vomitoria,* channeling processions into Hawkaypata (figure 13.1). They also formed the initial ceremonial routes for the dispersal of runners at *sitwa* and for the carriage of *qhapaq hucha* to the provinces. The large terraced expanse of Kusipata was the viewing area from which foreigners and others, excluded from certain ceremonies, could watch and to a limited extent participate.

In Hawkaypata, Limaqpampa, and Qorikancha there is much evidence for feasting, drinking, and the burning of llamas. However, the archaeological record is much more equivocal with regard to the identification of either particular annual festivals or periodic ceremonies, mainly because the historical details of specific offerings are not clear and not all materials were buried. Nevertheless, there are patterns that can be recognized as offerings in both the placement of items and their association within an assemblage and the importance of the place in which they are deposited, but none of these can be attributed to any specific ceremony.

For example, a pattern recognized in Qorikancha, involving either figurines or human cranial material surrounded by *tupu,* may have been related to the *qhapaq hucha* ceremony, although similar finds in the spaces around the temple and at Tumibamba may suggest quite a different ritual. A second pattern of a line of llama figurines found at Hawkaypata in front of the *usnu* platform is similar to finds at Wallatapampa near Saqsaywaman and on top of Misti and Llullaillaco, which are also associated with a male figurine. Ceruti and Reinhard have argued that on the mountain tops this forms part of the *qhapaq hucha* offerings. However, this may not be the case for all examples of this pattern.

Other ceremonies, rituals, and meanings may be represented by various other types of assemblage or individual finds. One pattern now recognized at many sites is the use of a focal object surrounded by various broken artifacts and surmounted by a burnt wooden effigy. Figurines have been found in significant places, invariably with no contextual description. In certain contexts, caches of objects have been found within a structure or patio, such as the *urpu* containing thirteen fine pots in Banco Wiese (Hatunkancha) or the one containing mica in Paraninfo (Amarukancha) that are clearly offerings. The meaning and location of each of these objects need to be carefully assessed.

Various inka ceremonies and rituals involved the sacrifice of animals, particularly llamas and guinea pigs and humans that were buried, while

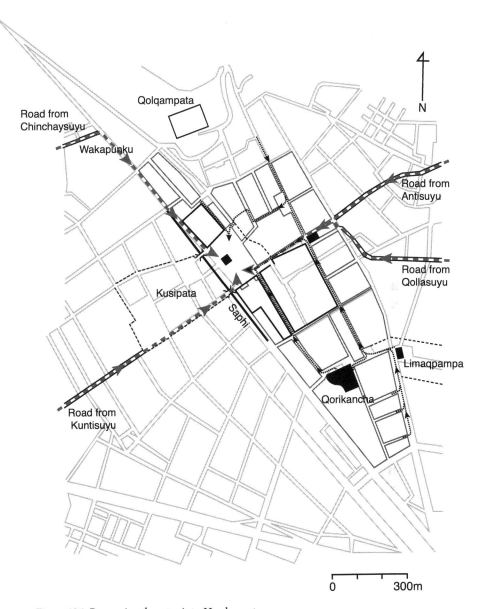

Figure 13.1. Processional routes into Hawkaypata.

llamas were also burned. Sub-floor, in-wall, or sub-threshold offerings could be dedicatory in function, as part of the construction rituals of a building, or protective of the structure. Others on hilltops, terraces, or alongside *waka* were in veneration of the gods or protective of the city over which they looked. Cobo (1990: 51–84) listed more than thirty-five *waka* where children were sacrificed and twelve at which llamas were burned or buried or had the blood drawn and sprinkled. In the city, possible dedicatory or protective human burials have been found as offerings in prominent positions, such as at Waynapata, while human bone has been found beside the carved rock of Sapantiana. The nature of sub-floor burials in the residential areas remain equivocal, although some may have been dedicatory in function.

The archaeological record from the open areas surrounding Qorikancha indicates that the Sun temple was a focus of much ritual activity for those people who could not enter it. In these areas numerous offerings can be recognized, as well as several burials, pottery from many parts of Tawantinsuyu, and burnt llama bone.

While certain classes of offering can be identified because they are found adjacent to or within prominent places in the city, there are problems when such assemblages are observed in residential contexts. More work needs to be done to assess the types of assemblage found in various contexts throughout Cusco in order to isolate other patterns of offering and be able to distinguish those from ordinary domestic activity.

The Symbolism of the City

A fundamental aspect of the ancient city is the study of urban symbolism, that within its own cultural world, the city displays characteristics that demonstrate the interplay between its political and economic functions on the one hand and the practice of religion on the other. Wheatley (1971) considered that there were four factors that needed to be considered for each realm of urbanism: geomantic precautions; cardinal orientation and alignment; the symbolism of the center; and the parallelism of the macrocosmos and microcosmos. For the inkas, Cusco represented the quintessential settlement where all aspects of their worldview from their origins to their relationship with their gods, ancestors, and the land came together at the "navel of the world."

The myths of world and inka origins were linked by the inkas to establish themselves as the children of the Sun and legitimate heirs to the world created by Tiqsi Wiraqocha Pachayachachiq on the Island of the Sun in Lake Titiqaqa and to the earlier urban civilization of Tiwanaku. The places that their ancestors visited, the things they witnessed that led to their geomantic foundation of their city at Wanaypata, and the rock of *cusco wanka* gave them absolute political and spiritual control of Cusco. It made them inviolable rulers of the existing inhabitants. Their association with the natural world of springs, mountains, ravines, rocks, and the cycle of fertility, rains, and sunshine brought them an animated world of spirits and deities in which they lived and developed. The defense of Cusco during the Chanka war and the subsequent systematic replanning of the city and its region by Pachakuti Inka Yupanki established a new series of important places to be remembered and revered. Indeed, the refoundation of Cusco began with the reconstruction of Qorikancha and a reaffirmation of the importance of the Sun religion within inka society before the city or rural districts were rebuilt.

The use of the term *Cusco* for both the king and the city and its definition "in the middle" and "the center about which the world revolves" underlines the inkas' belief in their own supremacy, legitimated by their perceived association with the Sun and as the mediators between their god and the people. The memorialization of places and place-names associated with the origin myth became critical and was repeated in the landscapes around the city and later further afield.

The parallelism between the world of men, *kay pacha*, the upper world, *hanan pacha*, and the underworld, *uku pacha*, were emphasized in myths about the heavens and underworld but also could be observed at the December solstice sunrise. At that time the sun rose from behind Awsangati and the direction of Titiqaqa through the Milky Way, the celestial river, while on the meridian high in the sky stood Alpha Crucis, the star perhaps considered Cusco at the point where the two rivers join and in the direction of the inka's own *paqarina*. This too places the inkas and their ancestors at the center of the world.

Cusco was not planned or oriented toward the cardinal directions, although important mountains lie cardinally placed to the city within the outer heartland, including the Puma Urqo, the inka origin place. However, cardinal planning became a trait that they exported as they built new *cusco*, such as El Shincal, in distant provinces.

Unlike many ancient cities, Cusco did not have massive monumental architecture. Instead, it had a subtle blend of well-planned and well-crafted single-story buildings. Monumentality is discerned in low platforms and the use of open space to emphasize them, such as in Hawkaypata and Li-maqpampa, and in construction on relatively high ground or in prominent locations, such as Qorikancha.

Two *axes mundi* can be recognized within Cusco, and both are located in plan-seams. Qorikancha, in plan-seam B, was the main Sun temple of Tawantinsuyu and the residence of the statue of Punchaw. It was where one founding brother turned to stone in *cusco wanka* during the origin story and where Pachakuti initiated the reconstruction program after the Chanka war. As such, the most important ceremonies in honor of the Sun were performed inside it, such as the llama sacrifices and the live burial of the *qhapaq hucha* children during its dedicatory celebrations. Its participants and walls were painted in llama blood. Qorikancha was also the center from which the *seqe* system of *waka* radiated across the city and its hinterland, controlling therefore much of ritual and religious life. Its symbolism was enhanced by its elevated position on the ridge and because it was clad in gold panels, which would have transformed its fine andesite architecture into a brilliant light-filled place for those privileged to be inside (Saunders 2002).

The second was the *usnu* complex in Hawkaypata, which played the major politico-religious role in the city and the empire. There, Pachakuti had a second image of the Sun erected as a shaped stone sheathed in gold in order that the ordinary people could enjoy and participate in the replication of those ceremonies held at the dedication of Qorikancha. According to the chronicles, it was there that the Sapa Inka viewed the parades and processions, received tribute, consulted with the ancestors, and announced political decisions. This more secular center was also engaged in Sun worship by proclaiming and legitimizing the actions and deeds of the king. It was the main focus of popular ceremony, and its events could be viewed from Kusipata and even from the suburban villages from beyond. It was this architectural complex and its plaza and the role it played that formed the planning template for the new *cusco*, which took the politico-religious symbols of the city, its ceremonies, rituals, and myths to other parts of Tawantinsuyu as Cusco.

The Social and Economic Status and Activities of the Residential Population

The documentary sources describe several sociological differences within the urban population. For example, the city was divided into two moieties,

Hanan and Hurin, as well as into various social groups, including ten *panaqa*, ten *ayllu*, *yanakuna* (servants), *aqllakuna*, and members of provincial elite delegations. Unfortunately, there is no archaeological evidence in terms of material culture or architecture to separate the city clearly into Hanan and Hurin Cusco. There have been insufficient excavations in the palaces and temples to determine any differences, although in the plan-seams at the Houses of Waskar and Qorikancha there is a great deal of highly decorated and finely made inka pottery, which contrasts markedly from the general pattern observed in the *kancha*. This could be explained by the fact that most of the plan-seam data comes from public areas and rubbish dumps and not from living areas, such as at Kusikancha or Intiqawarina #620.

In his chronicle, Sancho (1917: 192) stated that the city was occupied by the inka elite, who lived in palaces and that there were no poor people. This archaeological analysis has revealed that there were three types of residence within the city: the royal palaces surrounding Hawkaypata; the *kancha* in the plan-units; and a walled compound called Hatunkancha, adjacent to the plaza, that housed the *aqllakuna inter alia*. These appear to have performed different roles within the governance of inka life. Nevertheless, it is clear from the limited archaeology that the elite had servants, and therefore each architectural group would have had people from different social grades, including *yanakuna*.

Comparing the architecture and assemblages from the residential compounds, there is a notable difference between Hatunkancha and the other *kancha*. The former stands out because it was a closed community with a single entrance, a special arrangement of structures in rows and a small plaza flanked by *kallanka*. It is similar in plan to a compound at Huánuco Pampa that Morris (1974) considered on the basis of its finds to be an *aqllawasi*. Two elite burials, an offering cache of well-made pottery, and another of metal objects have been found within it, while in the *kancha* the occupation is more basic and the burials are relatively poor in terms of grave goods. This would suggest that inhabitants of Hatunkancha were of higher status, including *aqllakuna*, than those in the *kancha*.

The burial evidence from four *kancha* excavations demonstrates that the residents were women, men, and children, possibly family groups, and that they also had pet dogs. These were generally healthy people who had not suffered childhood stress or arthritic injury from heavy workloads. Whether these were inkas or other local people is not known, but at least one Kusikancha individual had annular oblique cranial vault modification, suggesting a Titiqaqa origin (Andrushko 2007). The use of foreign or provincial pottery could also be seen as an indicator of ethnic origin of the inhabitants. Within Cusco the majority of wares from all over the empire are found as offerings in the open spaces around Qorikancha and on the Salesianos terraces overlooking the city, as well as in Kusipata and at Saqsaywaman Muyuqmarka. In the residential areas, various inka plain and decorated wares and some killke ones dominate the ceramic assemblages. However, chimú potsherds have been found in Hatunkancha in the excavations at Triunfo #392, and an elite male burial at Casa Concha contained a complete chimú vessel, suggesting that there were people of North Coast ancestry located in that compound. In the residential *kancha*, chimú potsherds have been recovered in an offering in Nazarenas, while sherds from a pacajes-inka vessel were found in Intiqawarina #620. In the suburban village of Wakapunku, a two-handled chimú dish was found as part of an offering.

There is plenty of evidence from the *kancha* and Hatunkancha for domestic activities in kitchens, such as food preparation, cooking, and brewing. These contain grindstones, chopping tools, clay ovens, stoves and stands, reddened floors, ash and charcoal, food remains, and cooking, storage, and serving ceramics. The only substantial excavation in Qasana has also revealed a similar kitchen complex, but this is thought to have catered for feasts held in the adjacent first patio of the palace. The *kancha* excavations also reveal evidence for meals, drinking, and storage.

It is presumed that the *kancha* inhabitants not only served the elite but were also engaged in craft industry. While textile making tools, such as spindle whorls and *ruki*, are found throughout the city, there is no archaeological evidence for any specific workshop. Similarly, there are hints that metal working and pottery making may also have taken place, but there is no concentration of artifacts to suggest the scale of operation.

The social patterns revealed in the archaeology of the city do not conform to the pattern derived from the historical documents or to those seen in other urban and palace archaeologies in the Cusco hinterland. However, this is a problem perceived because the disturbed contexts are thought not to reveal anything useful and because of the lack of an overall research strategy that would demand rigorous hypothesis testing. There is a need for further extensive research in those parts of the city that have hitherto lacked intensive investigation, such as Qasana, Hatunkancha, and Awaqpinta.

Burial and the Disposal of the Dead

The inkas generally disposed of their dead, irrespective of their status, by placing them in a walled hillside cave (*machay*), under a rock, or in a *chullpa* or burial tower. Even the Sapa Inka was mummified and kept in this way. The chroniclers mentioned that there were human sacrifices in which the corpse was buried. These included the killing of servants and officials on the death of the king and child sacrifices at *waka* for various reasons. The inkas therefore had contrasting practices for disposing of the dead, but clearly burial was reserved for special cases. There was no royal tomb; mummified remains were kept in ancestral houses.

Archaeology has revealed at least 840 burials and numerous miscellaneous collections of human bone found in prepared pits, cists, shaft tombs, large pots, or clay capsules in the city and the hinterland, although the majority have not been published in detail. They fall into two broad categories: those associated with residential areas and those found in more public places, such as temple surrounds, plazas, and terraces overlooking plazas and adjacent to *waka*.

In the city archaeologists have found the remains of fifty-five people as well as at least fourteen other groups of human bone. Of these, thirty-five were found in residential areas together with ten collections of bone. In the *kancha*, they were found in building interiors, in corners or against the footings, in entrance ways, on lateral patios, and some in the main patio. They were usually single burials in pits with few or no grave goods. It is argued that these were individuals who had been brought to Cusco as *yanakuna* or *aqllakuna* and who did not have access to traditional hillside cemeteries and therefore were buried where they lived and worked. The two burials in Hatunkancha were each in a prepared grave with more than fifteen ceramic offerings and other objects. These may have been elite *yanakuna* or *aqllakuna* without access to Cusco burial areas or foundation dedicatory burials for certain buildings or compounds.

The other twenty burials in the city were found in prominent places throughout the city. They include the Amarukancha palace, adjacent to Kusipata, in Limaqpampa, in the open spaces surrounding Qorikancha, *waka* such as Pumaqchupan, the carved rock at Sapantiana, and terraces that overlook the city, such as Waynapata. Many of these were elaborately furnished with grave goods and were almost certainly offerings placed to protect the city and appease the gods. As we have seen, in Qorikancha human bone was also used in very specific offerings, in situations similar to figurines, and in those cases may represent surrogate sacrifices.

The Relationships with, and the Planning of, the Hinterland Settlements

No city can exist in isolation and without its hinterland. A vital part of Pachakuti's reconstruction program was the remodeling of rural infrastructure and the channelization of the rivers. This entailed the construction of terraces, canals, and reservoirs for efficient cultivation, but also land reclamation through flood prevention and the draining of low-lying marshy lands. The combined effect of this program was that the rural hinterland was resettled by the important *panaqa* and *ayllu* of Cusco, who received better quality lands for farming and pasture, and that state land was set aside to build up surpluses to maintain the ceremonial, political, and building programs in the city.

This period of construction brought in workers as *mitayoq* and *mitmaqkuna* not only to farm the land for the *panaqa*, the *ayllu*, and the state but also to build the city. They were housed in *llaqta* that were distributed close to farmland or quarries throughout the valley. These settlements were ordered rows of uniform houses and open spaces, some with platforms. Excavation in several of these clearly shows domestic activities, including food preparation, cooking, brewing, and textile manufacture. Burials have been found in the houses and public areas in locations similar to those of the urban *kancha*, although one hut in Qotakalli had 427 secondary burials that had been hastily placed upon the abandonment of the settlement. This would imply that the inhabitants of these *llaqta* had no access to burial grounds in the Cusco valley.

The majority of pottery found in these villages is inka with some local killke or lucre styles. There is almost none from beyond the valley, suggesting that the settlers had been provided with household equipment when they arrived. However, skeletal analysis shows that at least one village, Qotakalli, had six individuals with tabular erect deformation and seventeen had annular oblique, implying that they were foreigners from the Titiqaqa region and the central or northern coast (Andrushko 2007).

It is known from the documents that Cusco was surrounded by storehouses and that Pachakuti had indicated on which hillsides they should be built in the valley. These state-built structures conform to two general patterns: elongated, multi-doored buildings in rows on terraces, and rows of small rectangular huts. Although the architecture of the two types is different, it is not known whether this is a function of what was being stored. From excavations in the first type, they also received dedicatory burials and offerings.

There is a distinct spatial relationship between the location of *llaqta* and *qolqa* and the other state-built structure, the isolated *kancha*. The latter were walled enclosures of inka buildings with a more elaborate range of artifacts than the *llaqta* and appear to have been inhabited by an elite who managed the agricultural and storage resources of the valley. These buildings had both dedicatory burials and a spatial distribution of graves similar to that in Kusikancha.

In contrast, the suburban villages were closer to the city, located on or near the main roads into the capital from the *suyu*. According to the documents, they appear to have been populated by local non-inka *ayllu*, provincial elite, and *mitmaqkuna* brought as specialist craft communities, such as metalsmiths in Carmenqa and Chakillchaca. Only the royal suburb of Qolqampata is different.

Unfortunately, apart from Qolqampata, there has been very little archaeological excavation to determine the nature, composition, and functions of these settlements. There has been some focus on *waka* and associated burials and offerings that demonstrate a pattern of rich finds in prominent places overlooking the city.

The hinterland settlements functioned to supply the city with labor, food, and other materials from the fields, quarries, and storehouses. The hinterland was also integral to the practice of ceremony and ritual and the general belief system of the inkas. The *seqe* system extended across this area with its *waka* and the specific rituals and offerings that were made at them. In addition, there were other significant ceremonial locations, including four rural Sun temples and at least three ancestral houses. These were the focus of offering and ritual as well as processions to and from the city and between temples across the hinterland. Rich dedicatory burials have been found at them. Some ceremonies and processions traveled from mountains and sacred places into the city, such as the inauguration of a king, while others went out from it, such as *sitwa, mayucati,* and *qhapaq hucha.*

Conclusion

This book has successfully utilized the historical sources, field observation, and archaeological record and techniques to develop the notion of Cusco as a city that embraced the inka worldview and identity. The inkas' association with their ancestors, the natural world, Titiqaqa and Tiwanaku, and their intimate association with the Sun are paramount to this understanding. As urban and rural planners, the inkas were outstanding. They managed their resources of labor and materials well to construct their city as the navel of the world, the focus of the Sun worship, and the location of El Cusco, the son of the Sun. This analysis has revealed many new concepts and ways of assessing the inkas, their planning, and their city, but it is by no means the final word on the subject. More archaeological work needs to be done in understanding inka society, burials, and the villages they built for their workforce. More excavation, survey, and analytical work is needed in Cusco itself to elaborate and even challenge these ideas of the city and of the inkas.

Glossary

All words are quechua or aymara, except for a few in Spanish words (indicated by Sp.)

apu—a great lord or a deity, and therefore often refers to a mountain top.

apurucu—a large male llama used for breeding (González Holguín 1989: 32), although Cobo (1990: 128) suggests that they were "very old."

aqha—maize beer (quechua), also known as *chicha*.

aqlla—a woman who was specifically selected at an early age from the empire for service to the Sun and the Sapa Inka. After education in an *aqllawasi*, such women had diverse roles: to serve the Inka as a royal concubine, to be given as a wife to a provincial noble, to care for a royal mummy; to be a sacrificial victim; or to be a royal servant as clothing maker, cook, *chicha* maker, or simple waitress.

aqllakuna—women chosen as *aqlla*.

aqllawasi—house or convent for the *aqllakuna* or *mamakuna*.

aqorasi—a round polished metal mirror with a handle, or a pectoral, a metal plate worn around the neck and over the chest.

ayllu—an endogamous, territorially based lineage that claims descent from a mythical ancestor.

aysana—a flat-bottomed, narrow-necked jar.

cabildo—a town council and therefore the name of its building (Sp).

carpawasi—an inka building drawn by Guaman Poma (1980: 330 [332]) and described as a tent or pavilion. González Holguín (1989: 50) defined it as a three-sided building or passage. The stem *carppa* means covered in textiles or canes.

casona—a large colonial house with patio, usually with two stories adjacent to the street (Sp).

chachapuma—a stone statue of a seated puma found at Tiwanaku.

chakitaqlla—the andean foot-plow.

chaquira—a pendant or bead made of spondylus shell.

chicha—maize beer, also *aqha*.

chullpa—a burial tower, usually built of stone with a low, narrow entrance.

chuñu—a type of freeze-dried potato.

cuyusmango—an inka building drawn by Guaman Poma (1980: 330 [332]) and described as a large hall in a palace complex with a door and niches in a narrow end.

ekeko—a miniature object that contains the essence of the full-sized one it represents; also *illa*.

estado—a unit of measurement in colonial Spain, about 1.67m (Sp).

hanan—the upper part of a social division.

hanan pacha—in inka cosmology, the upper world, the heavens.

hurin—the lower part of a social division.

ichu—an andean native grass, *Stipa ichu*.

illa—a miniature object that contains the essence of the full-sized one; also *ekeko*.

inti raymi—inka month of June and festival for the June solstice.

itu raymi—an inka festival, held at any time of the year to counter the effects of environmental disasters, such as earthquake, plague, flood, or drought.

jiwaya—a stone hammer used for stone trimming.

kallanka—a long, narrow, building with several doors, usually facing a plaza.

kancha—a walled compound of houses with a central patio; an enclosure; it also means toasted or popped maize kernels.

kay pacha—in inka cosmology, the everyday world, the world of humans.

khipu—a knotted cord used as a mnemonic device for recording census details, stored goods, and social histories.

kiqllu—an urban street or lane.

kurpana—an agricultural tool for breaking clods of earth.

llaqta—an inka town, village, or settlement.

machay—a cave or rock shelter, often walled and used to house the dead.

maka—an inka bottle with a pointed base and flared rim used for the storage, transport, and serving of *chicha* and the storage of foodstuffs; also known as an aryballo.

makana—a heavy wooden or stone implement used to compact sediments, such as floors.

mallki—an ancestor; also a long-lived tree, the shape of which resembles an old person.

mamakuna—the chosen women, also known as *aqllakuna*.

manzana (mz)—a street block (Sp).

maran—a large rectangular or square bottom grindstone.

masma—an inka three-sided roofed building with one wall open; also *wayruna*.

mayu—a river or stream.

mita—tribute in the form of work or a work obligation.

mitayoq—a tribute or corvée laborer.

mitmaq—an inka policy to translocate an *ayllu* from its homeland for settlement elsewhere, where it replaced another group. It was used for political purposes to reduce unrest within Tawantinsuyu.

mitmaqkuna—persons or group translocated from their homeland and settled elsewhere by the inkas.

moraya—a type of freeze-dried potato.

mote—boiled maize kernels (*muti* in quechua).

mullu—the thorny oyster or spondylus shell; a large mollusc found in warm tropical waters and exploited by the inkas in the Gulf of Guayas (about 2°S), renown for its special qualities, particularly as beads or figurines, being red on one side and white on the other.

mutka—a polished stone vessel or mortar used for grinding.

ñandú—the flightless bird, *Rhea americana*, also known in quechua as *suri*.

ñañu waska—a cord, used for linear measurement, probably 6.46m (4r) long.

napa—a camelid prepared for sacrifice with a red cloth over its back.

ntin—A quechua word that means the totality, everything included, and "the spatial inclusion of one thing in another" (Platt 1986: 245), as found in the term *Tawantinsuyu*.

pachamanka—an earth oven; also *watiya*.

palmo—a colonial unit of linear measurement of 21.6cm (Sp).

pampa—a relatively level open space used for farming, grazing, or public gatherings.

panaqa—an endogamous, territorially based inka noble lineage that claimed descent from a mythical ancestor.

paqarina—the origin place from where an andean social group emerged to establish its village and territory.

pata—a terrace or open space.

picota—the gallows, often raised in the center of a Spanish town square (Sp).

pirka—an inka technique of random rubble wall construction.

pirua—a storage bin, usually made of clay; also *taqe*.

phiruru—a spindle whorl, usually made from ceramic, bone, stone, or wood. Also known as *fusayola*.

puku—a ceramic or wooden plate or dish, usually with opposing lugs, a bird-headed handle, or a loop handle.

pukullu—burial in a walled cave or rock shelter. Also *pukutu*.

punku—a natural or man-made gateway to an important place.

purucaya—the funeral ceremonies for the Sapa Inka.

pururauca—a stone *waka*, animated as a soldier in the defense of Cusco during the Chanka war that became petrified again after the victory.

qero—a wooden, metal, or ceramic beaker, used for drinking *aqha* (*chicha*).

qhapaq hucha—an inka ceremony first celebrated at the dedication of Qori-kancha in the reign of Pachacuti Inka Yupanki with the sacrifice of a boy and a girl; later a ceremony of redistribution between the Inka and the Sun and a province or provincial *waka* that involved blood from llamas of the Sun and child sacrifice.

qhapaq ñan—an inka main road.

qhapaq raymi—the inka month of December and festival for the December solstice.

qoa—a mythical feline thought to live in Awsangati, protecting the herds of the Creator; also associated with thunder, lightning, and hail.

qocha—a lake, pool, or inka reservoir.

qolqa—an inka storeroom.

qonopa—a stone or wooden animal figurine, usually a llama, with a hole in its back for grinding small quantities of important substances, such as coca or *vilka*; placed as an offering in certain locations.

qontay—a white sediment of decomposed limestone found in soils of the Cusco valley.

Qoya—the Inka queen.

qumpi—fine woven cloth made from vicuña wool.

raki—a large mouthed pot with a rounded or pointed base and flared rim, used for brewing or storage; also known as *urpu*.

rikra—an inka unit of linear measurement (1r); it is calculated to be 1.615m long.

rokro—an andean stew made from meat, potatoes, chili, and other herbs.

ruki—an andean weaving shuttle, usually made of animal bone or antler.

salamanca—a term used in Argentina to refer to a dangerous place (Sp).

sanku—a maize dough soaked in llama blood.

Sapa Inka—the inka king, literally the "Only Inka."

sapi—a tree root.

saruna—wall steps, protruding like pegs from the wall, to gain access to an upper story or terrace.

seqe—a road or line along which there are *waka*.

sikya—an inka unit of linear measurement, it is calculated to be 0.8075m (0.5r) long.

sinchiwasi—an inka building, a military barracks.

sitwa—an inka ceremony of cleansing or ridding the city of "evil" that took place in September when the *panaqa* and *ayllu* of the city and Inner Heartland ran a relay with their colleagues from the Outer Heartland as far as a prominent mountain beside one of the major rivers, the Vilcanota and the Apurimaq, where they washed their clothes and arms.

solar—a term used in both medieval England and Spain to mean "an urban plot, house, or compound"; in this case, it describes a group of individual houses or structures arranged around a courtyard, for which inka archaeologists use *kancha* (Hyslop 1990: 16–17). An alternative Spanish word, *corral*, was also used as "an enclosed space" to describe houses with a courtyard.

sunturpaucar—a wooden staff covered with colored feathers with three feathers sprouting out of the top, part of royal regalia.

suri—the quechua word for the flightless bird, *ñandu, Rhea americanus*.

suyu—a quarter or territorial division.

tambo—a colonial and republican term for an urban inn, derived from *tampu*, that provided food, lodging, stabling, and warehousing for traders from the Cusco hinterland.

tampu—an intermediate stopping place along the inka road that provided lodging for passing inka officials, processions, tribute, and armies. These were effectively small urban centers, often with *kallanka*, plaza, *usnu* complex, and *qolqa*.

taqe—a storage bin, usually made of clay.

tticachurana—a tall-necked, flat-based inka bottle, often called a *florero*.

tullu—bones.

tumi—an inka metal knife with a handle and crescentic blade.

tupayauri—a wooden staff of office or authority.

tupu—a pin with a rounded head for fastening clothing, usually made of metal; also an andean unit of linear measurement of variable length and of areal measurement, generally about 0.25 to 0.33 of a hectare.

tunaw—a stone pestle or muller for grinding.

ukhu pacha—in inka cosmology, the underworld, entered through caves or water surfaces.

unku—an inka man's shirt.

urpu—a large, wide-mouthed pot with a pointed or rounded base and flared rim, used for storage or brewing; also known as *raki*.

usnu—a structural or natural complex, usually featuring a platform and an upright stone and a hole, pool, canal, or river, which is found in or adjacent to a plaza, serving both religious and political functions.

vilka—an hallucinogenic snuff from the seeds of the tropical leguminous tree *Anadenanthera colubrina* or *A. peregrina*; also added to *chicha* or given as a purgative enema.

waka—an inka shrine or sacred place.

warachiquy—the inka initiation ritual, held in the month of *qhapaq raymi* (December).

waska—an inka unit of linear measurement, calculated to be 6.46m (4r) long.

watiya—an earth oven (also *pachamanka*).

wawki—a statue or amulet maintained by the Sapa Inka as his surrogate, his "brother." These were carved in stone as animals or anthropomorphic effigies, or they were cast in gold as a human statue.

wayrana—a three-sided roofed inka building, also *masma*.

yanakuna—men and women who have been taken from their home communities to serve the Inka, Sun, or other nobility as farmers, craftsmen, or guards; slaves who have lost rights to their homeland.

Notes

Chapter 1. Urbanism in Prehispanic Andes

1. Direct quotations from the chronicles are taken from the most recent English translations of that work. Where no such work is cited, however, the translation is my own from the latest Spanish edition.

Chapter 2. Inka Architecture and Urban Buildings

1. The characteristic batter of inka structural walls, externally and internally, is generally between 2° and 7°, that is, between 3.5% and 12.25% (e.g., Protzen 1999: 196). The extremes can range from almost vertical, such as the internal rear wall of Qorikancha R-1, which is 1.5° (2.62%) for the lower 1.63m to the niche base and only 0.5° (0.88%) for the 1.84m above (Puelles 2005: 154), to as much as 15° (26.8%) (Kendall 1985: 23).

2. The trapezoidal form is characteristic of inka doorways, niches, and windows. It was aesthetically pleasing to the eye but also a subtle technique to add structural strength to those walls that have been perforated by a door, because the shape is achieved by corbelling. Such a form would also slightly reduce the required length of the lintel.

3. Tapia is a large adobe block, sometimes several meters in length and between 1m and 1.5m tall. It is generally manufactured *in situ* by building a wooden frame on top of footings or a wall, filling it with rammed clay, dried grass, and small stones, and allowing it to fully dry before removing the frame.

4. The *chakitaqlla* is the andean footplow with a fire-hardened or metal blade, generally used for digging heavy soils.

5. A stepped niche has the form of two stepped-frets side by side. It may be like a stepped-pyramid or the inverse.

6. Manyaraki is a district in Ollantaytambo with a plaza, located below the main temple on the opposite side of the Patakancha river to Qosqo Ayllu.

7. In her definition, Muñóz (2007: 257) suggested that a *kallanka* should have a minimum length of at least 40m.

8. Guaman Poma (1980: 330 [332]) listed the names of fourteen buildings associated with royal palaces: Cuyusmango Uaci, Quinco Uaci (curved house), Muyo Uaci (round house), Carpa Uaci (pavilion), Moyo Uaci, Uauya Condo Uaci, Marca Uaci (nobles' house), Punona Uaci (dormitory), Churacona Uaci (storehouse), Aca uasi (chichería), Masana Uaci (drying house), Camachicona Uaci (counsel house), Uaccha Uaci (almshouse), and Suntor uasi (round tower).

9. I have recorded the remains of eight large halls in the Outer Heartland (table 2.7). All can be readily identified in the field, although their subsequent reuse and remodeling as well as farming and road construction have meant that none are intact. For example, the Casa de la Ñusta in Yucay lacks its rear wall and part of its side walls, while the façade of Canchispukyo in the Qochoq valley was removed during road construction.

10. There are two *seqe waka* with this suffix: Warupuncu (AN-3:1), a bridge to enter the city near Qorikancha, and a pass, Puncu (QO-9:13), on the southern edge of the valley (Cobo 1990: 65, 77).

Chapter 3. Canons of Inka Settlement Planning

1. According to *Visitas*, compiled in the 1560s on the basis of interviews with provincial leaders who held *khipu* records of their obligations to the inkas, the province of Huánuco provided 400 stone masons for work in Cusco and 400 farmers to cultivate land there (Ortiz de Zuñiga 1967), while Lupaqa province provided people to build houses and walls in Cusco and elsewhere as well as others to prepare fields and to farm there, too (Garci Diez de San Miguel 1964).

2. Following Gibaja's 1982 work, Lisbet Bengtsson (1998: 79–85) excavated under a large stone block, weighing about 70 metric tons, on the road at the base of the ramp in Ollantaytambo. She found evidence of several poles used lengthwise as a track on which to slide the rock.

3. Its name combines an ethnographically known unit of length (*waska*) and the word *ñañu* or *llañu*, which means a narrow thing; the translation may be a "narrow measuring cord."

4. *Trichocereus cuzcoensis*, known today as *hawak'ollay*, is probably the cactus that Betanzos (1996: 70) referred to as *haguacolla quisca*. Gade (1975: 192) recorded that it is a tall columnar cactus that grows at altitudes between 2,800m and 3,600m in the Vilcanota valley, where its gum is used as a glue and that it is also mixed with gypsum to make a whitewash.

5. The inkas essentially used a decimal system, although the largest number in any set tends to be a unit around forty, such as the *seqe* system of forty-one lines and a *waranqa* of 40,000 people.

6. It is clear that areal measurement is important for calculating the size of urban or rural property. Unfortunately, little work has been done on the inka system of areal measurement, probably called a *tupu*. The modern agricultural *tupu* in the Cusco region is thought to be the area sufficient to sustain a family for one year. Therefore, it varies between 2,000sqm and 3,696sqm, according to terrain, soil type, aspect, and water provision (Valencia 1982).

7. Using the principles of cosine quantogram (D. G. Kendall 1974), Robert Porteous from the ANU Research School of Physical Sciences wrote a computer program to test for a quantum in my field data.

8. Calca has been continually occupied since 1534; today it is a small regional center with a population of about 9,200.

9. Ollantaytambo has been continually occupied since the conquest; today it is a very small regional and tourist center. The Qosqo Ayllu sector has a population of about 1,000.

10. In excavations along the line of Lari calle on the eastern side of Qosqo Ayllu, several

cyclopean blocks were found, suggesting that the outer wall was continued in that style on that side of the town (Soto and Cabrera 1999).

11. In sixteenth-century documents, Ollantaytambo was called simply Tambo (see Glave and Remy 1983).

Chapter 4. Archaeology and the Town

1. There have been limited excavations in Ollantaytambo Qosqo Ayllu, Calca, and Vilkaswamán, while the World Heritage city of Cuenca has recently begun a major urban archaeological program, directed by Jaime Idrovo (2009), following on from some pioneering test pits dug by Jamieson (1999). The latter has already discovered pre-inka, inka, colonial, and republican tombs, walls, structures, and canals. It is noted that the inka settlement stretched from Pumapongo to the city center.

2. *Townscape* has come to mean many things since it was coined, but the most appropriate definition is the urban built environment, its visual appearance; in other words, its physical form, architectural styles, and geographical setting (see definition in Larkham and Jones 1991).

3. Strictly speaking, a plan-seam is a line separating plan-units (Larkham and Jones 1991); in this book, it is used to describe the irregular space between the regular plan-units, characterized by open spaces and building complexes on various alignments and with functions different from those of the plan-units.

4. Town plans were popular components of atlases of the sixteenth and early seventeenth centuries. Perhaps the most famous of these is *Civitates Orbis Terrarum*, edited by Georg Braun and Franz Hogenburg (2011) and published as six volumes in Cologne between the years 1572 and 1617. Overall, it contained 546 color maps, bird's-eye views, and urban prospects by more than 100 cartographers of 286 towns in Europe, the Mediterranean, the Near East, and India. Volume 1 contains the only two illustrations of American towns: Cusco and Mexico City.

Chapter 5. A Historical Topography of Cusco

1. The source for 2007 urban population is the Municipality of Cusco website: http://www.municusco.com.pe

2. In order to locate changes and various features in the city, I have used a system of numbered street blocks (*manzana*), devised by the Municipality of Cusco. In the text, these are written with the prefix *mz*, followed by the block number, e.g., mz37, as a convenient shorthand. This system was used by Agurto (1980) and Aparicio and Marmonilla (1989).

3. Guaman Poma (1980: 31[31], 84[84]) stated that *aqhamama*, mother beer, was an early name for Cusco.

4. It is thought that the three men were Martín Bueno, Pedro Martín de Moguer, and Juan de Zárate. They left Cajamarca on 15 February and arrived back on 15 May 1533.

5. The main eyewitness chronicles are by Juan Ruiz de Arce (2002 [1545]), Miguel de Estete (1924 [1534]), Diego de Trujillo (1948 [1571]), Pedro Sancho de la Hoz (1917 [1534]), and Pedro Pizarro (1986 [1571]). Cristóbal de Mena (1967 [1534]) and Francisco de Xerez (1985 [1534]) did not travel to Cusco, choosing to return to Spain. They interviewed the three men who had and used their descriptions in their accounts.

6. The total amount of gold was only half of what had been melted in Cajamarca, only 588,266 pesos, but the amount of silver was more than double, 164,558 marks of good and 63,752 of poor quality (Hemming 1970: 132).

7. MacCormack has argued that many sixteenth-century Spaniards (Betanzos 1996; Cieza de León 1959; Anonymous Jesuit 1968) saw Cusco and Tawantinsuyu in terms of their understanding of ancient Rome and its empire, including its urban buildings, functions, and laws as well as its roads, provinces, and provincial cities.

8. There has been some confusion in the documents of the intended dedication of the church. However, in the earliest document (1534), Pizarro is recorded as declaring that it was to be called Nuestra Señora de la Asunción (Rivera Serna 1965).

9. *Solar* is a medieval Spanish word used for an urban house or property.

10. Atabilca was probably a name the Spaniards used for Atawallpa.

11. Despite differences, omissions, and tears in the manuscript, the two lists of settlers, dating to March and October 1534, each tally about 100 men (Rivera Serna 1965).

12. For example, Juan Pizarro received two *solares* "on the terraces which can be taken" (Rivera Serna 1965). This suggests that these were vacant, not built upon. From later documents it is clear that these were one or two terraces in Kusipata.

13. The colonial Spanish foot was about 27.9cm in length.

14. The name Qora Qora was used in the Acta de Fundación for the houses or fortress of Waskar (Rivera Serna 1965). This site has a commanding position above the plaza. It is not to be confused with the large hall of the same name that lay immediately below it between the streets Procuradores and Suecia.

15. Garcilaso de la Vega left Cusco to live in Spain in 1560. He never returned. His chronicle was not published until 1609. He is the only chronicler to report on a "fine round tower" that stood in front of Amarukancha but was pulled down before he left the city (Garcilaso 1966: 426, 701). His description is detailed, but there is some confusion about its location. As Bauer (2004: 127) pointed out, it could have been one of the towers described by Pizarro as part of Qasana.

16. My translation of this statement is "the greater part is an inka building, and it is in good order."

17. The Carmelitas Descalzas order had originally been established in Cusco in a private house in Wakapunku in 1561 and chose to move to their new location nearby.

18. It is important to note the dates of survey, not simply those of publication. Therefore, the Pentland map was surveyed between 1827 and 1838, that of Hohagen in 1861, that of Squier in 1865, and that of Wiener in 1876–77.

19. The market hall was built between 1922 and 1925. It is attributed to Gustave Eiffel, as architect and constructor.

20. In 1951, there were 15 Peruvian soles to 1 US dollar. Therefore, the damage costs were private housing, $20 million, and public buildings, $6.67 million. At today's rates, this would be the equivalent about $180 million and $60 million.

Chapter 6. Analysis of the Cusco Town Plan

1. This street currently has four names: San Agustín from Limaqpampa Chico to Ruinas; Herrajes from Ruinas to Triunfo; Palacio from Triunfo to Plazuela de Nazarenas;

and Pumacurco from there to the end. In this book, San Agustín will be used to refer to the street from Limaqpampa Chico to Triunfo, and Pumacurco to the length above Triunfo.

2. PER-39 was the name commonly used for a project officially known as PER-71/539, a joint enterprise between the Peruvian government and UNESCO that began in 1973. It was concerned with the conservation and restoration of the historical monuments of the Cusco-Puno region.

3. Both andesite and diorite have a Mohs hardness of 6 and a compression of 1,200kg per sqcm. In contrast, limestone has a Mohs hardness of only 3 and a compression of 200 to 500kg per sqcm (Agurto 1987: 120).

4. Very few inka locations on the coast have any worked stone blocks in their structures. For example, Cerro Azul has two retaining walls, laid in sedimentary style, on the sea cliff face (Marcos 1987: fig. 69); Paredones in Nasca has several walls of fine rectangular, well-fitting blocks in sedimentary style topped with adobe bricks (Herrera 1997); in contrast, there is only a single fine ashlar in a door jamb at La Centinela (Santillana pers. comm.). In all cases, the rock types have not been determined.

5. All measurements were made and checked on several occasions between 1984 and 2009, using a 30m tape measure.

6. This measurement, 807.84m (500.21r), is made up of numerous shorter lengths, which probably accounts for the error of only 34cm in over 800m.

Chapter 7. Inka Public Spaces, Palaces, and Temples

1. A *palmo* in Spanish America measured about 21.6cm in length (Hemming 1970).

2. These are the June solstice, the passage of the sun through zenith, the equinoxes, the day of the passage of the sun through anti-zenith (nadir), and the December solstice (table 12.3).

3. Seda Qosqo is the municipal utility company, specializing in the installation of water and sewage infrastructure in Cusco.

4. Betanzos (1996: 48) wrote that the stone font stood half an *estado* high; a Spanish *estado* measured 1.67m.

5. The data for the *seqe* system of shrines around Cusco was collected by Polo de Ondegardo, but his original manuscript is lost. Fortunately, it was reproduced by Cobo (1990: 51–84). It is organized by *suyu, seqe,* and then *waka* on each *seqe*; hence the shorthand for the fourth *waka* on the fifth *seqe* of Chinchaysuyu is CH-5:4. This scheme is used throughout this book. The prefixes CH, AN, QO, and CU refer to the *suyu*: Chinchaysuyu, Antisuyu, Qollasuyu, and Kuntisuyu.

6. The excavated data would suggest that, with no side walls and the possibility that a staircase would have been located in the middle, its façade length must have been much longer than the 19.25m exposed. Its height was at least 1.8m. It is not known which direction it was facing. However, given its location, this must have been among the largest *usnu* platforms in Tawantinsuyu (cf. table 2.5).

7. Over 300 "bags" of cultural materials were recovered, including large amounts of inka, colonial, and republican pottery, animal bones, and other items (Cornejo 1996).

8. A common place for an inka offering pit was at the threshold of a building or complex. For example, at the Coast gate in the Third Wall of Pachacamac, an offering was

placed in a pit that contained ceramic figurines, spondylus beads, and a figurine with the skeleton of a young girl (Cornejo 1999).

9. Garcilaso de la Vega (1966: 69, 426–27) attributed Amarukancha to Wayna Qhapaq. Sarmiento (2007: 187) thought it had been built by Waskar, while Murúa (1987: 154) stated that it was his residence.

10. The Spaniards reopened this room—only for it to be struck again by lightning (Garcilaso 1966: 69).

11. No other chronicler mentioned this tower. John Rowe (1991: 90) thought that Garcilaso's memory of the Sunturwasi was faulty and that since he had claimed that Amarukancha had belonged to Wayna Qhapaq, he had confused it with Qasana, which indeed did belong to him and which did have two towers standing in front.

12. According to Garcilaso (1966: 749 pt. 2 bk. 2 ch. 7), Altamirano's horse stumbled into a hole in the courtyard of his property and exposed the treasure.

13. The original dimensions of the extant walls of Hatunrumiyoq were 47.8m (29.6r) on the northern side, 69.45m (43r) on the eastern, and 66.25m (41r) on the western. The southern wall was about 48.45m (30r) long.

14. Given its excavated dimensions, 18m in length, with a walled 2m wide staircase at its western end, then, by using the principles of inka symmetry, the platform must have continued a similar distance to the west, making it very large indeed, certainly in excess of 38m in length (cf. table 2.5). An underground site museum now shows two walls and a terrace of the platform façade, steps, and the excavation finds. Among the metal working objects, there are a heavy black volcanic *jiwaya* and an andesite anvil, *yunki*, used in hammering metal leaf. Whether these represent activities conducted on the platform is not known.

15. Some of these gold objects reached Seville between 1533 and 1538 as gifts to the king of Spain. They are listed by Xerez (1985: 158–59) in documents summarized by Lothrop (1938) and in the 1534 Relación Francesa (Porras Barrenechea 1967: 73–77). They include thirty-one gold panels used to decorate doors and benches, a life-sized statue of a 10-year-old boy, twenty dressed female statues, four life-sized llamas, two maize stalks with three leaves and two cobs, as well as 116 gold vessels and eight lids.

16. Given the dimensions of the Spanish foot (27.9cm), then Qorikancha would have been either 111.76m or 139.69m square.

17. The west wall of R-3 was demolished during the colonial period to build monks' cells; it was rebuilt during the PER-39 conservation process in the 1970s.

18. *Vilka* is a hallucinogen derived from the ground dried seeds of the tropical leguminous tree *Anadenanthera colubrina* (Torres and Repke 2006). It was generally either snuffed or used as an enema by shamans (Guaman Poma (1980: 71 [71], 119 [119]), although Albornoz (1989: 172) reported that it was ground in a wooden or stone *qonopa* and was also added to *chicha*. It is a term that also came to mean something sacred, such as the Sun. For an archaeometric perspective, Cortella and Pochettino (2001) have concluded that a wooden *qonopa* in the Museo de La Plata, with a Cusco provenance, had coca leaves ground and burned within it.

19. From Pumapungo in Tumibamba, Jaime Idrovo (2000: 231, 263, 277) reported the following finds: in Tomb VI in the patio of the Aqllawasi Occidental *kancha*, there was an arrangement of four silver *tupu* around a copper pectoral; in tomb II in Qorikancha

patio, there were four gold *tupu* associated with a gold figurine and four copper ones with another; and in pit III in another patio of Qorikancha, there was a gold male figurine with three gold *tupu*.

Chapter 8. *Kancha* and Streets: The Residential Plan-Units

1. The green diorite blocks of this corner were vandalized by hammer blows, flaking its outer faces, during the second half of the twentieth century.

2. In 1993, it was possible to measure the width of Intiqawarina (lane 3) between two short lengths of limestone footings and lower wall, both of which have since disappeared. Lanes 4 and 5 are short passageways, entering mz73 from Tullumayu.

3. The inkas generally referred to the coastal lowlands as the Yungas.

4. The overall dimensions of Hatunkancha are as follows: Loreto, 219.65m (136r); Maruri, 175.92m (109r), San Agustín, 232.45m (144r), Triunfo, 144.4m (89.5), Portal Carrizos, 47.78m (29.6r).

5. This sector of mz3 has been further excavated in advance of the development of a commercial center. Unfortunately, several walls have been dismantled and the development has been delayed (El Sol 02/21/2008).

6. However, Albornoz (Duviols 1967: 26) stated that Kusikancha Pachamama was the house where Thupaq Inka Yupanki had been born.

7. The outer dimensions of Kusikancha today are Romeritos, 139.25m; Intipampa, 104.9m (65r); Pampa del Castillo, 97m; Maruri, 130.4m.

8. Nowadays, the Casa del Almirante houses the UNSAAC Museo Inka, the Casona Cabrera is the Museo de Arte Precolombino, and in 2009 the Beaterio de las Nazarenas was being converted into a hotel.

9. This means about 11% of the total property of the Casa del Almirante was excavated.

Chapter 9. Urban Life

1. The Sapa Inka invariably chose his heir from among his legitimate male children, although this was often challenged, causing struggles between *panaqa* and even civil war.

2. González Holguín (1989: 319) defined *rokro* as a stew made of potatoes and chili peppers, and as *locro* today it also contains meat and maize.

3. In the sixteenth-century dictionary of González Holguín (1989: 188), *huatiyana* is defined as a hole in the ground used for baking.

4. According to Nicholson (1960), nowadays each liter of traditionally made *chicha* is made from about 1.2kg of dried maize.

5. An *obraje* was a colonial textile manufacturing mill.

6. There was a third grave in this location that contained only a dog (CF22).

7. It has been noted that in many of the high altitude graves, pottery vessels are generally found with females, while the males tend to be accompanied by only a small number or none at all (Reinhard and Ceruti 2005: 30, 32).

Chapter 10. Suburbs and the Inner Heartland

1. Although Zuidema (1981) and Aveni (1981) agree with chroniclers, such as Molina, that the *seqe* lines of *waka* followed a basically straight course, both Niles (1987) and Bauer (1998) have claimed that their evidence suggests otherwise. However, there are problems

with their logic and evidence for the assignment of certain *waka* names to particular locations and, therefore, the overall acceptability of their evidence.

2. In terms of location and function, these inka suburban villages were not unlike the classic suburbs of the medieval European town (see Keene 1987: 71).

3. The mummies and *wawki* of two other Inkas, Lloque Yupanki and Qhapaq Yupanki, were found in a village near Cusco (Sarmiento 2007: 81, 87; Cobo 1979: 117, 123), which could have been either Cayaokachi or Wimpillay.

4. Higgs and Vita-Finzi (1972) developed site catchment analysis, based on the geographical ideas of von Thünen and Chisholm, in which intensity of land use declines with distance from a site, suggesting that circles with radii of 1.0 and 5.0km about each village would indicate the extent of intensively and extensively cultivated farmland.

5. *Peska*, *pichca* or *píchica* is a game of chance played throughout the Andes with a numbered die and a marked board (Gentile 1998). Cobo (1979: 148) described a game played by Thupaq Inka Yupanki, and Guaman Poma (1980: 243 [245]) mentioned that it was played by inka nobles at harvest time. Bingham (1930: 211: fig.172) found several peska dice at Machu Picchu.

6. When first excavated, archaeologists had expected an occupation dating to the earlier Qotakalli period but instead discovered that the site was inka (table 1.1).

7. Radiocarbon dates for the inka secondary burials in R-75 imply a late LIP or early inka period date (1290–1420, a 2 sigma calibrated date), but no information has been published for the nature of the material that has been dated or the laboratory number of the assay (Andrushko 2007: 64).

8. The dimensions of Pukakancha's three buildings are as follows: B-1 measures 24.0m (14.9r) by 11.4m (7r); B-2 is 17.6m (11r) by 9.6m (6r); B-3 is 27.4m (17r) by 11.4m (7r). The patio is 20.8m (13r) by 26.2m (16.25r).

9. A wood charcoal sample [AA 34936] from UE 4 in structure B-1 at Pukakancha yielded a date of 440±45 BP (calibrated 95.4% probability: AD 1400 [85.3%], AD 1530, AD 1570 [10.1%], AD 1630) (Bauer and Jones 2003: 6).

10. Urbanization, in the form of uncontrolled residential sprawl and waste disposal, now threatens the surviving lengths of the Suriwaylla and Santutis schemes.

Chapter 11. Ceremony and Ritual

1. As an insignia of their status, nobles (initiated inka men) were entitled to wear decorated ear plugs and, as a consequence, were called *orejones* by the Spaniards. The term "broken ears" refers to those whose earlobe had subsequently been torn; this reduced their status, and they became regarded as imperfect specimens.

2. On the basis of his published maps, Bauer only located 57 (17.4%) of the 328 *seqe waka* precisely. He placed a further 82 (25%) in a general "area of shrine" category, while he failed to locate the remainder (189 57.6%), simply giving a potential area for their location.

3. The mummies and *wawki* of the Inka kings of Hanan Cusco were not found at these locations by the Spaniards, as they had been hidden elsewhere within their lands and properties. For example, those of Pachakuti Inka Yupanki were found in the suburban village of Totoqachi, just below Patallaqta (Sarmiento 2007: 155), that of Viracocha Inka in his rural palace of Huchuy Cusco (Sarmiento 2007: 104, 122), and those of Inka Roca in a village near Larapa (Sarmiento 2007: 89). The mummy and *wawki* of Yawar Waqaq

were not discovered and were thought to be in the village of Paullu (Sarmiento 2007: 96). The mummy of Thupaq Inka Yupanki had been burned during the civil war before the Spanish occupation, although his ashes were found buried with his *wawki* at Qalispukio (Sarmiento 2007: 171).

4. This tunnel through the limestone outcrop was dynamited during the early part of the twentieth century.

5. The two *waka* on Mantocallas hill were Mantocallaspa (AN-3:5), a fountain of good water in which the Indians bathed, and Caripuquiu (AN-3:7), another fountain that received offerings of shells (Cobo 1990: 65).

6. Dance (*taki*), accompanied by drumming and song, was fundamental to all inka ceremonies. Specific dances are mentioned associated with certain ceremonies, such as the *wari* with the *warichiquy* initiation rituals of December. *Cayo* was a dance that was performed four times a day during the June solstice *inti raymi* festivities and at the conclusion of *qhapaq raymi*, the celebration of the December solstice (Cobo 1990: 133, 142).

7. Niles (1987: 199) suggested that Choqekancha was the site of Arkawasi, in the Rumiwasi group, while Sherbondy (1982: 47) thought it was Kusikallanka, part of the same complex. While these are significant locations, neither is a hilltop. In contrast, Zecenarro (2001: 78–79) placed it further east on a terraced hill, Wayraqpunku, above the Tambillo terraces, an interesting area but not strictly "above San Sebastián."

8. This description would suggest that these bodies were probably placed in clay capsules.

9. According to Cobo (1990: 51–84), anthropomorphic figurines were offered at Chuquipalta (CH-4:8), Llulpactuto (QO-3:9), and Catonge (QO-5:1); zoomorphic ones at Sucanca (CH-8:7); Pirquipuquio (AN-8:2), and Cuipanamaro (AN-8:3); and miniature clothing at Guamansaui (QO-1:7), Llulpactuto (QO-3:9), Wanakawri (QO-6:7), and Quiquijana (QO-6:9).

10. On his website, Luis Barreda has noted that during the 1972 excavation campaign in Qorikancha, "tens of marine shell sculptures were found, that represented small llamas and humans" (www.luisbarredamurillo.galeon.com).

11. In 2004, Sabino Quispe and Gloria Choque announced that in their excavations at Muyuqmarka they had found a miniature workshop that yielded evidence of the manufacture of anthropomorphic figurines out of spondylus, gold, and silver (Xinhua News Agency, 16/11/2004). There has to date been no publication of this work.

Chapter 12. The Navel of the World

1. On the day of the December solstice, the sun has an azimuth of 112°, which means a person standing on the summit of Wanakawri would see the rainbow center on a bearing of 292°. Cusco is about 11km from this observation point, and at this distance the rainbow would have a radius of about 7.4km, encompassing the location of the old city at the head of the valley.

2. This motif is significant in the symbolic imagery of Cusco for two reasons. First, a rainbow was seen shortly after dawn near the December solstice to arch over the location of the city from Wanakawri. Second, just before dawn at the same time of the year, the Milky Way would have arched across the southern sky with its apex, marked by the star Alpha Crucis, above the city and the origin place. A stone block with a bas-relief carving of

a human standing beneath an arch is found in Siete Culebras on the andesite wall Beaterio de las Nazarenas (mz12) (van de Guchte 1990).

3. Sarmiento (2007: 69) called this stone Ayar Awka cuzco wanka, which he glossed as the "boundary marker of marble" but which can also be translated as Ayar Awka, the sacred stone at the navel of the world.

4. Fourteen groups of rocks around Cusco turned into soldiers, *pururauca*, to resist the Chanka invasion. Following victory, they were repetrified and forever revered as *waka* (Cobo 1990: 51–84).

5. The type of tree was transcribed in the Cobo texts (e.g., 1990: 58) as a "quinoa." This cannot be correct because quinoa (*Chenopodium quinoa*) is an annual pseudo-cereal crop plant. The more appropriate transcription would be the *q'euña*.

6. A second definition of Wanakawri was given by González Holguín (1989: 73), who translated *huayakauri* as "rainbow," and by Sarmiento (2007: 66), who translated his transcripted word, *wanakawri*, also as "rainbow." In his analysis of Wanakawri, Szeminski (1988) translates it as "the fertilizing *waka*."

7. The toponym *churucana*, which also appears in ancient text as *churucani, churuncani, churicalla*, has not been specifically translated by Beyersdorff (1998: 186, 219) because neither of the possible stems matches the topographical features observed. These are the verb *churukay*, meaning to place or put an object, to store, or *churukuna*, meaning a place or the ground between two rivers. Alternatively, it could also be derived from the quechua word *churi*, which means "the son of an important man."

8. Research by Zawaski and Malville (2007–2008) confirms that the inkas made observations of the sun on the horizon on eight critical days of the year: the solstices, equinoxes, zenith, and anti-zenith. In fieldwork at many sites in the Cusco area, they have recorded that from each site several of these risings or settings could have been viewed, occurring behind various important mountains or other landscape features (table 12.3).

9. Londres (London) was founded in 1558 in the vicinity of El Shincal; its name commemorates the marriage in London of Mary, queen of England (daughter of Henry VIII), to Philip, the heir to the Spanish throne.

10. The inventory also includes inka provincial ceramics, regional ceramics, a *maka* rim, the bird handle of a plate, two inverted plates, an inverted pot; a bronze *tumi*, a bronze spangle; obsidian flakes, quartz core; carbonized maize, beans, peanuts, squash, coca leaves; adult camelid bone, bird and rodent bone, deer antlers, *suri* (*Rhea americana*) eggshell; fish scales; an *Argopecten purpuratus* shell (peruvian scallop); and a *Conus ximenes* shell (Raffino et al. 1997).

11. Two drinks are made from *Prosopis sp.* seeds in Argentina: *añapa*, an alcoholic drink, and *aloja*, a nonalcoholic one (Capparelli 2011).

12. In northwest Argentina, Prosopis flour is made into a flatbread called *patay* (Capparelli 2011).

13. The term *salamanca* is used in Argentina to refer to a cave in which the devil is thought to live and practice. Its use comes from a medieval legend of the dangers of such a cave in the Spanish city of Salamanca.

Bibliography

Adams, R. E. W., and R. C. Jones

1981. Spatial patterns and regional growth among Classic Maya cities. *American Antiquity* 46: 301–22.

Adams, R. McC.

1966. *The Evolution of Urban Society: Early Mesopotamia and Prehispanic Mexico.* Weidenfeld and Nicholson. London.

Adamska, A., and A. Michczynski

1996. Towards radiocarbon chronology of the Inca state. *Andes: Boletín de la Misión Arqueológica Andina* 1: 35–58. University of Warsaw. Warsaw.

Aguilar Laguna, C. R.

2002. Colegio Particular Salesiano. *Informe de Evaluación Arqueológica Sector Antigua Construcción.* Informe presentado al Instituto Nacional de Cultura. Cusco.

Agurto Calvo, S.

1978. Medidas de longitud en el Incario. In *III Congreso Peruano El Hombre y la Cultura Andina, Actas y Trabajos, tomo 1,* ed. R. Matos Mendieta, 5–36. Lima.

1980. *Cuzco—la Traza Urbana de la Ciudad Inca.* Proyecto Per 39. UNESCO and Instituto Nacional de Cultura. Cusco.

1987. *Estudios Acerca de la Construcción, Arquitectura y Planeamiento Incas.* Cámara Peruana de la Construcción. Lima.

Albornoz, Cristóbal de.

1989 [1583–84]. Instrucción para descubrir todas las guacas del Pirú y sus camayos y haziendas. In Cristóbal de Molina and Cristóbal de Albornoz, *Fábulas y Mitos de los Incas,* ed. H. Urbano and P. Duviols, 163–98. Crónicas de América 48, Historia 16. Madrid.

Alcina Franch, J.

1976. *Arqueología de Chinchero. 1. La Arquitectura.* Memorias de la Misión Científica Española en Hispanoamerica ll, Ministerio de Asuntos Exteriores, Madrid.

Allison, P. (ed.)

1999. *The Archaeology of Household Activities.* Routledge. London.

Amado, D.

2003. De la casa señorial al Beaterio Nazarenas. *Revista Andina* 36: 213–36. Cusco.

Andrushko, V. A.

2007. *The Bioarcheology of Inca Imperialism in the Heartland: An Analysis of Prehistoric*

Burials from the Cuzco Region of Peru. PhD dissertation, University of California. Santa Barbara.

Andrushko, V. A., and J. W. Verano

2008. Prehistoric trepanation in the Cuzco region of Peru: A view into an ancient Andean practice. *American Journal of Physical Anthropology* 137: 4–13.

Anonymous Chronicler

1906 [1570]. Discurso de la sucesión y gobierno de los Yngas. In *Juicio de Límites entre el Perú y Bolivia*. Prueba peruana presentada al gobierno de la República Argentina, vol. 8, ed. V. M. Maúrtua, 149–65. Tipografía de los Hijos de M. G. Hernández. Madrid.

Anonymous Jesuit

1968. De las Costumbres Antiguas de los Naturales del Pirú. In *Crónicas Peruanas de Interés Indígena*, ed. E. Barba. Biblioteca de Autores Españoles 209. Ediciones Atlas. Madrid.

Aparicio Flores, M. O., and E. Marmonilla Casapino

1989. *Cusco Sismo 86: Evaluación de Inmuebles del centro histórico.* Instituto Nacional de Cultura. Cusco.

Ardiles Nieves, P. E.

1986. Sistema de drenaje subterráneo prehispánico. *Allpanchis* 27: 75–97. Cusco.

1988. *Informe sobre Pampa del Castillo "Lote C."* Informe presentado al Instituto Nacional de Cultura. Cusco.

Arellano, C., and R. Matos Mendieta

2007. Variations between inka installations in the Puna of Chinchaycocha and the drainage of Tarma. In *Variations in the Expression of Inka Power*, ed. R. L. Burger, C. Morris, and R. Matos Mendieta, 11–39. Dumbarton Oaks. Harvard University Press. Cambridge.

Arroyo Abarca, P. M.

2005a. *Proyecto de Evaluación Arqueológica del Inmueble No 473 Limac Pampa Chico.* Informe presentado al Instituto Nacional de Cultura. Cusco.

2005b. *Proyecto de Evaluación Arqueológica del Inmueble No 620 calle Intiqawarina.* Informe presentado al Instituto Nacional de Cultura. Cusco.

Aston, M., and J. Bond.

1976. *The Landscape of Towns.* J. M. Dent and Sons. Cambridge.

Astuhuamán Gonzáles, C.

1998. *Asentamientos Inca en la Sierra de Piura.* Tesis para optar el grado Licenciado en Arqueología, Universidad Nacional Mayor de San Marcos. Lima.

2000. ¿Qué es un acllawasi? Respuestas de la arqueología y la historia. *Comunidad; Tierra-Hombre-Identidad* 4: 20–34. Piura.

2004. Identificación y función de las edificaciones inca: El caso de los acllawasi de la sierra de Piura. http://www.unfv.edu.pe/site/fondo_documentario/acllawasi/.

Aveni, A.

1981. Horizon astronomy in Incaic Cuzco. In *Archaeoastronomy in the Americas*, ed. R. Williamson, 305–18. Ballena Press. Menlo Park.

Azevedo P.O.D. de

1982. *Cusco Ciudad Histórica: Continuidad y Cambio.* Coedición Proyecto Regional de Patrimonio Cultural PNUD / UNESCO. Cusco.

Barker, P.

1982. *Techniques of Archaeological Excavation.* 2nd ed. B. T. Batsford. London.

Barnes, M., and D. Slive

1993. El puma de Cuzco: ¿plano de la ciudad ynga o noción europea? *Revista Andina* 11 (21): 79–102. Cusco.

Barraza Lescano, S.

2010. Redefiniendo una categoría arquitectónica inca: La kallana. *Boletín del Instituto Francés de Estudios Andinos* 39: 167–81. Lima.

Barreda Murillo, L.

1973. *Las Culturas Inka y Pre-Inka de Cusco.* Tesis doctoral, Universidad Nacional de San Antonio Abad del Cusco. Cusco.

n.d.a. *Bronces del Qorikancha.* http://luisbarredamurillo.galeon.com/index.html.

n.d.b. *Oro de Qorikancha.* http://luisbarredamurillo.galeon.com/aficiones1355383.html.

Barreda Murillo, L., and A. Valencia Zegarra

2007. Introducción a la etnología y arqueología de Saqsaywaman. In *Saysaywaman: Estudios fundamentales,* 85–151. Instituto Nacional de Cultura. Cusco.

Baudin, L.

2003. *Daily Life of the Incas.* Translated from the French by W. Bradford. Dover Publications. Mineola.

Bauer, B. S.

1992a. *The Development of the Inca State.* University of Texas Press. Austin.

1992b. Investigaciones arqueológicas recientes en los asientos de Maukallaqta y Puma Orqo, Departamento del Cuzco, Perú. *Avances en Arqueología Andina,* ed. B. S. Bauer, 65–108. Centro de Estudios Regionales Andinos "Bartolomé de las Casas." Cusco.

1998. *The Sacred Landscape of the Inca: The Cusco Ceque System.* University of Texas Press. Austin.

2004, ed. *Ancient Cuzco: Heartland of the Inca.* University of Texas Press. Austin.

Bauer, B. S., and R. A. Covey

2004. The development of the Inca state (AD 1000–1400). In *Ancient Cuzco: Heartland of the Inca,* ed. B. S. Bauer, 71–90. University of Texas Press. Austin.

Bauer, B. S., and D.S.P. Dearborn

1995. *Astronomy and Empire in the Ancient Andes.* University of Texas Press. Austin.

Bauer, B. S., and B. M. Jones

2003. *Early Intermediate and Middle Horizon Ceramic Styles of the Cuzco Valley.* Fieldiana Anthropology New Series No. 34. Publication 15212. Field Museum of Natural History. Chicago.

Béjar, I. S.

2003. La cantera de Rumiqolqa, Cusco. *Boletín de Arqueología PUCP,* 7: 407–17. Lima.

Béjar Luksic, L. F., M. F. Ccoa Cruz, N. J. Tacuri Portugal and K. X. Durand Cáceres

2011. The study of the ancient city of Cusco: a case study of Cora Cora. Paper read at the Binational Symposium on Inka Studies. Australian National University. Canberra.

Béjar Navarro, R.

1976. Un entierro en T'oqokachi. *Revista del Museo Nacional* 42: 145–51. Lima.

1990. *El Templo del Sol o Qorikancha.* Imprenta Yañez. Cusco.

1998. Excavaciones en el sector occidental del Qorikancha. Manuscript.

Benavente García, P.

2009. Rescate muro fino de la Plaza de Limacpampa. *Saqsaywaman* 9: 203–22. Cusco.

2011. Wayna Tauqaray centro de almacenamiento. DRC Cusco. www.drc.cusco.gob.pe/dmdocuments/publicaciones/ARTICULO%20DE%20WAYNA%20TAUQARAY%202011.SDI-MC.pdf. Accessed 06/13/2011.

Benavides, M.

2003. *Informe de investigación arqueológica Qotakalli*. Informe presentado al Instituto Nacional de Cultura. Dirección de Investigación y Catastro. Cusco.

Bengtsson, L.

1998. *Prehistoric stonework in the Peruvian Andes: A case study at Ollantaytambo*. Gotarc Series B no. 10. Gothenburg.

Beorchia Nigris, A.

1984. El enigma de los santuarios indígenas de Alta Montaña. *Revista del Centro de Investigaciones Arqueológicas de Alta Montaña* 5. San Juan.

Berry, B.J.L.

1967. *Geography of Market Centers and Retail Distribution*. Prentice-Hall. Englewood Hills.

Betanzos, Juan de

1996 [1551]. *Narrative of the Incas*. Translated and edited by R. Hamilton and D. Buchanan. University of Texas Press. Austin.

Beyersdorff, M.

1998. Suggested glosses of huaca names. In *The Sacred Landscape of the Inca: The Cusco Ceque System*, ed. B. S. Bauer, appendix 3, 179–96. University of Texas Press. Austin.

Biddle, M.

1968. Archaeology and the history of British towns. *Antiquity* 42: 109–16.

1976a. *Winchester in the Early Middle Ages*. Oxford University Press. Oxford.

1976b. The evolution of planned towns: Planned towns before 1066. In *The Plans and Topography of Mediaeval Towns*, ed. M. W. Barley, 19–22. Council for British Archaeology, Research Report no. 14. London.

1984. *The Study of Winchester: Archaeology and History in a British Town*. Oxford University Press. Oxford.

Bingham, H.

1930. *Machu Picchu, a Citadel of the Incas*. Memoirs of the National Geographic Society, Yale University. New Haven.

Bolívar, W.

2004. *Proyecto de evaluación arqueologica en el inmueble 208 de la calle Loreto. Informe final*. Instituto Nacional de Cultura. Cusco.

Bond, C. J.

1987. Anglo-Saxon and medieval defences. In *Urban Archaeology in Britain*, ed. J. Schofield and R. Leech, 92–116. Council for British Archaeology Research Report 61. London.

1990. Central place and medieval new town: The origins of Thame, Oxfordshire. In *The Built Form of Western Cities*, ed. T. R. Slater, 83–106. Leicester University Press. Leicester.

Bonnett Medina, P.
2003. Hallazgos en Muyuqmarka de Saqsaywaman: Protesis dental inka. *Saqsaywaman* 6: 113–61. Cusco.

Bouchard, J. F.
1976a. Patrones de agrupamiento arquitectónico del Horizonte Tardío. *Revista del Museo Nacional* 42: 97–111. Lima.

1976b. Charpentes andines inca et modernes: Observations et reflexiones. *Bulletin de l'Institut Français d'Études Andines* 3–4: 105–17. Lima.

1983. *Contribution a l'Étude de l'Architecture Inca: Établissements de la vallée du Rio Vilcanota-Urubamba.* Fondation de la Maison des Sciences de l'Homme. Paris.

Bourget, S.
1995. Los sacerdotes a la sombra del Cerro Blanco y del arco bicéfalo. *Revista del Museo de Arqueología, Antropología e Historia* 5: 81–125. Trujillo.

Braun, G., and F. Hogenburg
2011. *Cities of the World. Complete edition of the colour plates of 1572–1617.* Taschen Cologne.

Bray, T. L.
2000. Inca iconography: The art of empire in the Andes. *Res. Anthropology and Aesthetics* 38: 168–85.

2003a. Inca pottery as culinary equipment: Food, feasting, and gender in imperial state design. *Latin American Antiquity* 14 (1): 3–28.

2003b. To dine splendidly: Imperial pottery, commensal politics, and the Inca state. In *The Archaeology and Politics of Food and Feasting in Early States and Empires*, ed. T. L. Bray, pp. 93–142. Kluwer Academic/Plenum. New York.

Brown, D. O.
1992. *Administration and Planning in the Inka Empire: A Perspective from the Provincial Capital of Pumpu, Central Peru.* PhD dissertation, University of Texas. Austin.

Burger, R. L., J. A. Lee-Thorp, and N. J. van der Merwe
2003. Rite and crop in the Inca state revisited: An isotopic perspective from Machu Picchu and beyond. In *The 1912 Yale Peruvian Scientific Expedition Collections from Machu Picchu: Human and Animal Remains*, ed. R. L. Burger and L. C. Salazar, 119–37. Yale University Publications in Anthropology 85. New Haven.

Burgos Guevara, H.
1995. *El Guamán, el Puma y el Amaru: Formación estructural del gobierno indígena en Ecuador*, Biblioteca Abya-yala. Quito.

Bustinza Espinoza, R.
2003. *Informe de investigación arqueológica Qhataqhasapatallacta.* Informe presentado al Instituto Nacional de Cultura. Dirección de Investigación y Catastro. Cusco.

2004. *Informe de investigación arqueológica Qotakalli.* Informe presentado al Instituto Nacional de Cultura. Dirección de Investigación y Catastro. Cusco.

2008. Arqueología en el Templo de Santa Ana. *Saqsaywaman* 7: 131–55. Instituto Nacional de Cultura. Cusco.

Cabello Valboa, Miguel
2011 [1586]. *Miscelánea Antártica: Una historia del Perú antiguo.* Edited by I. Lerner. Fundación José Manuel Lara. Sevilla.

Cahua, J.

1998. *Informe final de investigación arqueológica en la Iglesia del Triunfo del Cusco*. Informe presentado al Instituto Nacional de Cultura. Dirección de Investigación y Catastro. Cusco.

Candia Gomez, A.

1992a. *Arquitectura de Qhataqasapatallaqta*. Tesis para optar al Título Profesional de Licenciados en Arqueología, Universidad Nacional de San Antonio Abad Cusco. Cusco.

1992b. Ocupación killki en Qhata Q'asallaqta. *Saqsaywaman: Revista Arqueológica* 4: 122–32. Cusco.

Candia, M. R.

2008. La ocupación inka en Urqo-Calca: Una visión de su función y abandono a través de un contexto ritual. *Saqsaywaman* 8: 72–84. Instituto Nacional de Cultura. Cusco.

Capparelli, A.

2011. Elucidating post-harvest practices involved in the processing of algarrobo (*Prosopis* spp.) for food at El Shincal Inka site (Northwest Argentina): An experimental approach based on charred remains. *Archaeological and Anthropological Sciences* 3: 93–112.

Carrasco, D.

1999. *City of Sacrifice: The Aztec Empire and the Role of Violence in Civilization*. Beacon Press. Boston.

Carter, H.

1983. *An Introduction to Urban Historical Geography*. Edward Arnold. London.

Carver, M. O. H.

1987a. *Underneath English Towns: Interpreting Urban Archaeology*. B. T. Batsford. London.

1987b. The nature of urban deposits. In *Urban Archaeology in Britain*, ed. J. Schofield and R. Leech, 9–26. Council for British Archaeology Research Report 61. London.

Castillo Tecsi, T.

1999. *Informe Final de las Excavaciones Arqueológicas realizadas en inmueble no 348 de la calle Plateros de la Ciudad del Cusco*. Informe presentado al Instituto Nacional de Cultura. Cusco.

Castillo Tecsi, T., and K. M. Jurado Chamorro

1996. *El Centro Urbano Prehispánico de Calca*. Tesis para optar al Título Profesional de Licenciados en Arqueología, Universidad Nacional de San Antonio Abad del Cusco. Cusco.

Ceruti, M. C.

2001. Recientes hallazgos en los volcanes Quehuar (6.130 m) y Llullaillaco (6.739 m). *Actas del XIII Congreso Nacional de Arqueología Argentina* 1: 313–20. Córdoba.

2003. *Llullaillaco: Sacrificios y ofrendas en un santuario inca de Alta Montaña*. Universidad Católica de Salta. Salta.

2004. Human bodies as objects of dedication at Inca mountain shrines (north-western Argentina). *World Archaeology* 36: 103–22.

Chávez Ballón, M.

1970. Cuzco, capital del imperio. *Wayka* 3: 1–15. Cusco.

Christie, J. J.
2007. Did the Inka copy Cusco? An answer derived from an architectural-sculptural model. *Journal of Latin American and Caribbean Anthropology* 12: 164–99.

Cieza de León, Pedro
1959 [1553]. *The Incas of Pedro Cieza de León.* Translated by H. de Onis, ed. V. W. von Hagen. University of Oklahoma Press. Oklahoma City.
1986 [1553]. *Crónica del Perú, Primera Parte.* Introduction by F. Pease G. Y. Fondo Editorial. Pontificia Universidad Católica del Perú. Lima.

Claros Centeno, D., and A. Mormontoy Atayupanqui
1992. *Arqueología de Qontaymoqo y Sillkinchani.* Tesis para optar al Título Profesional de Licenciados en Arqueología, Universidad Nacional de San Antonio Abad del Cusco. Cusco.

Coben, L. S.
2006. Other Cuzcos: Replicated theatres of Inka power. In *Archaeology of Performance: Theaters of Power, Community, and Politics,* ed. T. Inomata and L. S. Coben, 223–59. Altamira Press. Oxford.

Cobo, Bernabé
1979 [1653]. *History of the Inca Empire: An Account of the Indian's Customs and Their Origin Together with a Treatise on Inca Legends, History, and Social Institutions.* Translated and edited by R. Hamilton. University of Texas Press. Austin.
1990 [1653]. *Inca Religion and Customs.* Translated and edited by R. Hamilton. University of Texas Press. Austin.

Colque Enríquez, M.
2001. *Informe de Investigación Arqueológica Ex Beaterio de las Nazarenas, Cusco.* Informe presentado al Instituto Nacional de Cultura. Cusco.

Concha Olivera, C. G.
2011. Zona arqueológica Qhataqasapatallaqta. DRC. Cusco. www.drc.cusco.gob.pe/dmdocuments/publicaciones/Articulo%20de%20Qhataqasapatallaqta%202011SDI-MC.pdf. Accessed 06/13/2011.

Connell, S. V., C. Gifford, A. Lucía González, and M. Carpenter
2003. Hard times in Ecuador: Inka troubles at Pambamarca. *Antiquity* 77 (295). http://antiquity.ac.uk/ProjGall/Connell/connell.html. Accessed 07/27/2006.

Conrad, G. W.
1982. The burial platforms of Chan Chan: Some social and political implications. In *Andean Desert City,* ed. M. E. Moseley and K. Day, 87–117. University of New Mexico Press. Albuquerque.

Contreras y Valverde, V. de
1982. *Relación de la Ciudad del Cusco 1649.* Prólogo y transcripción de M. C. Martín Rubio. Amauta. Cusco.

Conzen, M. R. G.
1960. *Alnwick Northumberland: A Study in Town-Plan Analysis.* George and Son. London.

Cornejo Guerrero, M. A.
1999. *An Archaeological Analysis of an Inka Province: Pachacamac and the Ischma Nation of the Central Coast of Peru.* PhD dissertation, Australian National University. Canberra.

Cornejo Gutiérrez, M.

1996. *Informe Preliminar de Investigación Arqueológica Plaza de Armas*. Informe presentado al Instituto Nacional de Cultura. Cusco.

1998. Plaza Mayor de Cusco. *Saqsaywaman* 5: 165–84. Cusco.

Cortella, A. R., and M. L. Pochettino

2001. *Erythroxylum coca*: Microscopical identification in powdered and carbonized archaeological material. *Journal of Archaeological Science* 28: 787–94.

Covey, R. A.

2003. A processual study of Inka state formation. *Journal of Anthropological Archaeology* 22: 333–57.

2009. Domestic life and craft specialization in Inka Cuzco and its rural hinterland. In *Domestic Life in Prehispanic Capitals: A Study of Specialization, Hierachy, and Ethnicity*, ed. L. R. Manzanilla and C. Chapdelaine, 243–54. Memoirs of the Museum of Anthropology 40, University of Michigan. Ann Arbor.

Crummy, P.

1979. The system of measurement used in town planning from the ninth to the thirteenth centuries. In *Anglo-Saxon Studies in Archaeology and History*, ed. S. C. Hawkes, D. Brown, and J. Campbell, 1: 149–64. British Archaeological Reports British Series 72. Oxford.

1982. The origins of some major Romano-British towns. *Britannia* 13: 125–34.

1985. Colchester: The mechanics of laying out a town. In *Roman Urban Topography in Britain and Western Europe*, ed. F. Grew and B. Hobley, 78–85. Council for British Archaeology Research Report no. 59. London.

Cumpa Palacios, C. V.

1988. *Prospección Arqueológica en Qoripata*. Tésis presentado por el grado de Bachiller en Arqueología, Universidad Nacional de San Antonio Abad del Cusco. Cusco.

2000. *Informe preliminar. Investigación arqueólogica: Muro Inca calle Loreto sector Poder Judicial*. Informe presentado al Instituto Nacional de Cultura. Cusco.

D'Altroy, T. N.

1992. *Provincial Power in the Inka Empire*. Smithsonian Institution Press. Washington, DC.

2002. *The Incas*. Blackwell. Oxford.

Dean, C. S.

1998. Creating a ruin in colonial Cusco: Sacsahuamán and what was made of it. *Andean Past* 5: 161–83.

Delgado González, C. M.

1998. Excavaciones arqueológicas en Tipon (Pukara): Parafernalia de una ofrenda inka. *Saqsaywaman* 5: 147–63. Cusco.

Demarest, A. A.

1981. *Viracocha: The nature and antiquity of the Andean High God*. Peabody Museum Monographs 6, Harvard University. Cambridge.

Diáz Yampi, A. M., and C. R. Farfán Delgado

2000. *Arqueología de Rumiwasi*. Tesis para optar al Título de Licenciados en Arqueología, Universidad Nacional de San Antonio Abad del Cusco. Cusco.

Donahue-Wallace, K.

2006. *Art and Architecture of Viceregal Latin America, 1521–1821.* University of New Mexico Press. Albuquerque.

Donnan, C. B.

1997. A Chimú-Inca manufacturing center from the north coast of Peru. *Latin American Antiquity* 8: 30–54.

Durand Cáceres, K. X., and L. E. Verastegui Gibaja

2009. *Análisis de Alfarería Inca Procedente del Inmueble Intiqhawarina 620, Ciudad del Cusco.* Tesis para optar al Título Profesional de Licenciados en Arqueología, Universidad Nacional de San Antonio Abad del Cusco. Cusco.

Duviols, P.

1967. Un inédit de Cristóbal de Albornoz, Instrucción para descubrir todas las guacas del Pirú y sus camayos y haziendas. *Journal de la Société de Américanistes* 56: 17–39. Paris.

1976. La capacocha: Mecanismo y función del sacrificio humano. *Allpanchis* 9: 3–57. Cusco.

Eaton, G. F.

1916. The collection of osteological material from Machu Picchu. *Memoirs of the Connecticut Academy of Arts and Sciences* 5: 1–96. New Haven.

Ellis, S. P.

1995. Prologue to a study of Roman urban form. In *Theoretical Roman Archaeology: Second Conference Proceedings,* ed. P. Rush, 92–104. Worldwide Archaeology. Avebury.

Elson, C. M., and M. E. Smith

2001. Archaeological deposits from the Aztec New Fire ceremony. *Ancient Mesoamerica* 12: 157–74.

Espinosa Soriano, W.

1970. Los mitmas yungas de Collique en Cajamarca, siglos XV, XVI y XVII. *Revista del Museo Nacional* 36: 9–57. Lima.

1983. Los mitmas plateros de Ishma en el país de los Ayarmacas, siglos XV–XVI. *Boletín de Lima* 30 (5): 38–52. Lima.

Espinoza Galarza, M.

1979. *Topónimos Quechuas del Perú.* Lima. Imprenta Noriega. Segunda Edición.

Esquivel y Navia, D. de

1980. *Noticias Cronológicas de la Gran Ciudad del Cuzco.* Edited by F. Denegri Luna. Biblioteca Peruana de Cultura. Lima.

Estete, Miguel de

1924 [1534]. *Noticia del Perú.* In *Historia de los Incas y Conquista del Perú,* ed. H. H. Urteaga, 8: 3–56. Colección de Libros y Documentos referentes a la Historia Peruana. Sanmartí. Lima.

Farfán Acuña, D.

2009. Investigaciones arqueológicas en Lucerinas. *Saqsaywaman* 9: 127–48. Cusco.

Farfán Acuña, D.

2011. Avances de las investigaciones arqueológicas en Wimpillay. DRC. Cusco. www.drc. cusco.gob.pe/dmdocuments/publicaciones/ARTICULO%20DE%20WIMPILLAY%202011SDI-MC.pdf. Accessed 06/13/2011.

Farrington, I. S.

1984a. Prehistoric intensive agricultural schemes: River canalization in the Sacred Valley of the Incas. In *Drained Field Agriculture in Central and South America*, ed. J. P. Darch, 221–35. British Archaeological Reports International Series 189. Oxford.

1984b. Medidas de tierra en el Valle de Yucay, Cusco. *Gaceta Arqueológica Andina* 11: 10–11. Lima.

1992. Ritual geography, settlement patterns, and the characterization of the provinces of the Inka heartland. *World Archaeology* 23: 368–85

1995. The mummy, estate, and palace of Inka Huayna Capac at Quispeguanca. *Tawantinsuyu* 1: 55–65. Canberra.

1998. The concept of Cusco. *Tawantinsuyu* 5: 53–59. Canberra.

1999. El Shincal: Un Cusco del Kollasusyu. In *Actas del XII Congreso Nacional de Arqueología Argentina*, 22–26 September 1997, ed. C. Diez Marín, 53–62. La Plata.

2002. Puma and jaguar: Cosmology, identity, and ceremony in the landscape of Inka Cusco. Paper read at the symposium Landscape and Symbol in the Inka State, held at the Humanities Research Centre, Australian National University. Canberra.

2010a. The houses and "fortress" of Waskar: Archaeological perspectives on a forgotten building complex in Inka Cusco. *Journal of Iberian and Latin American Studies* 16: 87–99.

2010b. The urban archaeology of Inka Cusco: A case study of Hatunkancha. In *Arqueología Argentina en el Bicentenario de la Revolución de Mayo*, ed. Simposio 26: Tawantinsuyu 2010, tomo III, ed. J. R. Bárcena and H. Chiavazza, 1247–52. Universidad Nacional de Cuyo. Mendoza.

2010c. The puma on the rock: Monuments, felines, origins, and identity among the inkas. Paper read at the symposium "Monumental Landscapes" of the Australian Archaeological Association annual meeting. Bateman's Bay.

Farrington, I. S., and C. R. Farfán Delgado

2002. Rocks, caves, and ancestors: Archaeological perspectives on the origin places of ayllus and inka royal panacas. Paper read at the Simposio: Identidad y transformación en el Tawantinsuyu y en los Andes coloniales. Perspectivas arqueológicas y etnohistóricas, August 2002. Lima.

Farrington, I. S., and J. Zapata Rodríguez

2003. Nuevos cánones de arquitectura inka: Investigaciones en el sitio de Tambokancha-Tumibamba, Jaquijahuana, Cuzco. *Boletín de Arqueología PUCP* 7: 57–77. Lima.

Fernández Carrasco, O.

2001. Saqsawaman Santuario Andino. *Visión Cultural* 1 (3): 39–45. Cusco.

Fernández Carrasco, S. O.

2004. *Plaza Inka de Hanan Hauk'aypata del Cusco*. Tesis para optar al Título Profesional de Licenciados en Arqueología, Universidad Nacional San Antonio Abad del Cusco. Cusco.

Fox, R. A.

1997. *Archaeology, History, and Custer's Last Battle: The Little Big Horn Reexamined*. University of Oklahoma Press. Norman.

Franco Inojosa, J. M.

1935. Janan Kosko. *Revista del Museo Nacional* 4 (1): 209–33. Lima.

1937. Janan Kosko II. *Revista del Museo Nacional* 6 (2): 201–31. Lima.

1941. Arqueología cusqueña: Un cateo en Cusipata (Plaza de Regocijo). *Revista del Museo Nacional* 10 (1): 108–9. Lima.

Franco Inojosa, J. M., and L. A. Llanos

1940. Saysawaman: Una excavación en el edificio sur de Muyumarca. *Revista del Museo Nacional* 9 (1): 22–32. Lima.

Fraser, V.

1990. *The Architecture of Conquest: Building the Viceroyalty of Peru, 1535–1635*. Cambridge University Press. Cambridge.

Fresco, G. A.

1983. Arquitectura de Ingapirca (Cañar-Ecuador). *Miscelánea Antropológica Ecuatoriana: Boletín de los Museos del Banco Central del Ecuador* 3 (3): 195–212. Quito.

Gade, D. W.

1975. *Plants, Man, and the Land in the Vilcanota Valley of Peru*. Biogeographica IV. W Junk. The Hague.

García Calderón, E.

2005. *Informe del proyecto de evaluación arqueológico del inmueble ubicado en Santa Catalina Ancha #342*. Instituto Nacional de Cultura. Cusco.

Garci Diez de San Miguel

1964 [1567]. *Visita hecha a la Provincia de Chucuito*. Casa de la Cultura, Lima.

Garcilaso de la Vega

1966 [1609]. *Royal Commentaries of the Incas and General History of Peru*. Edited by H. V. Livermore. University of Texas Press. Austin.

Gasparini, G.

1993. The pre-Hispanic grid system: The urban shape of conquest and territorial organization. In *Settlements in the Americas: Cross-Cultural Perspectives*, ed. R. Bennett, 78–109. University of Delaware Press. Newark.

Gasparini, G., and L. Margolies

1980. *Inca Architecture*. Translated by P. Lyon. Indiana University Press. Bloomington.

Gentile Lafaille, M. E.

1998. La pichca: Oráculo y juego de fortuna (su persistencia en el espacio y tiempo andinos). *Boletín del Intituto Francés de Estudios Andinos* 27: 75–131.

Gibaja Oviedo, A.

1982. Secuencia cronológica de Ollantaytambo. In *Current Archaeological Projects in the Central Andes: Some Approaches and Results*, ed. A. Kendall, 225–45. British Archaeological Reports International Series 210. Oxford.

1990. Estudio etnoarqueológico sobre las ofrendas al agua. *Saqsaywaman* 3: 217–27. Cusco.

Giovannetti, M.

2009. *Articulación entre el sistema agrícola, redes de irrigación y áreas de molienda como medida del grado de ocupación Inka en El Shinkal (Prov. Catamarca)*. Tesis para optar al grado de Doctor en Ciencias Naturales, Facultad de Ciencias Naturales y Museo, Universidad Nacional de La Plata. La Plata.

Gisbert, T., J. C. Jemio, R. Montero, E. Salinas, and M. Soledad Quiroga

1996. *Los Chullpares del Río Lauca y el Parque Sajama*. Revista de la Academia Nacional de Ciencias de Bolivia 70. La Paz.

Glave, L. M., and M. I. Remy

1983. *Estructura Agraria y Vida Rural en una Región Andina: Ollantaytambo entre los siglos XVI y XIX.* Centro de Estudios Rurales Andinos "Bartolomé de Las Casas." Cusco.

González Corrales, J. A.

1981. *Informe de los Trabajos de Investigación Arqueológica, Proyecto 'Libertador' Cusco, Ampliación.* Informe presentado al Instituto Nacional de Cultura. Cusco.

1984. La arquitectura y cerámica Killke del Cusco. In *Current Archaeological Projects in the Central Andes: Some Approaches and Results,* ed. A. Kendall, 189–220. British Archaeological Reports International Series 210. Oxford.

González Holguín, Diego

1989 [1608]. *Vocabulario de la Lengua General de Todo el Perú llamada Lengua Qquichua o del Inca.* Universidad Nacional Mayor de San Marcos. Lima.

Gordon, R. B.

1985. Laboratory evidence of the use of metal tools at Machu Picchu (Peru) and environs. *Journal of Archaeological Science* 12: 311–27.

Grimes, W. F.

1968. *The Excavation of Roman and Mediaeval London.* Routledge and Kegan Paul. London.

Guaman Poma de Ayala, Felipe

1980 [1615]. *El Primer Nueva Corónica y Buen Gobierno.* Edited by J. V. Murra and R. Adorno. Siglo Veintiuno. México DF.

Guevara Carazas, L.

2008. *Proyecto de Investigación Arqueológica Wallatapampa (Qalispugio waka).* http://www.inc-cusco.gob.pe/webPAS/PIAS/Proy5/default.aspx.

Guillén Naveros, J. W.

2008. *Proyecto de Investigación Arqueológica Salonniyoq o Templo de la Luna.* Informe. Cusco. http://www.inc-cusco.gob.pe/webPAS/PIAS/Proy4/default.aspx.

2009. Investigación arqueológica en Salonniyoq, Templo de la Luna. *Saqsaywaman* 9: 52–71. Cusco.

Gyarmati, J., and A. Varga

1999. *Chacaras of War: An Inka State Estate in Cochabamba, Bolivia.* Museum of Ethnography. Budapest.

Haggett, P.

1965. *Locational Analysis in Human Geography.* Arnold. London.

Hardoy, J. E.

1973. *Pre-Columbian Cities.* Translated from the Spanish by J. Thorne. George Allen and Unwin. London.

Harris, E. C.

1979. *Principles of Archaeological Stratigraphy.* 2nd ed. Academic Press. London.

Harth-Terré, E.

1964. *Técnica y Arte de la Cantería Incaica.* Editorial Garcilaso. Lima.

Hastorf, C. A.

1993. *Agriculture and the Onset of Political Inequality before the Inka.* Cambridge University Press. Cambridge.

Hastorf, C. A., and S. Johannessen

1993. Pre-Hispanic political change and the role of maize in the Central Andes of Peru. *American Anthropologist* 95: 115–38.

Hayashida, F.

1999. Style, technology, and state production: Inka pottery manufacture in the Leche valley, Peru. *Latin American Antiquity* 10 (4): 337–52.

Heffernan, K. J.

1990. *Limatambo in Late Prehistory: Landscape Archaeology and Documentary Images of Inca Presence in the Periphery of Cusco.* PhD dissertation, Australian National University. Canberra.

1996a. *Limatambo: Archaeology, History, and the Regional Societies of Inca Cusco.* British Archaeological Reports International Series 644. Oxford.

1996b. The mitimaes of Tilka and the Inka incorporation of Chinchaysuyu. *Tawantin-suyu* 2: 23–36. Canberra.

Helsley-Marchbanks, A. M.

2004 (1987–89). The Inca presence in Chayanta, Bolivia: The metallurgical component. *Ñawpa Pacha* 25–27: 251–60. Berkeley.

Hemming, J.

1970. *The Conquest of the Incas.* Macmillan. London.

Herrera, F.

1997. Trabajos preliminares en Paredones en el valle de Nasca, *Tawantinsuyu* 3: 119–26. Canberra.

Higgs, E. S., and C. Vita-Finzi

1972. Prehistoric economies: A territorial approach. In *Papers in Economic Prehistory*, ed. E. S. Higgs, 27–36. Cambridge University Press. Cambridge.

Huaycochea Nuñez de la Torre, F. de M.

1994. *Qolqas. Bancos de Reserva Andinos. Almacenes Inkas. Arqueología de Qolqas.* UNSAAC. Cusco.

Hume, I. N.

1964. Handmaiden to history. *North Carolina Historical Review* 41: 215–25.

Hyslop, J.

1984. *The Inka Road System.* Academic Press. New York.

1985. *Inkawasi, the New Cusco.* British Archaeological Reports 234. Oxford.

1990. *Inka Settlement Planning.* University of Texas Press. Austin.

Idrovo Urigüen, J.

2000. *Tomebamba: Arqueología e Historia de una Ciudad Imperial.* Banco Central del Ecuador. Dirección Cultural Regional. Cuenca.

2009. Arqueología urbana: Una práctica indispensable. *INPC: Revista del Patrimonio Cultural del Ecuador* 2: 24–28. Quito.

Isbell, W. H.

1978. Cosmological order expressed in prehistoric ceremonial centers. *Actes du LXII Congrès International des Américanistes* 4: 269–97. Paris.

Jamieson, R. W.

1999. *Domestic Architecture and Power: The Historical Archaeology of Colonial Ecuador.* Kluwer/Springer. New York.

Janusek, J. W.

2004. *Identity and Power in the Ancient Andes: Tiwanaku Cities through Time.* Routledge. London.

Julien, C. J.

1982. Inca decimal administration in the Lake Titicaca region. In *The Inca and Aztec States, 1400–1800,* ed. G. A. Collier, R. I. Rosaldo, and J. D. Wirth, 119–51. Academic Press. New York.

1995. Documentación presentada por la ciudad del Cuzco sobre el terremoto de 1650. *Revista del Museo Inka e Instituto de Arqueología* 25: 293–373. Cusco.

1998. La organización parroquial del Cusco y la ciudad incaica. *Tawantinsuyu* 5: 82–96. Canberra.

2000. *Reading Inca History.* University of Iowa Press. Iowa City.

2004 (1987–89). Las tumbas de Sacsahuaman y el estilo Cuzco-Inca. *Ñawpa Pacha* 25–27: 1–125. Berkeley.

Kaulicke, P.

2000. *Memoria y Muerte en el Perú Antiguo.* Pontificia Universidad Católica del Perú. Fondo Editorial. Lima.

Keene D. J.

1987. Suburban growth. In *The Plans and Topography of Mediaeval Towns,* ed. M. W. Barley, 71–82. Council for British Archaeology, Research Report no. 14. London.

Kendall, A.

1973. *Everyday Life of the Incas.* Batsford. London.

1985. *Aspects of Inca Architecture.* British Archaeological Reports International Series no. 210, Oxford.

1991. The Cusichaca Archaeological Project, Cuzco, Peru: A final report. *Bulletin of the Institute of Archaeology* 28: 1–97. London.

Kendall, A., R. Early, and B. Sillar

1992. Report on archaeological field season investigating early Inca architecture at Juchuy Coscco (Q'aqya Qhawana) and Warq'ana, Province of Calca, Dept. of Cuzco, Peru. In *Ancient America: Contributions to New World Archaeology,* ed. N. J. Saunders, 189–255. Oxbow Monograph 24. Oxford.

Kendall, D. G.

1974. Hunting quanta. *Philosophical Transactions of the Royal Society of London* A276: 231–66.

Kolata, A. L.

1982. Chronology and settlement growth at Chan Chan. In *Andean Desert City,* ed. M. E. Moseley and K. Day, 67–86. University of New Mexico Press. Albuquerque.

Kubler, G.

1952. *Cuzco: Reconstruction of the town and restoration of its monuments.* Report of the UNESCO Mission of 1951. Museums and Monuments III. UNESCO. Paris.

Ladron de Guevara Aviles, O.

1967. La restauración del Ccoricancha y Templo de Santo Domingo. *Revista del Museo y Instituto de Arqueología* 14 (21): 29–93. Cusco.

Larkham, P., and A. Jones

1991. *A Glossary of Urban Form Research.* Monograph 26. Historical Geography Research Group. Institute of British Geographers. London.

Lee, V. R.

1997. Design by numbers: Architectural order among the Incas. *Tawantinsuyu* 3: 103–18. Canberra.

LeVine, T. Y.

1992. The study of storage systems. In *Inka Storage Systems*, ed. T. Y. LeVine, 3–28. University of Oklahoma Press. Norman.

Lilley, K. D.

2000. Mapping the medieval city: Plan analysis and urban history. *Urban History* 27 (1): 5–30.

2008. Digital mappings. In *Medieval Chester Project*, ed. M. Faulkner. www.medieval chester.ac.uk. Accessed 08/22/2011.

Lilley, K. D., C. D. Lloyd, and S. Trick

2005. *Mapping Medieval Townscapes: A Digital Atlas of King Edward I's "New Towns" of England and Wales.* Archaeological Data Service. York. http://ads.ahds.ac.uk/cata logue/resources.html?atlas_ahrb_2005. Accessed 08/22/2011.

2007. Designs and designers of medieval "new towns" in Wales. *Antiquity* 81: 279–93.

Llanos. L. A.

1943. Hallazgo en el Cusco. *Revista del Museo Nacional* 12: 109–14. Lima.

López Gómez, A., and C. Manso Porto

2006. *Cartografía del siglo XVIII: Tomás López en la Real Academia de la Historia.* Real Academia de la Historia, Madrid.

Lorandi, A. M.

1984. Soñocamayoc: Los olleros del Inka en los centros manufactureros del Tucumán. *Revista del Museo de La Plata (Antropología)* 7 (62): 303–27. La Plata.

Lothrop, S. K.

1938. *Inca Treasure as Depicted by Spanish Historians.* Publications of the Frederick Webb Hodge Anniversary Publication Fund. Southwest Museum. Los Angeles.

Lozano Castro, A.

1991. *Cuenca: Ciudad prehispánica, significado y forma.* Ediciones Abya-yala. Quito.

MacCormack, S.

1991. *Religion in the Andes: Vision and Imagination in Early Colonial Peru.* Princeton University Press. Princeton.

2001a. Cuzco, another Rome? In *Empires: Perspectives from Archaeology and History*, ed. S. Alcock et al., 419–35. Cambridge University Press. Cambridge.

2001b. History, historical record, and ceremonial action: Incas and Spaniards in Cuzco. *Comparative Studies in Society and History* 43: 329–63. Cambridge.

MacCurdy, G. G.

1923. Human skeletal remains from the highlands of Peru. *American Journal of Physical Anthropology* 6: 217–330.

Magli, G.

2005. Mathematics, astronomy and sacred landscape in the Inka heartland. *Nexus Network Journal—Architecture and Mathematics* 7 (2): 22–32. Basel.

Marcos, J.

1987. *Late Intermediate Occupation at Cerro Azul, Perú: A Preliminary Report.* University of Michigan Museum of Anthropology Technical Report 20. Ann Arbor.

Mar Ismodes, R. del
  1992. Ofrenda Inka en el Paraninfo Universitario. Manuscript.
Matos Mendieta, R.
  1994. *Pumpu: Centro administrativo inka de la Puna de Junín.* Editorial Horizonte. Lima.
Maza Hirpahuanca, J.
  1995. *Excavaciones Arqueológicas en Pukamarca, Local Banco Wiese, Inmuebles no. 315 y 341, calle Maruri.* Informe presentado al Instituto Nacional de Cultura. Cusco.
  2003. *Proyecto de Puesta en Valor "Kusikancha" Sectores I y II.* Informe presentado al Instituto Nacional de Cultura. Cusco.
McEwan, G. F.
  1998. The function of niched halls in Wari architecture. *Latin American Antiquity* 9 (1): 68–86.
  2006. *The Incas: New Perspectives.* ABC-Clio. Santa Barbara.
McEwan, G. F., M. Chatfield, and A. Gibaja
  2002. The archaeology of inka origins: Excavations at Chokepukio, Cuzco, Peru. In *Andean Archaeology I: Variations in socio-political organization,* ed. W. H. Isbell and H. Silverman, 287–301. Kluwer Academic. New York.
Meddens, F.
  1994. Mountains, miniatures, ancestors, and fertility: The meaning of a Late Horizon offering in a Middle Horizon structure in Peru. *Bulletin of the Institute of Archaeology* 31: 127–50. University College. London.
Meddens, F., C. McEwan, and C. Vivanco Pomacanchari
  2010. Onca "stone ancestors" in context at a high altitude *usnu* platform. *Latin American Antiquity* 21: 173–94.
Meinken, A. K.
  2000–2001. Trabajos arqueológicos efectuados en edificios largos tipo kallanka: Maucallacta Tompullo 2, Achaymarca. Informe preliminar campaña 1999. In *Proyecto Arqueológico Condesuyos, Vol. 1,* ed. M. Ziólkowski and L. A. Belan Franco, 127–81. Universidad de Varsovia. Warsaw.
Mena, Cristóbal de
  1967 [1534]. La Conquista del Perú. In *Las Relaciones Primitivas de la Conquista del Perú,* ed. R. Porras Barrenechea, 79–101. Instituto Raúl Porras Barrenechea. Lima.
Menzel, D.
  1964. Style and time in the Middle Horizon. *Ñawpa Pacha* 2: 1–105. Berkeley.
  1976. *Pottery Style and Society in Ancient Peru: Art as a Mirror of History in the Ica Valley, 1350–1570.* University of California Press. Berkeley.
Merma Gomez, L. M.
  2001. *Proyecto de Evaluación Arqueológica. Pukin La Pradera.* Informe Final, presentado al Sub-Dirección de Investigación, Dirección de Investigación y Catastro. Instituto Nacional de Cultura. Cusco.
Meyers, A.
  1976. *Die Inka in Ekuador.* Bonner Amerikanistische Studien 6. Bonn.
Meyers, A., and C. Ulbert
  1997. Inka archaeology in eastern Bolivia: Some aspects of the Samaipata Project. *Tawantinsuyu* 3: 79–85. Canberra.

Miller, G. R.

2003. Food for the dead, tools for the afterlife: Zooarchaeology at Machu Picchu. In *The 1912 Yale Peruvian Scientific Expedition Collections from Machu Picchu: Human and Animal Remains*, ed. R. L. Burger and L. C. Salazar, 1–63. Yale University Publications in Anthropology 85. New Haven.

Miranda Ayerbe, A., and W. Zanabria Alegria

1994. *La Cantera de Huaqòto: Una introducción a su estudio tecnológico.* Tesis para optar al Título Profesional de Licenciados en Arqueología, Universidad Nacional de San Antonio Abad del Cusco. Cusco.

Molina, Cristóbal de

1873 [1573]. An Account of the Fables and Rites of the Yncas. In *Narratives of the Rites and Laws of the Yncas*, ed. C. R. Markham, 3–64. Hakluyt Society. Burt Franklin. New York.

1989 [1573]. Relación de las Fábulas y Ritos de los Incas. In *Fábulas y Ritos de los Incas*, ed. H. Urbano and P. Duviols, 47–134. Crónicas de América, Historia 16. Madrid.

Montesinos, Fernando de

2007 [1642]. Memorias Antiguas Historiales y Políticas del Pirú. In *The Quito Manuscript: An Inca History Preserved by Fernando de Montesinos*, ed. S. Hyland, 106–54. Yale University Publications in Anthropology no. 88. New Haven.

Moore, J. D.

1989. Prehispanic beer in coastal Peru: Technology and social context of prehistoric production. *American Anthropologist* 91: 682–95.

1996. The archaeology of plazas and the proxemics of ritual. *American Anthropologist* 98 (4): 789–802.

2005. Andean processions: Dynamics of sound, display, and power. In *Cultural Landscapes in the Ancient Andes: Archaeologies of Place*, 123–73. University Press of Florida. Gainesville.

Moorehead, E. L.

1978. Highland Inca architecture in adobe. *Ñawpa Pacha* 16: 65–94. Berkeley.

Mormontoy, A.

1994. Investigaciones arqueológicas en Sillkinchani (San Jerónimo—Cusco). *Andes* 1: 77–96. Facultad de Ciencias Sociales, UNSAAC. Cusco.

2000. *Informe de la Investigación Arqueológica en el Sitio de Silkinchani. Sector II.* Informe presentado al Instituto Nacional de Cultura. Cusco.

Mörner, M.

1978. *Perfil de la Sociedad Rural del Cuzco a Fines de la Colonia.* Universidad del Pácifico. Lima.

Morris, C.

1967. *Storage in Tawantinsuyu.* PhD dissertation, University of Chicago. Chicago.

1971. The identification of function in Inca architecture and ceramics. *Revista del Museo Nacional* 37: 135–44. Lima.

1974. Reconstructing patterns of non-agricultural production in the Inca economy: Archaeology and documents in institutional analysis. In *Reconstructing Complex Societies*, ed. C. B. Moore, 49–68. Bulletin of the American Schools of Oriental Research. Supplemental Series no. 20. Cambridge.

1979. Maize beer in the economics, politics, and religion of the Inka empire. In *Fermented Food Beverages in Nutrition*, ed. C. F. Gastineau et al., 21–34. Academic Press. New York.

1987. Arquitectura y estructura del espacio en Huánuco Pampa. *Cuadernos* 12: 27–45. Instituto Nacional de Antropología, Buenos Aires.

2004. Enclosures of power: The multiple spaces of Inca administrative palaces. In *Palaces of the Ancient New World*, ed. S. T. Evans and J. Pillsbury, 299–323. Dumbarton Oaks. Washington, DC.

2008. Links in the chain of Inka cities: Communication, alliance, and the cultural production of status, value, and power. In *The Ancient City: New Perspectives on Urbanism in the Old and New Worlds*, ed. J. Marcus and J. A. Sabloff, 299–319. School of Advanced Research Press. Sante Fe.

Morris, C., and R. A. Covey
2003. La plaza central de Huánuco Pampa: Espacio y transformación. *Boletín de Arqueología PUCP* 7: 133–49. Lima.

Morris, C., and D. E. Thompson
1985. *Huánuco Pampa: An Inca City and Its Hinterland*. Thames and Hudson. London.

Morris, C., R. A. Covey, and P. Stein
2011. *The Huánuco Pampa Archaeological Project. Volume 1: The Plaza and Palace Complex*. Anthropological Papers of the American Museum of Natural History, no. 96. New York.

Morris, R.
1987. Parish churches. In *Urban Archaeology in Britain*, ed. J. Schofield and R. Leech, 177–91. Council for British Archaeology Research Report 61. London.

Moseley, M. E., D. J. Nash, P. R. Williams, S. D. DeFrance, A. Miranda, M. Ruales
2005. Burning down the brewery: Establishing and evacuating an ancient imperial colony at Cerro Baúl, Peru. *Proceedings of the National Academy of Sciences* 102 (48): 17264–71.

Muñóz Collazos, M. de los Angeles
2007. The kallanka at Samaipata, Bolivia: An example of Inka monumental architecture. In *Variations in the Expression of Inka Power*, ed. R. L. Burger, C. Morris, and R. Matos Mendieta, 255–65. Dumbarton Oaks. Washington, DC.

Murra, J. V.
1960. Rite and crop in the Inca state. In *Culture in History*, ed. S. Diamond, 393–407. Columbia University Press. New York.

1982. The mit'a obligations of ethnic groups to the Inka state. In *The Inca and Aztec States, 1400–1800*, ed. G. A. Collier, R. I. Rosaldo, and J. D. Wirth, 237–62. Academic Press. New York.

Murra, J. V., and G. J. Hadden
1966. Informe presentado al Patronato Nacional de Arqueología sobre la labor de limpieza y consolidación de Huánuco Viejo (20 de julio a 23 de noviembre 1965). *Cuadernos de Investigación* 1: 129–44. Universidad Nacional Hermilio Valdizán. Huánuco.

Murúa, Martín de
1987 [1615/1590–1600]. *Historia General del Perú, origen y descendencia de los Incas*. Edited by M. Ballesteros Gabrois. Crónicas de América 35, Historia 16. Madrid.

Nair, S.

2003. *Of Remembrance and Forgetting: The Architecture of Chinchero, Peru, from Thupa Inka to the Spanish Occupation.* PhD dissertation, University of California. Berkeley.

2007. Witnessing the in-visibility of Inca architecture in colonial Peru. *Buildings and Landscapes* 14: 50–65.

Nicholson, G. E.

1960. Chicha maize types and chicha manufacture in Peru. *Economic Botany* 14: 290–99.

Niles, S. A.

1987. *Callachaca: Style and Status in an Inca Community.* University of Iowa Press. Iowa City.

1988. Looking for "lost" Inca palaces. *Expedition* 30 (3): 56–64.

1999. *The Shape of Inca History: Narrative and Architecture in an Andean Empire.* University of Iowa Press. Iowa City.

2004. The nature of inka royal estates. In *Machu Picchu: Unveiling the Mystery of the Incas*, ed. R. L. Burger and L. C. Salazar, 49–68. Yale University Press. New Haven.

Oberti Rodríguez, I.

2002. *Informe de la Excavación de Arqueología realizado dentro de la Casa N° 526 ubicada en la calle Teqseqocha—Manzana N°25 correspondiente al "Centro Histórico de la Ciudad del Cuzco."* Informe presentado al Instituto Nacional de Cultura. Cusco.

2004. *Informe de Exploración de Arqueología realizado dentro del Inmueble N° 366 ubicado en la calle Procuradores de la Ciudad del Cuzco: Propiedad de la familia Vizcarra.* Informe presentado al Instituto Nacional de Cultura. Cusco.

Odaira, S.

1998. El mirador de Mullupungo: Un aspecto del control inca en la costa sur del Ecuador. *Tawantinsuyu* 5: 145–52. Canberra.

Ogburn, D. E.

2004a. Evidence for long-distance transportation of building stones in the Inka empire, from Cuzco, Peru, to Saraguro, Ecuador. *Latin American Antiquity* 15 (4): 419–39.

2004b. Power in stone: The long-distance movement of building blocks in the Inca empire. *Ethnohistory* 51: 101–35.

Ortiz de Zúñiga, Iñigo

1967. *Visita de la Provincia de León de Huánuco en 1562 (1569).* 2 vols. Universidad Nacional Hermilio Valdizán. Huánuco.

Pardo, L. A.

1941. Un hallazgo en la zona arqueológica del Awsangati (Cusco). *Revista del Museo Nacional* 10 (1): 110–12. Lima.

1957. *Historia y Arqueología del Cuzco.* Imprenta Colegio Militar. Leoncio Prado. Callao.

1959. Informe sobre una tumba incaica. *Revista del Museo e Instituto Arqueológico* 18: 101–14. Cusco.

1970. Saqsayhuamán: Enterramiento en el sector de Rumipunku. *Revista Saqsaywamán* 1: 179–80. Cusco.

Paredes García, M. S.

1999. *Registro Informatizado de Restos Prehispanicos en el Centro Historico de Cusco.*

Diagnóstico e Interpretación. Tesis para optar al Título Profesional de Licenciada en Arqueología, Universidad Nacional San Antonio Abad del Cusco. Cusco.

2001. *El Cusco Incaico*. Ediciones El Santo. Surco.

2003. Prácticas funerarias incaicas en Sacsayhuamán: Enterramientos ceremonials y complejo funerario. *Boletín de Arqueología PUCP* 7: 57–77. Lima.

Parker-Pearson, M.

1999. *The Archaeology of Death and Burial*. Sutton Publishing. Stroud.

Paternosto, C.

1989. *The Stone and the Thread: Andean Roots of Andean Abstract Art*. University of Texas Press. Austin.

Paz Flores, P., and E. Allcacontor Pumayalli

2002. *Excavación Arqueológica y Exploración de Pisos Informe Final Casa Concha*. Universidad Nacional San Antonio Abad del Cusco. Informe presentado al Instituto Nacional de Cultura. Cusco.

Perez Trujillo, A.

2001. *Informe Final de la Investigación Arqueológica realizada en la Iglesia Catedral de la Ciudad del Cusco: Sectores A y B*. Informe presentado al Convenio Arzobispado del Cusco-Telefónica del Perú. Instituto Nacional de Cultura. Cusco.

Perring, D.

1987. Domestic buildings in Romano-British towns. In *Urban Archaeology in Britain*, ed. J. Schofield and R. Leech, 147–55. Council for British Archaeology Research Report 61. London.

Pilares Daza, J.

2002. *Informe de investigación arqueológica Qhataqhasapatallacta*. Informe presentado al Instituto Nacional de Cultura. Dirección de Investigación y Catastro. Cusco.

2008. Las qolqas de Muyu Orqo. *Saqsaywaman* 7: 110–30. Cusco.

Pilco, R.

2004. *Informe Anual de Investigación Arqueológica de Wayna Tauqaray*. Informe presentado al Instituto Nacional de Cultura. Cusco.

Pizarro, Pedro

1986 [1571]. *Relación del Descubrimiento y Conquista de los Reinos del Perú*. 2nd ed. Fondo Editorial. Pontificia Universidad Católica del Perú. Lima.

Platt, T.

1986. Mirror and maize: The concept of yanatin among the Macha of Bolivia. In *Anthropological History of Andean Polities*, ed. J. V. Murra, N. Wachtel, and J. Revel, 227–59. Cambridge University Press. Cambridge.

Polo de Ondegardo, Juan

1965 [1571]. *On the Errors and Superstitions of the Indians, Taken from the Treatise and Investigation Done by Licentiate Polo*. Translated by A. Brunel, J. V. Murra, and S. Muirden. Human Relations Area Files. New Haven.

1990 [1571]. *El Mundo de los Incas*. Edición de L. González y AS. Alonso, Crónicas de América 58, Historia 16. Madrid.

Porras Barrenechea, R. (ed.)

1967. *Las Relaciones Primitivas de la Conquista del Perú*. Instituto Raúl Porras Barrenechea. Lima.

Prada Honor, R.

1986. *Titiqaqa: Huaca Prehispánica*. Tesis para optar al Título Profesional de Licenciados en Arqueología, Universidad Nacional San Antonio Abad del Cusco. Cusco.

Prescott, W. H.

1862. *The History of the Conquest of Peru*. Vol. 3. Routledge. London.

Protzen, J-P.

1980. Inca stonemasonry. *Scientific American* 254 (2): 94–103.

1993. *Inca Architecture and Construction at Ollantaytambo*. Oxford University Press. Oxford.

1999. Inca architecture. In *The Inca World: The Development of Pre-Columbian Peru, AD 1000–1534*, ed. L. Laurencich-Minelli, 193–218. University of Oklahoma Press. Norman.

2008. Inca city planning. In *Encyclopaedia of the History of Science, Technology, and Medicine in Non-Western Cultures*, vol. A-K, ed. H. Selin, 587–90. Springer. Berlin.

Protzen, J-P., and C. Morris

2004. Los colores de Tambo Colorado: Una re-evaluación. *Boletín de Arqueología PUCP* 8: 267–76. Lima.

Protzen, J-P., and S. Nair

1997. Who taught the Inca stonemasons their skills? *Journal of the Society of Architectural Historians* 56: 146–67.

Protzen, J-P., and J. H. Rowe

1994. Hawkaypata: The terrace of leisure. In *Streets: Critical Perspectives on Public Spaces*, ed. Z. Celik, D. Favro, and R. Ingersoll, 235–45. University of California Press. Berkeley.

Puelles Escalante, E.

2005. *Qorikancha: Construcción Inka*. Lima.

Raffino, R. A.

1981. *Los Inkas del Kollasuyu*. Ramos Americana Editorial. Buenos Aires.

Raffino, R. A.

1988. *Poblaciones Indígenas en Argentina: Urbanismo y proceso social precolombino*. Tipográfica Editora Argentina. Buenos Aires.

1993. *Inka: Arqueología, historia y urbanismo del altiplano andino*. Corregidor. Buenos Aires.

1993–98. Requiem por Watungasta. *Xama* 6–11: 113–26. Mendoza.

Raffino, R. A. (ed.)

2004. *El Shincal de Quimivíl*. Editorial Sarquis. Catamarca.

Raffino, R. A., R. Alvis, L. Baldini, D. Olivera, and M. Raviña

1983–85. Hualfín-El Shincal-Watungasta: Tres casos de urbanización inka en el N.O. argentino. *Cuadernos del Instituto Nacional de Antropología* 10: 425–558. Buenos Aires.

Raffino, R., D. Gobbo, R. Vázquez, A. Capparelli, V. G. Montes, R. Itturriza, C. Deschamps and M. Mannasero

1997. El ushnu de El Shincal de Quimivil. *Tawantinsuyu* 3: 22–39. Canberra.

Raffino, R. A., and I. S. Farrington

2004. Atlas del ushno en el territorio del Tawantinsuyu. In *El Shincal de Quimivil*, ed. R. A. Raffino, 255–59. Editorial Sarquis. Catamarca.

Ramírez, S. E.

2005. *To Feed and Be Fed: The Cosmological Bases of Authority and Identity in the Andes.* Stanford University Press. Stanford.

Ramos Gavilan, Alonso

1976 [1621]. *Historia de Nuestra Señora de Copacabana.* Academia Boliviana de Historia. La Paz.

Reinhard, J.

1991. *Machu Picchu: The Sacred Center.* Nuevos Imágenes. Lima.

2005. *The Ice Maiden: Inca Mummies, Mountain Gods, and Sacred Sites in the Andes.* National Geographic Society. Washington, DC.

Reinhard, J., and C. Ceruti

2005. Sacred mountains, ceremonial sites, and human sacrifice among the Incas. *Archaeoastronomy* 19: 1–43. Austin.

Rivera Serna, R.

1965 [1534]. Libro Primero del Cabildo de la Ciudad del Cuzco. *Documenta* 4: 441–80. Lima.

Rodríguez Carreño, E.

2005. *Informe de Evaluación Arqueológica. Calle Maruri Inmueble no. 256.* Instituto Nacional de Cultura. Cusco.

Rojas C., J. H.

2006. *El Complejo Arqueológico de Ingapirca.* Vol. 3. Offset Color Cuenca. Azogues.

Rosell, C.

2004. *Informe Final de Evaluación Arqueológica: Inmueble de la Plazoleta de Santo Domingo No. 263 (fronterizo al Templo de Santo Domingo).* Instituto Nacional de Cultura. Cusco.

Rostworowski de Diez Canseco, M.

1962. Nuevos datos sobre tenencia de tierras reales en el Incario. *Revista del Museo Nacional* 31: 130–59. Lima.

1988. Mediciones y computos en el Antiguo Perú. *Cuadernos Prehispanicos* 6, Seminario Americanista, Universidad de Valladolid. Valladolid.

Rowe, J. H.

1944. *An Introduction to the Archaeology of Cuzco.* Papers of the Peabody Museum of American Archaeology and Ethnology, 27 (2). Harvard University. Cambridge.

1946. Inca culture at the time of the Spanish Conquest. In *Handbook of South American Indians*, ed. J. H. Steward, 2: 183–330. Bulletin of American Ethnology 143. Cooper Square. New York.

1963. Urban settlements in ancient Peru. *Ñawpa Pacha* 1: 1–26. Berkeley.

1968. What kind of city was Inca Cuzco? *Ñawpa Pacha* 6: 59–76. Berkeley.

1990a. Machu Picchu a la luz de documentos de siglo XVI. *Histórica* 14: 139–54. Lima.

1990b. El plano más antiguo del Cuzco. Dos parroquias de la ciudad vistas en 1643. *Histórica* 14: 367–77. Lima.

1991. Los monumentos perdidos de la Plaza Mayor del Cuzco incaico. *Revista del Museo e Instituto de Arqueología* UNSAAC 24: 83–100. Cusco.

2003a. El barrio de Cayau Cachi y la parroquia de Belén. In *Los Incas del Cuzco: Siglos XVI–XVII–XVIII*, 135–42. Instituto Nacional de Cultura. Cusco.

2003b. Hawkaypata: Como fue la plaza de los Incas. In *Los Incas del Cuzco: Siglos XVI–XVII–XVIII*, 231–35. Instituto Nacional de Cultura. Cusco.

Rueda Sosa, D, and E. Gonzales Costillas
2004. *Poblaciones que Estuvieron a Cargo de las Guacas de Ccachona*. Tesis para optar al Titulo Profesional de Licenciado en Arqueología. Universidad Nacional de San Antonio Abad del Cusco. Cusco.

Ruiz de Arce, Juan
2002 [1545]. La Memoria. In *La Memoria de Juan Ruiz de Arce: Conquista del Perú, saberes secretos de caballería, y defensa del mayorazgo*, ed. E. Stoll, 58–123. Vervuert Iberoamericana. Madrid.

Salazar, L. C.
2006. Machu Picchu's silent majority: A consideration of the inka cemeteries. In *Variations in the Expression of Inka Power*, ed. R. L. Burger, C. Morris, and R. Matos Mendieta, 165–83. Dumbarton Oaks. Washington, DC.

Salceda, S. A., and R. A. Raffino
2004. El hombre de "El Shincal." In *El Shincal de Quimivil*, ed. R. A. Raffino, 165–77. Editorial Sarquis. Catamarca.

Sancho de la Hoz, Pedro
1917 [1534]. Relación. In *Colección de Libros y Documentos Referentes a la Historia del Perú*, ed. H. H. Urteaga, 5: 122–202. Sanmarti, Lima.

San Román Luna, W. et al.
2002. *Evaluación e Investigación Arqueológica del "Kusikancha" (Ex-Cuartel 27 de Noviembre)*. Informe presentado al Instituto Nacional de Cultura. Cusco.
2003. *Evaluación e Investigación Arqueológica del "Kusikancha" (Ex-Cuartel 27 de Noviembre)*. Informe presentado al Instituto Nacional de Cultura. Cusco.

Santa Cruz Pachacuti Yamqui Salcamayhua, Don Joan de
1992 [1613]. Relación de antigüedades deste reyno del Perú. In *Antigüedades del Perú*, ed. H. Urbano and A. Sánchez, 123–269. Crónicas de América 70. Historia 16. Madrid.

Santillan, Hernando de
1968 [1563]. *Relación del Orígen, Descendencia, Política, y Gobierno de los Incas*. Biblioteca de Autores Españoles, vol. 209. Madrid.

Santillana, J. I.
2001. *The Inka Province of Vilcaswaman: Religious Dynamics and the Expansion of the Inka State*. PhD dissertation, Australian National University. Canberra.

Sarmiento de Gamboa, Pedro
2007 [1572]. *The History of the Incas*. Translated and edited by B. S. Bauer and V. Smith, University of Texas Press. Austin.

Saunders, N. J.
2002. The colours of light: Materiality and chromatic cultures of the Americas. In *Colouring the Past: The Significance of Colour in Archaeological Research*, ed. A. Jones and G. MacGregor, 209–26. Berg. Oxford.

Schjellerup, I.
1997. *Incas and Spaniards in the Conquest of the Chachapoyas: Archaeological and Ethnohistorical Research in the North-eastern Andes of Peru*. GOTARC, series B, Gothenburg Archaeological Theses 7. Göteborg.

Schofield, J.

1987. Recent approaches in urban archaeology. In *Urban Archaeology in Britain*, ed. J. Schofield and R. Leech, 1–8. Council for British Archaeology Research Report 61. London.

Scott, D. D., R. A. Fox Jr., M. A. Connor, and D. Harmon

2000. *Archaeological Perspectives on the Battle of Little Bighorn.* University of Oklahoma Press. Norman.

Segovia, Bartolomé de (Cristóbal de Molina)

1968 [1552]. *Relación de muchas cosas acaescidas en el Perú*, Biblioteca de Autores Españoles, tomo 209. Madrid.

Senchysyn Trever, L.

2005. *Slithering Serpents and the Afterlives of Stones: The Role of Ornament in Inka Style Architecture of Cusco, Peru.* MA dissertation, University of Maryland. College Park.

Shady Solis, R.

2006. America's first city? The case of a Late Archaic caral. In *Andean Archaeology III: North and South*, ed. W. H. Isbell and H. Silverman, 28–66. Springer. New York.

Sherbondy, J. E.

1982. *The canal systems of Hanan Cuzco.* PhD dissertation, University of Illinois. Urbana-Champaign.

1986a. *Mallki: Ancestros y cultivo de árboles en los Andes.* Proyecto FAO-Holanda/INFOR GCP/PER/027/NET. Documento de Trabajo No. 5. Lima.

1986b. Los ceques: código de canales en el Cusco incaico. Allpanchis 27: 39–74. Cusco.

Sillar, B.

1994. Playing with God? Children, play, and the ritual use of miniatures in the Andes. *Archaeological Review from Cambridge* 13: 47–63. Cambridge.

2002. Caminando a través del tiempo: Geografías sagradas en Cacha/Raqchi, departamento del Cuzco (Perú). *Revista Andina* 35: 221–45. Cusco.

Silva Hurtado, M. A.

1982. *Excavaciones Arqueológicas en el Hostal Alhambra II de Yucay.* Informe presentado al Instituto Nacional de Cultura. Cusco.

Silverblatt, I.

1987. *Moon, Sun, and Witches: Gender Ideology and Class in Inca and Colonial Peru.* Princeton University Press. Princeton.

Slater, T. R.

1990. English medieval new towns with composite plans: Evidence from the Midlands. In *The Built Form of Western Cities*, ed. T. R. Slater, 60–82. Leicester University Press. Leicester.

Smith, M. E.

2007. Form and meaning in the earliest cities: A new approach to ancient urban planning. *Journal of Planning History* 6 (1): 3–47.

2010. The archaeological study of neighborhoods and districts in ancient cities. *Journal of Anthropological Archaeology* 29: 137–54.

2011. Empirical urban theory for archaeologists. *Journal of Archaeological Method and Theory* 18: 167–92.

Smith, R. C.

1955. Colonial towns of Spanish and Portuguese America. *Journal of the Society of Architectural Historians* 14: 3–12.

Socualaya Dávila, C.

2008. *Proyecto de Investigación Arqueológica de los Sectores Chincana Grande y Qocha.* Informe presentado al Instituto Nacional de Cultura. Cusco.

Solis, F.

1999. *Informe de las Excavaciones Arqueológicas en el Cementerio de Suchuna-Saqsaywaman.* Informe presentado al Instituto Nacional de Cultura. Cusco.

Solling, L. A.

2007. *An Archaeological Study of Inka Cusco.* PhB (Hons) thesis, Australian National University. Canberra.

Soto Huanco, M., and D. Cabrera Carrillo

1999. *Arquitectura Inca en Ollantaytambo. Registro, descripción y análisis técnico-morfológico del área urbana de un tambo Inca.* Tesis para optar al Título Profesional de Licenciados en Arqueología. Universidad Nacional San Antonio Abad del Cusco. Cusco.

Spurling, G. E.

1992. *The Organization of Craft Production in the Inka State: The Potters and Weavers of Milliraya.* PhD dissertation, Cornell University. Ithaca.

Squier, E. G.

1877. *Peru: Incidents of Travel and Exploration in the Land of the Incas.* Harper and Brothers. New York.

Stehberg, R.

1995. *Instalaciones Incaica en el Norte Centro Semiárido de Chile.* Dirección de Bibliotecas Archivos y Museos. Santiago.

Szeminski, J.

1991. Wana Kawri waka. In *El Culto Estatal del Imperio Inca,* ed. M. S. Ziolkowski, 35–53. Estudios y Memorias 2. Centro de Estudios Latinoamericanos. University of Warsaw. Warsaw.

Tantalean, H., and C. Pérez Maestro

2000. Muerte en el Altiplano Andino: Investigaciones en la necrópolis Inka de Cutimbo (Puno, Perú). *Revista de Arqueología* 228: 26–37. Madrid.

Tomayconsa, L., and R. Pilco Vargas

1994. *Investigación Arqueológica del Inmueble N° 263 [Plazoleta de Santo Domingo] Manzana 037.* Informe final presentado al Instituto Nacional de Cultura. Cusco.

Topic, J. R.

1990. Craft production in the Kingdom of Chimor. In *The Northern Dynasties: Kingship and Statecraft in Chimor,* ed. M. E. Moseley and A. Cordy-Collins, 145–76. Dumbarton Oaks. Washington, DC.

2009. Domestic economy as political economy at Chan Chan, Perú. In *Domestic Life in Prehispanic Capitals: A Study of Specialization, Hierachy, and Ethnicity,* ed. L. R. Manzanilla and C. Chapdelaine, 221–42. Memoirs of the Museum of Anthropology 40, University of Michigan. Ann Arbor.

Torres, C. M., and D. B. Repke

2006. *Anadenanthera: Visionary Plant of Ancient South America.* Haworth Herbal Press. New York.

Torres, J.

2001. *Excavaciones arqueológicas en el sector Suchuna del Parque Arqueológico de Saqsaywaman.* Tesis para optar al Título de Licenciado en Arqueología de la Facultad de Ciencias Sociales, Universidad Nacional de San Antonio Abad del Cusco. Cusco.

Torres Ccahuana, R. L.

2011. Contextos funerarios del Horizonte Tardío—Cheqollo San Jerónimo. DRC. Cusco. www.drc.cusco.gob.pe/dmdocuments/publicaciones/ARTICULO%20CHEQOLLO%202011SDI-MC.pdf. Accessed 06/13/2011.

Tovar Cayo, J. L.

1996. *Cantería Inka en Waqoto-Cusco.* Tesis para optar al Título Profesional de Licenciado en Arqueología. Universidad Nacional de San Antonio Abad del Cusco. Cusco.

Trujillo, Diego de

1948 [1571]. *Relación del Descubrimiento del Reyno del Perú.* Edited by Raúl Porras Barrenechea. Imprenta de la Escuela de Estudios Hispano-Américanos. Sevilla.

Uhle, M.

1930. El Templo del Sol de los Incas en el Cuzco. *Proceedings of the 23rd International Congress of Americanists* (1928): 291–95. New York.

Urbano, H.

1981. *Wiraqocha y Ayar: Héroes y funciones en las sociedades andinas.* Biblioteca de la Tradición Oral Andina 3. Centro de Estudios Rurales Andinos 'Bartolomé de las Casas.' Cusco.

Urton, G.

1978. Orientation in Quechua and Incaic astronomy. *Ethnology* 17: 157–67.

1982. *At the Crossroads of the Earth and the Sky: An Andean Cosmology.* University of Texas Press. Austin.

1984. Chuta: El espacio de la práctica social en Pacariqtambo, Perú. *Revista Andina* 2: 7–43. Cusco.

1990. *The History of a Myth: Pacariqtambo and the Origin of the Inkas.* University of Texas Press. Austin.

Uscachi Santos, I.

2009. Investigación arquelógica Sector Wayrapunku Qowiqarana "waka" Pachakuti. *Saqsaywaman* 9: 72–82. Cusco.

Valcárcel, L. E.

1934. Los trabajos arqueológicos del Cusco: Sajsawaman redescubierto (I) and (II). *Revista del Museo Nacional* 3: 3–36, 211–33. Lima.

1935. Los trabajos arqueológicos del Cusco. Sajsawaman redescubierto (III) and (IV). *Revista del Museo Nacional* 4: 1–24, 161–203. Lima.

Valencia Espinoza, A.

1982. *Pesos y Medidas en Canas.* Cusco.

Valencia Zegarra, A.

1970a. Dos tumbas de Saqsaywaman. *Revista Saqsaywaman. Revista del Patronato Departamental de Arqueología del Cuzco* 1: 173–78. Cusco.

1970b. Los microesculturas de Saqsaywaman. *Revista Saqsaywaman: Revista del Patronato Departamental de Arqueología del Cuzco* 1: 159–71. Cusco.

1979. *Colección Arqueológica Cusco de Max Uhle.* Instituto Nacional de Cultura. Cusco.

1984. Arqueología de Qolqampata. *Revista del Museo e Instituto de Arqueología* UNSAAC 23: 47–62. Cusco.

1991. *Informe Final Arqueológico de las Excavaciones Realizadas en la Iglesia Compañia de Jesus.* Informe final presentado al Instituto Nacional de Cultura. Cusco.

Valencia Zegarra, A., and A. Gibaja Oviedo

1992. *Machu Picchu: La investigación y conservación del monumento arqueológico después de Hiram Bingham.* Municipalidad de Qosqo. Cusco.

van de Guchte, M. J.

1990. *Carving the World: Inca Monumental Scupture and Landscape.* PhD dissertation, University of Illinois. Urbana-Champaign.

Vargas Paliza, E.

2007. *Kusikancha. Morada de las momias reales de los Inkas.* Instituto Nacional de Cultura. Cusco.

Verano, J.

2003. Human skeletal remains from Machu Picchu: A reexamination of the Yale Peabody Museum's collections. In *The 1912 Yale Peruvian Scientific Expedition Collections from Machu Picchu: Human and Animal Remains,* ed. R. L. Burger and L. C. Salazar, 65–117. Yale University Publications in Anthropology 85. New Haven.

Villacorta Oviedo, Y.

2011. Análisis de la Cerámica Inca: formas y diseños. Tesis para optar al Título de Licenciada en Arqueología. Universidad Nacional de San Antonio Abad del Cusco. Cusco.

Vince, A.

1987. The study of pottery from urban excavations. In *Urban Archaeology in Britain,* ed. J. Schofield and R. Leech, 201–13. Council for British Archaeology Research Report 61. London.

Viñuales, G. M.

2004. *El Espacio Urbano en el Cusco Colonial: Uso y organización de las estructuras simbólicos.* CEDODAL. Epigrafe. Lima.

Wheatley, P.

1971. *The Pivot of the Four Quarters: A Preliminary Enquiry into the Origins and Character of the Ancient Chinese City.* Edinburgh University Press. Edinburgh.

Whitehand, J. W. R., and K. Gu

2007. Extending the compass of plan analysis: A Chinese exploration. *Urban Morphology* 11: 91–110.

Whittle, A., J. Pollard, and C. Grigson

1999. *The Harmony Symbols: The Windmill Hill Causewayed Enclosure.* Oxbow. Oxford.

Wiener, C.

1993 [1880]. *Perú y Bolivia.* Instituto Francés de Estudios Andinos. Lima.

Wurster, W.

1999. Dos mundos, una ciudad: El Cuzco, capital de los Incas y ciudad colonial española. In *L'Amérique du Sud. Des chasseurs-ceulleurs à l'Empire Inca,* ed. A. Chevalier, L. Velarde, and I. Chenal-Velarde, 129–36. Actes des journées d'étude d'archéologie précolombienne, Genève, 10–11 octobre 1997, British Archaeological Reports International Series 746. Oxford.

Xerez, Francisco de

1985 [1534]. *Verdadera Relación de la Conquista del Perú*. Edición a cargo de C. Bravo Guerreira. Historia 16. 2nd ed. Madrid.

Yaeger, J., and J. M. López Bejerano

2004. Reconfiguración de un espacio sagrado: Los inkas y la pirámide Pumapunku en Tiwanaku, Bolivia. *Chungara. Revista de Antropología Chilena* 36 (2): 337–50. Arica.

Zanabria Alegría, W.

1997. *Rehabilitación y Renovación de Redes de Distribución de Agua Potable de la Ciudad del Cusco. Informe Arqueológico*. Informe presentado al Instituto Nacional de Cultura. Cusco.

1998a. *Informe del Proyecto de Investigación Arqueológica del Inmueble No. 392 Esquina de las Calles Triunfo y Herrajes-Cusco*. Informe presentado al Instituto Nacional de Cultura. Cusco.

1998b. *Informe de Investigación Arqueológica del Inmueble No 107 esquinas de las calles Amargura y Saphy*. Informe presentado al Instituto Nacional de Cultura. Cusco.

Zapata Rodríguez, J. M.

1983. *Investigación Arqueológica en Machupicchu. Sector Militar*. Tesis para optar Licenciatura. Universidad Nacional de San Antonio Abad del Cusco. Cusco.

1992. *Informe Final de las Excavaciones Realizadas en el Inmueble ubicado en la esquina que forman las calles Tigre y Saphy*. Informe presentado al Instituto Nacional de Cultura. Cusco.

1993. *Informe Final de las Excavaciones Arqueológicas Realizadas en el Terreno sin Construir del Palacio del Almirante*. Universidad Nacional San Antonio Abad del Cusco. Informe presentado al Instituto Nacional de Cultura. Cusco.

1997. Arquitectura contextos funerarios wari en Batan Urqu, Cusco. *Boletín de Arqueología PUCP* 1: 165–206. Lima.

1998a. *Excavaciones Arqueológicas en el Barrio de San Cristóbal de la Ciudad del Cusco. Informe Final*. Informe presentado al Instituto Nacional de Cultura. Cusco.

1998b. Los cerros sagrados: Panorama del periodo formativo en la cuenca del Vincanota, Cusco. *Boletín de Arqueología PUCP* 2: 307–36. Lima.

2002. Casas, hombres y protectores en un pueblo de la periferia del Cusco incaico, Paper read at the symposium: Landscape and Symbol in the Inka State, held at the Humanities Research Centre, The Australian National University, Canberra.

2003. *Informe Final del Proyecto de Evaluación Arqueológica Realizado en Inmueble Número 348 de la Calle Suecia*. Informe presentado al Instituto Nacional de Cultura.—Cusco. Cusco.

Zawaski, M. J., and J. M. Malville

2007–2008. An archaeoastronomical survey of major inca sites in Peru, *Archaeoastronomy* 21: 20–38.

Zecenarro Benavente, G.

2001. *Arquitectura Arqueológica en la Quebrada de Thanpumach'ay*. Municipalidad del Cusco. Cusco.

Zegarra Solis, F.
2008. Proyecto de Investigacón Arqueológica de Qochapata. http://www.inc-cusco. gob.pe/webPAS/PIAS/Proy2/default.aspx.

Zuidema, R. T.
1964. *The Ceque System of Cuzco.* International Archives of Ethnography, Supplement to volume 50. Brill. Leiden.

1973. Kinship and ancestorcult in three Peruvian communities: Hernández Príncipe's account of 1622. *Bulletin de l'Institut Français d'Études Andines* 2: 16–33. Lima.

1977. The Inca calendar. In *Native American Astronomy*, ed. A. F. Aveni, 219–59. University of Texas Press. Austin.

1978. Shafttombs and the Inca empire. *Journal of the Steward Anthropological Society* 9: 133–77. Urbana-Champaign.

1980. El ushnu. *Revista de la Universidad Complutense* 28: 317–62. Madrid.

1981. Inca observations of the solar and lunar passages through zenith and anti-zenith at Cuzco. In *Archaeoastronomy in the Americas*, ed. R. Williamson, 319–42. Ballena Press. Menlo Park.

1982. The sidereal lunar calendar of the Incas. In *Archaeoastronomy in the New World*, ed. A. F. Aveni, 59–107. Cambridge University Press. Cambridge. Zanabria

1983. The lion in the city: Royal symbols of transition in Cuzco. *Journal of Latin American Lore* 9: 39–100.

1986. Inka dynasty and irrigation: Another look at Andean concepts of history. In *Anthropological History of Andean Polities*, ed. J. V. Murra, N. Wachtel, and J. Revel, 177–200. Cambridge University Press. Cambridge.

1990. Ceques and chapas: An andean pattern of land partition in the modern valley of Cuzco. In *Circumpacifica: Festschrift für Thomas S. Barthel. Band 1 Mittel- und Südamerika*, ed. B. Illius and M. Laubscher, 627–43. Sonderdruck Peter Lund. Frankfurt am Main.

1999. Pilgrimage and ritual movements in Cuzco and the Inca empire. In *Pilgrimage: Sacred Landscapes and Self-Organized Complexity*, ed. J. M. Malville and B. Saraswati, 248–64. Indira Gandhi National Centre for the Arts. New Delhi.

2003. The astronomical significance of a procession, a pilgrimage and a race in the calendar of Cuzco. In *Current Studies in Archaeoastronomy: Conversations across Time and Space: Selected Papers from the Fifth Oxford International Conference at Santa Fe, 1996*, ed. J. W. Fountain and R. M. Sinclair, 353–66. Carolina Academic Press. Durham.

Newspapers and Press Agencies

Andina. Agencia Peruana de Noticias.
07/19/2006: Hallan fardo funerario con 15 vasijas de cerámica en Centro Histórico de Cusco.

09/10/2006: Encuentran restos óseos de niño y mujer en tumba inca.

10/03/2006: Descubren restos arqueológicos preíncas cerca de la Plaza de Armas de Cusco.

09/13/2007: Confirman que restos óseos hallados en templo San Cristóbal pertenecen a Paullo Inca.

09/09/2008: Hallan miles de objetos ceremonias en fortaleza de Sacsayhuamán.

09/21/2008: Descubren 277 objetos de bronce en el Parque Arqueológico de Saqsaywamán.

12/17/2008: Descubren depósito de cerámica ceremonial en huaca de Parque Arqueológico de Saqsaywamán.

07/10/2009: Descubren muro prehispánico en subsuelo de calle del Centro Histórico del Cusco.

07/16/2009: Descubren contexto funerario en calle de la ciudad del Cusco.

09/16/2009: Descubren muro inca durante excavación para adecuación de hotel de lujo.

10/07/2009: Descubren 12 contextos funerarios y recintos prehispánicos en zona urbana marginal de Cusco.

10/14/2009: Descubren más extructuras incaicos en el subsuelo del antiguo convento de los agustinos.

Comercial (Cusco)in the Archivo de la Municipalidad del Cusco

25/06/1926: Descubrimiento de objetos arqueológicos

26/06/1926: El tesoro de los Incas

Diario El Sol (Cusco)

02/21/2008: Destruyen muro histórico en Cusco.

08/08/2008: Restos arqueológicos de Limacpampa pertenecieron a edificio ceremonial.

04/18/2009: Encuentran muro inca durante construcción de hotel Marriott.

06/16/2009: Municipalidad de Santiago depredó restos arqueológicos.

06/17/2009: Hallan contexto funerario y cimentación de muro inca.

09/01/2009: Hallazgo arqueológico en Wayna Tauqaray San Sebastián.

12/30/2009: En plaza Limacpampa INC exhibe muros incas en museo de sitio subterráneo

El Comercio (Lima)

03/28/2008: Hallan muro inca en el centro del Cusco.

09/04/2008: Hallan sistema de vivienda inca a dos cuadras de la Plaza de Armas de Cusco.

09/06/2008: Arqueólogos hallan restos de lo que sería el palacio de una esposa de Pachacútec.

07/10/2009: Hallan muro prehispánico en subsuelo del Centro Histórico de Cusco.

10/11/2009: Cusqueños están divididos por la construcción de nuevos edificios.

Instituto Nacional de Cultura, Cusco press release

08/05/2008: Hallan muro inca y escalinatas bajo el asfalto cusqueño.

Xinhua News Agency (Beijing)

11/16/2004: Hallan taller de adornos en miniatura de época incaica.

Index

IAN FARRINGTON is senior lecturer in archaeology at the Australian National University, Canberra. He has conducted research in Peru since 1971, initially on the north coast and later in the Cusco region. He has been twice decorated by the Peruvian government, receiving the medals of the Order of Merit for Distinguished Service (Orden al Mérito por Servicios Distinguidos) in 1984 and El Sol del Perú in 1990. In 1995, he was the founding editor, with Rodolfo Raffino, of *Tawantinsuyu: An International Journal of Inka Studies*. He has edited a collection of essays on prehistoric agriculture in the tropics, coauthored a popular book on New World civilizations, and written several academic papers. His most recent project, with codirector Julinho Zapata, is an excavation program at the impressive site of Tambokancha near Zurite on the Pampa de Anta.

ANCIENT CITIES OF THE NEW WORLD

Edited by Michael E. Smith, Arizona State University; Marilyn A. Masson, University at Albany, SUNY; John W. Janusek, Vanderbilt University

Ancient Cities of the New World is devoted to the study of the ancient urban sites of Mesoamerica and South America. This series is designed to present theories, models, and approaches that shed light on the region's diverse, ancient urban patterns and polity organization. Major, overarching topics to be explored in the series are urban form (size, architecture, and layout) and urban lifestyles (ethnicity, gender, households, neighborhoods, and craft activities). Books include important works focused on a single key ancient city or analyzing a collection of cities and towns within their regional contexts. The series features cross-disciplinary works in archaeology, art history, and ethnohistory written for a broad scholarly audience.